MI5

BRITISH SECURITY
SERVICE OPERATIONS
1909–1945

M I 5

BRITISH SECURITY
SERVICE OPERATIONS
1909–1945

NIGEL WEST

Frontline Books

MI5: BRITISH SECURITY SERVICE OPERATIONS, 1909–1945
The True Story of the Most Secret Counter-Espionage Organisation in the World

This edition published in 2019 by Frontline Books,
an imprint of Pen & Sword Books Ltd,
47 Church Street, Barnsley, S. Yorkshire, S70 2AS

First published by The Bodley Head Ltd., 1981.

Copyright © Nigel West
ISBN: 978-1-52675-570-4

Typeset in 10.5/12.5 point Palatino by Dave Cassan.
Printed and bound by TJ International, Padstow, Cornwall

Pen & Sword Books Ltd incorporates the imprints of Pen & Sword Archaeology,
Air World Books, Atlas, Aviation, Battleground, Discovery, Family History,
History, Maritime, Military, Naval, Politics, Social History, Transport, True Crime,
Claymore Press, Frontline Books, Praetorian Press, Seaforth Publishing and
White Owl

For a complete list of Pen & Sword titles please contact:

PEN & SWORD BOOKS LTD
47 Church Street, Barnsley, South Yorkshire, S70 2AS, UK.
E-mail: enquiries@pen-and-sword.co.uk
Website: www.pen-and-sword.co.uk

Or

PEN AND SWORD BOOKS,
1950 Lawrence Roadd, Havertown, PA 19083, USA
E-mail: Uspen-and-sword@casematepublishers.com
Website: www.penandswordbooks.com

Contents

Acknowledgements

I owe a debt of thanks to the following:

The former members of the Security Service, the Secret Intelligence Service, the Naval Intelligence Department, the Radio Security Service, the Joint Intelligence Committee, the Combined Services Detailed Interrogation Centre, MI9 and the Security Executive who were kind enough to tell me of their wartime experiences.

The former members of the American Office of Strategic Services and the Irish Intelligence Service, G2.

The Federal Bureau of Investigation and the Central Intelligence Agency.

The MI5 double agents who granted me interviews, including BALLOON, BRUTUS, DREADNOUGHT, FREAK, GARBO, GELATINE, JEFF, METEOR, MUTT, TATE, TRICYCLE and ZIGZAG.

The family of SUMMER.

The four former MI5 officers who read my manuscript.

Rear-Admiral W.N. Ash of the Ministry of Defence's 'D' Notice Committee for his guidance.

The Departmental Records Office and the Service archivists who patiently answered my questions.

The Chief Constables of Essex, Greater Manchester, Northamptonshire, South Wales and Strathclyde who authorized searches of their records.

ACKNOWLEDGEMENTS

The staff of the Public Records Office in Kew, the Imperial War Museum, the British Museum, the Hoover Institute at Stanford University and the Netherlands State Institute for War Documentation.

The Embassies of Belgium, Luxembourg, Spain, Sweden and Switzerland.

Julian Allason of ACT for his data processing skills.

John Moe in Sweden (himself a wartime double agent) who devoted many hours of his spare time to this project, as did Detective Joseph J. Gannon of the New York Police Department.

Sir William Stephenson, H. Montgomery Hyde, Winston Ramsey, and Professor M.R.D. Foot for their encouragement.

My researchers, Veronique LeJeune in Brussels, Maria Vidal in Spain and Camilla Van Gerbig in London.

Venetia Pollock for her editorial skills.

Abbreviations

BRCA	Bureau Central de Renseignements et d'Action
BSC	British Security Co-ordination, New York
BUF	British Union of Fascists
BUPO	Bundespolizei: Swiss Security Service
C	Chief of the Secret Intelligence Service (MI6)
CID	Committee of Imperial Defence
CID	Criminal Investigation Department
COS	Chiefs of Staff
CPGB	Communist Party of Great Britain
CSDIC	Combined Services Detailed Interrogation Centre
DMI	Director of Military Intelligence
DNI	Director of Naval Intelligence
DPP	Director of Public Prosecutions
DSO	Defence Security Officer
FBI	Federal Bureau of Investigation
FSP	Field Security Police
FSW	Field Security Wing
FUSAG	First United States Army Group
G2	Irish Military Intelligence Department
GC & CS	Government Code & Cypher School
GPO	General Post Office
GPU	Soviet Military Intelligence
GSP	Gibraltar Security Police
HDE	Home Defence Executive
IPI	Indian Political Intelligence
IRA	Irish Republican Army
ISK	Intelligence Services Knox
ISLU	Inter-Services Liaison Unit (MI6)
ISOS	Intelligence Services Oliver Strachey
JIC	Joint Intelligence Committee

LDV	Local Defence Volunteers
LIU	Letter Interception Unit
MEW	Ministry of Economic Warfare
MOI	Ministry of Information
NID	Naval Intelligence Department
NKVD	Soviet Security Service
NYPD	New York Police Department
001	Camp 001, HM Prison Dartmoor
020	Camp 020, Latchmere House, Ham Common
OGPU	Soviet Political Intelligence Service
OSS	Office of Strategic Services
PCO	Passport Control Office
PIDE	Portuguese Security Service
POW	Prisoner of War
PWIS	Prisoner of War Interrogation Service
PUS	Permanent Under-Secretary
RSHA	Reich Security Agency
RSLO	Regional Security Liaison Officer
RSS	Radio Security Service (MI8)
RUC	Royal Ulster Constabulary
RVPS	Royal Victoria Patriotic School
SD	Sicherheitsdeinst: Nazi Security Service
SHAEF	Supreme Headquarters Allied Expeditionary Force
SIME	Security Intelligence Middle East
SIS	Secret Intelligence Service (MI6)
SOE	Special Operations Executive
VI	Voluntary Interceptor
WX	Camp WX, Isle of Man
YCL	Young Communist League

Military Intelligence Designations

MI_1	Directorate of Military Intelligence
MI_3	German Section, Military Intelligence
MI_5	Imperial Security Intelligence Service
MI_6	Secret Intelligence Service
MI_8	Radio Security Service
MI_9	Escape and Evasion Service
MI_{11}	Field Security Police
MI_{19}	Combined Services Detailed Interrogation Centre
MI(L)	War Office Liaison with Allied Intelligence Services

Introduction

'Writing to the War Office is like having intercourse with an elephant. There is very little pleasure to be derived from it; you are very likely to be squashed; and there will be no result for two years.'

UNKNOWN MILITARY SAGE

In spite of all the books published since the last war on the subject of intelligence, very little has ever been written about the role of Britain's premier counter-intelligence organization, the Security Service, known once as 'The Imperial Security Intelligence Service', and now more widely referred to by its military intelligence 'cover' designation of MI5.

In 1963 John Bulloch wrote *M.I.5* with the help of Lady Kell, the widow of the first Director-General, but he devoted less than seven pages to the 1939-1945 era. Indeed, one part of the book deals with the German spy who masterminded the sinking of HMS *Royal Oak* at Scapa Flow in October 1939. In fact, no such spy ever existed.

Many people interested in the subject of counter-intelligence hoped the long-awaited *Official History of British Intelligence in the Second World War*, researched by a team of Cambridge historians headed by Professor Hinsley, would set matters right, but this was not to be the case. In the first volume of nearly five hundred pages there were only ten references to the Security Service. They chiefly concerned MI5's relations with other British intelligence organizations and gave no details of MI5's operations.

There is of course a good reason for the dearth of information about what is arguably Britain's most secret government department. Its staff are prohibited from publishing their memoirs and there are virtually no relevant papers stored at the Public Records Office. Uniquely, Sir Percy

Sillitoe, MI5's Director-General from 1946 to 1953 included nearly thirty (unrevealing) pages about the Security Service in his 1955 autobiography *Cloak Without Dagger*.

His first attempt, largely ghosted by his Personal Assistant Russell Lee, was vetoed by the government. The real breakthrough for students of counter-intelligence came with Sir John Masterman's publication in 1972 of *The Double Cross System in the War of 1939-1945*, an account of the wartime Twenty Committee over which he presided. Predictably the book caused protests from the Security Service but in the end the Cabinet, led by Mr Heath, decided to authorize a British edition. Its release was indisputably in breach of a long-established embargo and created considerable resentment amongst some of the MI5 officers who had actually been directly responsible for the handling of double agents, about whom Masterman wrote so freely. The book proved to be a best-seller and a fascinating insight into the workings of just one of MI5's many branches. It also brought into perspective some of the other tales of MI5's wartime activities, which ranged from Ewan Montagu's *The Man Who Never Was*, through *The Real Eddie Chapman Story* to Dusko Popov's *Spy Counterspy*. All the B1(a) case officers were consulted during Masterman's struggle for permission to publish (although the agents themselves were not), and one of them, Christopher Harmer, even acted as his legal representative in the long negotiations.

The picture which emerged of the Security Service was, however, inevitably an unbalanced one. Masterman dealt with B1(a) in depth, but never once mentioned B1(b) or B1(c), each an important sub-section of the Counter-Espionage ('B') Division. Similarly, there was no account of the work of 'A' Division or, for that matter, 'C', 'D', 'E' or 'F'.

Some critics have also commented on the practice of naming posts rather than the individuals who held the posts. Masterman talks of case officers and the Director of 'B' Division but does not tell the reader who these remarkable people were.

There are of course many dangers in 'naming names', as Chapman Pincher discovered when Mrs Thatcher branded his book, *Their Trade is Treachery*, 'inaccurate . . . distorted . . . and wrong.' I have tried to steer a middle course, avoiding the pitfalls of depersonalizing events in historical interest and importance while checking and double-checking the information I received. Masterman had the advantage of access to his own post-war report on the Twenty Committee and was able to draw on his own experience of the Security Service, based on his own intimate involvement over a period of four and a half years, 1941-1945. I have enjoyed neither of these benefits. But I have been able to trace many of the double agents and hear their version of events. Quite a number of retired MI5 officers too were quite willing to be interviewed, perhaps in the hope that the record might be set straight.

When I began my research, I was told by a former Director-General of the Security Service that the task was virtually impossible, especially for an outsider. It was this, more than anything else, which encouraged me to embark on the most interesting three years of my life. Although I found little published material to help me I was not short of advice. Malcolm Muggeridge, himself a wartime SIS officer, warned in his autobiography: 'Diplomats and Intelligence agents, in my experience, are even bigger liars than journalists, and the historians who try to reconstruct the past out of their records are, for the most, dealing with fantasy'. Nevertheless, I was determined to make the attempt and was encouraged by a comment by Sir Percy Sillitoe: 'MI5 has alternatively intrigued and infuriated the public by the aura of "hush-hush" with which it has seemed to be surrounded'. I knew this to be true and was fascinated by his opinion that 'its popular reputation was in no way exaggerated'.

I soon found myself agreeing with Sir Percy. Even the more recent articles and books dealing with MI5 were loaded with inaccuracies. Philby's *My Silent War*, generally considered to be a reliable source on at least the structure of Britain's wartime secret services, incorrectly named 'Sir Charles Petrie' as 'head of MI5 during the war'. He had meant Sir David Petrie, but in fact even he did not join MI5 until November 1940, more than a year after the declaration of war. Andrew Boyle, the principal 'mole-hunter' during the Blunt revelations, was erroneously referring to 'MI5's B Section' six months after Mrs Thatcher had confirmed the art historian's guilt. Others claimed Blunt had 'risen to become number three in MI5'. Equally inaccurate was Chapman Pincher's assertion that Roger Hollis had initially joined 'Section F of MI5'. In spite of all the alleged 'informed comment', no one with a knowledge of MI5 had pointed out the glaring flaws.

The simple explanation was that few outside MI5 had any idea of the organization's structure or even its responsibilities. Some claimed that the Security Service was limited to an internal security role within the boundaries of the United Kingdom. Others made a parallel with the American FBI. Neither turned out to be true.

The cornerstone of my project was the creation of an organizational chart of the wartime Security Service. Few have attempted to describe the structure of a British intelligence department and even fewer have succeeded. The wartime 'need to know' policy meant that I would receive little help, even from those whom I assumed had been in a position to take an overall view of MI5's structure. The staff were deliberately compartmentalized so that those at the Divisional Director level either were not aware of the activites of other branches, or did not wish to know. This made my task well-nigh impossible, but by checking and counter-checking a general picture gradually developed.

The resulting organizational tables appear at the end of this Introduction and include the names of many of the outstanding members of MI5's staff.

Having established the areas of MI5's responsibilities and its internal structure I turned to look at some of the organization's leading personalities. One confusing problem connected with this was the matter of rank. Guy Liddell, for example, held the commission of Captain in the Royal Artillery throughout the war, even after he had been promoted to Director of 'B' Division (known simply as 'DB') in May 1940. Furthermore, many of his subordinates were, in military terms, senior to him. Len Burt, the Chief Inspector from Scotland Yard who was brought into MI5 in September 1940, was commissioned into the Intelligence Corps with the rank of Major. By the end of hostilities, he had achieved the rank of Lieutenant-Colonel. Similarly, when Sir David Petrie was appointed Director-General of the Security Service in November 1940 he too was commissioned into the Intelligence Corps with the rank of 'Second Lieutenant, Acting Colonel, Local Brigadier'. Uniforms and their badges of rank were of little significance internally and many of the staff rarely wore anything other than civvies. Indeed, on one memorable occasion shortly after the war, Dick White's reluctance to wear uniform actually resulted in a unique newspaper story. On 28 October, 1946 the *Daily Telegraph*, under the heading 'TROOPSHIP HAD MYSTERY MAN', reported Colonel D.G. White, 'an important civilian passenger', embarking on the *Duchess of Bedford* at Liverpool on his way to rejoin his unit in the Middle East. 'Coded messages' apparently awaited his arrival at the docks. No doubt somewhat embarrassed, the War Office commented that Colonel White of the Intelligence Corps 'was entitled to travel in civilian clothes when not with his unit'.

Those MI5 officers who liaised with other units were given local ranks to help them extract maximum co-operation. This was especially true of the DSOs posted abroad. However, as one might expect, the lack of military discipline in some of these 'temporary officers, temporary gentlemen' or 'civilians in uniform' caused some friction with the regular soldiers.

Having learnt to ignore MI5 ranks I was confronted with the difficulty of identifying former MI5 officers. All are obliged to sign an undertaking that they will not reveal their employment or duties with the Security Service. In exchange they receive a promise from the government that it will never 'blow their cover'. However, distinguished their record, most ex-MI5 officers with entries in such reference books as *Who's Who* have had to confine themselves to such brief descriptions as 'Civil Assistant, War Office, 1939-1940' and other apparently mundane disguises. This tradition has only once been breached, by Sir Percy Sillitoe who listed 'Director-General, Security Service, 1946-1953'. His own staff had to content themselves with the usual 'Attached War Office'. As well as hiding their 'attachment' staff were also expected to maintain tight individual security. Boyfriends dropped their lunch-dates off in Piccadilly rather than risk identifying MI5's office in St James's Street. Relatives were expected not to enquire too deeply into exactly which department in the War Office a person worked in, and when asked an MI5 employee would always give the standard explanation: 'I work for a rather dull department in the War Office'.

While writing this book I was never given access to files in MI5's famous Registry but over a period of three years I succeeded in obtaining interviews with enough ex-Security Service officers to build up the organizational charts and identify some two hundred of the principal people. I also became more aware of the mystique surrounding my chosen subject.

To my surprise I realized that MI5 had actively promoted its own image and frequently encouraged myths about its power and influence. One example was the instruction given to MI5 officers who came into contact with partially initiated outsiders, such as Chief Constables, never to show surprise, no matter what the circumstances. Another was the rule on codes. All communications with MI5 headquarters were to be sent by telegram in code, however prosaic the contents.

Supporting the air of mystery surrounding the Security Service was its unique standing in Britain, apparently bridging the Civil Service and the Military. Although officially a department of the War Office, and answerable to the Secretary of State for War, MI5 achieved independent status, with direct access to the Home Secretary and Prime Minister, shortly after the Great War. The first Director-General, Major-General Sir Vernon Kell, KBE, CB, developed close links with those at the most senior level of government, the Secretary to the Cabinet, the Permanent Under-Secretaries and the Chiefs of Staff. A secret telephone exchange connected him directly to 'C' (the SIS Chief), the Metropolitan Police Commissioner, the Director of Naval Intelligence (DNI) and the Special Advisers of the day at the Foreign Office. As his obituary notice in *The Times* in April 1942 commented, 'Though his name was probably not generally well known to the public, few men were better known in the official world.' The personalities within the intelligence 'Establishment' changed from time to time, just as Prime Ministers did, but the posts remained. For some intelligence bureaucrats like Admiral 'Blinker' Hall the Whitehall structure helped build personal empires. Hall was DNI for longer than any other DNI this century; his father achieved the same record for the previous century. Both men had tremendous influence, but neither's tenure of office was even a fifth of Kell's thirty-one years.

Describing a series of events with the benefit of some forty years' hindsight is hardly an onerous task if all the documentation is available to the researcher. On this subject however, there is virtually no source of relevant papers, which inevitably requires the undeterred to rely on the memories of others. When accepting these recollections, however faulty, one has to be mindful of the prejudices and opinions which naturally colour conversations about events long past. With the Security Service, two identifiable dogmas have established themselves, mainly because of the lack of anybody willing to 'go public' and voice a contrary view.

Perhaps the most widely held is what could be termed the 'Indian policeman' syndrome, namely, that MI5 was staffed in part by colonial policemen who were either inept or had simply not kept pace with modern intelligence techniques. As with most good propaganda, there is indeed an element of truth in this view. The Security Service during the war did employ many ex-colonial police officers, and more than a few came from India, but those aware of the labyrinthine qualities of Indian politics will not belittle the achievements of the Indian police, surrounded as they were by plots, intrigues and disturbances. The British-controlled intelligence system in the sub-continent is even today held up by some of those qualified to judge as an enviable model of an intelligence-gathering organization. It was no mean boast that practically every village in India contained a knowledgeable source for the British. It was men with experience of this unique system who were drawn into MI5 by Kell.

A second, widely-held assumption is connected with this: that old Sir Vernon Kell was quite unsuited to head a counter-intelligence organization, and that his methods were, to put it politely, quaint. There are naturally stories which develop this theme. One MI5 officer, John Maude, recalled a memorable interview with the Director-General. He had been sent up to Scotland to investigate a spy rumour and fell into conversation with a young artillery officer in the same train who was rejoining his unit. Maude was travelling in civvies and was appalled to hear the man opposite discuss details of HMS *Nelson's* present location and other indiscretions. As the two men struck up a conversation the officer became less and less security-conscious. When the MI5 man returned to London after completing his task he reported the incident to Kell, Kell asked him if he had encouraged the officer to be indiscreet. The future judge agreed that he had in fact tried to lead the young man on, at which Kell told him to drop the matter, warning him never to repeat the exercise.

This almost paternal approach to counter-espionage resulted in accusations of being old-fashioned, but there is another worthwhile observation. MI5 was never accused of behaving like the Gestapo. Nor, for that matter, did MI5 become the tool of any one politician or party. Britain's Security Service would certainly appear to have fared better in this respect than some of its European counterparts during the same period. Both the French and the Dutch governments in exile were bedevilled by politically motivated security organizations.

Finally, a word concerning jargon. Like every other organization or institution MI5 developed its own terms which instantly identified those who were on the inside and those who were outside. An illustration of this is that during the three years I spent researching this book, the word 'spy' was never used by anyone in the know.

Throughout this book 'MI5' and 'Security Service' are used interchangably. Both refer to the same organization although members of other intelligence organizations would simply talk of 'Five' and 'Six' when discussing the Security Service or the Security Intelligence Service. For obvious reasons the initials of the Security Service were never used.

The first internal principle to understand is the difference between the agents and the officers. MI5 officers were the full-time professionals who worked in MI5 headquarters or one of the sub-offices. The term 'office' had a wider meaning than simply a building where work is done. Agents were not 'in the office', officers were. An individual agent rarely visited MI5 premises and generally only came into contact with his case officer. Beyond the case officer were other officers, but none should ever be described as 'MI5 agents'.

The agents themselves divide into three groups. The straightforward agents work for X against Y. Double agents and those who admit to Y that they are working for X, change their loyalties, and work for Y against X. A 'triple' is the most complicated of all. He is employed by X and confesses this to Y in the hope that Y will use him as a double agent, although in reality he remains loyal to X: X know that if they continue to hear from him his messages will be under the control of Y.

The business of running double agents is extremely difficult, and has been analysed brilliantly by J.C. Masterman. One area that he did not discuss was the actual process of 'turning', the method by which an agent is persuaded to reverse his loyalties. Coercion and brute force are counter-productive because the agent will appear to co-operate, but will resent this treatment and will change sides again as soon as he has an opportunity. Experience shows that a good double agent must sincerely believe in his new role. It matters little whether the agent originally volunteered to 'turn' or whether he underwent what might have appeared an age of quiet persuasion. Once turned, the agent must convince his new case officer that the transformation has been successful.

Much confusion has been caused by mistakenly referring the MI5 officers as agents, and referring to the occasional officer who has been working as an agent for the opposition as a double agent. Once the reader has mastered these subtle distinctions he is ready to tackle the complicated history of MI5 from 1909 to 1945.

I have divided the book into three parts. The pre-war part deals with the general build-up of MO5 and MI5 under Kell until 1939. The central part covers the outbreak of war, Kell's dismissal and the interregnum. The final part describes in detail the double cross agents and their networks, those spies who were caught and executed in Britain, Soviet wartime efforts and MI5's overseas activities, in which I include Ireland.

The Wartime Organization of the Security Service

The Organization of MI5

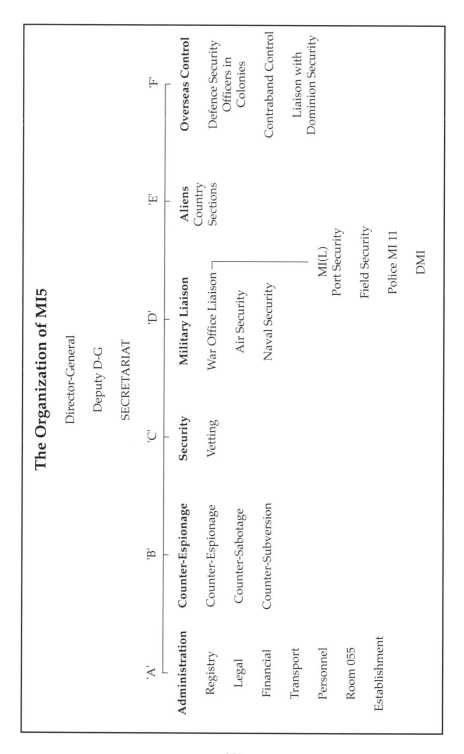

Director-General

Deputy D-G

SECRETARIAT

'A'	'B'	'C'	'D'	'E'	'F'
Administration	**Counter-Espionage**	**Security**	**Military Liaison**	**Aliens**	**Overseas Control**
Registry	Counter-Espionage	Vetting	War Office Liaison	Country Sections	Defence Security Officers in Colonies
Legal	Counter-Sabotage		Air Security		
Financial	Counter-Subversion		Naval Security		Contraband Control
Transport			MI(L)		Liaison with Dominion Security
Personnel			Port Security		
Room 055			Field Security		
Establishment			Police MI 11		
			DMI		

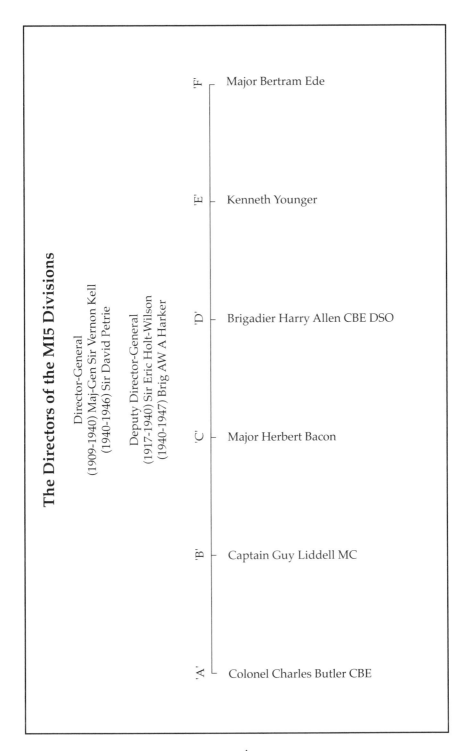

The Directors of the MI5 Divisions

Director-General
(1909-1940) Maj-Gen Sir Vernon Kell
(1940-1946) Sir David Petrie

Deputy Director-General
(1917-1940) Sir Eric Holt-Wilson
(1940-1947) Brig AW A Harker

'F' — Major Bertram Ede

'E' — Kenneth Younger

'D' — Brigadier Harry Allen CBE DSO

'C' — Major Herbert Bacon

'B' — Captain Guy Liddell MC

'A' — Colonel Charles Butler CBE

'A' Division of MI5

DIRECTOR OF A
Butler

Assistant Director
Cumming

REGISTRY	LEGAL	FINANCE	PERSONNEL	TRANSPORT	ROOM 055	ESTABLISHMENT
Edwards	Pilcher	Marshall	Dicker	Wheatley	Dunsterville	Cusack
Paton-Smith	Hale	Webster	Constance	Horsfall	Horsfall	
Withers	Crocker		Mounsey	Cottenham	Lennox	
Smythe	Shelford				Cussen	
Bird					Watts	
Morgan						

The names shown are those of some of the leading personalities who served; but not necessarily contemporaneously

'B' Division of MI5

DIRECTOR OF B
Liddell

Assistant Director
White

DOUBLE AGENTS	ENEMY ANALYSIS	COUNTER-SABOTAGE	ENEMY WIRELESS	ENEMY MAIL	'THE WATCHERS'	POLICE UNIT	RUMOUR
Robertson	Milmo	Rothschild	Reid	Brander	Ottaway	Burt	Maude
Marriott	Stamp	Mayor	Lee		Hunter	Fish	
Wilson	Hart		Poulton			Spooner	
Harmer	Day		Reason			Skardon	
Astor	Gwyer					Smith	
Ashley						Davies	

The names shown are those of some of the leading personalities who served; but not necessarily contemporaneously

RSLOs	Military Subversion	Political Subversion	Press	SHAEF	Soviet Affairs	Financial Inteligence	Home Forces
MacIver	Alexander	Knight	Tangye	Blunt	Saunders	Reid	Mountain
Glover	Bodington	Bingham		Furnival	Bagot		
Dykes	Watson	Gillson		Jones	Sisemore		
Lane	Curry	Younger			McCulloch		
Johnson		Brocklehurst					
Dixon		Glass					
Hope		Darwall					
Ryde		Himsworth					
Wethered		Poston					
Perfect		Land					
Maude							
Phipps							

Ireland	Iberian	Balkan	Norwegian	Double Agents in Canada	Double Agents in South Africa	Country Sections	'W'
Liddell	Brooman-White	Haldane-Porter	Liversidge	Mills	Luke	Young	Frost
Caroe	Harris	Caulfield				Ramsbotham	Arnold
Stephenson						Carr	Ritchie
						Younger	

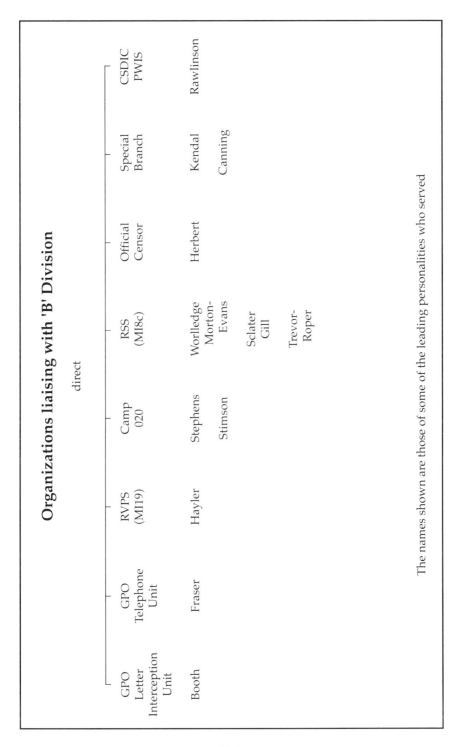

Organizations liaising with 'B' Division

direct

GPO Letter Interception Unit	GPO Telephone Unit	RVPS (MI19)	Camp 020	RSS (MI8c)	Official Censor	Special Branch	CSDIC PWIS
Booth	Fraser	Hayler	Stephens	Worlledge	Herbert	Kendal	Rawlinson
			Stimson	Morton-Evans		Canning	
				Sclater Gill			
				Trevor-Roper			

The names shown are those of some of the leading personalities who served

'D' Division of MI5

DIRECTOR OF A
Allen

Assistant Directors
Percival
Hill

Military Liaison	FSP	Air Security	Naval Security	Port Security
Speir	Davies	Archer	Bennett	Adam
			Burton	Burne
			Money	Bardwell
				Ferguson
				Kane
				Mare
				Noble

The names shown are those of some of the leading personalities who served

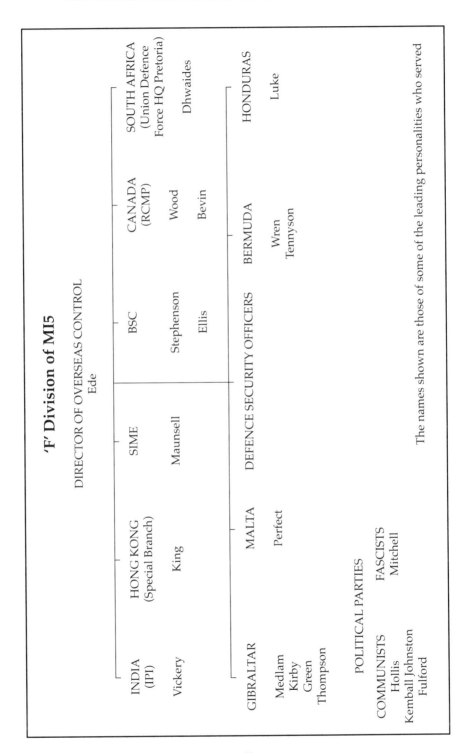

'F' Division of MI5

DIRECTOR OF OVERSEAS CONTROL
Ede

INDIA (IPI)	HONG KONG (Special Branch)	SIME	BSC	CANADA (RCMP)	SOUTH AFRICA (Union Defence Force HQ Pretoria)
Vickery	King	Maunsell	Stephenson	Wood	Dhwaides
			Ellis	Bevin	

DEFENCE SECURITY OFFICERS

GIBRALTAR	MALTA	BERMUDA	HONDURAS
Medlam	Perfect	Wren	Luke
Kirby		Tennyson	
Green			
Thompson			

POLITICAL PARTIES

COMMUNISTS	FASCISTS
Hollis	Mitchell
Kemball Johnston	
Fulford	

The names shown are those of some of the leading personalities who served

PART ONE:

MI5 1909-1939

1

The Early Years

In 1887 Great Britain recognized the importance of intelligence work by creating, for the first time, the posts of Director of Military Intelligence and Director of Naval Intelligence. The Intelligence Branch of the War Office, under the leadership of the DMI, concerned itself with gathering information on foreign armies and also took charge of mobilization and home defence. Anti-invasion planning stayed with the Admiralty, as it had done since the Napoleonic Wars.

Inevitably the Royal Navy's domination of the world's trade routes meant that the Naval Intelligence Department became Britain's best-funded intelligence organization. After the Boer War the military and naval establishment came under fierce criticism. The post of DMI was abolished in 1904 and responsibility for counter-espionage was placed with the Special Duties Division of the War Office's Military Operations Directorate. This directorate was itself a sub-division of the Intelligence and Mobilization Department, and experience proved the arrangement to be unsatisfactory. The Foreign Office were less than happy at having to depend on the War Office for information and some intensive lobbying went on in Whitehall.

The Cabinet then set up the Committee of Imperial Defence, or CID, which had two important roles. The first was to have direct civilian control over matters of service strategy and policy. The second was to encourage co-ordination between the Services and their various intelligence organizations. Locked away in the minutes of the CID lie the origins of the British Imperial Security Intelligence Service which was later to become known as MO5 and then MI5.

The CID was to include the Chiefs of Staff and meet under the chairmanship of the Prime Minister or one of his senior Cabinet colleagues. The important innovation was the granting to the CID of a permanent staff so that decisions taken by the Committee could be pursued in Whitehall. As soon as the CID was established it embarked on a lengthy study of Britain's intelligence arrangements; the need for change was widely recognized and the CID's recommendations were implemented quickly.

In 1907 the retiring Director of Naval Intelligence (DNI), Sir Charles Ottley, was appointed Secretary of the CID. His Assistant was a young Marine named Maurice Hankey, a man destined to become one of the most powerful in Britain. In August 1909 Ottley recommended, with the backing of the CID, that a Secret Service Bureau be created to take charge of all matters relating to intelligence gathering.

The proposal, which was approved by the Cabinet, divided the Secret Service Bureau into two parts with quite separate areas of interest: foreign and home. The Foreign Section was to be headed by Captain Mansfield Cumming RN, and it was this Section which was later to grow into the Secret Intelligence Service or MI6. The Home Section was to be organized by Captain Vernon Kell, late of the South Staffordshire Regiment.

Kell was chosen for the job by Colonel James Edmonds, a member of the CID Secretariat, and Kell's future close friend and next-door neighbour. Kell was a remarkable man who was to run MO5 – and later MI5 – for over thirty years, building up the Service from small beginnings in 1909 into the large department with its many specialist branches that it had become by 1939. To understand how MO5 grew, and how it was staffed and run, it is necessary to discover what influenced Kell and look at the events which confronted him during the Great War and the Twenties and Thirties: the pressures of international Communism and the rise of the Nazis.

He was born on 21 November 1873, the son of Major Waldegrave Kell, a regular officer in the South Staffordshires. His mother was the daughter of Count Konarska, a refugee aristocrat from Poland. He was brought up at Ruckley Grange in a small village near Shrewsbury and was educated at home. By the time he went to Sandhurst in 1892 he could speak German, Italian, French and Polish, all fluently. Two years later he joined his father's regiment at their depot in Lichfield. During the next four years he qualified as an Army interpreter in French and German, and then began learning Russian while on leave in Moscow. He then rejoined his regiment in Cork, having passed further language exams. In Cork he met Constance Scott, the daughter of a local landowner, and they married on 5 April 1900. Later that year Kell was posted to China where he was to spend the following three years, seeing his first action during the Boxer Rebellion.

When Kell eventually returned to Britain via Moscow in 1904 he was in poor health and was therefore instructed to report for duty to the War

Office. In 1907 he was transferred to the CID Secretariat where he worked under Colonel Edmonds. He had suffered from dysentery while in the Far East and now became increasingly vulnerable to the attacks of asthma which he had endured from childhood. All of this denied him a future with his regiment, so when Edmonds offered him the new post of Director of the Home Section of the Secret Service Bureau with responsibility for investigating and countering espionage in the United Kingdom, he accepted.

Kell's new section now carried the Military Operations designation MO5, a label which was to stick until 1916. Within twelve months the Foreign Section was removed to the Admiralty and Kell achieved a clerk and his first assistant, Stanley Strong, who had been an official in the Boy Scout movement.

Kell's initial mandate was to study Britain's vulnerability to foreign espionage and recommend to the CID what steps should be taken to prevent the theft of secret information. Within this brief was a request to assess the dangers of home-grown subversion from those political extremists bent on undermining the established system of government. This latter area of responsibility had previously been the exclusive province of Scotland Yard's Special Irish Branch, which had been created in 1883 to deaf with the Fenians and other Irish Nationalists. Kell turned to this forerunner of today's Special Branch for help in compiling the information he needed. He received strong support from Superintendent Patrick Quinn, the fifty-eight-year-old Irishman from County Mayo who had led Scotland Yard's Special Branch since 1903. Another close collaborator was to be Basil Thomson, when the latter became Deputy Commissioner of the Metropolitan Police in 1913. Before this appointment Thomson, who had trained as a barrister, had joined the Colonial Office (serving for a time as the Prime Minister of Tonga). He had also been a Governor of Dartmoor Prison and Wormwood Scrubs.

These two influential figures were to prove valuable allies for Kell as he argued for his own, independent recruitment of staff. Initially MO5 had to rely on 'attachments' from other departments such as Inspector Melville from Scotland Yard, Captain Reginald Drake from the North Staffordshire Regiment, William Haldane Porter from the Home Office Aliens' Department and Captain Frederick Clark from the War Office. In 1912 Kell was joined by Eric Holt-Wilson RE, an instructor from the RMA Woolwich; he was to serve as Kell's Chief of Staff for twenty-three years.

Kell continued to request additional staff but his pleas were turned down on the grounds of expense. He was later to joke to friends that he spent months without a secretary because the Treasury would not sanction the recruitment of one. Eventually Kell decided to use his own resources – or rather the War Office's – to bring his department up to reasonable strength. For MO5 was nominally still under the aegis of the War Office. Whenever he met a suitable young officer he contacted his Commanding Officer and had him transferred to General Staff duties. The new recruit would then find himself being ordered to report to Kell at the War Office. All candidates were personally interviewed by him in depth until 1939. This procedure enabled the Security Service to increase its numbers without attracting unnecessary attention but it established a recruitment policy which was later to be misunderstood. Kell maintained very strict standards of 'reliability' for his staff which meant in short that they were all drawn from his social circle. His officers and his secretarial staff could generally be summed up as having a 'military and county' background.

The policy was to be attacked at various times as arrogant and snobbish but actually its basis was financial. His officers were appallingly badly paid and the secretaries fared even worse. Whitehall restrictions prevented Kell from paying anyone more than pocket-money but he calculated that most of them enjoyed a private income. However, as a compromise Kell negotiated a tax-free arrangement with the Inland Revenue. It was agreed that to preserve security none of his staff should pay income tax, and a system developed whereby a special code-number could be added to any tax return. This effectively exempted the recipient from further demands or enquiries.

Having fought and partially won the battle for personnel, Kell turned his attention to the political matter of changing the law. In July 1910 he joined a CID sub-committee, chaired by the then Home Secretary Winston Churchill, to make recommendations and consider the treatment of aliens in the event of war. Next Kell and the CID looked at the 1889 Official Secrets Act, which was in need of revision because it required a prosecution to show unlawful intent, which was virtually impossible to prove. A photographer found taking pictures of a Naval dockyard merely had to claim to be working for an industrial interest (as opposed to a foreign military power) and a case would collapse. Just such a case occurred during the summer of 1910 when a German lieutenant was caught redhanded sketching the harbour defences of Portsmouth. The trial of Siegfried Helm opened in Winchester on 14 November 1910 before Mr Justice Eldon Bankes. The Attorney-General, Sir Rufus Isaacs, prosecuted for the Crown and the jury returned a verdict of Guilty, the first such conviction under the Official Secrets Act of an officer in a foreign army. Helm admitted to holding the rank of Lieutenant in the 21st Battalion of the Nassau Regiment, and his offences had been witnessed by two British officers, Captain H. de C. Martelli (later Major-General Sir Horace Martelli) and Lieutenant Hugh Salmon. Their first-hand evidence persuaded the jury to convict, as did the accused's notebook, but the judge discharged the prisoner because he had already spent four weeks in custody.

The case served to highlight the inadequacy of the law and persuaded the CID to press for new legislation. The following year a wide-reaching Bill was presented to Parliament and received the Royal Assent in August 1911. From this date the mere possession of official or sensitive information became a serious offence.

The 1911 Act was a powerful weapon but it did not apparently deter the Kaiser's General Staff from despatching agents to Britain. In 1912 MO5 dealt with their first defector, a German named Karl Hentschel. He had been refused a pay rise by Berlin and in a fit of pique volunteered a lengthy confession concerning his activities. As a result, a Royal Navy gunner, George Parrott, was imprisoned for four years. The case was not a total success because Hentschel reappeared, having been paid off and allowed to settle in Australia. He turned up in London and successfully managed to get himself arrested by the City of London police after a volunteered confession, having failed to extract further payment from the Security Service. Hentschel was charged with offences under the Official Secrets Act but the prosecution was withdrawn once the defendant started to relate his experiences from the dock. Hentschel was quickly discharged but it was an embarrassing moment for Kell and the Director of Public Prosecutions.

Another case about this time was that of Wilhelm Klauer. A German-born dentist practising in Portsea, he was convicted of espionage in 1913 after paying a police nominee £30 for what he thought was test data on torpedoes. Klauer went to prison for five years. Klauer, like many of the cases handled at this time by MO5, was an example of a referral from the civil police authorities. Other intelligence originated from information volunteered from the public; as yet the infant security service hardly had the manpower to do much sleuthing in its own right.

But Kell did not always have to rely on information from others: he began to collect his own. He knew that the charter granted to him by the CID gave him responsibility for counter-espionage, counter-sabotage and counter-subversion both in the United Kingdom and in Britain's overseas interests; the department had a preventative role as well as an investigative one. With this in mind he had initiated a card-index system on all potential subversives in conjunction with Special Branch which was to be the basis of an intelligence *coup* on 5 August 1914. He also had another great success the day before on 4 August.

In 1909 Quinn of the Special Branch had identified the main German Intelligence 'post office' in Britain. It was run from a barber's shop at 402A Caledonian Road, London, by Karl Gustav Ernst, the forty-five-year-old son of a German surgical instrument maker who had come to live in Britain in the 1860s. Kell obtained a warrant from the Home Secretary to intercept all the mail to and from the barber's shop and was soon able to identify every member of Ernst's spy ring. Early in the morning of 4 August 1914 the shop was raided by Special Branch and Ernst was arrested. At the same time other raids were taking place and twenty suspected agents were taken into custody. The Kaiser's network was in ruins and the reputation of MO5 was made. Ernst was charged with 'conspiring with Parrott, Graves, Gould, Grosse and others to obtain information on the movements, armament and disposition of Naval ships'. After a two-day trial at the Old Bailey in November 1914 Ernst was sentenced to seven years' imprisonment.

On 5 August 1914 the Aliens Restriction Act which Kell and Churchill had discussed in 1910 came into force, requiring every alien in the country to register with their local police station. But even as these regulations were being enforced Special Branch detectives were rounding up some two hundred suspected German agents. They in fact were the first of more than 32,000 internees who were to be taken into custody on the orders of the Home Secretary, Reginald McKenna. By the end of 1915 the country's Chief Constables received instructions to detain all Germans between the ages of seventeen and fifty-five. Those over military age were repatriated.

The controversial round-up lent the Security Service a reputation for quiet and mysterious efficiency, and many of the principles created in the early Great War investigations became accepted standards for the department. For the first time records were kept of the entry of foreigners and their addresses were registered with the Home Office.

The Security Service expanded greatly following the declaration of war and the influx of new talent helped to develop unusual techniques. One innovative officer was Edward Hinchley-Cooke who became, in 1915, the first MO5 'stool pigeon', masquerading with considerable success as a German prisoner of war and mixing with genuine prisoners.

All the services now tightened up on their gathering of intelligence both in those countries where the Crown had possessions to defend and in the rest of the world, where Britain could gather information with or without the consent of the government concerned. At home MO5 hunted for spies, traitors and saboteurs; intelligence gathering elsewhere was divided between SIS and the NID, who also encompassed the code-breakers in Room 40 of the Admiralty, under Alastair Denniston.

In January 1917 the Room 40 decrypters unravelled a secret telegram from the Kaiser's Foreign Minister Arthur Zimmermann, to the German ambassador in Mexico. The 155 coded groups announced that the German navy was about to begin 'unrestricted warfare' which would mean the sinking of neutral vessels in the war zone. Admiral Reginald ('Blinker') Hall provided the Americans with the text of the message 'in clear' and gave them the key for them to decipher their own intercepted copy. One passage, which President Wilson found disgraceful, contained Germany's promise to help Mexico 'to regain by conquest her lost territory in Texas, Arizona and New Mexico'. The United States joined the war on 21 March 1917.

Altogether eleven German spies were executed in Britain during the Great War, the majority of whom were bona fide soldiers and thus tried by court martial. Their individual cases have been well documented but in contrast to the Second World War, only one Briton was prosecuted for treason, Sir Roger Casement, arrested in Ireland in 1916. Nine of the Great War spies were shot in the Tower of London whereas, as shall be seen, only one such execution took place there between 1939 and 1945.

Sabotage of Royal Navy ships was suspected thrice but not proven. On 26 November 1914 the battleship HMS *Bulwark* blew up at Sheerness with the loss of 700 officers and men. The following year an auxiliary cruiser exploded at the same place killing both the crew and some seventy dockyard workers who were carrying out repairs on board. HMS *Natal* blew up on 30 December 1916 at Cromarty in Scotland. On 9 July 1917 the battleship HMS *Vanguard* blew up with the loss of 700. No explanations were ever found for these disasters so sabotage was presumed and precedents of what to look out for were established to be acted upon during the next year.

In 1916 the Directorate of Military Intelligence was formed and MO5, which had been answerable to Major-General Spencer Ewart, became MI5, a bureaucratic change which did not affect status, activity or personnel. Although officially a department of the War Office still, and answerable to the Secretary of State for War, MI5 had now achieved independence, with direct access to the Prime Minister. In practice Kell rarely came into personal contact with the Prime Minister of the day or any of his ministers, but in the post-war years he slowly began to develop closer relations with those at the most senior level of government, the Secretary to the Cabinet, the Permanent Under-secretaries and the Chiefs of Staff. He was soon to be constantly in contact with the First Secretary to the Treasury and the various special advisers to the government of the day, and maintained excellent contacts in industry, the City and even with the Press barons. A secret telephone exchange connected him directly to 'C', the chief of the SIS, the Foreign Office, the Metropolitan Police Commissioner and the DNI.

Power and political muscle however seemed to be more obviously connected with SIS and Naval Intelligence. MI5 attracted little glamour, for the officers generally worked far from the limelight and all too often saw credit given to others, Scotland Yard 'fronting' their more important *coups* and the end of their careers frequently occurring without recognition or thanks.

Such publicized literary figures as Compton Mackenzie, Somerset Maugham and Graham Greene preferred the glories of foreign service with the SIS. But MI5 did have one literary giant, John Buchan. He was Kell's nominee for the sensitive post of Press liaison when he returned to London in 1917 after a spell at the front in France as an intelligence officer. Buchan was appointed Director of Intelligence at the Ministry of Information and was assisted by Harold Baker (then Liberal MP for Accrington) and Hugh Macmillan (later Lord Macmillan). Buchan commented in his autobiography *Memory Hold-the-Door*:[1]

> 'I have some queer macabre recollections of those years – of meeting with odd people in odd places, of fantastic duties which a romancer would have rejected as beyond probability.'

Another MI5 author who was to draw on his own experiences was John Dickson Carr, the American-born thriller writer, who served with Kell before joining the BBC as a playwright in 1942.

The post-war period saw MI5 contract from its 1918 strength of eight hundred but in spite of this it managed to develop in new spheres. It was a time to learn from the past, a time to consolidate MI5's position amongst the secret intelligence communities, a moment to look around for new recruits who could be trained in specialist fields. It was a period, too, which was bedevilled with the growing activities of German and Soviet infiltration.

First, Kell consolidated his links with Scotland Yard and the various other intelligence units. To strengthen these important contacts Kell invented an exclusive club known as the I.P. Club. The I.P. stood either for Important Person or Intelligence Person, depending upon who asked. The club held regular informal meetings and each Christmas threw a dinner at the Hyde Park Hotel. In the interests of liaison some senior foreign (Allied) intelligence figures were invited to these functions, but all the guests were first carefully screened by the I.P. Club Secretary, Stanley Strong.

Then, ever mindful of his initial brief to maintain security in Britain's overseas interests, Kell forged stronger links with the Colonies and the Dominions. Commands overseas would second a Staff officer to act as a liaison or Defence Security Officer who reported back to Kell in London. Gradually the Dominions and the Colonies developed their own security organizations, and where these existed MI5 attached a liaison officer. The largest Dominion intelligence was the IPI, an independent body nominally within the Home Department of the Government of India. The IPI was run by Sir Horace Williamson, a barrister with more than thirty years' experience in the Indian police. At the same time, as shall be seen, SIS built up their own overseas network with 'Passport Control Offices'.

Changes in the law called for a specialist section to prepare cases for prosecution. The first legal adviser, and the future basis of 'A' Division's legal department, was a barrister from the Inner Temple, Walter Moresby. As the son of Admiral Moresby, he satisfied Kell's strict requirements concerning a 'reliable background', and as a man of some financial standing did not become a burden on MI5's meagre resources. Another recruit from the legal profession was Joseph Ball, a twenty-eight-year-old barrister from Gray's Inn.

There were those in high places who did not always like to see one department of the secret services growing unduly powerful and there were others who often thought that intelligence gatherers should all be together under one roof and one control. So, from time to time attempts were made to merge the various branches. The persistent refusal of governments to offer proper finance inevitably meant confining the department's activities. As an economy measure, Churchill as Secretary of State for War even suggested merging MI5 with SIS and what was then the Home Office Directorate of Intelligence, but the plan never gained acceptance even though Admiral Sinclair of SIS tried to resurrect it several times between 1915 and 1927. Kell bore no animosity for this take-over bid and later employed Sinclair's son Derek in MI5. Kell defended his department's position from all comers: he was determined to see that any attempt at amalgamation was effectively discredited and that his section, albeit small, was efficient and independent. Others too failed to absorb MI5 and on the rare occasions when a separate domestic intelligence organization was set up, as happened with Basil Thomson's 'Directorate of Intelligence' in 1919, Kell's department swallowed the interloper and took on its best officers.

Much as it may have annoyed Kell at the time to have his erstwhile friend Thomson try a *coup*, he must have been delighted later on when he discovered what an outstanding recruit he had gained from Scotland Yard in Guy Liddell. Like his two brothers, Cecil and David, Guy Liddell had won the Military Cross during the Great War in the Royal Field Artillery. He had been twenty-seven when Thomson asked him if he would like to work directly under him to accumulate information about extremists. This post was part of the reorganization of Special Branch that Thomson had masterminded when he became the head. Liddell at the Yard worked closely with Kell at MI5, whose own department had shrunk to a mere skeleton of its wartime size, and Sinclair at SIS who had actively engaged in anti-Soviet operations since the 1917 revolution. At first Liddell's office had a very small staff: Hugh Miller, Bunty Saunders (who later was to remain on the Foreign Office List as a 'clerical officer'), Miss McCulloch and his secretary Margo Huggins. The job entailed few field investigations, which were generally left to the rest of Special Branch, and mainly consisted of collating intelligence that had been received by the various other organizations in the field, NID, Foreign Office and the cypher and communications branch. The office developed a powerful collection of dossiers on political extremists and rank and file members of the Communist Party of Great Britain which Liddell considered a prime target of Comintern manipulation. This division of labour worked well until March 1927 when Liddell and Kell launched the first anti-Soviet counter-intelligence operation described in Chapter II.

Guy Liddell then moved from the police to MI5 where he was destined to become one of the most remarkable of counter-intelligence officers. Short, with thinning hair, he seemed to be either very mysterious or extremely shy. In fact, he was both. He was also a vain man, always conscious of his appearance. When interviewing subordinates, he had the disconcerting habit of staring into the distance and avoiding direct personal contact; at the same time, he would pluck thoughtfully at some invisible hair on his head. Liddell had married Calypso Baring, Lord Revelstoke's youngest daughter who, like himself, had strong Irish connections; Lord Revelstoke lived on Lambay Island near Dublin. Liddell's family were a source of anxiety to him and he took refuge in his work and in his music. He was an accomplished musician, probably the best amateur cellist in the country, and the occasional musical soirées held at his home were very popular. One of his assets was to spot talented young staff and encourage them. He trained Tar Robertson and Dick White, both of whose names will appear with considerable frequency later in these pages.

Upon joining MI5 Liddell went to work in 'B' Division, under Brigadier A.W.A. Harker, a regular soldier since 1910, known to his friends as Jasper. In 1933 Tar Robertson, a friend of Kell's son John, was invited to join the organization. A Sandhurst graduate, Robertson was commissioned into the Seaforth Highlanders and shared an office in MI5's Cromwell Road headquarters with Liddell and his assistant Millicent Bagot. At first his counter-espionage duties appeared to be limited to trailing the Japanese Military Attaché round the country, from one Army field exercise or Fleet review to another. He also served an apprenticeship with Colonel Alexander, which consisted in the main of buying drinks for informers on potential troublemakers in the ranks in Aldershot pubs. Those were indeed early days.

Dick White was first introduced to Guy Liddell by Malcolm Cumming. At the time White, a young school teacher, was conducting a party of boys to Australia and Cumming was on the same liner on his way to an Army exercise. The two men struck up a friendship and as a result White was appointed Liddell's assistant. White was already a graduate of Christ Church, Oxford and the Universities of Michigan and California; now Liddell asked him to extend his contacts abroad by travelling through Germany. White eventually returned to Britain having made several useful friends in Munich and Bavaria. He also returned convinced that war with Hitler was inevitable. White possessed a formidable brain and was quick to perceive the advantages of a network of double agents. He was later to become Director-General of the Security Service (1953-1956), Chief of the Secret Intelligence Service (1956-1968), and finally Intelligence Co-ordinator to the Cabinet, a post specially created for him (1968-1972).

Liddell, Robertson and White were all important new recruits to MI5 during the inter-war period and were all destined to play vital roles during the ensuing war.

Another name to conjure with at this time, already mentioned as MO5's first 'stool pigeon' in 1915, was Edward Hinchley-Cooke. His mother had been German and his command of the language was so good that in 1920 Kell lent him to the Prime Minister, Lloyd George, as his simultaneous translator for the Spa Conference. He acted in the same capacity for Lord Birkenhead and for several other Cabinet Ministers. Later he became unrivalled as an interrogator although he did at times appear to suffer from what some considered to be a rather exaggerated hatred of the enemy. Kell relied upon him to represent MI5 at all the pre-war espionage cases.

Harker and Liddell sat at their desks quietly collating information and maintaining essential contact with other interested departments.

Like spiders they built a web and sat waiting for the flies to show themselves. Should a fly appear they called in Special Branch. For although MI5 was responsible for discovering sabotage and subversions, it could neither arrest nor prosecute. The only positive action MI5 could take was to recruit and run individual agents, and this was now initiated by Charles Henry Maxwell Knight.

Max Knight was a remarkable ex-Naval officer who joined MI5 in 1924 and was to have considerable influence with the intelligence hierarchy and indeed the government. He was also to keep Churchill informed of intelligence developments through his personal assistant Major Desmond Morton, who had become a close friend. When Churchill became Prime Minister, Knight retained his ear and friendship.

It was inconceivable to think of the tall elegant Harker keeping a secret rendezvous with an agent but his close friend Knight thrived on the intrigue and greatly enjoyed the trappings of counter-espionage. He only met his agents on neutral territory such as the lobbies of second-rate hotels and used a whole dictionary of code names to cloak his identity. Different agents knew him simply as 'M', 'Captain King' or 'Mr K'. Knight was a successful author of natural history books, sharing Kell's passion for ornithology, and was also a talented zoologist, author, fencer, cricketer, magician and jazz drummer, quite apart from his more mysterious qualities. He instilled tremendous confidence and loyalty in all of his staff, in spite of some bizarre eccentricities. As a keen naturalist his pockets were often filled with live insects and he boasted of sleeping with grass snakes to keep them warm.

Knight directed many of his anti-Nazi campaigns from a small office in Dolphin Square which he had purchased in his wife's name. This was 308 Hood House, which retained the name 'Miss Coplestone' on the doorbell throughout the war. Later Knight bought a second flat, also in Dolphin Square, 10 Collingwood House, where he established his secretary, Joan Miller. Knight moved into Dolphin Square in 1937 and was thus conveniently located close to MI5 at Thames House on Millbank, and the Anglo-German Information Service in Parliament Street.

The rise to power of Hitler was watched and speculated upon within the War Office but it did not herald any new German intelligence offensive against the United Kingdom. MI5 still concentrated their meagre resources on the more certain – and, by this date, proven – Russian-inspired espionage. Other departments within the Directorate of Military Intelligence, principally MI3 (later MI14), were responsible for monitoring the growth of German militarism. MI5 were limited to the somewhat superficial surveillance and infiltration of the political groups which were in effect to become Nazi front organizations. The first of these was the Anglo-German Association, a movement founded by Lord D'Abernon after his six years in Berlin as British Ambassador. He left in 1926 having seen the Weimar Republic at first hand, and was determined to fight for better treatment for the Germans under the Treaty of Versailles. The tactics of infiltration employed by the Security Service in respect of these organizations are examined in Chapter III.

Between the wars the British intelligence services had to deal not only with problems raised by the rise of Nazism but also with those created by Irish nationalists. SIS had kept clear of Ireland since 1919, when a number of their professionals had been butchered on a day that became known as Bloody Sunday. The British Combined Intelligence Service under Colonel Ormonde Winter operated a number of 'safe houses' in the Dublin area and on 21 November they were raided by Michael Collins's IRA murder squads. Fourteen CIS men were killed in the gun battles that followed, along with two Royal Irish Constabulary policemen. Only one member of the IRA was hit during the raid.

Bloody Sunday had a devastating effect on MI5 and MI6 and from that date onwards neither organization displayed any great enthusiasm to become involved in Irish affairs. Anyway, the Security Service could only operate with the active help of the local police and after Lloyd George's partition of Ireland in 1921 this became impossible, even though the southern twenty-one counties were granted Dominion status. Then in June 1922 sixty-seven Fenians were rounded up in England and interned after the murder of Field-Marshal Sir Henry Wilson. The government defended its action by quoting the 'Restoration of Order in Ireland Act' but eventually after an adverse decision in the House of Lords agreed to pay the internees substantial damages. A major row ensued.

Another great furore about this time, which had nothing to do with MI5 but which unhappily seemed to taint it in some people's minds, was the mutiny at Invergordon. This was really a matter for Naval Intelligence but Charles Butler and Colonel W.A. Alexander of MI5 were dispatched to the North to assess whether it was a limited minor incident or a matter of great moment. Despite their suggestion that it was only a storm in a teacup, the DNI himself, Rear-Admiral C.V. Usborne, was sacked. The only useful aspect of the affair was that the names of the 400-odd seamen who were purged in the aftermath of this mutiny were forwarded to MI5 by Naval Intelligence and formed a fruitful addition to the Registry's card index for future reference.

During the early Thirties, when MI5 was based in London's Cromwell Road, there was a staff establishment of fewer than twenty-five officers, a figure which included some secretarial personnel who also carried out occasional investigative duties. This small number of people were expected to collect and collate all intelligence data and to put out sensitive antennae to learn of any attempts by hostile intelligence services to undermine loyalty or to penetrate positions of power or importance which might have later implications. There was alert concern for the stability of British institutions, particularly the armed forces, for they were thought to be the target of Communist-inspired subversion. Three incidents in the Thirties attracted an embarrassing amount of adverse press coverage although they had nothing whatever to do with MI5 as such: Kell again however caught considerable side flak.

In 1933 the *Oleander* and the *War Afridi* were apparently sabotaged. In 1935 the submarine *Oberon* suffered unexplained damage to its electrical gear. HMS *Cumberland*, a cruiser, experienced a similar attack and the ill-fated *Royal Oak* reported a deliberate attempt to knock out her fire-control system. The final straw occurred the following year when the main diesel engines of the submarine *L-54* were tampered with in Devonport and HMS *Velox* nearly had some mine-release gear stolen in the Naval dockyard at Chatham.

MI5 were called in on all these investigations in an advisory capacity only, as the nature of the damage clearly pointed to its being an internal matter for the Royal Navy. Major Horace F. ('Con') Bodington (who, with Charles Butler and Colonel W.A. Alexander, had previously tried to get to the bottom of the Invergordon Mutiny without much success) was given a watching brief as the Naval Intelligence Department conducted a search for the elusive saboteurs. With the aid of MI5's Registry and Special Branch they were able to name five dockyard workers whose left-wing political affiliations gave cause for concern. The men were dismissed early in 1937 without any explanation and a mighty scene erupted in Parliament. These men were definitely not responsible for some of the earlier incidents (which were considered to have been caused by Naval ratings with grievances, probably devoid of political motives) in the opinion of the NID, so the suspicion lingered that there was a sabotage ring within His Majesty's Senior Service which Kell had failed to detect.

MI5 have often been thought to have been paranoid about Communist-inspired subversion but this was always considered to be more likely than infiltration from Germany in the inter-war period because of the nature and stated aims of the Soviet Communist

International and because there was a legitimate Communist political party extant in Great Britain openly dedicated to furthering the cause of Communism. Moreover, after 1921 there were Soviet envoys and diplomats officially present in London, who it was feared would provide cover for subversive agents. The man appointed by Kell to counter this menace was Colonel W.A. Alexander, a wealthy Regular Army officer who had good reason to loathe the Comintern as he had lost most of his fortune by backing the anti-Soviet North Russian Expeditionary Force. The way in which MI5 coped with the Communists up to 1939 is described in Chapter II.

In 1937 the staff of MI5 transferred – all twenty-eight of them – from Cromwell Road to two floors in Thames House, Millbank. They then moved to shared accommodation around the corner in Horseferry Road. By the time this move was completed Kell was certain that war was unavoidable. He became increasingly alarmed at the flood of refugees arriving in Britain. More than 20,000 Germans had registered with the police by mid-1937 and the number was growing daily. With this volume the Director-General warned that the security situation was becoming untenable and at one point urged the Cabinet to think in terms of 3,000 possible agents. Chapters IV and V explain how MI5 dealt with aliens and possible Fifth Columnists in 1939.

Kell did eventually succeed in gaining permission to expand his organization but matters had been left so late that MI5 found it difficult to increase in size and keep good security. To meet the need for a bigger Security Service Kell dispensed with one of his ground-rules, that he should interview every potential employee. In the eighteen months preceding the war MI5 grew faster than at any time in its history. Once war was declared on 3 September, 1939, it was to experience yet another traumatic change.

However before covering MI5's wartime activities I would like to discuss first the Soviet Union's attempts to penetrate into Britain before the war and then those made by the Nazis.

II
MI5 and the CPGB

'The loyalty of a Party Member lies primarily with the Party and secondarily with his country.'

ALEXANDER FOOTE, a CPGB member recruited into the NKVD by Douglas Springhall in 1938, commenting on his experiences in his memoirs, *Handbook for Spies*.

In 1924 Ramsay MacDonald's government allowed the Soviet Union to establish a permanent diplomatic representative in London, thus setting the scene for a covert conflict between the British and Russian intelligence services. The secret war had many participants, including the Communist Party of Great Britain, the Comintern, the Secret Intelligence Service, the Government Code and Cypher School and the Security Service. The task of monitoring the activities of the CPGB and keeping an eye on the Russian envoys was divided amongst several British organizations. To clarify this, it is necessary to go back in time to recap some significant events.

In 1923 the DNI, Sir Hugh ('Quex') Sinclair succeeded Mansfield Cumming as Chief of the Secret Intelligence Service ('C'). Cumming was a remarkable Naval officer who frequently disconcerted those who met him by his habit of absent-mindedly tapping his wooden leg during a conversation. Sinclair's move from the Admiralty to 21 Queen Anne's Gate, 'C's official office and residence, also brought about a change in the organization entrusted to maintain surveillance on the country's wireless traffic, the Government Code and Cypher School. GC & CS were the peacetime successors to the famous cryptographers of Room 40, headed by Commander Alastair Denniston, a Scottish professor of German with an insatiable appetite for mathematical puzzles.

GC & CS were supposed to provide secure codes for British official communications but much of their duties involved the breaking of foreign wireless traffic. When in 1919 GC & CS had been authorized by the Cabinet to continue the work of Room 40, it had consisted of twenty-five officers, all poring over captured German code-books under the DNI's supervision.

Now, in the Twenties, GC & CS were housed in Broadway Buildings which conveniently backed on to the office of the SIS Chief in Queen Anne's Gate, so they were firmly under SIS control. Denniston and his team occupied two floors of the office building while the main SIS headquarters were located directly above them.

The actual interception of signals took place in several Foreign Office ground stations but the battle against the Soviet codes was concentrated in a small, discreetly secluded radio station, Grove Park, in Camberwell, South London. Here transmissions to and from the Russian Chargé d'Affaires office in Chesham Place were recorded in secret and then decrypted by Denniston's experts. One of his 'brains' was F. Fetterlein, a Russian who had helped devise many of the Tsarist codes inherited by the Communists.

While the GC & CS code-breakers plucked Soviet messages from the ether another secret organization received the final 'clear' versions and acted on the information gained. This special anti-subversion office, named the Directorate of Intelligence, ran Grove Park and was masterminded by Basil Thomson, the head of Special Branch. As already explained, in 1919 Thomson's 'private' intelligence service had been left largely in the hands of Guy Liddell, his secretary, Margo Huggins, and a small staff consisting of Hugh Miller, Bunty Saunders and Miss McCulloch. Liddell and his team were housed in Scotland Yard and, with the aid of SIS who had been actively engaged in anti-Soviet operations since the 1917 revolution, they had developed an impressive collection of dossiers on political extremists.

Although Guy Liddell and MI5 were later to be particularly successful in dealing with Soviet-inspired subversion, their first effort was something of a blunder. On Saturday, 25 October 1924, *The Times* and the *Daily Mail* published the full text of the Zinoviev letter which, dated 15 September 1924, purported to be a secret directive from the Comintern addressed to the Communist Party of Great Britain. The British Central Committee were urged:

'In the event of danger of war, with the aid of the latter (Communist cells within British troop units) and in contact with the transport workers it is possible to paralyse all the military preparations of the bourgeois, and make a start in turning an imperialist war into a class war.'

The publication of the letter ensured Ramsay MacDonald's government would suffer a humiliating defeat at the General Election, which was only days away. The implications were particularly damaging for the Labour administration because the Comintern were apparently organizing within the British Army. The Prime Minister and the Cabinet had fought hard for a treaty with Moscow, and their pronouncements on the subject now dramatically backfired. If ever there was a well-timed leak, the Zinoviev letter was it. The impact was particularly effective because the Foreign Office itself released the copy document to the newspapers. Even the Prime Minister believed in its authenticity, although he badly misjudged the consequences of its publication.

MacDonald did not question the content or the origin off the letter because he had been advised by Kell, Liddell and Sinclair that it was genuine. In fact, they were all wrong. A copy of the 'original' had come into the possession of Donald im Thurn, a wealthy ex-MI5 officer with close connections with several influential emigré families, from a mysterious source. The letter was passed to the Foreign Office and Kell for an opinion, and both sent it on to Scotland Yard for Liddell's consideration, since he was effectively the sole expert on covert Bolshevik policy. The letter was examined by Bunty Saunders and Guy Liddell, and both reported that it contained few surprises for the intelligence community. The contents merely served to confirm what they already knew concerning the intentions of the Comintern.

The matter would probably have remained confidential if Sir Reginald ('Blinker') Hall, the Unionist MP for Eastbourne and ex-Director of Naval Intelligence (and decrypter of the Zimmermann Telegram) had not been tipped off. He was informed, as was Conservative Central Office, that the Labour government were planning to suppress evidence of a 'Soviet plot' because of the forthcoming General Election. Hall was very close to Admiral Sinclair (they had both been DNI) and both fell headlong into a classic deception operation. Kell accepted Liddell's opinion that the letter was probably genuine but agreed, at Sinclair's request, not to pursue the matter. Sinclair and Hall also believed in the authenticity of the letter and recognized that, however conveniently, it provided proof of Moscow's sinister intentions. They were determined to take action and felt duty-bound to prevent the affair from being hushed up.

The Labour Party were caught completely unprepared by the ensuing scandal and were duly crushed on polling day, 28 October. The *Daily Herald*, Labour's standard-bearer, commented on the eve-of-poll:

'THE RED PLOT WILL BECOME LABOUR'S RED LETTER DAY'

The domestic political consequences of the Zinoviev letter were all too clear as the new Prime Minister, Stanley Baldwin, formed his Cabinet. The Soviet Union was not to be trusted and had been hoist with its own petard. The Labour Party tried to revive the affair on several later occasions but there was never enough support to launch a proper enquiry. A 1966 investigation by three *Sunday Times* journalists commented:

> 'Without stretching causation too far, it is possible to see the effect of the Zinoviev affair on the whole broad future of democratic socialism in Britain. The decision to refuse Communists the Labour umbrella in electoral politics was a critical moment in the transformation of the Labour Party into the mass democratic organization which permanently replaced the Liberals in the two-party system.'[2]

The letter is now thought to have been forged in Berlin by two Russian exiles, but was nevertheless accepted as genuine by Donald im Thurn, Liddell, Miss Saunders, Kell, Hall, Sinclair, the Foreign Office and the Prime Minister, to say nothing of the newspapers involved.

It was to be the same MP, Admiral 'Blinker' Hall who was to spark off one of the great pre-war intelligence *coups*. In March 1927 he had been introduced to George Monckland, a Lloyds underwriter who had served in the Black Watch during the war and had been invalided out of the Army in 1918 after being wounded. Monckland told a strange story. A young friend of his named Wilfred Macartney, who also worked in Lloyds, had asked him to find out about shipments of arms to Finland from cargo documents lodged with various insurers. Monckland saw no harm in carrying out this simple request but was surprised when he was handed £25 for the information. Macartney then explained that he was working for the Russians. This news thoroughly alarmed Monckland, who made up some fictitious details for Macartney. Macartney then produced a long questionnaire on matters concerning the RAF and asked Monckland to complete it.

It was at this point that Monckland had decided to seek advice, and had obtained an introduction to Sir Reginald Hall, who lived nearby in

Curzon Street. Hall in turn passed the questionnaire on to his old colleague Vernon Kell, and a major investigation began. At Scotland Yard Liddell discovered that Macartney had already acquired a sizeable file and criminal record. He had first come to the attention of the police in February 1926 when he had been sentenced to nine months for smashing a jeweller's shop window in Albemarle Street. His Army record revealed an extraordinary career which included a spell as an intelligence officer.

In 1915, at the age of only sixteen, Macartney failed an Army medical because of poor eyesight, but managed to join the RAMC 3rd Field Ambulance as a driver and be sent to France, where he secured a commission in the Royal Scots. After some months his eyes deteriorated and he was forced to resign his commission. After treatment he was recommissioned in the Essex Regiment, then stationed in Malta. From there he went to Egypt where he was taken on by the Staff as a censor. His first posting was to the Aegean, under the command of Captain Compton Mackenzie, the Royal Marines officer who headed British Intelligence operations in the Eastern Mediterranean theatre. Macartney worked directly for Compton Mackenzie in the cover of a Port Control Officer until September 1917 when he returned to France with the 52nd Division. In September the following year he was taken prisoner at Cambrai but made a daring escape from the Germans by jumping out of a train near Aix-la-Chapelle. This achievement was rewarded with a Certificate of Merit from the Army Council.

After the Armistice Macartney, now aged nineteen, was attached to the Berlin-Baghdad Railway Mission in Constantinople where he was appointed Railway Transport Officer, He left the Army as a lieutenant in August 1919. His criminal record showed his February 1926 conviction and two fines for being drunk and disorderly in the West End in January and February 1927.

Liddell's intelligence file also identified Macartney as a contributor to the *Sunday Worker* newspaper. After his release from prison in October 1926 he wrote an article entitled 'Boss propaganda in the Scrubs' and three weeks later 'The fate of the good union men' in the same paper.

Eventually Liddell interviewed Monckland, the Lloyds underwriter, and was offered further valuable information; Macartney had shown him a typewritten letter dated 22 March from a 'K.J. Johnson', apparently the Russian master-spy in London. Macartney explained that this was the name used by whoever was directing Soviet operations in Britain.

Kell was determined to identify the whole network before the Yard closed in, and arranged an elaborate deception for Macartney. The points raised in the RAF questionnaire Monckland had been asked to fill in demonstrated that the author had considerable military knowledge. Very likely it was the work of the Soviets. The decision was therefore taken to provide Monckland with a genuine secret document and keep a close watch on Macartney. An RAF handbook marked 'secret' and entitled 'Regulations for Training the Flying Personnel of the Royal Air Force' was given to Monckland for onward transmission to the Russians. The risk in offering this particular document was insignificant because the Air Ministry had assured Kell it was obsolete and about to be replaced by an up-to-date issue. Special Branch were mobilized to follow Macartney after he had left Monckland's flat in Hertford Street, Mayfair, but the matter took on an altogether more complex aspect when Macartney was observed to pass the RAF manual to a Russian who was known to be a member of the USSR Trade Delegation. The complications were two-fold. The Trade Delegation had diplomatic immunity and, secondly, it was difficult to maintain close surveillance on the Delegation's offices unless the City of London police and the Foreign Office were informed, thus increasing the risk of a leak.

The Soviet Trade Delegation had been the subject of Guy Liddell's interest since they first moved into their premises at 49 Moorgate in the City. The building itself had cost over £300,000, a substantial sum, and had several unique features. These included concrete-lined vaults which were off-limits to anyone other than the most senior of the Russian staff. The Trade Delegation, under the chairmanship of Mr L. Khinchuk, employed a staff of over 400, 233 of whom were Russians. A little research revealed that the Delegation paid the wages of only 35, the rest being 'attached' to the All Russian Co-operative Society Limited, better known as Arcos. The intercepts broken by the GC & CS had long ago proved the diplomatic mission, the Trade Delegation and Arcos to be involved in subversive activities in Britain. To date no action had been taken, but now the situation changed. The Secretary of State for War, Kell's direct superior, went to Sir William Joynson-Hicks, the Home Secretary, on the evening of 11 May 1927 and explained how MI5 were sure the Russians were in possession of a secret RAF document. He proposed a massive police raid on the Russian Trade Delegation with a warrant issued by a magistrate under the Official Secrets Act.

The Home Secretary agreed, but only after he had been reassured on a few important points and after consultations with the Prime Minister, Mr Baldwin, and the Foreign Secretary, Sir Austen Chamberlain. Not least of these points was the diplomatic immunity enjoyed by Mr Khinchuk and his Soviet staff. Sir Wyndham Childs, the Metropolitan Police Assistant Commissioner and head of Special Branch, was persuasive. The police, he said, would exploit a loophole previously overlooked by the Russians. The Soviet Trade Delegation certainly had immunity from search but they shared offices with Arcos Ltd, a company registered in Britain with limited liability, which of course did not enjoy any protection. If a magistrate issued a search warrant on Arcos, Special Branch would achieve their goal. Enquiries had shown that there was no physical division between the two Russian offices. When the Trade Delegation Chairman made his protest about an illegal search, as he surely would, the police could reply that they had only entered the premises of Arcos.

Joynson-Hicks agreed to the manoeuvre and the City of London police were contacted. Colonel Turnbull, their Chief, agreed to send one of his men, Chief Superintendent Halford, to a City Magistrate's Court to apply for a warrant under Section 9 of the Official Secrets Act. The application was supported by the sworn evidence of Special Branch detectives who stated that the missing RAF manual had definitely been located in the Arcos buildings. A close watch had been kept on the agent delivering the document (Macartney), they disclosed, and the lodgings of the various Soviet personnel involved had been 'surveyed'. A warrant was issued on the morning of 12 May and at 4.25 PM a mass of policemen congregated outside Soviet House at 49 Moorgate. The raiding party consisted of about 100 uniformed City of London policemen, 50 Special Branch officers and a small contingent of Foreign Office interpreters who were to translate the documents seized.

At 4.30 PM the police, some brandishing revolvers, swept into the building and secured the main corridors. Then a second wave entered all the individual offices and ordered the staff out into open areas where they were obliged to turn out their pockets and handbags. Every scrap of paper was recovered and examined. A long search started through all the offices and the British staff were questioned and then released. In the basement the raiders met some opposition. The centre of the building contained a specially protected room with no handle on the door. The detectives hammered on the door but were warned to keep away by shouts from within. Eventually the police managed to force an entry and found two men pushing documents into a blazing fire. After a brief struggle the men surrendered and a box stuffed with important papers was recovered. The two were identitified as Anton Miller, a cypher clerk, and Mr Khudiakov, both members of the Russian Trade Delegation.

Once the building had been sealed off and the telephone lines disconnected the police marshalled the staff into the entrance hall and began releasing them, first the women and then the men. The heads of each department, however, were detained and asked for their keys so that all the safes on the premises could be opened. The searchers continued their work, poring over mounds of files until 11 PM, when it was decided to resume the operation in the morning. To dissuade anyone planning on going into Arcos before the authorities, a massive police guard was mounted on the building for the night. Meanwhile Mr Rosengolz, the Soviet Chargé d'Affaires, began to telephone those involved or implicated in the raid. He registered a protest with Sir Austen Chamberlain, the Foreign Secretary, and arranged to see him the following day. He then tried to apply pressure on the government by asking the Labour Party to table a series of urgent questions in the House to the Home Secretary. Mr Arthur Henderson MP duly obliged, but the next morning the police kept their nerve and resumed their search. In the course of the morning Colonel Turnbull and Sir Wyndham Childs went on a conducted tour of the building and had all the places of interest pointed out to them. Two of these were large concrete storerooms which had resisted all attempts to gain entry. The Russians refused to give up the keys and the steel doors looked impregnable. They were also shown a quantity of Soviet propaganda films and a collection of weapons that the Chargé d'Affaires later claimed were 'samples of hunting rifles' waiting for shipment back to Moscow. The team of interpreters discovered a wealth of papers relating to Soviet espionage and subversion and were busy making copies and translations. Nevertheless, the RAF manual was not found and it seemed likely that it had been among the papers burnt in the first moments of the raid.

Later that afternoon Sir Wyndham Childs went to report to the Home Secretary and obtained permission to force a way into the two remaining strongrooms. MI5 then arranged for a demolition company to move into the vaults of the offices and start drilling through the reinforced walls. By midnight on the second day of the raid, after more than two hours' work, the police burst into the strongrooms and seized a mass of files stacked inside.

The raid eventually came to an end at midnight on 16 May 1927, after just over 103 hours and several protests from the Russians. Macartney had made a panic-stricken telephone call to Monckland soon after the raid had started, telling him to destroy any incriminating papers he might have collected. Monckland passed this news on to Liddell, even though arrangements had already been made with the GPO to intercept Monckland's mail and telephone conversations. The Foreign Office GC & CS code-breakers then made their report. They had managed to decrypt several of the secret telegrams sent by Rosengolz to the Commissariat for Foreign Affairs in Moscow. On 18 May one reported on the raid:

> 'Your No 126. There were none of our ciphers or very secret material at the Trade Delegation. On special instructions the Chargé d'Affaires acquainted the Trade Delegate with the content of certain cipher messages. (signed) YAKOVLEV'

Another stated:

> 'Among a number of rumours as to the nature of the missing document, there is also a supposition that it relates to the Aerial Bombardment of (DELETED). I consider it expedient for you to publish as a rumour a statement that it refers to the aerial bombardment of a certain European capital.'

The RAF handbook was never found but Kell reckoned that the raid had been more than justified. The regular Soviet courier between Chesham House and Moorgate, Robert Koling, had been searched and several compromising letters relating to future trade union plans in the United Kingdom were recovered. They made fascinating reading and enabled Liddell to expand his growing pile of dossiers on political extremists and Communist front organizations. The Trade Delegation cypher clerk, Anton Miller, was caught carrying a list of Comintern cover addresses in such far-off countries as Canada, Argentina, Colombia, Guatemala, Uruguay, Mexico, Brazil, Chile, South Africa, Australia and the United States. Some of the personal files read during the raid also gave a fascinating insight into the Comintern's behaviour. One letter the Cabinet decided to publish quoted 'Comrade Karl Bahn' telling 'Comrade Jan Jilinsky' that the members of the CPGB who were employed on Soviet steamers as seamen were 'idle and drunken'. Evidently the 'Ships-arco's' division had decided to enlist Communists on three Soviet merchant vessels which flew British flags. The results were laughably unsatisfactory. Comrade Bahn itemized the records of many of the men involved and complained:

> '… the British Communist Party recommends none but the refuse of the Labour Party, people who are not seamen. The few satisfactory British seamen, Communists, who are rarely found, never dream of darkening the threshold of the Communist Party on the score of work and a good sailor has always so far been sure of finding work.'

Some of the individual dossiers of the seamen proved highly entertaining:

> 'Adams. Stoker. A good orator but a bad stoker and a slacker. The other stokers had to do his work for him. Deserted in Odessa and is now employed in the Seamen's Club there, presumably as an organizer.
>
> Ralph. Stoker. Was summoned by telegram from Dublin by Burns. A bad worker and the Party comrades distrusted him. Drank and left the ship on his own or would have had to be dismissed.'

On 26 May the government published a remarkable White Paper and announced that diplomatic relations with Moscow, which had been originally initiated by Ramsay MacDonald in 1921, would be severed forthwith. Evidence of the Soviet Union's attempts at subversion were included in the two-part document. The first reproduced various incriminating letters found during the Arcos raid; the second dealt with decrypted telegrams intercepted by the Foreign Office. Liddell passed on copies of these to other European counter-intelligence agencies who made their own raids on local Arcos branches. A Parliamentary motion of censure on the government's action tabled by a group of Socialists was roundly defeated by a majority of 248.

An unexpected result of the Arcos raid was Macartney's confidence. After his hasty telephone call to Monckland he recovered himself and was soon in contact again, in spite of a slight brush with the law caused by another drinking session. Liddell intervened behind the scenes and all charges against Macartney were quietly dropped to prevent his being sent to prison, an event Liddell understandably wished to avoid for a while. For the next six months Monckland tried to extract more information from Macartney about the network with which he was involved. Special Branch were stretched to their limits following the young Russian agent on his travels, which included a trip to Berlin. During the early part of August Macartney made a couple of visits to a secretarial firm in the Edgware Road and had several letters and reports typed up, apparently for the elusive 'Mr Johnson'. Each time he went to the typists Special Branch detectives called in shortly afterwards and took away the dictation notes.

Gradually, the evidence mounted that a spy-ring really did exist. A copy of one report for the spy-master recorded 'expenses paid' and 'Davis' and 'Barton' were mentioned as having received sums from Macartney. It seemed likely that Davis was a sergeant in the Tank Corps and had provided Macartney with some basic intelligence about British mechanized armour during a visit to Aldershot and on a later trip to Tidworth, timed to coincide with military exercises.

Keeping track of Macartney proved a difficult task because he had managed to obtain a false passport in the name of William Frank Hudson. He once boasted to Monckland that he had access to genuine passports, issued by the Passport Office but without any record remaining at Petty France. MI5 immediately contacted the Passport Office and to their amazement got confirmation of his claim. A valid passport had been issued to a William Frank Hudson but mysteriously there was no copy of the original application.

By November 1927 Macartney had arranged for Monckland to exchange letters with 'Mr Johnson' and a meeting was set up for the afternoon of 16 November 1927 in the Marble Arch Cinema Café. Monckland was to sit alone at a table reading a book and 'Mr Johnson' would come over and introduce himself.

Monckland complied with the instructions and sat down to read a copy of *The Spy* by Upton Sinclair. He was soon approached by a young foreigner in his early twenties who announced himself as 'Mr Johnson' and enquired about shipments of arms to the Baltic States and the quality of information Monckland might be able to provide. After a brief conversation Monckland agreed to a second rendezvous the following day when, he claimed, he would provide 'Mr Johnson' with some examples of the intelligence to which he had access. The meeting would also be attended by Macartney.

MI5 now decided the charade had been allowed to go on for long enough as the two principal characters had been identified. The following day 'Mr Johnson' was arrested by Inspector Cosgrove of Special Branch while he waited for his two companions. Macartney was intercepted at Hampstead tube station, right across the road from the agreed meeting place. Both men were taken to Scotland Yard where they were interrogated by the Assistant Commissioner, Colonel Carter, and Superintendents Parker, Byrne and McBride. 'Mr Johnson' was found to be Georg Hansen, a twenty-four-year old German student who had registered as an alien at Bow Street Police Station in July 1927. Clearly, he was a replacement 'Mr Johnson', instructed to bypass the usual route of communication to Moscow which had been compromised by the White Paper's publication. Both men were charged with offences under the Official Secrets Act and remanded to Brixton where they stayed until their trial at the Old Bailey in January the following year.

The prosecution at the Old Bailey offered a great weight of evidence. George Monckland described how he had become friendly with Macartney and had been pressed into gathering intelligence for the

Russians. Special Branch detectives related the long surveillance operation that had been mounted to keep track of Macartney and identify 'Mr Johnson'. Two typists from the Edgware Road secretarial firms recognized Macartney as the author of various technical reports on aircraft. Finally, Post Office officials from MI5's Letter Interception Unit presented photographs of incriminating correspondence between Macartney and Monckland.

A substantial amount of damning evidence came from Macartney himself, or rather from his rooms. Special Branch detectives recovered a formidable quantity of documents including a notebook full of observations made during the Army exercises at Tidworth in September 1927.

The defence were in difficulties right from the beginning. So much depended on Monckland's testimony that he was repeatedly questioned about his relationship with Macartney and his circle of friends who, it was suggested, were mainly criminal types. Monckland denied he spent time playing *chemin de fer* in an illegal club but did not elaborate on how close a friend he was of the younger man. Macartney stated that he had known Monckland for about five years, 'more intimately than anyone else in London'. The manoeuvre to discredit Monckland failed because of the respectable picture the Attorney-General, Sir Douglas Hogg, painted of his chief witness. Monckland had been educated at Marlborough and articled in his father's firm of solicitors before joining the Black Watch in 1914. He worked at Lloyds and disclosed that his income was in excess of £1,000 per year. He certainly made a better impression than the young spy, who was accidently revealed as a young man with several previous convictions (the judge, the Lord Chief Justice, instructed the jury on this occasion to forget what they had heard) and a fully-paid-up member of the CPGB. The search of Macartney's rooms produced a membership card which showed he had joined the CPGB's Paddington Branch on 30 April 1927. The defence claimed Macartney was a part-time journalist contributing to various leftist newspapers and it was because of this interest he had followed up several offers of 'scoops' from Monckland. Some of Monckland's ideas for 'exposures' were fairly mundane, such as the claim that Britain was making huge covert deliveries of arms to Baltic states bordering the Soviet Union.

But potentially far more dangerous was Macartney's claim that Monckland had offered to obtain evidence from 'Locker-Lampson' that 'the Zinovieff letter had been forged'. The reference was to the Right Honourable Godfrey Locker-Lampson CMG DSO, the Unionist Member of Parliament for Wood Green and, at the time of the trial, the

Under-Secretary of State for Foreign Affairs. The prosecution quickly denied that Monckland had made any such suggestion and moved on to other matters.

Macartney was attempting to introduce a political bombshell into the proceedings which could well embarrass MI5, Scotland Yard and SIS. But he was trying to put life into a long-dead issue. Since 1924 there had been many other momentous political events, including the Conservative defeat of the General Strike of 1926. The Tories showed no inclination to pursue the intelligence aspects of the Zinoviev affair and the unofficial Labour Party enquiry's conclusions did not carry much weight with anyone except the Party faithful.

Undaunted, Macartney tried to use every weapon at his disposal. He attacked Monckland's version of everything, accused the Letter Interception Unit photographer of perjury and swore that all the other witnesses were mistaken. The effort was in vain. The jury was all too ready to believe in a wide-scale Russian conspiracy even though 'Barton' and 'Davis' were never produced in Court.

Georg Hansen was rather more muted in his defence. He told the Court that he was neither a Communist nor a Bolshevist but merely a journalist from Germany who wished to improve his English. He had come to London, he explained, to enrol at the Regent School of Languages. He did manage to surprise the prosecution on the second day of the trial by bringing a third character into the affair. He claimed that he had met a 'Dr Odenbach' in the Piccadilly branch of Lyon's Corner House and had been asked by him to assist with research on a book about disarmament. His meeting with Monckland at the Marble Arch Cinema Café was, he said, an appointment he was keeping for 'Dr Odenbach'. He was using the English name 'Johnson' so as not to alarm the Lloyds underwriter.

Unfortunately, this belated idea failed the following day when Inspector Cosgrove told the jury that overnight he had searched the Register of Aliens at the Home Office and there was no record of any 'Dr Odenbach'. The defence ploy, such as it was, crumbled and both men were declared guilty after the jury had retired for only fifteen minutes.

They were convicted of various charges under the Official Secrets Act including 'attempting to obtain information on the RAF', 'collecting information relating to the mechanized force of His Majesty's Army' and persuading Monckland to do the same. Each man received ten years, to be served concurrently with a further sentence of two years' hard labour.[3]

The conviction was never really in doubt but it was nevertheless a considerable victory for Kell and Liddell. The two separate intelligence offices had liaised well together and the Arcos raid had proved a dramatic success. Both men were satisfied that for at least the time being the Russians would carefully reconsider before committing further agents to Britain. The two intelligence officers also recognized that the Comintern were particularly interested in the recruitment of ideological traitors who would certainly prove more difficult to detect. Nigel Watson, a Russian linguist who had joined MI5 to sift through the piles of confiscated Soviet papers, reported that although the Russians had apparently failed to influence the General Strike or turn Communist seamen into reliable agents and couriers, they did attach importance to their relationship with the CPGB and British trade unions.

One of the letters confiscated from Robert Koling, the Arcos courier, was from Atchkanov, Secretary of the International Propaganda Committee of Transport Workers, addressed to 'Comrade Atkins' in London, dealing with the distribution of *Seafarer* magazines in the United States of America. Perhaps the longest letter seized was from G. Sloutsky, Secretariat, Miners' International Propaganda Committee, addressed to 'Comrades Aitken and Bob Ellis' in London. The contents concerned a forthcoming meeting of the Miners' Federation of Great Britain, the question of the Anglo-Soviet Committee of Miners and the attitude they would adopt in connection with future 'conflict'.

Not all the correspondence related to trade union activity in Britain. The General Secretary of the Revolutionary Leather Workers' International Committee of Propaganda and Action, Comrade Jusefovitch, wrote to 'Comrade Bixby' of the Workers' Party of the United States, requesting information on 'the position' of left-wing activists in the boot and shoe industry in America.

Watson's analysis of the documents stated that the GPU and the OGPU would concentrate their efforts on subverting the CPGB and covertly recruiting sympathizers. The view was confirmed by one of the first Soviet defectors, General Alexander Orlov, author of the basic Soviet espionage handbook. Orlov had been head of the Economic Section of the CHEKA, and had fled from Spain to the United States where he had published *The Secret History of Stalin's Crimes*. Orlov was a prolific source of intelligence, as was another defector, Georgi Agabekov, an OGPU officer who had fallen in love with a twenty-year-old English girl named Isabel Streater who was living with her parents in Constantinople. Agabekov and Miss Streater married in November 1931 and went to live in Brussels. Eventually their marriage broke up, and in 1938 he was kidnapped and murdered by the OGPU. He had previously been the OGPU 'Resident' in Persia under diplomatic cover at the Soviet Legation in Teheran. In December 1930 he volunteered information to the Fish investigation of Communism in the United States. Isabel Streater joined the British Foreign Office after the war and died in New York in November 1971.

The most interesting intelligence to be gleaned from these defectors was the claim that there was an ideological traitor in the Foreign Office, known to Moscow as 'B3'. Kell's growing concern about the influence of the Comintern in Britain was translated into action. Liddell, Miller, Bunty Saunders and Miss McCulloch were brought formally into MI5 and allocated offices in its Cromwell Road headquarters. This move was to mark a significant moment in the development of MI5's ability and determination to combat Soviet subversion. Kell also strengthened MI5 by recruiting Max Knight, who proceeded to set up a special operation unit to plant agents inside the CPGB.

For some time, the telephones at the CPGB headquarters in King Street, Covent Garden, had been monitored at the Temple Bar Telephone Exchange, on the authority of a warrant from the Home Secretary, and Knight's name was now added to the distribution list of the MI5 transcripts, Guy Liddell and Hugh Miller had also organized an embryonic vetting procedure to compare names in CPGB files with those employed by the government in sensitive areas. This led to a series of dismissals of leftist workers up and down the country. One of those sacked was Percy Glading, an engineer employed as an examiner in the Navy Department of Woolwich Arsenal. Glading had achieved a dossier at Scotland Yard because he had attended the Communist International in India in 1925. He had become known to MI5 after he had been implicated in a conspiracy by Colonel (later Sir Cecil) Kaye of the Indian Central Intelligence Bureau, the IPI 'umbrella', who had supervised the arrest of fifty-six Bolshevist agitators led Manandranath Roy, a Comintern agent living in Germany. The conspirators had been tried in Cawnpore, Bengal, and sentenced to varying terms of imprisonment.

The CPGB had, of course, been the subject of Special Branch scrutiny since its first inception, and members of the Party's Executive had been convicted of such crimes as sedition and breach of the peace as long ago as 1919. Indeed, the veteran General Secretary, Harry Pollitt, had earned his first entry on his criminal record in June 1921.

Surveillance on the CPGB in the early days had been directed by Detective Chief Inspector Parker, who placed his men at most Party rallies, but his methods were thought to be rather less sophisticated than was required for the task. On one embarrassing occasion in April 1924 Special Branch men rented rooms in Bedford Street directly below a

CPGB conference. By opening a trapdoor in the ceiling, they were able to sit underneath the speaker's platform and take shorthand notes of what was said. Unfortunately, the two detectives were discovered and the local police called to the scene. A young constable found, when he brought his prisoners to Bow Street, that he had apprehended Detective Sergeant Hopley of Scotland Yard!

In a once-and-for-all effort Parker organized a raid in October 1925 on 16 King Street, the Young Communist League at 38 Great Ormond Street and the *Workers' Weekly* office in Fleet Street. They hauled away more than 250,000 letters, documents, books and pamphlets and arrested ten members of the Party's Executive Committee and two others. They were Albert Inkpen (CPGB Secretary), Ernest Cant (CPGB London Organizer), John Campbell (editor of *Workers' Weekly*), William Rust (YCL Secretary), Tom Wintringham (assistant editor of *Workers' Weekly*), Harry Pollitt (member of the Comintern Executive in Moscow), William Gallacher (later Communist MP for West Fife), Thomas Bell (member of the CPGB Executive Committee), John Murphy (British Delegate to the 1924 Congress in Moscow), Robert Arnot (Director of Labour Research) and Walter Hannington and Arthur McManus (both CPGB Executive Committee members).

All twelve were eventually sent for trial at the Old Bailey on 17 November, 1925 in a blaze of publicity, with such celebrities as Bernard Shaw, Lady Warwick, Colonel Josiah Wedgwood (the Labour MP for Newcastle under Lyme), Shapurji Saklatvala (the Communist MP for Battersea), and the redoubtable George Lansbury MP standing as sureties for the defendants.

The twelve Communists were charged with seditious conspiracy and incitement to mutiny and were found guilty after an eight-day trial. The jury took only twenty minutes to reach their verdict.

Mr Justice Swift sentenced five of the men with previous similar convictions to twelve months, in spite of the objections of their Counsel, Mr Arthur Henderson. The remaining seven refused to be bound over and received six months each.

The trial certainly took the top of the CPGB hierarchy out of circulation temporarily but, more importantly, it failed to prove that the CPGB was run by Moscow's hirelings. The CPGB finances were examined in depth and there was little evidence to show large sums arriving from the Soviet Union. The prosecution made as much as they could of a mysterious £14,000 sum shown as bookshop income but none of the defendants appeared very sinister. It was altogether a poor performance for an admitted six years of intermittent observation by Special Branch.

Guy Liddell and Max Knight had the task of preparing a new strategy to deal with the reformed CPGB but unfortunately the anti-Comintern section had virtually no information from inside the new CPGB. Max Knight set about correcting this oversight. In April 1930 Percy Glading reappeared from a long trip abroad to the Lenin School in Moscow and became a rather obvious target for MI5 surveillance.

Knight's first move was to recruit Olga Gray, the nineteen-year-old daughter of a chemical worker from Gateshead. She was to become a close confidante of Glading's. After some initial hesitation Miss Gray agreed to help MI5 and from that moment onwards neither Glading nor the CPGB escaped Knight's close attention. She also joined The Friends of the Soviet Union and the following year became a typist at the Anti-War Movement's headquarters in Gray's Inn Road. For the next seven years she gave details of Communist activities in Britain, and in February 1937 achieved a breakthrough when Glading asked her to be the nominee tenant for a safe house. Glading was never given any reason to doubt her sincerity. In 1934 he had entrusted Olga with a courier mission to the Soviet Union and she had done her job well. Now he told her to find a 'neutral' address, preferably one without a porter, and after consultations with Knight she found a ground floor flat at 82 Holland Road, Kensington. During the next two months Glading and Olga Gray became visitors to the new flat and she was allowed to meet 'Mr Peters', an important Russian contact. When Knight read the report of the meeting he started enquiries to identify the mysterious foreigner: in the course of conversation 'Peters' had revealed that during the war he had served in a Russian cavalry regiment although he was an Austrian. Knight pegged him as Theodore Maly, a Soviet intelligence officer from the NKVD.

On 20 May, 1937 the long wait started to pay dividends. Glading asked Miss Gray to leave her new job (one which Glading had asked her to get to spy on another political organization) so that she could take a more active role in the secret work ahead. This, he explained, was going to involve a great deal of photography and she would therefore have to be given lessons in the subject by an expert. The experts turned out to be 'Mr and Mrs Stephens', two foreigners who spoke to each other in French. Matters came to a head on 18 October. There was a 'trial run' at 82 Holland Road when, for three and a half hours, the plotters practised taking photographs of underground railway maps. Clearly the big event was imminent. Three days later 'Mrs Stephens' visited the flat again clutching what looked to the MI5 watchers like a large plan. The plan was then photographed with the equipment supplied by Glading. The forty-two exposures were later shown to portray details of a new fourteen-inch Naval gun being developed at the Woolwich Arsenal where Glading had been employed as a grinder during the war, and then again from June 1925 until his dismissal in 1928 because of his Communist activities.

The two MI5 watchers assigned to the case by Max Knight followed 'Mrs Stephens' when she left the flat, apparently still carrying the plan. She made her way to Hyde Park Corner by taxi and was met by 'Mr Stephens' and an unknown man. The party walked up Piccadilly where 'Mrs Stephens' passed over the plans to the unidentified conspirator. At this point the group took a taxi to Charing Cross Station and split up. 'Mr and Mrs Stephens' were followed to Fonset House, a block of flats in the Edgware Road while their companion retrieved an attaché case from the left luggage and caught a train to Welling in Kent. He was then followed to an address in Olyffe Avenue. The following day it was established that the man's name was George Whomack, a mechanical examiner at Woolwich Arsenal where he had worked since 1918. The Arsenal considered him a good worker and in June the previous year he had been promoted to assistant foreman.

A full-scale alert was now sounded and Knight reported on the implications of the latest developments. A permanent watch was put on Glading's home in Warwick Avenue, South Harrow, but it was thought too dangerous to let Special Branch put a full-time team on him twenty-four hours a day. No thefts were reported from the Arsenal so MI5 assumed whatever had been photographed by 'Mrs Stephens' had been replaced by Whomack. Knight confirmed this when Olga examined the film negative before Glading collected them the following day. She managed to note various numbers on the plans and they were soon traced to the latest blueprints of the new fourteen-inch Naval gun. It was a document Whomack had easy access to. Glading obviously considered the whole affair a success. He told Knight's agent on 2 November that 'Mr and Mrs Stephens' were 'returning to Moscow because their small daughter was ill' and that it was unlikely that a replacement would arrive before Christmas.

This sparked off a debate about the advisability of allowing two proven Soviet agents to leave the country, but eventually it was decided that, since they both could claim diplomatic immunity if arrested, there would be little to gain by taking them into custody. Thus, on 6 November MI5 watched the two spies pile luggage into a taxi in the Edgware Road and then transfer to the Paris boat train at Victoria, destined for the Gare du Nord and, presumably, Moscow. In fact, Stalin was conducting a purge of the NKVD. Theodore Maly had already been recalled and disappeared shortly after his arrival in Moscow.

The next burst of espionage activity from Percy Glading took place in the New Year of 1938. On 12 January he had warned Olga, Knight's agent, to prepare for more action and the MI5 teams duly took up their positions outside the homes of the two suspects. On 15 January, 1938 Glading was observed to leave his house at 2.40 PM and return three and a half hours later with a bulky newspaper under his arm. He made no attempt to go to the flat in Holland Road but the following day was trailed to Charing Cross Station, still carrying the bulky newspaper. He went down into the public lavatory and handed the rolled paper to a much younger man. The two men were then followed to the Corner House in the Strand where they bought a meal. Afterwards, at 6.30, they split up, Glading returning home to South Harrow, the second man going by train to Woolwich and then by bus to an address in Swingate Lane, Plumstead. The next day MI5 identified the young man as Charles Munday, a twenty-two-year-old assistant chemist in the War Chemist's department at Woolwich Arsenal.

The ring now definitely included Glading, Whomack and Munday, and it seemed likely there were others involved, according to Knight's agent. On the same day that Munday was identified (his home address being in Genesta Road, Plumstead, not far from Swingate Lane, a source of some confusion for the watchers) Glading telephoned Olga Gray and asked her to meet him the following day. There was, apparently, more work to be done. While they had lunch in a pub Glading revealed he was planning an important rendezvous that evening at Charing Cross. Would Olga prepare for a photographic session at the Holland Road safe house? The MI5 agent agreed to be at the flat by 6 PM when she was again met by Glading. By this time, she had managed to telephone Knight about the meeting place and warn him of a replacement for 'Stephens' who had arrived in Britain. The news was quickly passed on to Special Branch and a large operation was mounted to watch Glading at Charing Cross Station later that evening.

The decision was also taken to arrest anyone who turned up at the rendezvous. Glading had managed to photograph the Naval blueprints successfully and pass on the negatives to Moscow. His session on 15 January had apparently involved taking pictures of more than two hundred pages of a book and as yet MI5 had no idea what documents were involved. If he was passing on the films then the courier would be arrested; if he was taking delivery of a further batch of secret material, as Knight thought likely, then they would plug the leak by an arrest.

At exactly 8.15 PM Glading was approached by a middle-aged man carrying a brown paper parcel near the Strand exit of Charing Cross Station. The Special Branch watchers intercepted them and Inspector

Tommy Thompson seized the package. Both men were speechless. They were quickly bundled into waiting cars and driven to Scotland Yard where the package was opened. It was found to contain four blueprints, three dated 1927, the other 1928, of a special pressure bar apparatus designed to test detonators. They had been caught redhanded but Glading's contact was not a Russian spy-master. He was Albert Williams, a thirty-nine-year old carpenter working at the Woolwich Arsenal. The only record he had was an Army one, which showed that he had enlisted at the age of sixteen in the RFA, Territorial Army and had served in France, Flanders and with the North Russia Expeditionary Force. He had been demobbed in 1919 and had proved himself to be an excellent worker at the Arsenal since that date, even achieving some awards for innovation. Both men were immediately charged with possession of the blueprints but declined to comment on how they came to possess them.

Special Branch detectives then went to Glading's house (without a search warrant, an oversight commented on later) and carried out a thorough search, in spite of protests from Mrs Glading. They found a mass of incriminating evidence. Tommy Thompson supervised the operation and recovered two cameras, four spools of Leica film, part of an anti-tank mine wrapped in a piece of paper that bore a handwritten description of its function, five developed quarter-inch plates, some typewritten papers describing an aircraft bomb, a sheet of handwritten foolscap detailing a Naval torpedo and a 1937 diary that had the pages torn out until 3 November 1939. All were significant finds.

The film spools proved to be the negatives of a 1925 explosives textbook (marked 'Restricted'). It was quickly established that this was the item Charles Munday had passed to Glading at Charing Cross on 16 January. The anti-tank mine could be linked to Williams because his handwriting was on the paper wrapped around it.

Detective Inspectors Bridges and Birch then went to Williams's house where they found an improvised studio and darkroom equipped with two cameras and some unused quarter-inch plates similar to those found at Glading's home. Indeed, the Glading plates showed a tiny portion of background which, when magnified, perfectly matched the wallpaper in Williams's studio. The Special Branch men also found a piece of plywood propped up close to one of the cameras. The photographer had evidently pinned his subject materials against the screen to take the pictures. Bulldog clips exactly matching those overlapping on Glading's prints were found on the top of the board. The prints showed plans of a particular type of fuse used on anti-submarine bombs. There could be no denying the relationship between

Williams and Glading. The plans came from the department at the Arsenal in which Williams worked.

Instructions were given for Munday and Whomack to be arrested. All were, in some way, inextricably linked together. When the Holland Road safe house was searched a camera was found with Glading's fingerprints on it. Papers bearing Munday's name on them were taken from Williams' house. The common denominator was the Arsenal.

All four were charged with offences under the Official Secrets Act and remanded in custody, though not without some strong opposition from the defence which was presented by Dudley Collard, himself a Communist sympathizer, and Denis Pritt KC MP.[4] The case eventually came before Mr Justice Hawke at the Old Bailey on 14 May, 1938. Glading, Williams and Whomack all pleaded Guilty to five counts and all were sentenced to terms of imprisonment: Glading got six years, Williams four years and Whomack three years. Munday was acquitted by the jury because Sir Donald Somervell, the Attorney-General, decided not to offer any evidence against him.

The case was closed but the judge made this comment on the performance of Knight's agent who had faithfully reported back on Glading and the CPGB:

> 'I would like to say something about this lady, Miss "X". I do not propose to call her into Court to hear what I have to say for reasons which may be very good reasons, but I do desire to say that I think that this young woman is possessed of extraordinary courage, and I think she has done a great service to her country.'

Knight had undoubtedly scored a major success even if the main Soviet organizers were never caught. The Woolwich Arsenal plot failed because it had been infiltrated from the start. MI5 learnt the lesson well and gave Olga Gray a new identity in Canada.

While this operation was continuing an important Soviet official broke with Stalin and sought political asylum in the West. The OGPU officer concerned, Walter Krivitsky, had once been the head of Soviet Military Intelligence in Western Europe. He was known to SIS as 'Dr Martin Lessner', an Austrian dealer in rare books who maintained his networks from The Hague, a city which had first acquired the reputation of 'Spy Capital of the World' owing to its neutrality during the Great War. Krivitsky was based in his 'art gallery' in the fashionable Celebestraat and was naturally the target of some surveillance directed from the SIS Station, which at the time was led by the Passport Control Officer, Major

Chidson. Chidson had succeeded Major Dalton in the post and had an equally unhappy experience. The Hague was a senior SIS posting and unfortunately Dalton had fallen prey to some financial temptations. When he committed suicide Chidson replaced him but he found it difficult to hide his animosity towards the French Deuxième Bureau representative, a man who was supposed to be his ally. Chidson too had to be replaced – by Major R.H. Stevens. While the Hague Station was enduring all these internal rifts Krivitsky defected in France.

At the end of Septemoer 1937 he was ordered home to Moscow but the recent assassinations of General Miller (the head of the Paris-based Federation of Tsarist Army Veterans) and Ignace Reiss (a veteran OGPU agent) put Krivitsky on his guard. He quite rightly suspected a purge and approached the French Ministry of the Interior. After, several suspected attempts at kidnapping and murder Krivitsky eventually obtained passage to the United States, where he made lengthy statements concerning his former employees, the OGPU. His remarks naturally aroused the interest of Guy Liddell, who was by then Deputy-Director of 'B' Division, and Jane Sissmore,[5] an experienced MI5 officer and former barrister, was asked to prepare a report on Krivitsky's allegations. In theory this defector should have been better placed and possibly better motivated than previous converts to assist Western counter-intelligence forces, but this did not prove to be the case.

Walter Krivitsky was an uneasy defector. He knew he was a prime target for assassination and saw enemies everywhere. On Sunday, 9 February, 1941, at the Hotel Bellevue in Washington he was found locked in his fifth-floor room by a maid after he had allegedly shot himself. The Soviets were robbed of their prize but lost no time in planting rumours that he had finally been reached by the OGPU.

Jane Sissmore's report, 'Summary of Interviews with General Walter Krivitsky', dated January 1940. clearly showed that the GPU had well-established agents in a position to transmit the contents of important Foreign Office documents. None of Krivitsky's revelations were relevant to Burgess, Maclean, Philby or Blunt. They did suggest that some agents had been recruited amongst those who were involved in the anti-Fascist movements but this came as no surprise. The report also mentioned that an unnamed British journalist had been sent to Spain to spy against France but this too was not unexpected, although it was used as a lever against Philby during his cross-examination by 'Buster' Milmo and Jim Skardon in November 1951. Certainly, none of Krivitsky's hints were relevant to Maclean, who only joined the Foreign Office in 1938. Indeed, when investigation was undertaken in London and Washington in 1951 Philby suggested to the MI5 representative, Geoffrey Patterson, that

Krivitsky's profiles be compared with the list of suspects. He knew that such an exercise would rule out Maclean and his fellow conspirators. Burgess had joined the Foreign Office from the BBC much later in the war, in the autumn of 1943. Blunt was still a Cambridge don in 1937.

One misunderstanding that originated from Miss Sissmore's report was that it pointed a finger at Philby but was ignored. Philby was one of the many ideological sympathizers of the Thirties and a self-confessed Russian agent from 1936 (see *My Silent War*[6]), but again his first access to secrets was limited to his role as a journalist in France in 1940 when he attended briefings given by the BEF to War Correspondents. Even if the report had identified Philby as a spy it would have been difficult to take any action against him. *The Times* gave him his first job in Spain in May 1937; he was never in any position to compromise British secrets until he joined SOE in July 1940.

The real value of Krivitsky's information lay in his ability and willingness to identify NKVD men working under diplomatic cover in Britain and even a few of their sources. Most of the suspects were already quite familiar to MI5 but it was a tremendous intelligence *coup* to have been able to clear up all the 'loose ends' of earlier investigations.

Krivitsky offered a mass of intelligence, some of it detailed enough to have Jane Sissmore ultimately suggest the probable existence of at least two well-placed Russian agents passing secrets from London who had not yet been identified. An investigation was launched and eventually suspicion fell on Captain John King, a Foreign Office cypher clerk. King was arrested as soon as MI5 were sure of his guilt. Tar Robertson and William Codrington, the head of the Foreign Office's Security Department, intercepted King in the Bunch of Grapes pub in Curzon Street and bought him a series of large whiskies. He was soon intoxicated and mournfully admitted his involvement with the Russians. When King was arrested he made a complete confession and identified the Soviet diplomats who were his contacts. He was sent for trial *in camera* at the Old Bailey on 18 October, 1939, and pleaded Guilty to a charge under the Emergency Powers Act. Unusually, no press announcement was made at the time about the affair.

In prison King detailed how he had been suborned by the Russians, He had served in the Artists' Rifles during the Great War and had been commissioned with the rank of Captain. He became a cypher clerk and was posted to Damascus, Paris and, after the Armistice, Germany. He then joined the Foreign Office and was chosen to be part of the British Delegation to the League of Nations in Geneva. While there in May 1935 he fell in love with an American (he had by now separated from his wife Ethel whom he had married when he was twenty) and became indebted to a Dutch businessman (and a Russian agent) named Pieck who handed him on to another Soviet contact named 'Petersen'. Mr Justice Hilbery sentenced him to ten years.

King was released after the war with full remission for good conduct. His conviction did not become public knowledge until June 1956 when the Foreign Office issued a statement admitting that a cypher clerk had been prosecuted in 1939.

While the Foreign Office doubled their efforts to improve security Liddell, now without the aid of Hugh Miller who had died while MI5 were based in Cromwell Road, ordered an intensification of the King Street surveillance carried out by Max Knight's team and circulated instructions throughout the War Office about the employment of Communists, via MI5's 'vetting' department, 'C' Division.

One of these memos led to another investigation and prosecution. The embryonic 'vetting' procedure required sensitive government departments to forward the names of new employees to MI5's 'C' Division for a comparison check with Registry. The system was certainly not infallible but it did ensure that activists who overtly joined political organizations would be identified immediately. The obvious drawback to the system was that it only catered for those who were overt extremists. When Philby's name was passed to Registry on a 'check-slip' the reply was 'Nothing Recorded Against' (NRA) although the card showed that his father, Harry St John Philby, had been interned in 1939 for five months. One name however that did spark a reaction was that of Edward Walker Edwards, who achieved the rare distinction of being noticed and indeed investigated by Miss Paton-Smith of Registry, a lady known as 'Strength through Joy'.

Edwards was a thirty-seven-year-old clerk who had got a job with the headquarters of the 71st West Riding Regiment RATA in Sheffield in March 1939. He applied for a clerical vacancy and after a brief interview with the adjutant was taken on as a clerical assistant. His name was forwarded to London for confirmation but it was some time before the Registry staff got around to dealing with him. Part of the problem was that the Security Service had always been a relatively small organization and Kell had fought a losing battle to expand. When the time for rapid expansion came it inevitably meant a decrease in efficiency. MI5's new girls were assigned to Miss Paton-Smith as an introduction. Delays in dealing with the flood of check-slips were unavoidable. The staff were untrained and the number of people being inducted into sensitive posts enormous. In Edwards' case the system worked. His small card-index showed several cross-references. He was a member of the CPGB. He had served under Wilfred Macartney in the International Brigade in

Spain. His service record showed that he had joined the RAF in 1919 and had left in 1923. The case warranted further investigation because Edwards was no mere rank-and-file member of the CPGB. He was an activist and was last recorded working full-time for a Communist organization and living with a senior functionary in London. Now his address was given as Musgrave Place, Sheffield. Furthermore, his flat-mate merited a substantial MI5 dossier and had been convicted of incitement to mutiny after Invergordon. On 21 April Edwards was sacked from his job after just five weeks and his lodgings raided the same evening shortly before midnight. His possessions were searched and two documents were recovered from an overcoat pocket. The first was a War Office circular dated 21 January, 1939, consisting of Liddell's guidelines for Territorial Army recruitment policy. This memo dealt with the International Brigade in detail and listed veterans who might cause dissension in the ranks if they were allowed to join up. The second item was a broader document relating to the expansion of the services but none the less of interest to anyone following British military activities.

Edwards was immediately arrested and a further inventory taken in the office where he had been employed. It was discovered that two further papers were missing from the files. One was a War Office letter marked 'Secret' sent from Sheffield to London raising questions about the role of the Territorial Army in home security and the other was a similar letter dealing with duties that might be required of the regiment by the civilian authorities.

Edwards was sent for trial to the Manchester Assizes on 18 May, 1939 where he pleaded Guilty to four charges under the Official Secrets Act and Not Guilty to a further two charges. The prosecution accepted the pleas and Mr Justice Stable sentenced him to eighteen months' imprisonment with hard labour, commenting:

> 'I do not believe you were one of those debased citizens stealing confidential information for the purpose of selling it to a foreign power. But I am quite satisfied that your object in getting this employment in the Territorial Army was to find out what you could, and, having got as much information as you were able, to use that information for the purposes of having the forces of the Crown rotted from the inside.'

The Twenties and Thirties provided many lessons for MI5, not the least of which was to concentrate the business of counter-subversion in one well-informed department, rather than leave matters to a number of fragmented organizations. The efforts of George Monckland and Olga Gray also proved a further point: the best form of counter-subversion is active counter-intelligence, the recruitment of agents to infiltrate suspect pressure groups or parties. The Arcos raid owed its success to early, careful management by an MI5 agent. Similarly, it is doubtful that the Woolwich Arsenal case would ever have been discovered if Max Knight's agent had not been in on the affair before it had ever begun.

What is less easy to determine is the degree to which the early Security Service was in danger of becoming an arm of the political establishment. They were fooled by the Zinoviev letter although, however false it may have been, its contents did reflect the prevailing policy of the Comintern. Blame for stoking up the scandal has frequently been laid with Admirals Sinclair and Hall, and there can be little doubt that they enabled Conservative Central Office to make capital out of it. But were their motives laudable or otherwise? Neither man was power-crazed or ambitious for higher office. They believed they were blowing the whistle on a despicable cover-up which deserved to be publicized. Their timing was miraculous or satanic, depending on one's point of view.

But for MI5 the significance of the deception was Kell's skill in escaping involvement. He left the matter to SIS and the others, and therefore avoided criticism. Indeed, the fact that Kell remained in office so long is a measure of the trust politicians of most persuasions had in him. There is however a good deal of evidence to suggest that the Director-General did not reciprocate. It might well appear that successive Cabinets were so determined to grasp short-term advantages that they persistently ignored advice not to make public the achievements of their code-breakers. Time and again the decrypters were frustrated by Ministers anxious to announce the contents of secret Soviet telegrams. Moscow would invariably change their codes, having being warned of their insecurity, and thus force GC & CS to start their work from scratch.

When one takes into consideration the chronic shortage of funds for MI5 during this period, their limited staff and their inability to mount operations without the help and manpower of the regular police, it is perhaps astonishing that they achieved as much as they did. The Security Service during this period were never embarrassed by incompetence, acquittals or revelations of corruption. The cases that went to trial were never concluded by scathing criticism from the judge. The reverse, in fact, was generally the case. Perhaps the greatest accolade must come from D.N. Pritt, the leftist barrister who defended so many of MI5's clients. In 1958 he published *Spies and Informers in the*

Witness Box,[7] a review of the legal arguments and dangers of relying on the evidence of informers. In spite of this distinguished Counsel's many courtroom protests at hearings being held *in camera*, and the testimony of unidentified witnesses, Pritt reserved his harshest criticism for several American 'political' trials. He never once alleged that any of the defendants in Britain had received anything less than a fair trial.

III

The Abwehr's Preparations for War

'Spies betray themselves by their walk. A spy may effect a wonderful disguise in front yet be instantly recognized by a keen eye from behind. This is a point frequently forgotten by beginners.'

Sir Robert Baden-Powell

If the Secret Intelligence Service's motto was 'Above All, My Country', then MI5's was 'Slowly but Surely'. Kell's chauffeur-driven Invicta had a small flag on the bonnet; the emblem on the flag was a tortoise, a mascot for the slow-moving but painstaking character of the counter-espionage organization and its Chief.

In the Twenties and early Thirties the greater part of MI5's limited resources was devoted to the investigation of Soviet-inspired espionage and subversion, as shown in the last chapter. The Weimar Republic did not initially pose a great threat, but with the rise to power of the Nazis MI5's burden increased. MI5 had four proven cases of Germans found actively spying in Britain during this period and two cases of British subjects offering their services to the Germans, the tip of the iceberg of Nazi sympathizers whose members increased as the possibility of war loomed nearer.

MI5's first case involving a British subject collaborating with the ex-enemy was concerned with Captain Vivian Stranders, a General Staff officer who had joined the Royal Flying Corps in 1917. He fought on the Western Front as a gunnery officer in the early stages of the war but was transferred home after complaints from French officers about some of his rather more indiscreet remarks. He loathed the French and rarely lost an opportunity to voice his opinions.

Early in 1919 he was posted to Kiel as part of the Reparations Commission. Before the war Stranders had taught English at a language school in Frankfurt and his skill as a military interpreter led to promotion. In September 1919 he was given a junior appointment on the Inter-Allied Aeronautical Commission of Control, a body set up in Berlin's Hotel Excelsior to supervise the dismantling of Germany's war industries, as required by the terms of the peace treaty. The British section of the Commission soon found themselves trying to defend the Germans from the French, who seemed determined, in the opinion of Stranders and others, to enforce a kind of economic slavery. Industries with only remote military connections were dismembered at the insistence of the French contingent, who heavily outnumbered their Allies in the Commission.

When Stranders was demobbed in 1921 at the age of thirty-nine he returned to Germany and started a small business in Düsseldorf, importing motor-cycle engines. His venture prospered because the Treaty of Versailles limited the power and size of German aircraft. A motor-cycle engine was about the only unit allowed for light aircraft. Gradually his sales increased and he branched out into other aeronautical equipment. Just as his project was expanding well the French and Belgians occupied the Rhine and his partner began speculating between the different currencies. The galloping inflation brought disaster and Stranders found himself defrauded and broke. At about this time Stranders was recruited by the firms of Dornier, Heinkel and Junkers as a consultant. His main job was to act as their agent in purchasing materials specifically prohibited by the Treaty of Versailles. In this capacity he made a tour of the Bristol Aircraft factory at Filton. The Germans planned to circumvent the Treaty by sending the aeroplane engines to Sweden and then diverting them back to the Reich, but the scheme failed. The various licences required for such exports were owned by a French company and it was decided to procure the badly-needed equipment via Paris. Stranders was set up as an importer/exporter, apparently contracted to purchase samples and information for the Japanese. The French Deuxième Bureau quickly identified him as a covert supplier of prohibited material to the Weimar Republic and placed him under surveillance.

The sensitivity of the French about illicit arms dealing led to a series of prosecutions of foreign agents in 1926 but Stranders was left alone, at least for a white. A British ex-Army officer named John Leather and two other Englishmen, Ernest Phillips and William Fischer, were convicted of eliciting military information for a foreign power in March 1926 in Paris, but meanwhile Stranders started negotiating for the manufacturing rights of the Gnome-Rhone Jupiter engine on behalf of Berlin. By this time his dossier at Scotland Yard had grown considerably and a warrant had been issued for his arrest in Britain on a charge of bigamy.

Stranders avoided returning to Britain but was arrested on 21 December, 1927 by Superintendent Duclaux of the Deuxième Bureau. He was charged with espionage and remanded to the State Prison for interrogation. In a matter of days Special Branch detectives raided a house in Kellett Road, Brixton. A man named Pidsey and an Austrian were questioned about their relationship with Stranders. No evidence of espionage was found but the two men decided to leave the country immediately.

Stranders appeared before a closed court in Paris on 9 March, 1927 and was found guilty after a two-day hearing. He was sentenced to two years' solitary confinement and a fine of a thousand francs (about £8 at the time).

A transcript of the case was sent to Special Branch but Scotland Yard were confident the unfortunate incident was an isolated one. A certain amount of interest was generated in Britain by Stranders' conviction. Lord Sandon, the Tory MP for Shrewsbury, asked a question in the House and got confirmation from the Under-Secretary of State for Air that Stranders did not hold a rank in the RAF Reserve as had been reported in the press. When Stranders was released from gaol he went back to Berlin with his British passport and embarked on a career in journalism. His theme remained the same: support for the growing National Socialist movement and condemnation of the Versailles 'betrayal'. MI5 retained their interest in him and in May 1931 took steps to ensure the itinerant Englishman would receive an official welcome if he decided to come home. His passport, No. 2978, was blacklisted by the Foreign Office and consular officials in Europe were instructed to confiscate it. Stranders was to be furnished with a temporary document which would only allow him to travel to the United Kingdom. His activities in Germany had also come to the attention of a Labour MP, Rennie Smith, who had been lecturing in Stuttgart in January 1931. Stranders had become editor of *Steel Helmet*, the war veterans' magazine, and the Member for Penistone had been given a copy on his tour. As soon as he got back to London he delivered the magazine to Dr Hugh Dalton at the Foreign Office, who passed it on to MI5.

Stranders declined to visit Britain and instead became a naturalized citizen of Germany, a move that resulted in a discreet announcement in the *London Gazette* stating that Vivian Stranders no longer had any right to his former rank of Captain and henceforth should be known as 'Mr'.

This, however, was not the last MI5 heard of Stranders. He became extremely active in the Nazi cause but was to remain beyond the jurisdiction of Kell's organization. Later Stranders became an ardent supporter of Hitler and was appointed editor of *The Camp*, a propaganda newspaper circulated in German POW camps. He then became a founder member of the notorious British Free Corps. He achieved the rank of Obersturmbannfuhrer (Major) and toured many of the POW camps recruiting anti-Communists for the Legion of St George. After the war he was arrested by American forces in Austria along with several other renegades. As a naturalized German subject, he escaped prosecution for treason but underwent intensive MI5 interrogation. He died, aged seventy-eight, in 1959, still an unrepentant Nazi.

Meanwhile MI5 had to cope with a more overt case of German-inspired espionage. In August 1932 SIS, via the Berlin Air Attaché, Wing-Commander Justin Herring, reported that a man claiming to be a British officer had attempted to get an interview with the German War Office. The British Embassy in Berlin had tentatively identified the man as Second Lieutenant Norman Baillie-Stewart, a twenty-four-year-old officer in the Seaforth Highlanders. Kell ordered an investigation into the matter and passed the case to Major Hinchley-Cooke, his best interrogator, who quickly discovered that Baillie-Stewart was on quite legitimate leave and was due to return to Aldershot, where he was attached to the Royal Army Service Corps.

Baillie-Stewart was the son of an Indian Army officer, Colonel Hope Baillie Wright of the 67th Punjab Regiment. He had two sons, both of whom entered the Army. The younger one, Norman, was educated at the Royal Naval College, Dartmouth and then won a cadet scholarship to Sandhurst. In December 1928 he passed out of Sandhurst and changed his name by deed poll to Baillie-Stewart before joining the Seaforth Highlanders, which were garrisoned at Dover.

Second Lieutenant Baillie-Stewart went with his battalion to India and served on the north-west frontier until 1932 when he was granted a transfer to the Royal Army Service Corps based at Aldershot. On 16 July, 1932 he had obtained permission to holiday abroad and had gone to Berlin alone in August. The Embassy reported that Baillie-Stewart had booked into a hotel called the Stadtkiel on the Mittelstrasse, and had returned to Britain on 20 August, 1932.

Hinchley-Cooke obtained permission to search Baillie-Stewart's quarters but nothing incriminating was found. An interception of his mail, though, revealed that Baillie-Stewart started writing to a 'Herr Otto Waldemar Obst' at a Berlin cover address on his return.

On 13 November, 1932 the LIU opened a letter addressed to Baillie-Stewart at his home in Southsea. Inside were ten £5 notes and the following:

> 'My dear Boy, I often think of the nice days we spent together in Berlin last summer. I hope you are very well and you have not forgotten me. You were so kind in lending me some money. You remember my father stopped giving money to me because he did not wish that I should continue studying. Meanwhile he has altered his opinion and it is all right. Unfortunately I cannot pay you back the whole sum at once, but I hope I may be able to send you the rest before Christmas. I look forward to seeing you again next year. Please write me again if you can come. With very kind regards, yours, Marie Louise.'

This letter was answered by Baillie-Stewart on 26 November in his own handwriting, though it was addressed to 'Herr Obst' at a Berlin address. He signed it 'Alphonse Poiret'. It read:

> 'Dear Friend, Thank you for your letter and the prompt way in which you settled our small debt. It is very good of you to ask me to stay with you and I shall do my utmost to take a holiday. At the moment I think I shall be able to manage at the beginning of March.
>
> 'When you write to me in future may I make a suggestion that you use much smaller seals as such large ones are apt to arouse the curiosity of unscrupulous people. I say this because from the appearance of your last letter I should imagine someone had opened it to have a look inside before it reached my home address.
>
> 'The weather here is not too good at the moment and nearly everyone seems to have colds. I hope you are faring better in Berlin.
>
> 'I shall look forward to hearing from you soon and seeing you in the Spring. Many thanks again. Yours ever, Alphonse Poiret.'

During the autumn of 1932 Baillie-Stewart made three weekend trips to Holland, having first obtained permission to go to London. On these occasions he kept a rendezvous with a German in Rotterdam and then returned home after a few hours. These visits, however, escaped the notice of MI5, who had to rely on the officer's mail as their source of information.

On 7 December a further letter arrived from 'Marie Louise' and was found to contain four £10 banknotes.[8]

At the Cromwell Road headquarters of the Security Service Kell chaired a meeting to assess the situation that included Brigadier Harker, Major

Hinchley-Cooke, his assistant, Captain Phillips and Guy Liddell. Baillie-Stewart was now known to be in covert communication with a German agent. He was also known to have visited the Mechanical Warfare Experimental Establishment at Farnborough and a search was made of his library records at the military manuals section of the RASC library. The information that could be betrayed to an enemy was very limited although Baillie-Stewart was in a position to give details of tank and armoured car design and the intricacies of military tactics and military organization.

The young officer's offence was judged to be an indiscretion and Kell insisted that an opportunity should be provided for escape. If the War Office would agree, Baillie-Stewart would be asked to resign his commission quietly and warned about his activities shortly afterwards. There was no dissent recorded from those gathered.

On 20 January, 1933 Baillie-Stewart was summoned to the Adjutant's office at Aldershot where, without explanation, he was asked to resign. Baillie-Stewart refused and penned an angry letter to his Brigadier at Command Headquarters; almost immediately he received a reply ordering him to report with his Colonel. When Baillie-Stewart turned up at the appointed time the Brigadier made an excuse and left the room. At the same moment Colonel Syms of the Judge Advocate's Department walked in with Captain Phillips from MI5. Without much ado they presented the Second Lieutenant with two pages of closely typed allegations. They stated that he had stayed at a hotel in Berlin in August 1932 and made enquiries about how he could contact the German Secret Service; that he had later been visited by a German officer and that at least one interview had taken place in his room; that £50 had later been sent to him in the post by a person with a foreign code name; that Baillie-Stewart had acknowledged receipt of the money and messages by use of a similar code; that a further £40 had been received three weeks later; that Baillie-Stewart had again acknowledged receipt of the money and had indicated that he would make a further visit abroad at his next leave and, finally, that he had retained a restricted military manual from the RASC library for over a month.

Again Baillie-Stewart was offered the chance of resigning his commission quietly in exchange for information about his contact with the Abwehr. After a period of silence, the accusations were strongly denied; he was asked to sign a document giving permission for his quarters to be searched and this he did.

Hinchley-Cooke had remained outside the room waiting for the formal assent which Phillips then handed to him. Hinchley-Cooke supervised a thorough search of Baillie-Stewart's possessions with Captain Causton MC while the Provost Marshal, the head of the

Military Police, charged the bewildered young man with an offence against the Official Secrets Act.

After he had been charged Baillie-Stewart wrote a letter to 'Herr Obst' and handed it to his Adjutant for posting. The Adjutant surrendered the letter to Major Hinchley-Cooke. It read:

> 'Dear friend, I am afraid through making your acquaintance and that of Marie Louise that I am now involved in trouble with the Military Authorities here, who give me to believe that you are connected with the Intelligence activities in your country.
>
> 'As you know, nothing connected with such matter has passed between us.
>
> 'My affection for Marie Louise, which prompted her to finance me in the manner she did, has taken a direction I never dreamt of and has placed me in the terrible position which I am now in. In the face of things and the circumstances I must sever all connection with you and Marie Louise, to whom I send my love and ask her and you to forget me entirely.
>
> 'As I used to sign myself "Alphonse Poiret" I now sign myself by my proper name and regret very much that this is goodbye to both of you. Yours very sincerely, Norman Baillie-Stewart.'

On 20 March, six days after his interrogation and arrest Baillie-Stewart was driven up to London with a military escort and passed to the Coldstream Guards at the Tower of London. No British officer had ever been charged with such grave offences and the Army Council were in some difficulties to keep the lid on the affair. The Tower of London was chosen because it was the least open military establishment in London, the alternatives being Chelsea Barracks (notoriously insecure) and Wellington Barracks (equally impossible to secure against the determined). As it turned out the Tower of London was a disastrous choice. The Army took the view that Baillie-Stewart should be given every opportunity to prepare his defence and that his Counsel would be based in London. He was also too well known amongst his brother officers at Aldershot, who would be placed in a difficult position once the public had focused its gaze on the young man's predicament. The pressure for some kind of disclosure mounted and eventually, on 8 February, 1933, the War Office confirmed that an officer of the Seaforth Highlanders was being detained at the Tower.

This opened the flood-gates of newspaper speculation and eventually, some ten days later, they identified Baillie-Stewart and announced that he was to be court-martialled 'early in March'.

The promised court martial proved to be a sensation. An officer from a famous regiment was to be tried on a unique charge and was being held in the most privileged military establishment in the world. The charge against him was unprecedented in peacetime. Questions were asked in the House and Mr Duff Cooper, the Financial Secretary to the War Office, defended the Army Council's decision to house the prisoner in the Tower.

On 20 March, 1933 Baillie-Stewart's court martial began at the Duke of York's Headquarters in Chelsea before the President, Major General W.J. Dugan, Commander of the 56th Division Territorial Army, Mr P.N. Sutherland Graeme, the Judge Advocate, with Major H. Shapcott prosecuting.

The ten charges under the Official Secrets Act included having been associated with Otto Waldemar Obst in Berlin, obtaining information about tanks, armoured cars, automatic rifles and military organization which might be useful to an enemy and having made two journeys to Holland for purposes contrary to the Act.

Baillie-Stewart pleaded Not Guilty and the prosecution detailed the evidence against him. Major Hinchley-Cooke and Captain Phillips gave their evidence as Major 'A' and Captain 'B' to keep their identities secret and maintain the traditional anonymity of MI5 personnel. Much of it concerned the denials made by Baillie-Stewart when Colonel Syms and Captain 'B' first presented him with the allegations at Aldershot.

His explanation of the money from 'Marie Louise' was that it was a payment for 'services rendered' of an 'immoral nature'. The girl could not be identified beyond the fact that her age was about twenty-two and she had fair hair. He did not know her address or that of her relatives and had replied to 'Herr Obst' when acknowledging the £90 because that had been the arrangement.

Baillie-Stewart had offered no information about Herr Obst apart from saying that he looked about thirty-six years old. He denied that there had been any code used in the letters and expressed surprise when Hinchley-Cooke pointed out that 'Obst' was German for fruit, 'Marie Louise' was a type of small French pear and 'Poiret' was the French for a small pear. The defence claimed that the name 'Poiret' had been used merely to prevent blackmail at a later date.

The rest of the evidence concerned items found in Baillie-Stewart's room at Aldershot after his arrest. They included a piece of paper that had the Berlin address of the German Military Defence HQ and its telephone number on it, various notes about boat and train timetables to Harwich, a scrap of an invitation to an exhibition in a Berlin department store on which were written the words 'organisation, tanks,

AC's, equipment, arming and structure, automatic rifles, pattern extent'. The words 'organisation of brigade' and 'tanks' were also written on the paper. A photograph of a tank was also found which had been lent by a brother officer, Lt D.W.S. Miller, formerly of the Royal Tank Corps, and a copy of *Tactical Handling of Tank Battalions*.

The implication was that 'Herr Obst' was a German agent as was 'Marie Louise' (if she existed) and that he had dictated a list of his requirements to his young recruit. 'AC's' stood for armoured cars and 'extent' probably meant range or extent of distribution. Major 'A' would give evidence about the letter code and 'Herr Obst' while Captain 'B' would confirm that Baillie-Stewart's original statement contained many flaws. Further evidence would be given from an officer who had lent the defendant a copy of the 1929 *Textbook of Small Arms* and a surprise witness, Miss 'D'.

Miss 'D' was a young German girl, Lotte Geiller, who had met Baillie-Stewart on one of his trips to Holland. She had been visiting her fiancé in Glasgow and was on her way home to Heidelberg. She had written several letters to the dashing young Army officer and these had been intercepted by the LIU. Hinchley-Cooke persuaded her to come to London and confirm that he had accompanied her from Harwich to the Hook of Holland. For good measure she stated that Baillie-Stewart had told her that he was on his way to Holland 'to do the most difficult thing he had ever done'.

The other witnesses called when the court martial went into closed session were Army officers giving details of the sensitive information contained in various Army manuals that had been borrowed from the RASC library in Aldershot by the defendant on his return from Berlin.

The court martial lasted for a week at the end of which Baillie-Stewart was found guilty and returned to the Tower to await his sentence. Three weeks later he was informed that the General Court Martial had sentenced him to be cashiered and serve five years' imprisonment. He was immediately transferred to Wormwood Scrubs where he was interviewed a few days later by Brigadier Harker, the Director of 'B' Division.

Because MI5 have never had any official powers the department's policy has always been to leave initial interviews with suspects to the civil police and Special Branch, to avoid any awkward complication in the preparation of a case. A person suspected of offences is not obliged to answer any questions that have not been put by a police officer. The custom in MI5 is to assist the police as far as they can before a trial and then interview the prisoner after he has been convicted. The other advantage of this procedure is that once convicted the person concerned is less likely to fabricate answers. The prisoner has nothing to lose from co-operating with a post-mortem and he may feel that the authorities might grant him certain incentives in exchange for his help.

Baillie-Stewart's case was unusual for many reasons. His first interrogation at Aldershot had been conducted by Colonel Syms of the Judge Advocate's Department and Captain Phillips from MI5, with Major Hinchley-Cooke in the room next door. This break with usual procedure weakened the case of the prosecution and the defence did not fail to spot it and take some advantage from it. Mr Norman Parkes was able to exploit the situation by suggesting that Syms had made the offer that if Baillie-Stewart admitted the offence the matter would remain secret and he would be allowed to resign his commission quietly. Syms strongly denied this and accepted only that 'the military authorities wished to keep the matter secret at the time'.

The defence then suggested that Baillie-Stewart had offered to help MI5 in gathering further information about Herr Obst when he next visited Germany, as Colonel Syms had claimed that 'Obst' and 'Marie Louise' were 'Secret Service agents'. Syms denied that the defendant had made such an offer but agreed that he had promised to find out 'for the Army Council' more about the two Germans.

The confidential interview with Brigadier Marker at Wormwood Scrubs was not an unqualified success. Baillie-Stewart agreed to make a full statement but there were unpleasant repercussions for the department.

Baillie-Stewart changed his story and admitted that 'Marie Louise' was an invention and that 'Herr Obst' had really been a 'Major Muller' (also a fictitious name) and the Berlin address had been a cover address. His confession was detailed and was in complete contradiction to the various statements made by the defence during the court martial. Nevertheless, it was a useful document because it at last enabled Kell to assess the true significance of the officer's treachery. He was a foolish, naive young man whose services the Germans had accepted without protest. Shortly before the hearings at the Duke of York's Headquarters the defendant had received two further letters from 'Herr Obst' which had tried to support his story of the amorous but illicit liaison. 'Marie Louise' wrote to say that unfortunately she would be unable to give evidence on his behalf because of family problems, in spite of her burning desire to clear him. Baillie-Stewart himself claimed that his actions had been innocent and that he had next to nothing to betray in terms of secret military intelligence. The argument that any information might be useful to an enemy, however trivial, was completely lost on him.

His parents rallied to his cause and claimed that the Aldershot confrontation was unfair and that their son had been unable to demand his rights. In terms of public relations, the whole episode had been a disaster for the Army. One commentator noted that when the court martial was convened four of the officers had come from the Judge Advocate's Department (Colonel Syms, Mr P. Sutherland Graeme, Major H. Shapcott and the Deputy Judge Advocate) and two from the Intelligence Department of the War Office (Major 'A' and Captain 'B').

The real trouble started when Baillie-Stewart revealed that he had been interviewed by MI5 in prison and that an offer of freedom had been made in exchange for a full disclosure regarding the German Secret Service and their codes. No such inducement had been given but of course the newly-convicted prisoner was given the opportunity to tell the counter-intelligence service the truth. Baillie-Stewart was obviously displeased that his statement had not been immediately rewarded. On 23 November, 1933 Mr Duff Cooper was asked in the House if the authorities had not reneged on an agreement made with MI5. The reply stated:

'If Baillie-Stewart made a statement that he was induced to make a confession by a promise that he would be released, there is no truth whatever in that statement.'

The denial could hardly have been more categoric and allowed MI5 to escape the flak.[9]

The cases of Vivian Stranders and Norman Baillie-Stewart were sufficient to alert MI5 to the dangers of a British Fifth Column. Both men had offered their services to the Germans and as their future actions bore out, they were motivated by ideological aspirations. The potential value to Germany of a well-placed group of Nazi sympathizers in the British corridors of power was judged to be incalculable by Berlin. No opportunity was lost to promote German propaganda and build up influence with British politicians. The German intention was to develop those organizations that were anyway pro-German and increase their covert grip on the less obvious organizations which had influential members.

The British government's first step in the propaganda war was to expel a leading Nazi journalist in November 1935. He was Dr H.W. Thost, the London correspondent of the Nazi organs *Angriff* and *Voelkischer Beobachter*. The Home Office declined to renew his permit to stay in Britain on advice from MI5, thus effectively throwing him out of the country. The Germans reacted sharply to the announcement, thus confirming Thost's importance. The German Ambassador made a personal visit to the Foreign Office to protest but in vain. Thost was kept under observation until 12 November, 1935 when he climbed aboard an aeroplane at Croydon, bound for Berlin.

Much of Thost's work was taken over by three other Nazi journalists, Werner Crome of the *Lokal-Anzeiger*, a Berlin newspaper, Herr Wrede from the same paper, and a special replacement assigned to the Graf Reichschach News Agency, Herr von Langen. Von Langen had already experienced some difficulties with his political intrigues. The previous year the Italian government had found his presence 'undesirable'. Eventually this trio were also told to leave. On 9 August, 1937 they were given a fortnight to pack their bags. *The Times* commented wryly:

> 'the charges against these men have not been published but it is known that they are not concerned with journalistic work.'

The MI5 charge was not espionage, but subversion. Throughout the following year concern at Thames House rose about the activities of the Nazi propagandists. Kell was prevented from expanding his organization to cope with what he saw as a new threat. Special Branch placed various German Embassy personnel under routine surveillance but they could never provide evidence of spying. The Security Service simply were not equipped to deal with the different Pro-Nazi campaigns so they fell back on the well-established practice of planting informants close to the leaders of the organizations. Much of the infiltration work fell on Max Knight who had virtually become the operational arm of MI5.

It was now, in 1937, that Knight moved into his Dolphin Square flat which was conveniently situated close to Thames House on Millbank and the Anglo-German Information Service in Parliament Street. This so-called 'Information Service' was in fact the front for the leading Partei man in the United Kingdom, Dr R.G. Roesel. His official appointment in Britain was that of London correspondent of the *National-Zeitung*, Goering's Essen-based newspaper, but Roesel's main occupation was to keep up a constant flow of pro-Nazi propaganda to British parliamentarians and Fleet Street. All his staff earned large dossiers at Thames House and included Edmund Hillermann, Anna Wolf and the official head of the Nazi Party in Britain, O.G. Karlowa.

Roesel encouraged the various sympathetic groups and provided them with covert intelligence on pro-Bolshevik, pro-Semitic organizations in London. Roesel was ordered out of the country in May

1939. Three days after his expulsion the Home Secretary, Sir Samuel Hoare, gave a further five agents – Richard Frauendorf, Captain Adolf Jaeger, Ernst Lahrmann, Gunther Schallies and Friedrich Scharpf – their marching orders. These political warfare specialists were relatively easy to identify and the government had no difficulty in arranging for their work permits not to be renewed. It was their British contacts that proved more difficult.

Several groups found themselves receiving Dr Roesel's attentions. They included the Anglo-German Fellowship, the *Anglo-German Review* (founded in September 1936), the British Union of Fascists, the Imperial Fascist League, the Nordic League, the National Socialist League, the British People's Party, the Link and the Right Club. Between them these organizations exerted considerable influence and their membership was certainly not limited to the extreme Right.

On 14 July, 1936 the Anglo-German Fellowship threw a large banquet to honour the Kaiser's daughter, the Duchess of Brunswick. The distinguished guest-list included a wealth of influential figures, as well as Dr Roesel. Amongst those attending were Admiral Sir Barry Domvile, the ex-DNI. Lord Redesdale (father of the Mitford sisters), Lord Jellicoe (eldest son of the Jutland hero), General J.F.C. Fuller (the tank strategist), Prince and Princess von Bismarck, Dr Fritz Hesse, Baron Marshal von Bieberstein, Count Albrecht Montgelas, Baroness Bruno Schroeder and Mr Harold Philby.[10]

An equally influential pro-German body was the Link, headed by the Chairman, Admiral Sir Barry Domvile. It was governed by a Council which included the distinguished history professor Sir Raymond Beazley, Professor A.P. Laurie, another prominent academic from Edinburgh, and supported by a host of well-known political names.[11] The Link was formed in 1937 as an 'independent non-party organization to promote Anglo-German friendship'. In May 1939 it had thirty-five active branches and a membership of around 4,329. Its publication was the *Anglo-German Review*, a magazine with offices in the Strand and operated by Anglo-German Publications Limited, a company registered in London with an all-British board of directors. It started in September 1936 and acted as a mouthpiece for Dr Goebbels. A similar organ was *News From Germany*, a broadsheet frequently distributed at meetings of the Link. These overtly pro-Nazi publications quickly closed down of their own accord when war was declared but many other political newspapers continued in production well into 1940. The Chief Censor banned the export of the *Daily Worker* and *Action*, the British Union of Fascists' bulletin, in May 1940 and then the following month extended the embargo to a range of Left and Right publications. They included *The Week, Russia Today, Challenge, World News and Views, Inside the Empire, New Propeller, People's Post, Headline, Free Press, Angles, Moscow News, Die Welt* and the *British Union Quarterly*.

As he rose to power Hitler had seemed comparatively well disposed towards Britain, and had named Britain in *Mein Kampf* as one of the major bastions of resistance to Bolshevism (the other, apart from Germany herself, being Italy). Hitler's overt policy was, apparently, to woo Great Britain and her Empire, and to that end he decreed that the Abwehr should refrain from developing any networks there.

Initially it had seemed that the Abwehr were restricting their activities in line with Hitler's policy, but in November 1935 came the first sign of a change in attitude. Dr Hermann Goertz, a forty-five-year-old Doctor of Jurisprudence from Lübeck, was arrested in England. He was a lawyer from a well-known and respected family. His father, Dr Heinrich Goertz, was a Liberal Deputy in the Reichstag and chairmanl of the local lawyers' association in the old Hanseatic town which stood on the River Trave. As a boy Hermann Goertz had been taught by an English governess, and had once taken a walking tour of Scotland. After leaving school he volunteered for twelve months' service with the 5th Regiment of Foot Guards and then went to Heidelberg University to study law. He qualified as a barrister but had hardly started to practise his profession when he was called up for the Great War. He served in Russia and Belgium and was severely wounded in the arm. After recuperation he applied to join the new German Air Force and flew as an observer in over thirty sorties. He then transferred to a training squadron at Schwerin but eventually had to give up flying because of his health. Goertz then spent the rest of the war interrogating captured British and American pilots on the Western Front as an intelligence officer attached to the 5th Army's HQ.

In 1916 he married an admiral's daughter who had been to school in England with his sister and after the war returned to his father's law firm. He qualified as an assistant judge in Bremen and then, after an unsuccessful partnership in Hanover, and a brief spell in London, travelled to America with his wife. He spent nearly eighteen months practising in the United States before coming to London in 1929. In London he had represented the giant German firm of Siemens in a case that they had brought against the British government. The legal hearings had dragged on until March 1931 when the case was dismissed. Goertz then returned to Germany and apparently joined the Abwehr, via the newly-formed 'illegal' Luftwaffe. 'Illegal' because the Versailles Treaty limited the size of the German post-war air force but the restrictions were ignored with the use of the 'Storm Troopers' Flying Club'.

Goertz first came to the notice of MI5 when Detective Inspector Webb of the Special Branch informed Hinchley-Cooke that the police in Kent had found some very compromising documents in a bungalow. The owner of the bungalow in Stanley Road, Broadstairs, Mrs Florence Johnson, had called the local police because her foreign tenant had left the country without paying his rent. A detective from the Kent Constabulary, Frederick Smith, carried out a search of the bungalow and alerted his superiors to what he found. The following day, on 25 October, 1935, Hinchley-Cooke and Webb paid a visit to 'Havelock' in Stanley Road and made an inventory of all the spy paraphernalia they found. This included a detailed sketch map of RAF Manston hidden amongst some clothes in a trunk, an Ordnance Survey map of South-East England with all the RAF stations marked on it, a camera in some overalls, various air magazines and some letters and notebooks that contained very damaging records of the tenant's activities.

Mrs Johnson was interviewed and gave a description of Dr Goertz and his young 'niece' who, she had been told, was acting as his clerk and secretary while he was writing a book. Hinchley-Cooke translated the various diaries and notebooks and was able to reconstruct much of the movements of the two Germans. Goertz had rented the bungalow from Mrs Johnson from 14 September to 26 October but clearly the lawyer had been in England travelling around the countryside for much of August. A diary listed:

> 'Aug 29 1935 Mildenhall; Aug 31 Duxford; Sept 1 Mildenhall; Sept 2 Hunstanton; Sept 3 Feltwell; Sept 5 and 6 London; Sept 7 Hatfield; Sept 10 Martlesham; Sept 11 Broadstairs, Ramsgate; Sept 12 Broadstairs; Sept 13 Mildenhall; Sept 19 Broadstairs.'

Hinchley-Cooke's worst fears were realized when he read some of the letters in the bungalow. One was a six-page application to join the Luftwaffe, complete with details of Goertz's experience as an intelligence officer during the Great War. Another letter mentioned that 'It would perhaps be necessary to tell the Chamber the unvarnished truth and inform them regarding your activities in England'. Apparently Goertz was in danger of being struck off the roll of Hamburg solicitors and he was being advised by a business colleague on how to avoid this.

Other items found were a copy of the *Air Force Diary*, the *RAF List*, heavily marked in pencil with ticks against particular aerodromes, and a book called *The Air Pilot* which provided maps of British airstrips. The evidence was more than enough for Hinchley-Cooke. A notice was sent to all ports of entry instructing the Immigration Officers to detain Dr Hermann Goertz of Hamburg and his 'niece', Marianne Emig, should they return to the United Kingdom. Hinchley-Cooke was confident that he would reappear because Goertz had left his motorcycle combination at 'Havelock' and Mrs Johnson stated that she had received a postcard from her tenant from Belgium telling her that he was going to come back, and incidentally instructing her on what to do with the motorcycle in the meantime.

On 8 November Goertz turned up alone at Harwich and was promptly arrested on a warrant and taken to Broadstairs where he made a long statement under caution. He admitted that all the maps, sketches and notebooks were his but claimed that his interest in flying was quite innocent. He explained that he had come to England on 19 July, 1935 and had spent a month in the Isle of Wight, Devon and Cornwall before continuing his holiday with Miss Emig to Suffolk. All the notes about the various RAF airfields were to be used in a novel he was preparing, entitled *Bridge Over the Grey Waters*.

Goertz was duly charged on 18 November with three offences under the Official Secrets Act, all relating to the sketches that had been found of the RAF station at Manston in Kent. The lawyer-novelist pleaded Not Guilty and his trial started on 4 March, 1936 at the Old Bailey. The prosecution stated that Goertz was a professional intelligence officer and produced in evidence all the materials recovered from 'Havelock' in Broadstairs. The defendant countered that all the documents seized were freely available to anyone willing to buy them. Pressed by the judge, Mr Justice Greaves-Lord, the police witness, Frederick Smith, admitted that most of the items were not restricted in any way. They included picture postcards of the aircraft carrier *Ark Royal*, the 1935 *RAF List* which had been bought from an Air Ministry bookstall during an air display, a reference book entitled *The Air Pilot* which contained maps of all the aerodromes in Britain. The same applied to the *Air Force Diary* found at Broadstairs though Goertz had written in it the address of the Nazi organization in London.

The prosecution then called 'Lieutenant-Colonel Cook' of the Directorate of Military Operations and Intelligence at the War Office, who was able to produce two pieces of evidence that were particularly damaging. Hinchley-Cooke had translated an application for a job from Goertz addressed to the German Air Force. It took the form of a six-page curriculum vitae which boasted that his success as an intelligence officer in the Great War had led to him being branded 'a particularly dangerous' interrogator by the Allies. The jury was suitably impressed. But most damning of all was a sketch of Manston airfield that had been made by Goertz. The original in *The Air Pilot* merely showed the runways and the contours. On the version found by the police each building at the RAF station had been identified as hangars, fuel dumps etc. Goertz had accurately identified all the airfield's installations and carefully marked them on his sketch, an action which, as the prosecution pointed out, was proof of more than amateur curiosity.

Counsel for the defence then challenged Hinchley-Cooke about the existence of an RAF station at Feltwell. The witness denied that there had been any mistake and confirmed that there was an airfield there. The defence, led by Reginald Croom-Johnson MP, an eminent King's Counsel, continued to challenge the MI5 officer and asked where he got his information. This proved an awkward question to answer. Hinchley-Cooke was obliged to fish a top-secret map from his briefcase and declared that it showed all the existing RAF fields and detailed those sites which were to be built on. The judge acknowledged the sensitivity of the line of questioning and promptly cleared the Court.

The next day, on 5 March, Hinchley-Cooke returned to the witness box and, with the Court *in camera* explained that Goertz had compiled a mass of intelligence about airfields in southern England that was both accurate and highly damaging. He was followed by an RAF Group Captain who confirmed that the German had correctly identified the location of such buildings as the bomb store at Manston. Both witnesses repeated that Goertz had accumulated information that was highly prejudicial to the Royal Air Force.

Once the Court came out of closed session the defence asked permission to recall Hinchley-Cooke. The judge agreed and Croom-Johnson entered into a long wrangle about the difference between a secret service agent and an intelligence officer. As an illustration of the point he was making the defence counsel instructed Hinchley-Cooke to write down in German his 'official designation' and his 'exact position at the War Office'. The veteran spy-catcher complied and read it over, in German, to the jury.

The prosecution were mildly put out by this exchange and asked for an expert definition of the word that the prosecution had translated as 'secret service' and the defence as 'intelligence service'. Hinchley-Cooke proceeded to give a masterly definition:

> 'The word had four possible meanings. It could mean "new service", "signal service", "intelligence service" or "secret service". The dividing line between intelligence service and secret service was

very indefinite and the interpretation depended on the context not only of the particular sentence in which it occurred but the whole document. The "intelligence service" was a collective designation of various services which collected and collated intelligence. That was information relating to armies, navies and air forces, and also information of a political nature. Such intelligence was usually obtained from open and readily available sources such as Naval Attachés, text books and other publications. Linked up with the Intelligence Service was the Secret Service. That service collected for the Intelligence Service such information as was not readily available but which had to be obtained in an underhand way, generally through secret service agents, commonly described as spies.'

In conclusion 'Colonel Cook' produced a copy of Colonel Nicolai's book on the German Secret Service and quoted a reference to espionage that confirmed his translation of Secret Service.

The case against Goertz was now virtually proved so the defence called him to the witness box to recover the situation. He described himself as a forty-five-year-old lawyer who had studied law at the universities of Heidelberg, Paris, Edinburgh and Kiel and a veteran of the Great War who had won the Iron Cross in 1917. He recounted at length how he had suffered much illness and had failed to get any remuneration for his work in a legal case for Siemens that had involved attending no less than forty sessions of the Law Courts in London. He explained that at the end of the case he was 40,000 marks in debt and had been advised to start writing in his spare time to earn some extra income. He dealt with the Air Force application found by Hinchley-Cooke by saying that he had tried to support his case by detailing his wartime experience. This, he had been advised, would be helpful because he was too old to be employed as a pilot. He concluded by stating that his request for a job had been turned down anyway on the grounds that he was too old.

Goertz did not however fare so well under cross-examination by the prosecution. He was forced to admit that the skeleton of his novel existed only in his head, and then he was questioned about various personalities in Berlin. This immediately put the German in an impossible situation. Counsel asked him if he had ever been to the Intelligence Branch of the Air Force in Berlin. The witness replied that he had not. He had only been to see his old squadron commander, Colonel Dressler. The prosecution demanded to know what position this officer held, and Goertz stumbled. He explained that he was 'in a difficult position' but could say that Colonel Dressler was 'not in the intelligence service or the secret service'. He added, 'I have to say things which may be harmful to the German law.'

At this point the judge intervened and asked if Goertz meant that it might be dangerous for him to state exactly what Colonel Dressler's post was. The witness agreed that so far he had not offended German law 'but I would not try to defend myself here if I thought that in Germany I would be tried for high treason.'

The judge then pressed again and asked, 'Does that mean it might be serious for you to disclose what he is?'

By now Goertz was in considerable trouble and quickly consulted his Counsel and his solicitor. The result was that Croom-Johnson got to his feet and explained that the consequence of 'answering the question would be that information about something in Germany would come out which would endanger this gentleman's position if the German authorities took a certain view of the matter'.

The prosecution accepted this and went on to ask: 'You say you saw this gentleman about whom you desire protection. Did you see anybody else?'

Goertz was again in difficulties. He replied that he had looked up a friend and had been to see his brother-in-law at the War Ministry. Counsel quickly asked who the friend was and the defendant admitted that this too was a difficult question to answer. He said, 'I cannot dare answer. It is impossible for me.'

By now the damage was done. Goertz was covered in confusion and no doubt concerned about the reception he would receive back in Berlin. The Court adjourned until Monday, 9 March but over the weekend Hitler ordered the occupation of the demilitarized zone of the Ruhr Valley. The jury wasted no time in returning a verdict of guilty and Goertz was sentenced to four years' imprisonment.[12]

The case received a huge amount of publicity and served to alert the public to the intelligence offensive that was about to be launched against Britain from the Continent. In fact, the expected offensive never materialized. MI5 turned their attention to the growing number of refugees and an intensification of surveillance on the Nazi front organization.

In documents recovered from the Abwehr after the war and interrogations conducted after the war the Security Service were able to establish that in September 1936 Hitler had indeed forbidden the Abwehr further adventures in Britain so as not to compromise relations. However, Kell did not know this at the time so he continued to log new arrivals registered under the Aliens Act and to add the names of suspects to the Registry list of undesirables. MI5 were unable to uncover further cases of German espionage until late in 1937 when Special Branch informed MI5 that the Dundee city police had passed on information relating to a fifty-one-year-old hairdresser, Mrs Jessie Jordan of Kinloch Street, Dundee.

The Jordan case became an important one because of the insight it gave Hinchley-Cooke and Phillips into the intentions of the Abwehr and the basis that it provided for a firm relationship with the American FBI.

Mrs Jordan was the widow of a German Great War soldier. After spending most of her adult life in Germany she had returned to Dundee to open a small business. At the age of sixteen she ran away from her mother (she never knew her father) and found a job as a domestic servant. Four years later she met a German named Jordan in Scotland and returned with him to Germany to get married. After the war she had married again but had subsequently obtained a divorce from her second husband. Eventually she had returned to Scotland, partly in disgust at the anti-Jewish treatment she had witnessed, although she was not herself a Jew. Apparently, the name Jordan, a name she had readopted after the failure of her second marriage, had Jewish significance. At the end of 1937 her postman asked whether he could keep the stamps from her overseas mail. She was receiving letters from all over the world and he was keen to build up his collection. Mrs Jordan refused in such strong terms that the postman reported the matter to his supervisor. The Post Office soon established that not only was the hairdresser getting an unusual amount of mail, but she was posting a great deal too. The bulk of her post went to America but she received letters from Holland, France, Germany, Sweden and South America.

'B' Division of MI5 obtained a warrant from the Home Secretary to intercept Mrs Jordan's mail and quickly established that she was acting as a post-box for the Abwehr. Hinchley-Cooke obtained Kell's permission to copy the letters Mrs Jordan received and posted.

All the cover addresses were listed with Registry as Abwehr centres though mail originating from the United States gave cause for concern. At the end of January 1937, the Deputy Director of 'B' Division, Guy Liddell, went to Washington and explained to the Director of the FBI, J. Edgar Hoover, that Mrs Jordan had been in communication with a 'Mr Kron' in New York.

Hoover checked the address and established that 'Herr Kron' was Günther Rumrich, a Sudeten German who had become a naturalized

American. His record showed that he had served seven years in the Army and had been sentenced for desertion and embezzlement of mess funds from Fort Missoula in Montana. The FBI agreed to keep Rumrich under surveillance so the Jordan post-box could be operated by 'B' Division staff, but unfortunately, he was arrested by detectives from the Aliens Squad on 16 February 1937 after a tip-off from the State Department. Rumrich had been taken into custody after a bizarre attempt to obtain a quantity of blank American passports by impersonating a senior State Department official, Edward Weston, an Under-Secretary of State. The plot was so hamfisted that Rumrich never stood a chance of success. The Abwehr had instructed him to obtain fifty passports via a steward on the *Europa*, Karl Schleuter. Just as the FBI were being told about MI5's suspicions concerning Rumrich the State Department's New York Passport Office were asking the Aliens Squad to investigate a phoney request for fifty blanks which were to be delivered to the Taft Hotel.

When the FBI finally got hold of Rumrich he told the whole story. He had read a copy of Colonel Nicolai's book and had immediately written to the Berlin *Voelkischer Beobachter*, the major Nazi daily, offering his services. He asked that if the Germans were interested in the information that 'a high official in the United States Army' could pass they should place an advertisement in the *New York Times*. It was to read: 'Theodor Koerner – Letter received' and give an address where he could contact the Abwehr. In the event the Abwehr had instructed him to reply to 'Sanders, Postbox 629, Hamburg 1, Germany.'[13] The announcement duly, appeared on 6 April, 1936 and 'Herr Kron' and Rumrich went into action. He operated for twenty months between May 1936 and February 1938 and succeeded in passing a considerable amount of intelligence back to Hamburg via Dundee.

Rumrich was interrogated by the FBI[14] and revealed that apart from Mrs Jordan his contact with the Abwehr had been via two employees of the *Europa*, Karl Schleuter and his girlfriend, Johanna Hofmann, an American from Queens who was working on the ship as a hairdresser. With the arrest of Johanna Hofmann, the FBI were able to eliminate a major German network in America. Others implicated in the spy-ring were William Lonkowski, an aircraft mechanic from Silesia who had worked in various American aircraft factories until an incident with US Customs in September 1935,[15] Werner Gudenberg, a young engineering draughtsman and Otto Voss, who worked for the Sikorsky factory at Farmingdale, Long Island. In turn Dr Ignatz Giebl, a Great War artillery officer and graduate of medicine at Fordham University, was implicated in the Nazi conspiracy. A Grand Jury investigation was started and the

Abwehr officer at the centre of the operation, Lieutenant Commander Erich Phieffer (alias 'N. Spielman', 'Dr Erdhoff' and merely 'Herr Doktor') was identified as the major conspirator, based at Wilhelmshaven.

MI5 received no public thanks for their contribution to this *coup* but it cemented relations between Hoover and Liddell. Mrs Jessie Jordan was arrested on 2 March 1938 and charged with offences under the Official Secrets Act. When her house in Kinloch Street was searched the police found a rather amateurish sketch map of Fife and a list of Coast Guard stations between Montrose and Kirkcaldy. This provided further ammunition for the prosecution which originally could only provide evidence to show that she had been 'in communication with foreign agents between 1 June and 2 March, 1938, for purposes prejudicial to the purposes and interests of the State'.

Mrs Jordan admitted the charge and confirmed she had received various small sums for her service to the Abwehr. Her Counsel pointed out that she now held German nationality and had spent so long in Germany that she found it difficult to speak English fluently. The Scottish Lord Justice Clerk Lord Aitchison commented that 'in considering what sentence   to impose the governing consideration must be what is required in the national interest', and dealt her four years at Perth Prison on 15 May, 1938.

Six months after Mrs Jordan's conviction in November 1938 the Letter Interception Unit reported a letter intercepted on its way to a known Abwehr cover address in Hanover. Hinchley-Cooke soon established the sender to be Donald Adams, a fifty-five-year-old racing journalist who lived in Friars Stile Road, Richmond. Adams had recently returned from Germany and Hinchley-Cooke assumed he had been recruited by the Abwehr while abroad. (It was later established that Adams had once worked as a salesman for a German export firm, Feodor Burgman of Dresden.) His mail was opened on a Home Office warrant for nearly eight months and allowed to continue its journey because the information he was providing was easily obtained from the daily newspapers, a fact that was not lost on his German contact 'Herr B. Skuch', who commented on his agent's inability to communicate more than once a month. Adams was arrested on 30 June, 1939 and pleaded Guilty to a total of eight charges under the Official Secrets Act at Richmond Police Court. Mr Justice Oliver sentenced him at the Old Bailey on 25 September, 1939 and commented: 'I spent last week trying people for murder. I do not really know if a man like you is not worse than any of those murderers because you took your part for pay for murdering your countrymen if you could.' Adams received seven years, and proved that the expanded LIU and postal censorship section were operating effectively.

The major German spy case of 1939 broke when the Royal Ordnance Factory at Euxton in Lancashire reported that an office had been broken into and two site plans of the establishment stolen. The theft had taken place on 2 March and the police were called in immediately. One of the first suspects in the case was an Irish bricklayer, Joseph Kelly, who had been working in the Ordnance Factory's compound since September the previous year. He was put under surveillance while MI5 investigated his background.

Kelly was a thirty-year-old labourer living in Rigby Street, Bolton. He was married with three children and was paid between £5 and £6 per week. The IRA 'English Campaign' was in full swing in March 1939 and naturally the Special Branch connected the two events. As a precaution the LIU were alerted to Kelly's address and this manoeuvre paid dividends. On 9 March Kelly received a letter from the Netherlands which attracted MI5's attention:

> 'Re your letter of 2nd inst. As I cannot arrange to go to Osnabruck I suggest we meet on the 17th or 18th. Perhaps you can book at the Hohenzollern, where I will ask for you.'

A German visa and $10 were included. This letter was intercepted at the same time as a passport application arrived from Kelly. Special Branch detectives learnt that Kelly was explaining to friends that he was due to visit Germany shortly to conclude a boxing deal.

Arrangements were made to keep the surveillance operation going even when Kelly went on his trip to Germany. He was followed to Holland and then over the frontier to Cologne where Kelly was observed to meet a German agent and accompany him to the local Abwehr out-station.

While he was abroad his home in Bolton was searched and his correspondence with cover addresses recovered. One letter dated 2 February seemed to indicate that Kelly was not necessarily a member of the IRA as at first suspected but a recent Abwehr recruit. In part the letter stated:

> 'Dear Sir, I owe your address to a friend. Referring to the previous application I would be pleased to take up communication with you. If you still feel inclined to take charge of my agency in the UK I would like to discuss matters and conditions.'

A warrant was issued for Kelly's arrest and he was detained as soon as he stepped off the cross-Channel ferry on 20 March. He was then driven to Bolton Police Station where, as he got out of the police car, he was spotted removing something from his mouth and throwing it away. A small piece of paper was recovered on which were printed instructions about future communications with the Abwehr. Kelly admitted the theft of the Royal Ordnance Factory plans and was charged with that and an offence under the Official Secrets Act. He then made a long statement explaining what had happened.

It seemed that in November 1938, after he had been working at Euxton for two months, he obtained an interview with the German Consul in Liverpool, Herr Walther Reinhardt, who was reluctantly persuaded to send Kelly's name to the Foreign Ministry in Berlin as a likely source of intelligence. After some months Kelly received a letter from Holland suggesting a rendezvous. Kelly went to London by train and made his offer to supply intelligence from the Lancashire munitions factory. The burglary took place on 1 March and the Irishman immediately wrote to his cover address asking for a second meeting. The Germans paid him £30 for the lay-out plan of the establishment. Kelly left the second one behind in England because it was apparently out of date.

When Kelly appeared before Mr Justice Stable in Manchester on 19 May, 1939 he pleaded Guilty but offered two statements of mitigation from his father and wife. The Judge commented:

> 'The Act of Parliament enables me to send you to penal servitude for fourteen years. I am not sure that that is any too much. I observed – whether the report is accurate or not I assume it was – in *The Times* newspaper last week that two men in another country were both executed. We have got in this country what I suppose is a more merciful course.'

He then sentenced Kelly to three years for the two charges of larceny and ten years for each of the charges under the Official Secrets Act.

Neither the Kelly prosecution nor any of the other espionage investigations of 1939 showed much evidence of a concerted effort against Britain from Berlin although in March MI5 had the hint of a big catch. An elderly German, Herr Walter Simon, was arrested and convicted on charges of failing to observe the Aliens Registration Act. Simon was interviewed by Colonel Hinchley-Cooke in prison but he declined to say anything about his work for the Abwehr. When Simon completed his sentence, he was deported back to Germany though this was by no means the end of his intelligence career, as will be seen in Chapter XII.

The best evidence of the Abwehr's pre-war intelligence offensive against Britain was obtained after the war as Allied counter-intelligence officers sifted through what remained of the Nazi records. The salvaging went on for some years after the final surrender just as the Allies probed the memories of their former adversaries.

The picture which emerged of the Abwehr's early efforts was undeniably impressive. Factories, mines, airfields, ports, harbour defences and military establishments throughout the British Isles had been surveyed, photographed and filed with meticulous attention to detail. The questionnaires supplied to their individual agents demonstrated a close knowledge of particular targets, information that frequently could not have come from aerial reconnaissance. Their instructions were precise and frequently embarrassingly accurate. In June 1941 part of a message from Hamburg for a German agent known to MI5 as TATE requested: 'Adjoining the aerodrome at Hawarden, west of Chester, there is at the south-west corner 1 km north of the village of Broughton, the Vickers factory on the surface. Where is the underground factory? Are the works in operation?'

Perhaps the most remarkable document recovered after the war was *Informationsheft Grossbritannien*, an intelligence summary of the United Kingdom compiled by the RSHA, the Reich Security Agency, early in 1940 in preparation for SEALION, the German invasion of Britain. The anonymous author[16] of the work covered aspects of British social, political and industrial life, and it included a 'Sonder-fahndungsliste' (Arrest List) of targets for the Gestapo and a pull-out section of aerial photographs spanning the whole of the south coast of England.

Of special interest to MI5 was the chapter commencing on page 85, entitled 'Der Britische Nachtrichtendienst', a concise explanation of the roles of all Britain's intelligence organizations and a commentary on some of their leading personalities such as Lord Hankey and Sir Robert Vansittart, the Permanent Under-Secretahes at the Foreign Office. Most of SIS's senior staff were accurately identify together with the locations of their London offices. The labyrinth of Britain's various intelligence organs was unravelled and the relationships between them explained. The Joint Intelligence Committee, a body largely unknown to the British public, was described, as were the methods used to distribute the information gathered to the relevant clients. The analysis of SIS was particularly thorough. Each of its departments was named, along with its precise location inside Broadway Buildings and the identities of the heads of each department. Admiral Hugh Sinclair was named as the late CSS and, 'according to Stevens' he had been succeeded by 'Oberst Stuart Menzies (pronounced Mengis), a Scot, on November 4, 1939'.

The document is equally remarkable for naming the sources it relied on. The names 'Captain Best' and 'Major Stevens' appear over forty times, sometimes with damning effect. The sensitive SIS Communications Section is described, and Colonel Gambier-Parry is correctly identified as being in command. One further comment adds: 'Stevens says … most of the staff have moved to Bletchley.' Stevens and Best, both SIS officers, were kidnapped by Nazi agents in November 1939 at Venlo on the Dutch-German frontier. Both were particularly knowledgeable about SIS operations, Stevens being the SIS Head of Station in The Hague, and Best running an extensive European network based in Paris and The Hague for Claude Dansey. Stevens was also in a position to know about the plan to site the GC & CS at Bletchley Park because the move had been practised during the Munich crisis of August 1938.

The passages create a comprehensive picture of the SIS, and if it had been used with the appendixed Arrest List as intended it would have been a formidable weapon. After the war both Stevens and Best were repatriated to Britain, interviewed by MI5, and allowed to retire without further action being taken against them.

Thanks to MI5's pre-war security *Informationsheft Grossbritannien* could shed relatively little light on MI5. The few paragraphs devoted to the Security Service explain its close relationship with Special Branch of Scotland Yard but the author admits that neither Best nor Stevens were ever in a position to learn the identity of its staff beyond those who had dealt with Section V of SIS run by Major Valentine Vivian. Nevertheless, the author confidently states that MI5's headquarters was in Thames House, Millbank, and its chief is named as Colonel Sir Vernon Kell. Kell's chief collaborator is named as 'Lt-Colonel Hinchley-Cook who has participated in many spy trials.' The author adds: 'His name does not appear in the Army List so therefore he is presumed to be a police officer.' He is described as 'wearing glasses, is strong and has a fresh complexion. He has a friendly nature and speaks German fluently with a mixture of a Hamburg and Saxon accent.'

Kell's other confederates are described as 'G. Liddel and one Mr Curry who concentrates on German National Socialist matters.' The final paragraph states: 'One of MI5's cover addresses is the office of Captain King, Flat 308, Hood House, Dolphin Square, in the name of Coplestone. MI5 staff can be found here. Captain King himself lives in Whitehall Mansions. He also has a proper office in the War Office.'

There is no indication where this piece of information had come from, but considering how candidly the author gives credit to Best and Stevens it may well be that the source for this intelligence was one of Captain King's more unreliable agents.[17]

The author noted that MI5's structure made it virtually impossible for outsiders to learn much about it. Thames House was judged to be the link with the outside world. MI5's strength at the outbreak of war was estimated to be about seventy-five.

One of the named sources of this information is a *Picture Post* article by Carl Olsson which in November 1938 described the Special Branch in an article as 'MI5's longest arm'. In total only five MI5 staff were actually identified by the Germans. Kell had achieved some fame during the Great War as a spy-catcher and it was not unreasonable his name should be known. Neither the Germans nor *Picture Post* were fooled by his 'retirement' which had been gazetted in 1924. Little secrecy could be expected over Hinchley-Cooke who had indeed been prominent in trials at the Old Bailey and had questioned Hermann Goertz at lengths after his imprisonment in 1936. 'Liddel' of course referred to Guy Liddell and 'Mr Curry' was clearly Jack Curry, who had also been active in pre-war counter-espionage (later Head of Section IX of SIS, Soviet Affairs).

This chapter of *Informationscheft Grossbritannien* was undeniably a devastating summary of the Secret Intelligence Service and indeed remained largely relevant and accurate well into the post-war period, identifying many senior long-serving officers. More than twenty years after the war, authors were requested by the War Office to delete references to Sir Stewart Menzies.

In the event of a German invasion there can be little doubt that the whole of the SIS structute known to Best and Stevens would have been quickly scooped up by the Gestapo. On the evidence of the relatively few passages relating to MI5, the Security Service might have hoped to escape such attention. To the Germans MI5 remained an unknown quantity.

PART TWO:

INTO WAR

IV
Aliens: The Enemy Within

'We expect to be attacked here, both from the air and by parachute and airborne troops in the near future, and are getting ready for them.'

Churchill to Roosevelt, 15 May, 1940

At the outbreak of war in 1939 MI5 retained its secretive nature and methods, but its powers were greatly enhanced. Kell was utterly determined to repeat his *coup* of 1914 and at one stroke eliminate the Abwehr's networks in Britain. It was an ambitious objective but he had all the necessary weapons at his disposal.

His principal weapon was the second Aliens Registration Act which had been passed by Parliament after the Great War to replace the 'temporary' 1914 measure. This legislation gave Immigration Officers complete control over whether or not a foreigner would be allowed to land in the United Kingdom. It also, most importantly, placed a responsibility on the alien to register with the police and keep them informed about his or her movements. Thus, through Special Branch Kell's men could keep Registry up to date on the whereabouts of suspected agents.

In September 1939 the numbers of enemy aliens had vastly increased. The police had a total of 71,600 registered on their books and to ensure wartime security every one of them would have to be interviewed with a view to possible internment. Quite apart from this large statistic MI5's Registry had accumulated a list of nearly 400 suspects who could not be allowed to retain their liberty. The majority of these were German nationals who had been living in Britain for a number of years, and several were employed as domestic servants in the homes of military personnel. Some thirty-five who held British nationality were served with detention orders under the new Defence of the Realm Act and lodged in Brixton Prison. The Home Office announced that all German and Austrian nationals would have to report immediately to their local police stations where their cases would be considered and processed.

This 'processing' would be undertaken by a special organization that the government had prepared in conditions of secrecy. One hundred and twenty King's Counsel and County Court judges were selected as one-man tribunals to hold informal hearings and decide on the cases of individual aliens. The tribunals sat with a senior police officer acting as secretary so that confidential information relating to the suspect could be passed on to the Chairman. Thus, the enemy aliens on MI5's index of suspects were ordered to internment camp reception centres without requiring Special Branch to make individual arrests. The system also allowed many Abwehr agents to be taken into custody without them suspecting that they had been identified as potential spies.

The internment procedure allowed for three categories of enemy aliens. The first, Category 'A' meant immediate detention. The internee would be taken under guard to a reception centre operated by the military before being transferred to one of the hastily-prepared internment camps across the country. The three largest camps were at Wharf Mills, a derelict cotton mill near Bury in Lancashire, a partly-built housing estate at Huyton, also in Lancashire, and the Isle of Man, where the Manx government had made several sites available to the War Office. The women internees were sent to the hospital wing of Holloway Prison in North London but as their numbers increased special provision for them (and their children under sixteen) was made at Port Erin and Port St Mary on the Isle of Man.

The camps all varied enormously in both the quality of the accommodation and security. Wharf Mills became notorious for its appalling conditions, while on the Isle of Man and at Huyton the internees enjoyed a measure of self-government with a structure of elected 'house leaders' and 'camp leaders'. The speed with which the internments were made caused many administrative problems. The authorities received a mass of complaints about the collection centre that had been located in the offices and buildings at Kempton Park Racecourse. Occasionally a tactless mixture of prisoners caused friction. Several Jewish internees received beatings at the hands of Fascist prisoners at Brixton and there were serious disturbances at Warner's Camp in Dorset where Nazi sympathizers rubbed shoulders with veterans from the International Brigade of the Spanish Civil War, Austrian Socialists and several German Communists and Trade Unionists.

German seamen captured on merchant vessels were sent to internment camps rather than POW camps as they were not strictly military personnel according to international law. Some 250 from the *Adolf Woerman* were sent to Warner's Camp where they clashed with the 200 Category 'A' Jews who had been there since the beginning of the war. Eventually the Nazi element were sent to Canada on the ill-fated *Arandora Star*.

The majority of the 71,600 enemy aliens examined by the tribunals were classified as Category 'C' which gave them complete freedom, but 6,800 fell into an intermediate group, Category 'B' and were subject to certain restrictions. They were unable to possess a car, bicycle, aircraft or boat and were not allowed to travel more than five miles from home (except in London) without a police permit. Cameras, firearms and carrier pigeons had to be surrendered and a 10.30 PM curfew (midnight in London) imposed. Of the initial 600 Category 'A' internees 120 were judged to be 'refugees from Nazi oppression'. This status was given to 4,100 in Category 'B' and 51,200 in Category 'C'.

By May of the following year the situation had changed dramatically. The Phoney War had come to an end and the Germans were advancing towards the Channel ports. The threat of invasion grew daily and the military authorities became increasingly concerned about the number of enemy aliens still resident in the coastal areas of Britain. The news-papers were filled with stories about the Nazi Fifth Column in Belgium and Holland and spy mania gripped the country.

The government responded by declaring a wide coastal belt from Inverness to Dorset 'protected' and announced that all German and Austrian males in Category 'B' between the ages of sixteen and sixty were to be interned immediately. All the remaining Category 'B' females were to report for their cases to be re-examined. By June 1940 there was a record number of people interned; the newspapers persisted in pointing out the dangers of 'the enemy within' and various public figures demanded further restrictions. The Registrar of Oxford University complained that there were over 1,000 foreigners in the city, of which 477 were enemy aliens. 'Aliens are a potential menace and we feel they should be interned,' he told *The Times*. 'They can be sorted out after internment if necessary.'

Again, the Internment Orders were extended. All 'B' Category German and Austrian women between the ages of sixteen and sixty were interned and a massive police operation took place to get the 3,500 females involved to the Isle of Man. Added to this group were the 300 Category 'B' men who had so far been exempted from internment. They were aged between sixty and seventy.

On the Isle of Man further areas were set aside to house the influx. Some of the resorts on the island's south coast were declared 'internment areas' although the local landladies were permitted to remain in their homes to supervise the newcomers.

The Manx authorities coped well with the shipments of internees that arrived and generally the facilities continued to be good. The women, of course, remained under the jurisdiction of the Home Office and Dame Joanna Cruickshank, the Matron in Chief of Princess Mary's Nursing Service was put in overall charge of the new arrivals, liaising closely with the MI5 office in Ramsey (which was to become known as 'the library' because of the frequency with which requests for information were referred there from St James's Street).

Kell was confident that with the secure internment of over 7,000 men and 4,000 women much of the Abwehr's networks had been eliminated and when, at the end of June 1940, all the Category 'C' males were ordered to report to the collection centres, the indications were that the lid had been sealed tight.

Moreover, Kell actually had a means of telling whether his surmise was correct or not, for since 1936 the intelligence services had had a part-time agent working for them obtaining information from the Germans. Arthur George Owens was code-named SNOW, a part anagram of his name. By means of SNOW, MI5 hoped to find out if there were any other Abwehr networks left in Britain or if SNOW was the sole survivor. (For more details about SNOW later on see Chapter VII.)

SNOW was also able to tell Robertson that he had made contact with the Hamburg Abstelle during a visit to Rotterdam in September 1939 and had been put in touch with another agent, a British subject of German origins who had been recruited in Cologne in 1938 (and given the Abwehr designation 3527) along with his two brothers. He was an expert photographer and was instructed by SNOW to develop the microdots which were to be carried through the British controls. When interviewed by Tar Robertson he proved entirely co-operative and agreed to help the authorities in any way he could. Thus 3527 was enrolled as CHARLIE while his less co-operative brother 3528 was assessed Category 'A' and interned.

3528 was drowned on 2 July, 1940 on his way to Canada when the *Arandora Star* was torpedoed in mid-Atlantic by Günther Prien, the U-boat commander responsible for sinking the *Royal Oak*. Prien himself was killed in March 1941 when the *U-47* was sunk by British depth charges in the Atlantic.

Kell was just celebrating the success of the internments when SNOW received a sum of money through the post, as payment for his services to the Abwehr. The immediate assumption was that the packet had been posted by a diplomat in London but further investigation ruled this out. SNOW, Robertson and Richmond Stopford, Robertson's assistant, examined the notes with Mrs Funnell, SNOW's mistress, who was herself of German descent, speculating about the ink marks on two of the £20 notes. They were clearly marked 'S & Co.'. Mrs Funnell suggested that they might have come from Selfridges and sure enough the department store confirmed that their cashiers marked bundles of £10 and £20 notes with 'S & Co.'. and the totals in the bundles. Richmond Stopford spent an afternoon in Selfridges and by luck managed to track down the assistant who had handled the notes. She distinctly remembered a middle-aged foreign woman asking for several £5 notes to be changed into larger denominations. This was an unusual request and the assistant had later taken down the woman's address when she ordered some goods to be delivered. The woman was Mrs Mathilde Krafft and she was working near Bournemouth as a housekeeper to a Naval officer. Richmond Stopford immediately reported the news to Colonel Robertson who arranged for Mrs Krafft's arrest and internment in Holloway. Once this particular leak had been plugged evidence mounted to suggest that the SNOW network was the only one left intact after the mass internments of May, June and July 1940.

On 10 June the numbers suffering internment were increased yet again. Mussolini declared war on Great Britain that evening and within an hour the Italian Club in Charing Cross Road had been raided by a force of 100 policemen and Special Branch detectives. The Italian community in Britain had anyway been subject to the restrictions imposed on all foreigners, such as reporting daily to the police, so the authorities were in a position to act swiftly. Detention Orders under the Aliens Act were served in Liverpool, Birmingham and Glasgow, though in a few places the police had to fight their way through angry crowds to get to bewildered and frightened café proprietors.

The fall of France to the Germans coincided with Sir John Anderson's announcement that all Chief Constables were forthwith empowered to intern any enemy alien they considered 'suspect'.

Kell accepted that the tribunal system was far from perfect and that certain regions seemed to act with perverse severity (in East Anglia all German domestic servants were assessed as Category 'B' thus preventing them from travelling to jobs in factories further afield) and the newspapers frequently criticized the procedures. When all the Category 'C' Certificate holders were interned in June, H.G. Wells wrote to *The Times* to complain that the internment of this group, who were mainly refugees, was indefensible and counter-productive. He accused the Home Office of being run by Nazi sympathisers and pointed out that one of his friends who had been interned, a naturalized British citizen, had a well-publicized anti-Fascist political record.

The outcry continued in some circles but the government became more aggressive in their attitude towards internment as the military situation deteriorated. In September 1939 the Home Office had been almost apologetic about the necessity for the detention orders but by the following year this attitude had changed. They no longer expressed regret for the inevitable inconvenience caused to the innocent, but rigorously enforced the regulations. Fines of £100 or six-months' imprisonment were imposed on Aliens Act offenders. Refugees who failed to produce their Alien's Registration Certificate to the police when asked for it were dealt with severely.

During the autumn of 1940 concern mounted again as large numbers of refugees fled the Continent. After the evacuation of Dunkirk, the position became even more precarious. The flood now included Poles, Danes, Belgians, the Dutch and the French, and every one had to be screened for reliability. At first five reception centres were established in London, at Balham, Bushey Park, Norwood, Crystal Palace and the Fulham Road. They were organized by the London County Council and all new arrivals were directed to them. Medical officers examined each one for lice and infectious diseases and then intelligence officers satisfied themselves about their bona fides. Once cleared the refugee was issued with a registration card and a ration book. By January 1941 three further establishments had been opened to cope with the influx of foreign escapees. A somewhat makeshift camp at Tunbridge Wells in Kent operated by an MI5 nominee, Major Grassby, was superseded by the Royal Victoria Patriotic School in Wandsworth. The foundations of this gigantic building were laid by Queen Victoria in 1857 when it was named The Royal Victoria Patriotic Asylum for the Orphan Daughters of Soldiers and Sailors killed in the Crimean War. Officially the RVPS came under the authority of MI9, the escape and evasion organization, but many of the staff, including the Director, Ronnie Haylor, were MI5 nominees. At first there were only five interrogators to screen the refugees but gradually the numbers increased and encompassed counter-intelligence officers from Allied forces.[18] Other RVPS offices were set up at Poole, where a seaplane service operated twice weekly to Lisbon, and at Bristol, Glasgow and Liverpool. In London the Oratory School was requisitioned and turned into a refugee processing centre.

Some of the first prisoners of war and internees were shipped across the Atlantic to Canada and a few went to Australia. Later on, many of the Category 'C' refugees were recruited into the newly-formed

Auxiliary Pioneer Corps and set to work building coastal defences and repairing bomb damage.

By and large, considering the size of the problem and its complexity, MI5's system of internment and screening could be said to have been remarkably efficient and successful, as later chapters will show.

V
The British Fifth Column

'We cannot be too sure of anybody.'

Field-Marshal Sir Edmund Ironside, Commander-in-Chief,
Home Forces, 5 June 1940

'There are tendencies, conspiracies and movements totally unknown in the case of previous encounters between countries.'

The Right Honourable John Clynes MP, Labour Member of
Parliament for Manchester (Platting) speaking on the Treachery Bill,
22 May, 1940

'If I erred in seeking a friendly understanding with Germany, I erred in good company.'

Lord Redesdale, April 1940

'Anyone who says the Germans will not invade is mad.'

The Director of Military Intelligence, Major-General F.G.
('Paddy') Beaumont-Nesbitt, addressing the Joint Intelligence
Committee, 13 September, 1940

General Mola's famous remark on 6 October, 1936 about his 'Fifth Column' already being in position in Spain's capital created a spectre which was to become the nightmare of Europe's counter-subversion organizations for years to come. The prospect of fighting an unseen enemy in the rear as well as the identified opponent was, and indeed still is, an anathema to conventional soldiers.

As already seen in Chapter III, MI5 had had dealings before the war with Vivian Stranders, Baillie-Stewart, Dr Goertz, Adams and Kelly, all of whom had collaborated with the Abwehr. MI5 also had long lists of those British people who were Nazi sympathizers or who at the very least thought that the Bolshevik menace was greater than that of Fascism.

In September 1940 MI5 and the security departments of the individual services devoted a large part of their resources to investigating the supposed treachery of British nationals, doing this in part through their Regional Security Liaison Officers, who were MI5's 'B' Division representatives scattered throughout Britain. Before the war the country had been divided into geographical regions, each with a Regional Commissioner who was empowered to rule by decree in the face of an invasion or general breakdown of government. The twelve Commissioners worked closely with their RSLO, the local Army Commanders and the Chief Constables in the area. Having identified and interviewed some of the RSLOs I realized their own experiences alone would fill an entire book. As the MI5 man 'in the field' and the most relatively accessible Security Service representative, the RSLO was generally the first to investigate claims of strange lights at night and allegations of spies landing from submarines in deserted coves. The public inundated the police with such scares and each bizarre claim had to be investigated by MI5.

The RSLO network was commanded by Colonel Alan MacIver, who hand-picked his men and instructed them never to appear surprised, no matter what they might be told during the course of their duties. To do so, he said, would undermine the confidence outsiders had in MI5.

The RSLOs enjoyed a very colourful war, even by MI5 standards. Two in particular were nicknamed 'Major Veuve' and 'Major Clicquot' because of their habit of having champagne sent up to their rooftop perch on Blenheim Palace while firewatching. Very occasionally the RSLOs themselves were guilty of lapses in security. One was actually arrested by a sharp-eyed constable who noticed a submachine-gun lying on the back seat of his car which was parked in St James's Street. The RSLO concerned was making an urgent call on MI5 headquarters and emerged into the arms of the law. The police released the man after a diplomatic intervention by a fellow RSLO. Generally, however, security was extremely rigid. An illustration of this is the experience of a newly-recruited RSLO due to report to Colonel MacIver at Blenheim Palace prior to taking up his post in Kent. The day beforehand he found himself chatting to an old friend in the bar of White's Club. Each asked the other what he was doing, and each evaded the question, saying vaguely that he was 'looking around for a useful war job'. The next day they spotted each other in the Blenheim Palace canteen queue.

RSLOs travelled back and forth across their territories interviewing suspects who had been denounced and supervising police raids on 'unreliables' believed to be aiding the enemy. In the absence of evidence to the contrary MI5's 'B' Division assumed that there were hundreds if not thousands of Nazi sympathizers at large willing to promote a German victory. What led them to believe such a state of affairs could be possible?

There never was in fact any shortage of evidence that such a group existed. During the previous February a 'New British Broadcasting Station' started transmitting programmes to Britain. Its clear purpose was to sow confusion and create dissension. One of its predominant themes was the imminent invasion and the help the German forces could expect from those 'loyal' Britons opposed to the warmonger Churchill. This 'patriotic' line was reinforced by signing off the broadcasts with the National Anthem and playing the 'Bonnie, bonnie banks of Loch Lomond' as a preliminary to each bulletin. Three other fake British stations joined in the propaganda. Radio Caledonia used 'Auld Lang Syne' as a signature tune and concentrated its news north of the Border. Worker's Challenge aimed itself at the factory shopfloor and denounced members of the Cabinet as exploiters and traitors. Finally, the Christian Peace Movement, clandestinely operated from Hamburg, urged all church-going folk to oppose the war effort. It was an almost impossible task to judge how many people listened to these stations or to monitor listeners' reactions. Nobody though could deny there were supporters for the propaganda line. Leaflets and posters were left in public places giving details of the enemy wavelengths and the times of their news programmes. Small stickers were surreptitiously placed in telephone booths. Occasionally an offender would be caught but there seemed little to support the idea of a widespread plot. One of those caught fly-posting was William Saxon-Steer, a forty-two-year-old violinist and enthusiastic member of Mosley's British Union of Fascists. He pleaded Guilty to advertising the New British Broadcasting Service in a telephone kiosk and was sentenced at the Old Bailey to seven years to discourage others. The broadcasts continued throughout the war but during the summer of 1940 their demoralizing message struck a somewhat raw nerve in Whitehall. Every broadcast emphasized the strength of the elusive Fifth Column. Easily-decipherable messages to covert supporters were mixed in with the commentaries. The news bulletins themselves were equally mischievous. Bank of England notes, one report alleged, had been forged in their thousands. The currency was worthless. Similarly, it was authoritatively stated that foot-and-mouth disease had broken out in the country, sabotage was crippling industry and imported tins of meat had been deliberately contaminated.

The newspapers carried out surveys to discover how many people even bothered to listen to the broadcasts but their findings obviously lost some of their validity because of the willingness of the censors to allow such material to be published at all. Nevertheless, the belief in a Fifth Column's existence was widespread. A secret sub-committee of the Joint Intelligence Committee named the 'Invasion Warning Sub-Committee' met for the first time in the Admiralty on 31 May, 1940. Commander Colpoys RN was appointed Chairman, assisted by Lt-Commander Denning (later Sir Norman Denning, DNI 1960-64). The DMI was represented on the Committee by Major L.H. Sanderson, a wartime recruit into MIl(c). They learnt that Admiral Sir Bertram Ramsey, the Naval officer commanding Dover, had telephoned London about

> 'indications of numerous acts of sabotage and Fifth Column activities in Dover, e.g. communications leakages, fixed defences sabotage, second-hand cars purchased at fantastic prices and left at various parking places.'

Spy fever became a national epidemic. On the same day as the Invasion Warning Sub-Committee were meeting, an order went out for the removal of all signposts and place names throughout the country. The Germans were believed to be on their way and it was thought the offensive would be spearheaded by parachutists who would create disruption behind the lines. This theory was given more credence than some of the reports on Nazi soldiers disguised as nuns, Red Cross nurses, monks, tramcar conductors, policemen and postmen (as reported by the Dutch Foreign Minister Mr van Kleffens at a press conference on 21 May, 1940). A popular explanation of the speed with which the Blitzkrieg had overwhelmed France, Belgium and Holland was treachery in the rear. Pro-German collaborators had made secret arrangements to secure bridges intact and cause widespread panic, thus aiding the enemy.

Although in a poor position to prepare elaborate fortifications for the invasion the government responded to the challenge with typical 'amateur' inventiveness. The nine hundred or so vulnerable beaches on the South Coast were booby-trapped and special Auxiliary Units were formed under the leadership of General Gubbins to hinder the enemy's progress.[19] Special plans were also made to prevent the centre of government being overwhelmed in a surprise attack. Sensitive departments were allowed to plan the evacuation of their offices and transfer to secret, less vulnerable locations. The operation was code-named BLACK MOVE and limited to five crucial ministries.

The Cabinet War Room was to move from beneath Great George Street to PADDOCK, the Post Office Research Station at Dollis Hill. The Admiralty was to go to Cricklewood, the War Office to Kneller Hall, Hounslow (the Army School of Music), the Air Ministry to 'Z' at Harrow (actually the Stationery Office Annexe) and the Ministry of Home Security to Cornwall House, Stamford Street. The Cabinet decided that a wholesale move into the regions would be bad for morale and so ordered certain sub-basements in the capital to be reinforced. Very few were let into the secret of PADDOCK or the 'CWR 2'. For the BLACK MOVE only 184 people were aware of its exact position in north London. The Prime Minister visited PADDOCK on 13 September, 1940, but BLACK MOVE was abandoned as a contingency plan after PADDOCK was bombed during an air raid on 20 September, 1940. The underground accommodation at PADDOCK consisted of fifty rooms on three levels.

Throughout the summer of 1940 MI5 concentrated their efforts on the second-echelon internments and the business of investigating the reports of Fifth Column activity that poured into Wormwood Scrubs via the War Office's room 055. Hundred of hours were spent following up tip-offs but not one resulted in the conviction of an enemy agent. When H.L.A. Hart joined MI5 his first job was to make an inspection of the telegraph poles in the southern counties and submit a security report on each of them. Someone had written to the War Office claiming that coded messages had been left on the poles to guide invading parachutists! The public were constantly warned about the dangers of careless talk and several prosecutions were publicized. An aerodrome labourer, William Jackson, was sent to prison for a month when his indiscreet conversation in a Welsh pub was overheard by a group of security-conscious soldiers in May 1940. The following month a mother and daughter were spotted on the banks of the Tyne discussing the passing ships. They were denounced by some schoolboys and fined £5 each. In July 1940 a twenty-five-year-old aircraftwoman went to prison for three months for starting rumours. A busman heard her say in a café that parachutists had landed near a particular town and comment that 'Hitler has a wonderful organization. It is the very thing we need in this country – someone with dictatorial powers.' The public responded with imagination to the government's pleas for vigilance. Police stations logged all the helpful telephone calls and passed on the information to the local RSLOs. Nevertheless, magistrates remained calm even if the rest of the country were seeing parachutists everywhere and on one occasion dismissed the case of a German-born woman who was prosecuted for flashing signals to enemy bombers with a torch.

The fear of a well-organized Fifth Column was experienced by all. General Ironside even stated as Commander-in-Chief, Home Forces, 'We have got examples of where there have been people quite definitely preparing aerodromes in this country.'

Max Knight had been concentrating on counter-subversion in 'B' Division since 1924. He had recruited agents in every walk of life and placed informants in most of the country's political organizations. One such agent was Tom Driberg, who joined the CPGB on Knight's instructions before being elected to Parliament in 1942. Knight had penetrated both the Right and the Left, and maintained strict security. Few MI5 officers were permitted to visit Knight's Dolphin Square sanctum: most of the agents were contacted elsewhere by his staff. His case officers included Philip Brocklehurst, who later switched to the Army and was drowned in Burma; Norman Himsworth, a newspaperman from Preston who supervised anti-Communist operations; Tony Gillson, a nightclubbing playboy and racehorse owner who transferred to SOE, only to be killed in an aircrash in 1943 en route for India; Rex Land, and Guy Poston. His deputy was John Bingham (later Lord Clanmorris), a successful journalist and thriller writer. Another of Knight's close friends was William (Bill) Younger, a polio victim, an MI5 agent since his undergraduate days at Oxford and a member of the brewing family. Bill Younger's mother, Joan Wheatley (Mrs Dennis Wheatley), his sister, Diana Younger, and his cousin, Kenneth Younger, were 'in the office'.

Knight's staff were an élite. They were generally youthful, attractive and rich. Knight himself had married twice, his first wife having taken an overdose of drugs in November 1936. His second wife, Lois, spent most of the war working at the headquarters of the Oxfordshire Constabulary. Perhaps his greatest talent, in spite of his eccentricities (which stretched to training cuckoos and sharing his flat with a bush-baby), was his ability to select and recruit very reliable women agents who became devoted to him, a feat remarkable because he was thought by some to have been a homosexual. Only two women penetrated his inner office at Dolphin Square: Joan Miller and his typist, Babe Holt who also commanded his diary, telephones and appointments. Miss Holt later married an early member of the office, Major Pyper, who was a particularly dashing figure. He had been scarred during a grenade practice and had joined MI5 as a convalescence duty. He later rejoined his regiment in Hong Kong, taking Babe Holt with him. Knight's office was unique within MI5 and was held in some awe by personnel based in St James's Street because of its mystery and the amount of autonomy granted to it. Other people in the organization knew only too well that an indiscreet reference to B5(b), as the office later came to be designated after the Petrie re-organization, would result in a scathing telephone call to Brigadier Harker, with whom Knight maintained a close friendship.

A latecomer to Knight's colourful department, brought in by Joan Miller, was Richard Darwall, a Royal Marines officer who was invalided out of active duty after a severe illness contracted in Iceland. At the end of April 1940 his unit had been awaiting orders in Pembroke Dock to commence the occupation of Southern Ireland. When their orders had arrived, they were instructed to join HMS *Belfast* at Gourock for the invasion of quite a different target – Iceland. This unpublicized event took place on 10 May, 1941. The only casualties were those Marines who were innoculated with defective vaccine in both arms. Darwall survived to capture the Reykjavik Radio Station single-handed from a taxi and arrest the German Consul-General, Herr Gerlach.

Joan Miller was an attractive young secretary who had joined MI5 from Elizabeth Arden. After a short stay at Transport in Wormwood Scrubs she had transferred to Dolphin Square. The first task that Knight had set her had been to befriend Krishna Menon, the Indian nationalist, but that had not been a success. Her second operation, which involved infiltration of the Right Club, was such a success that it became one of the few of Knight's operations to receive wartime publicity, although outside MI5 Joan Miller always had to be referred to as 'Miss X'.

The Right Club was a small select organization founded by Captain Archibald H.M. Ramsay, Unionist Member for Peebles since 1931. He had been educated at Eton and Sandhurst and had been severely wounded while serving in France during the Great War with the Coldstream Guards. He had been a founder member of the Link and had also subscribed to the Anglo-German Fellowship. Captain Ramsay made no secret of his strong political opinions. He had also gathered around him a number of influential figures, some of whom shared his extremist views. One of his followers was Anna Wolkoff, a passionate anti-Semite and fanatical anti-Communist. She was the thirty-eight-year-old daughter of Admiral Nicholas Wolkoff, an ex-Tsarist Naval Attaché who retired to London after the 1917 revolution. The Admiral, his wife and daughter opened a Russian Tea Room opposite South

Kensington tube station and this soon became a centre of right-wing political agitation, thus attracting the attention of MI5. Initially it seemed Miss Wolkoff confined her activities to the relatively harmless practices of organizing small discussion groups and occasionally printing and distributing inflammatory leaflets denouncing the war as a 'Jew's war', but as Joan Miller became more involved in the regular gatherings she learned more of Captain Ramsay's Right Club and his other, perhaps more overt, organization, the Link.

In the middle of May 1940 Joan Miller's infiltration of the Right Club paid an unexpected dividend. Her original task had been to monitor Ramsay's activities together with another MI5 agent, Mrs Amos, and build up a complete list of the members so MI5 could scoop up the whole group, rather than attack it piecemeal. She was completely accepted and trusted by Miss Wolkoff who at one point hinted that any information Joan Miller could remove from her 'dull filing job at the War Office' would be well received. The implication was that Miss Wolkoff was more than a political agitator. Max Knight decided not to take up the counter-intelligence opportunity but instructed his agent to learn more about her friend's covert interests. Gradually Knight was able to build up a detailed picture of Anna Wolkoff's contacts. She was holding secret meetings with Colonel Francesco Maringliano, an assistant Naval Attaché at the Italian Embassy, and was also seeing a twenty-nine-year-old cypher clerk from the American Embassy, Tyler Kent. The chain was enough to convince MI5 that the Italian Secret Service were using Miss Wolkoff as a conduit into the American code room in Grosvenor Square. This conclusion neatly dovetailed with the Government Code & Cypher School's intercept summaries which suggested that the German Ambassador in Rome, Hans Mackensen, had been reading Churchill's correspondence with President Roosevelt. If Kent had been passing copies of the telegrams to the Italians then the source of the German's information would be clear. Ambassador Joseph Kennedy agreed to waive Kent's diplomatic immunity and at ten in the morning of 20 May, 1940 his flat in Gloucester Place was raided by a Special Branch team which included an observer from the American Embassy. Inside they found some 1,500 classified American documents. Kent was taken into custody while Anna Wolkoff's rooms were searched. It was clear that Kent had first started taking secret copies of American telegrams home with him in October 1939. He admitted showing his collection to Captain Ramsay MP in March 1940. The evidence of the seized material and Kent's original statement to Special Branch provided the much-feared connection between the so-called British Fifth Column and the Germans.

Later that year Anna Wolkoff and Tyler Kent were sent for trial at the Old Bailey charged with offences under the Official Secrets Act and Defence Regulations. Kent was tried first, having been sacked by Kennedy from the American government service. He was found guilty on five counts, all relating to secret telegrams he had stolen from the Embassy cypher room. Anna Wolkoff was tried separately and found guilty on two charges after an eight-day hearing before Mr Justice Tucker. One charge concerned Kent, the other a coded letter she had tried to send William Joyce, 'Lord Haw-Haw', in Berlin. Kent was sentenced to seven years' imprisonment and Miss Wolkoff, partly because she had become a naturalized British subject in 1935, received ten years. From the dock she promised to kill Joan Miller.

By the end of the trial MI5 had discovered to their surprise that Miss Wolkoff's parents were employed at Wormwood Scrubs in the censorship department which was housed next door to MI5. The Official Censor had recruited the old White Russian admiral, who had lived in England since 1917, and his wife to read mail going overseas. Now great concern was expressed about the two organizations being sited so close together.

Regulation 18N of the Defence (General) Regulations, 1939 states

> 'If the Secretary of State has reasonable cause to believe any person to be of hostile origin or associations or to have been recently concerned in acts prejudicial to the public safety or the defence of the realm or in the preparation or instigation of such acts and that by reason thereof it is necessary to exercise control over him, he may make an order against that person directing that he be detained.'

Slowly, as the war progressed, the government's attitude towards aliens hardened, for military setbacks on the Continent brought the likelihood of invasion closer. The early internments under the Aliens Act had been designed to isolate the German and Austrian communities in Britain and to ensure the Home Office knew of their whereabouts and particulars. The Aliens Act was powerless to deal with home-grown subversives and so the 1939 Emergency Powers (Defence) Act was amended on 23 May, 1940. The new and drastic powers conferred on the Home Secretary under paragraph 18B now covered members of organizations that may have been 'subject to foreign influence or control' or 'persons in control of organizations' which have 'sympathies with the system of government of any power with which His Majesty is at war'. BUF organizers up and down the country were taken into custody, as were leaders of the Imperial Fascist League. The CPGB was left alone although a rally in Trafalgar Square was banned by the Home Secretary. John Beckett, the secretary of the British People's Party and ex-Labour MP for Peckham, was interned. Officials from the Nordic League and William Joyce's National Socialist League were rounded up and sent to Brixton. Joyce himself had renewed his passport on 24 August, 1939 and had gone to live in Berlin. He started his 'Lord Haw-Haw' broadcasts on 18 September, 1939.

The first arrest under the new strengthened 18B regulations was that of Captain Archibald H.M. Ramsay, MP, who was taken to Brixton Prison on 23 May, 1940, but the papers authorizing his detention had in fact been signed the previous day by the Home Secretary, Sir John Anderson, under the original 18B provisions. Captain Ramsay protested that his detention was a breach of Parliamentary Privilege but nevertheless remained in Brixton until 1944. (He resumed his seat the day after his release but failed to get re-elected in the General Election the following year.)

The new measures were described as 'drastic' by *The Times* and 'draconian' by some MPs, who protested when it was explained that detainees would have the right of appeal to a specially created Advisory Committee, to be chaired alternately by Sir Walter Monckton, KC and Mr Norman Birkett KC sitting with Sir Arthur Hazelrigg and Sir George Clerk, although they would be unable to cross-examine witnesses or even learn the names of those who had lodged information against them. Even the House of Commons had difficulty in obtaining details of internments beyond a routine announcement. The Prime Minister, replying to questions, stated that it would not be in the public interest to hear the matter debated.

Sir Oswald Mosley followed Captain Ramsay to Brixton Prison with other leading members of the British Union of Fascists including A. Raven Thomson, N. Francis Hawkins, F.E. Burdett, Captain U.A. Hick, C.F. Watts, H. McKechnie, G. Bruning and the veteran suffragette, Mrs Dacre Fox. Altogether 436 persons were detained under 18B in July 1940, bringing the total number to 1,373. Most were released by early 1941. Sir Oswald was allowed to join his wife in Holloway's preventative detention block in November 1941 and was released because of ill health in 1943.

The BUF headquarters in Sanctuary Buildings, Great Smith Street were raided in May 1940 by Special Branch but they gleaned little new information, save the membership records. Max Knight already had two informers at a high level in the party and MI5 were rather more confident than the government that the BUF presented little threat as a

Fifth Column. Mosley had of course opposed the war with Germany but once it had got under way he urged his Blackshirts to remain loyal to the Crown; an order that was almost completely obeyed.

The day after the declaration of war the Link had been dissolved by its Chairman, Sir Barry Domvile, who said, 'Naturally, we closed down on the declaration of war; that was essential, the King's enemies become our enemies. We had done our best for better Anglo-German relations and with the outbreak of hostilities there was no more to be done. All the branches are closed.' What was left of the Anglo-German Fellowship collapsed with the announcement of war. At the other end of the political spectrum the CPGB actively opposed the war until BARBAROSSA (the German codeword for the invasion of Russia) in June 1941. Several pacifist groups, such as the Peace Pledge Union, were manipulated by Moscow-line activists. All of these groups came under MI5 and Special Branch surveillance and by the middle of 1940 there had been several successful prosecutions. Six of the PPU's officials were bound over in June 1940 for attempting to cause disaffection with an anti-war poster. They were Alexander Wood, a Cambridge lecturer, Morris Rowntree, Stuart Morris, John Barclay, Ronald Smith and Sidney Todd. They were defended by John Platts-Mills (later MP for Finsbury and expelled from the Labour Party in May 1948). Various Communist Party public speakers were also convicted of using insulting language at Party gatherings. The CPGB limited their activities to describing the war as a 'Capitalists' war', although a few on the fringes of the Party went further. Montague Fyrth, a twenty-eight-year-old sub-lieutenant in the RNR, sent a copy of a British Expeditionary Force document to his brother Hubert, a left-wing student at Exeter University, who in turn passed it on to the *Daily Worker*. It was intercepted in the post and they were sentenced to six months' and twelve months' imprisonment respectively. They were defended by Mr Dudley Collard who had acted two years earlier for Percy Glading. He claimed that the two brothers 'were in no sense corrupt. They were honest and sincere from their point of view.' He went on to say that 'what they did was done in pursuance of ideas honestly held by them', at which the judge, Mr Justice Atkinson, commented drily, 'That can be said of any traitor here who wishes to assist the enemy.'

By the end of the war there had been only three significant prosecutions against Mosley's BUF members. The first took place in January 1940 when two Devon men were charged under the Official Secrets Act. They were Claude Duvivier, a naturalized British subject from Belgium; and Alexander Crowle, a Devonport dockyard worker. The two men had met through their support of the BUF and exchanged letters to each other mocking the BBCs propaganda. Some of the letters contained observations of Naval vessels made by Crowle which prompted a police search. In an envelope addressed to *Action*, the Blackshirt newspaper, the police found more material relating to the movements of shipping in the Plymouth area. The information was generally of a trivial nature but the case highlighted the dangers presented by BUF members unwilling to take Mosley's advice and serve the Crown loyally. Duvivier and Crowle originally pleaded Not Guilty to the charges under the Defence Regulations but after the Court had gone into closed session they changed their pleas and were sentenced to six months each.

The only Fifth Column investigation of the war that went beyond the trivial was sparked off by a Corporal Barron of the Royal Tank Corps stationed in Portsmouth who reported being approached for information by Fifth Columnists. He named two prominent local BUF members, William Swift and Archibald Watts, as being ringleaders and claimed that he had also been introduced to a middle-aged German woman who apparently was in communication with Germany. The woman was Marie Louise Ingram, aged forty-two, who was indeed German by birth but married to an RAF sergeant, which exempted her from internment the previous September. She lived at Marmion Road, Southsea and worked in the home of a senior Naval officer. Further evidence of a Fifth Column plot was provided by Cecil Rashleigh, the man who had introduced Barron to Mrs Ingram. He confirmed that Mrs Ingram appeared to be an ardent Nazi and was encouraging Swift to recruit sympathizers into the Local Defence Volunteers so they could participate if the German invasion took place. The Portsmouth police raided Mrs Ingram's house and recovered a quantity of Nazi paraphernalia but found no trace of a wireless transmitter or secret writing material. They settled for confiscating a pair of swastika flags and arrested her, Archibald Watts, who was unemployed but had previously worked on the trams in Portsmouth, and William Swift, who was a foreman in the Naval dockyard. All three were sent for trial at the Old Bailey in July 1940 and appeared before Mr Justice Singleton. After a three-day hearing the jury acquitted Watts, who had been the BUF District Leader in Southsea, but found Swift and Mrs Ingram guilty of various Defence Regulations charges.

Swift was jailed for fourteen years for 'communicating and associating with Mrs Ingram, having reasonable cause to believe that she was engaged in assisting an enemy, inciting Cecil Rashleigh to join the LDV in order to obtain arms and ammunition for the purpose of using them for the protection of enemy invaders, and endeavouring to cause disaffection in His Majesty's Service.' Mrs Ingram was cleared of an Official Secrets charge of conspiring to obtain blue-prints from Corporal Barron but jailed for ten years for acts calculated to assist an enemy.

By the end of this case the government were far from reassured about the existence of a Fifth Column. That Mrs Ingram, an apparently loyal German, could get a job as housekeeper with a senior Naval officer in a sensitive position (he worked in the Mines Development Department) and organize local Fascists into a potentially dangerous armed body was, on the face of it, an appalling breach of home security. Fortunately for MI5, it was virtually the only case of its kind. Later in the year Mrs Dorothy O'Grady, an Isle of Wight landlady, was investigated for Fifth Column activities and espionage and in fact was tried and sentenced to death at Winchester Assizes by Mr Justice McNaughten after pleading Guilty to a Treachery charge. It was only after she was sentenced to death that she admitted she had made up her confession and had deliberately drawn attention to herself so as to launch an MI5 enquiry. In February 1941 the Appeal Court quashed her conviction on the capital charge but sentenced her to fourteen years after John Trapnell, KC explained that MI5 were convinced that Mrs O'Grady had fantasized an imaginary role as a Nazi spy for herself.

The most straightforward case concerning the BUF was that of William Craven in April 1942. He was an agricultural worker from Gloucestershire who wrote offering his services to the German Ambassador in Dublin. As a matter of course, his letter was intercepted and passed on to Room 055 for following up. The result was that twenty-eight-year-old Craven appeared at the Old Bailey, pleading Guilty to a charge of intent to assist the enemy. He was sentenced to fourteen years. Ironically, Craven already featured as a BUF unreliable on his file in Registry, and had been one of the first to be interned under the original 18B Regulations in September 1939. He had been released the following month but had again been taken into custody during the crisis month of June 1940, only to be set free again the following April.

The summer of 1940 passed without an invasion being launched, though few on this side of the Channel realized how close the Wehrmacht came to initiating their attack. The German preparations are well documented by Peter Fleming and Ronald Wheatley.[20] On 26 May, 1940 the Chiefs of Staff were informed they would not receive advance warning of a German assault from intelligence sources. SIS networks had been crushed in Western Europe and the business of Signals Intelligence was still in its infancy. The authorities had to rely on aerial reconnaissance photographs taken by Spitfires but the RAF had few planes to spare for these intelligence gathering flights. In any case of the eleven aircraft available for photographic missions, only three were converted to long-range equipment suitable for the survey of Continental ports.

The first major invasion alarm in Whitehall began early in August 1940 when the Foreign Office's diplomatic sources and SIS suggested that an attack was imminent. The GC & CS had reported on 29 July that their Luftwaffe intercepts had included an order banning further missions against South Coast harbours, a restriction which had previously been imposed shortly before the attack on France relating to the French ports. On 12 August, 1940 they decoded a message to a Fliegercorps commander who had been closely involved in the French Blitzkrieg. He was told some thirty men 'with a perfect knowledge of English' were to be transferred to his command immediately. These were ominous signs and were taken extremely seriously. Some MI5 staff with knowledge of the organization and its agents were issued with 'L' (lethal) capsules which were to be taken to avoid interrogation. The guards on the capital's vulnerable points were doubled, and other precautions were taken to resist the invaders.

On the night of 13 August, the invaders arrived. Or rather, there was evidence to suggest that a large number of parachutists had arrived, perhaps eighty in total. This was the number of parachutes, some decorated with gigantic eagles, found throughout the Midlands. As well as sabotage paraphernalia, the Germans dropped maps, saddle-bags, wirelesses and lists of targets. A major operation began on the morning of 14 August to trace the invaders but they proved elusive. The Luftwaffe had apparently completed the drop for propaganda purposes.

In one sense they were successful. Most of the daily newspapers carried stories or pictures of the event for the following two days but the affair also served to warn the population, if they still needed any warning, of the dangers of talking to foreigners and being careful about letting slip valuable intelligence. By the time the first parachute spies did materialize, in September 1940, the populace were acutely aware of suspicious characters, even though there were tens of thousands of foreign refugees and soldiers within the United Kingdom,

The second and last invasion scare took place on the evening of 7 September, 1940, partly as a result of an urgent MI5 intelligence report to the Joint Intelligence Committee (JIC). The RAF's Photographic Reconnaissance Unit's flights during the latter end of August identified a marked increase in enemy activity in the Channel and logged a definite build-up in the number of invasion barges in Continental harbours. A fleet of landing craft was accumulating in certain occupied ports, such as Ostend and Calais, which tended to confirm German signal intercepts that something was about to break. Leave for the Wehrmacht was cancelled from 8 September and the meteorologists judged the tide and moon conditions of the period 8 September to 10 September to be particularly favourable for a seaborne assault on the South-East Coast.

The real clincher for the Chiefs of Staff was the capture early in the morning of 3 September of three Abwehr agents in Kent. They were quickly followed by a fourth, Jose Waldberg (see Chapter IX). All were subjected to intensive interrogation by Colonel Hinchley-Cooke and Colonel Stephens, who rushed their findings to Wormwood Scrubs. The agents confirmed their status as an advance guard for the invasion, which, they claimed, could be expected at any moment. Their task had been to radio details of the British defences in the area bounded by Oxford, Ipswich, London and Reading. The JIC accepted the MI5 report as confirmation of their other sources and passed on the opinion to the Chiefs of Staff at 5.30 PM on Saturday, 7 September, 1940. That evening, at seven minutes past eight, the code-word CROMWELL was flashed from the War Room to all the military units in Britain. Church bells were rung in some outlying districts and even a few bridges were destroyed by zealous Auxiliary Intelligence Officers who had been formed into resistance cells. In Scotland some of Gubbins's units disappeared underground at the signal and did not reappear for up to five days later. The code-word CROMWELL succeeded CAESAR which had been abandoned when General Ironside became general officer commanding the Home Forces on 5 June, 1940. In many areas CROMWELL was ignored. Some units were unaware of the change, others were staffed by weekend junior officers who had not been let into the secret.

The invasion scare was not a fantasy of hysterical imaginations. There were Abwehr agents in Kent. There were disloyal Britons. Those in authority really did also think that there might be thousands of Fifth Columnists in Britain. Despite the possible magnitude of the potential problem, the whole matter was handled quietly and legally. No concentration camps were built, there was no panic, simply the strengthening of Regulation 18B and the internment of slightly over 1,300 people, many of whom were only held for a matter of months and most of whom were released by the end of 1941. When this figure is considered in terms of the total population of the United Kingdom, it is not a very large one. The Fifth Column scare seems to have been dealt with by MI5 with remarkable calm, considerable efficiency and fairness.

Prominent Members of the Link

Sir Raymond Beazley (71) Professor of History, Birmingham University
The Duke of Bedford (82) 11th Duke
Brig R.G. Blakeney (68) Veteran of Khartoum
Col Sir John Brown, Deputy D-G of the Territorial Army
Archibald Crawford KC (58) Ex-Unionist candidate for Peebles
Sir John Crooke, Unionist MP for Deritend, Birmingham
Adm Sir Barry Domvile (62) DNI 1927-1930, Retired RN 1936
Viscountess Downe, Ex-BUF candidate for North Norfolk
Jasper Duff, Ulster MP
Maj-Gen J.F.C. Fuller (62) Military tactician
Ralph Gladwyn Jebb, Ex-BUF candidate for West Dorset
Sir Lionel Haworth (66) Ex-Indian political officer
Douglas Jerrold (47) Historian and publisher
Professor A.P. Laurie (79) Fellow of King's College, Cambridge
W-J. Bassett-Lowke, Labour Leader of Northants CC
Edward Rosslyn Mitchell (61) Ex-Labour MP for Paisley
Lord Nuffield (63) Chairman of Morris Motors Ltd
Vice-Adm R. St P. Parry (60) Retired RN 1931
Lady Pearson, Widow of Sir Edward Pearson[21]
Vice-Adm G.B. Powell (69) Retired RN 1926
Lord Redesdale (62) Father of the Mitford sisters
Lt-Col C.D. Roe (58) Indian Army, Retired 1931
Capt Edward Unwin VC (76) Hero of Gallipolli
Sir Lambert Ward (64) Unionist MP for Kingston-on-Hull
The Duke of Westminster (61) 2nd Duke
Maj-Gen H.S. White (78) Veteran of the Sudan Expedition
Frederick Wilshire (72) Recorder for Bridgwater
Sir Arnold Wilson (56) Tory MP for Hitchin
Col Francis Yeats-Brown (54) Author of *The Bengal Lancer*
(Ages in 1940 shown in parentheses)

Prominent Members of the Anglo-German Fellowship

Lord Aberdare (55) Chairman of *The Fortnightly Review*
The Earl of Airlie (47) Lord Chamberlain
Lord Arbuthnott (57) Lord Lieutenant of Kincardineshire
Lord Arnold (62) Former Labour MP for Penistone
Lord Barnby (56) Former Unionist MP for South Bradford
Sir Ernest Bennett, Former Labour MP for Cardiff
Viscount Bertie (67) Barrister

Sir Harry Brittain (67) Former Unionist MP for Acton
Lord Brocket (36) Former Unionist MP for Wavertree
Lord Ebbisham (70) Former Unionist MP for Epsom
Lord Eltisley (59) Former Tory MP for Cambridge
Earl of Glasgow (66) Ayrshire County Council Vice-Convenor
Lord Ernest Hamilton (78) Former MP for North Tyrone
Lord Hollenden (68) Former High Sheriff of London
Squadron-Ldr Norman Hulbert (37) Unionist MP for Stockport
Maj-Gen Sir Alfred Knox (70) Tory MP for Wycombe
Marquess of Londonderry (59) Former Tory Air Minister
Marquess of Lothian (56) Former Ambassador to Washington
Sir Jocelyn Lucas (50) Tory MP for Portsmouth
Viscount Lymington (47) Former Unionist MP for Basingstoke
Lord McGowan (65) Chairman of ICI
Jack Macnamara (35) Unionist MP for Chelmsford
Sir Thomas Moore (56) Unionist MP for Ayr
Lord Mottistone (66) Former Liberal War Minister
Lord Mount Temple (62) Former Tory Transport Minister
Lord Nuffield (63) Chairman of Morris Motors Ltd
Sir Harold Nutting (56) Former ADC to Gov-Gen of Australia
Sir Assheton Pownall (61) Unionist MP for Lewisham
Lord Rennell of Rodd (81) Former MP and Ambassador to Rome
Edward Rice, Former MP
Lord Sempill (46) Chairman of the Royal Aero Society
Lord Stamp (60) Director of the Bank of England
Sir William Strang (46) Foreign Office Chief Political Adviser
Adm Sir Murray Sueter (68) Tory MP for Hertford
Frank C. Tiarks (66) Governor of the Bank of England
The Duke of Wellington (66) Boer War veteran
(Ages in 1940 shown in parentheses)

VI
The Divisions of MI5

As war approached MI5 began to increase its staff, but even by September 1939 it was woefully ill-equipped to cope with the implications of a second European war. During the first ten months of the war the Security Service grew in size many times over, the phases of reorganization continuing until well into 1941.

A detailed chart of MI5's basic structure during this first twelve-month period is provided on page xx. It includes the names of many of the leading personalities, though it is certainly not complete. As a rule, there was considerable 'internal mobility' within the Security Service and, indeed, the whole wartime British intelligence community. The women generally started their MI5 service in the dread Registry, filing and cross-referring dossiers. They then progressed to secretarial positions, and a few lucky ones became intelligence officers in their own right. The men were also swopped from department to department, and even organization to organization. An MI5 background was considered a good qualification for a move to the Secret Intelligence Service or Special Operations Executive.

As the war progressed the nature of MI5's role changed. At the beginning the effort was concentrated on security measures within the British Isles and the Empire. Then Personnel were seconded to duty with many of the special operations groups which were formed in the overseas theatres. By the end of the war, when the emphasis had shifted to strategic deception, the running of agents and mopping-up operations, further internal changes were made and the importance, and therefore the staffing, of individual sections and sub-sections altered.

In spite of the great changes that occurred within MI5 in the first eighteen months of the war the fundamental structure of divisions remained intact. MI5 had six main Divisions, each with its own alphabetic letter, each headed by a Director, assisted by Deputy and Assistant Directors.

'A' Division was concerned with the administration of the entire Service and was headed by Colonel Charles Butler, a regular King's Royal Rifle Corps officer seconded to the Security Service from his regiment in 1926. He has already been mentioned in connection with an investigation he helped to conduct into the Invergordon Mutiny in 1931. His Division included such sections as Transport, Finance, Legal and the important Registry, the huge card-index system run by Miss Paton-Smith.

Butler's Assistant Director was Malcolm Cumming, whose duties included maintaining a motor pool of fast cars and ensuring that MI5 officers in the other Divisions received their supply of petrol coupons. He was assisted by Joan Wheatley, whose son, Bill Younger, was a wartime recruit. He had been crippled with polio as a child and was therefore unfit for military service. He was later to achieve some success as a thriller writer, using the pen-name William Mole. Others in the transport section included Ian Smith and Jock Horsfall, a brilliant though sometimes reckless driver who was killed after the war during an Isle of Man TT race. Another member of this section was Mark Pepys, the sixth Earl of Cottenham, a member of the pre-war Alvis racing team and one-time adviser to the Metropolitan Police Driving School. He eventually resigned from MI5 and went to live in America as he could not reconcile himself to a war against Germany. He was the author of *Motoring Without Fears* (1928) and *Steering Wheel Papers* (1932).

'B' Division was arguably the most important MI5 branch, being responsible for counter-espionage, first under Brigadier Jasper Harker and then under his successor, Guy Liddell. The many sub-sections in the Division included Tar Robertson's B1(a) which chiefly handled German espionage, B1(c) section which dealt with counter-sabotage and B5(a) and B5(b) which dealt with counter-subversion. Liaising closely with 'B' Division were all the other related intelligence groups, such as the Radio Security Service where Hugh Trevor-Roper worked, the Ham Common interrogation centre in Surrey and the Post Office's Letter Interception Unit. There is a detailed chart on pages xxiii - xxiv. Many of 'B' Division's sub-sections were staffed during the war by an extraordinary collection of lawyers, academics, playboys, regular soldiers and journalists who were drafted in.

The essential basis of 'B' Division's work in Britain was the network of Regional Security Liaison Officers or RSLOs. There were twelve RSLOs who worked closely with the Regional Commissioners, the local Army Commanders and Chief Constables, Colonel Alan McIver commanded the whole network. His deputy, and later successor, was a young solicitor, Gerald Glover (now Sir Gerald), who had spent the first months of the war as a King's Messenger carrying sabotage material into Rumania. Some of his fellow RSLOs were also drawn from the law: John Phipps (later a Metropolitan Magistrate), John Maude (later a judge), and Geoffrey Wethered. The other RSLOs were Basil Dykes, Richard Dixon, Major Lane, Mark Johnson (from a firm of City stockbrokers) and Peter Hope (later Sir Peter, a British Ambassador to Mexico and Alternate UK Representative to the UN). Hope transferred to MI5 from the Secret Intelligence Service (MI6) with whom he had served in pre-war Germany. During the course of his duties with MI5 he became an expert interrogator at the Royal Victoria Patriotic School and in 1945 arrested the notorious MI9 traitor, Sergeant Harold Cole.

'C' Division was run by Major Herbert Bacon, whose staff attempted the impossible by trying hurriedly to 'vet' recruits destined for sensitive positions.

Major Bacon's colleague in 'D' Division was Brigadier Harry Allen, a regular soldier who had served in the Great War in France and the Middle East. His role was primarily one of security liaison and it was with his department that the rest of the War Office generally had dealings. Within his Division were liaison officers from the RAF (Group Captain John Archer) and the Royal Navy (Commander Bennett). Other 'D' Division interests included the Field Security Police, headquartered at Mytchett Place near Aldershot, and Port Security, led by Colonel John Adam, a former Inspector General of Police in the North-West Frontier Province of India.

'E' Division was responsible for the supervision of aliens already in the United Kingdom. Each of the major countries with national's resident in Britain, be they refugees or long-term residents, had a section devoted to them. Thus, Kenneth Younger (later a Labour MP and Minister) liaised with the exiled French authorities and Peter Ramsbotham (later British Ambassador in Washington and Governor of Bermuda) kept discreet surveillance on suspect Americans. Younger had a particularly difficult task which was not helped by his arrest in January 1941 of Admiral Muselier, de Gaulle's deputy and Commander of the Free French Naval Forces. Muselier was the victim of an elaborate French plot involving forged pro-Vichy letters. He spent a week in custody in London and was released with Churchill's apologies when the letters were proved to be forgeries. Ramsbotham, a polio victim, remained in MI5 for only three years. As soon as he was fit enough he transferred to the regular forces and later won the Croix de Guerre.

Overseas Control, a part of 'F' Division, was headed by a Fourth Hussars officer named Bertram Ede. It was to him that MI5's representatives and liaison officers in British territories abroad, known as Defence Security Officers, reported.

The DSOs were generally regular soldiers who, having been posted to an overseas garrison, made contact with the local police and, when necessary, reported back to Overseas Control in London. Before the war this had been a somewhat informal arrangement with some officers, such as Kenneth Strong from the Royal Scots Fusiliers and Bertram Ede, who were, at various times, DSOs in Malta. Even in wartime when it came to choosing candidates from within MI5 to fill these posts abroad a certain amount of office politics entered the scene. When Tar Robertson fell foul of one of Lord Swinton's reorganizers in 1940 it was suggested that Jan Mayen Island might suit him since the position of DSO was vacant.

In 1939 the rapidly expanding Security Service outgrew its office space and Kell arranged a move to His Majesty's Prison at Wormwood Scrubs. He also made preparations to set up a special 'cage' so that MI5 prisoners could be isolated in a type of accommodation which the civil authorities could not provide. He appointed an ex-Special Branch officer, 'Stimmy' Stimson, to find a suitable detention centre close to MI5 headquarters but sufficiently secluded from prying eyes. The choice fell on Latchmere House on Ham Common, near Richmond.

The transfer to the Scrubs was a fairly chaotic affair but 'B' Division completed the move relatively unscathed since they had in part been housed in completely unsuitable offices in Horseferry Road, SW1, a matter of yards from the main headquarters in Thames House. At the time Guy Liddell was living in a beautiful house overlooking the Chelsea Embankment, conveniently close to his office, but he agreed with his colleagues that a move was essential, even though it involved a trek to west London. Most of the walls in their shared accommodation were flimsy partitions and it was difficult to avoid overhearing even the quietest of conversations being conducted in a neighbouring room.

It was a great misapprehension to think that siting MI5 in the Scrubs meant good security. Four-foot-thick walls certainly failed to protect the Registry, and the stream of Mayfair types turning up each morning at the gates succeeded only in attracting attention. Several people claim to have heard a bus conductor on the No 72 Scrubs route announce 'All change for MI5' when he reached the prison. The original wardens were responsible for manning the gate and maintaining security but most of the staff were so bemused by their change in role that they failed to take their jobs very seriously. If a secretary forgot to bring her War Office pass to work, the gatekeeper would invariably accept a letter or cheque book as proof of identity and let the miscreant in. Most of the MI5 girls favoured working in the Scrubs because during the hot summer of 1940 they could spend their lunch hours sunbathing on the grass outside the prison. They were drawn from the same social backgrounds and inevitably the mixture of wartime conditions, beautiful girls and eligible young men lent something of a party atmosphere to the office.

Neither was security improved by having the Official Censor's office inside the prison walls, in 'B' Wing. Admiral and Mrs Wolkoff were both employed there to read and censor mail going overseas which caused much consternation when their daughter Anna was sent for trial at the Old Bailey in 1940 with Tyler Kent.

Working in Wormwood Scrubs had many disadvantages. None of the cells were equipped with interior door-handles or, for that matter, telephones, so secure communication with either the outside world or even a colleague created problems. When cell doors accidentally shut they locked automatically, so private conversations sometimes had to be conducted in the canteen for absolute safety and security. The Signal Corps were brought in to supply telephones to some of the more important officers but the resulting mass of cables became a serious hazard to those who had to negotiate the spiral staircases between cell levels.

With the move to the Scrubs several senior MI5 officers expressed concern about the security of Registry, the major weapon in MI5's arsenal. Miss Paton-Smith who presided over Registry was an ex-store detective, who guarded the secrets of the massive card-index system with jealous enthusiasm. The files stored every kind of information, from cocktail party gossip to the more solid intelligence accumulated in the period since the Great War. Many suggestions were made for the duplication of the thousands of dossiers but Kell invariably refused permission for the exercise on the grounds of cost. It was estimated that the bill for photographing every item would be in excess of £4,000, a gigantic sum for the Director-General who had for years been obliged to operate with the minimum of financial support from the Treasury.

Eventually however Kell was won over and for several months teams of Registry personnel worked non-stop to reproduce the entire Registry so it could be sent to Blenheim, the original remaining in the Scrubs. This further move to Blenheim caused much confusion as records were still being copied when Miss Paton-Smith left for Oxfordshire with some of her staff, principally Janet Withers, the Small sisters and Grace Smythe, and left the recent wartime recruits battling to cope with their new duties.

Among the first to go to Blenheim with Registry was 'A' Division and the telephone interception unit, complete with its collection of old-fashioned wax recording drums. The stenographers who compiled transcripts of the tapped telephone conversations in conditions of great secrecy were moved into the tiny servants' rooms at the top of Blenheim Palace. Here, in some discomfort, the typists laboured, led by Pamela Eraser wife of the British Military Attaché in Paris, Brigadier the Hon William Fraser DSO, MC.

The MI5 'occupation' of Blenheim was a major affair. Convoys of Army trucks were escorted down the A40 from the Scrubs, through the village of Woodstock and whisked up to the Palace. Eric St Johnston, the county's Chief Constable, was instructed to maintain the tightest security about the operation but at the same time was asked to have his officers' line the route in case of any accidents. Needless to say, it was only a matter of time before the whole of the local population were aware of how important Blenheim had become.

The Tenth Duke of Marlborough (and Mayor of Woodstock to boot) declined to move out of his quarters in the western end of the Palace, so MI5, considering him to be patriotic, set up office all around him. Most of the ground floor was devoted to the Registry while the upper floors, which had recently been makeshift dormitories for 400 evacuees from Malvern College (whose own site had been earmarked for use by the Admiralty), were used to house departments that did not have an operational requirement to be in London. Colonel Adam's Port Security section (a part of 'D' Division) cleared room for themselves on the first floor while the RSLO unit found themselves in the room in which Winston Churchill had been born. Nissen huts and portable toilets were constructed in the garden and the western courtyard. Many of the women stationed at Blenheim have unhappy memories of these 'temporary' structures. The huts were extremely draughty and for some inexplicable reason the lavatory doors were delivered without locks. There were a number of incidents and complaints before the oversight was rectified.

Equally uncomfortable were many of the larger homes around Woodstock which were requisitioned to accommodate staff. As the organization mushroomed in size, so did the demand for secure accommodation. A few local country houses, such as Cornbury Park, were used as overflow offices and Keble College in Oxford was 'occupied' by secretarial staff who shared their rooms with women engaged in other secret work in the town.

There were many Oxford men among the MI5 wartime recruits so it was not unnatural that the university town should have been chosen to be the site for several secret departments. Amongst those sections located within the Colleges and libraries was the unit responsible for devising and printing the cypher books used by the different British Armed Services. All were finally printed using the facilities of the Oxford University Press.

The section entrusted with drawing up maps for the Chiefs of Staff was housed in the Bodleian Library. Details of future operations were sent down to Oxford under guard and the various plans were then prepared for distribution under conditions of extreme secrecy. There were flaws in the system, however. Officers from Blenheim were called in when top secret[22] orders for D-Day were found littered down the A40 shortly before the crucial time in June 1944. It turned out that one of the motor-cycle dispatch riders employed on the War Office to Oxford route had neglected to fasten the lid of one of his panniers. The plans were scattered all over the road but surprisingly there was no leakage of information.

The juxtaposition of so many secret departments with the University led to a wealth of marvellous stories. On one occasion the chaplain of Keble, a man named Stuart, picked up a secret MI5 telegram that had been put into his pigeon-hole at the porter's lodge by mistake. It simply read:

STUART STOP WILL YOU MARRY ME SATURDAY STOP SIGNED X

and caused great confusion to the chaplain as he had much difficulty in establishing just whose wedding he was being asked to officiate at. He eventually discovered that he shared a surname with an attractive young MI5 secretary who was receiving the attentions of an MI5 officer based in London.

The one disadvantage that Blenheim Palace had as a centre for counter-espionage was its relative lack of internal secrecy. The rooms on the first floor were so large that officers found themselves sharing space and sharing secrets. At one point before being posted to Washington, John Maude was in charge of a 'B' Division section, B19, which 'investigated the source of rumours'. He soon discovered that the unit, which consisted of about a dozen solicitors, was doing very little useful work and these legal brains spent much of their time answering letters that had arrived denouncing various individuals as enemy agents. Maude wrote a firm memo to Richard Butler and the greater part of B19 were transferred to more productive duties.

Just as Blenheim and Wormwood Scrubs seemed to be settling down an incendiary bomb landed on the roof of 'C' Wing of the Scrubs, where the Registry's treasures were stored, and for a while it seemed that all the dusty old cards would literally go up in smoke. The fire was extinguished before too much damage had been inflicted, which was indeed most fortunate because it was later discovered that many of the rolls of film at Blenheim had been over-exposed and were useless. The only casualty of the evening was Jock Horsfall, the racing driver from 'A' Division's transport section, who had been on fire-watch duty on the prison roof. While tackling the blaze he fell through a roof, badly injuring his neck. He survived the fall but the incident led to a number of rumours concerning the 'total destruction' of the Registry contents. The stories got wide circulation in intelligence and government circles and were soon being cited as examples of Kell's incompetence and resistance to change. In fact, the fire took place more than five months after he had left Wormwood Scrubs for the last time.

Internal communications at the Scrubs also left a great deal to be desired. Requested files had to be brought up from Blenheim by dispatch riders after the Registry fire. If an officer wished to use a particular dossier he would fill in a 'check-slip' and hand it to one of the messengers. He would then wait and hope for the best while the slip went to Oxfordshire. The situation got so bad it became a common practice for staff to deny having a recently-delivered file because 'if one admitted having it one might well have to return it there and then, and the chances of getting it back again were slim.'

One of the famous stories about missing files involved a newly-arrived secretary and two MI5 officers, Major Richard Comyns Carr[23] and Major Malcolm Cumming. The young girl was instructed to deliver a file personally to Major Comyns Carr. The next day she was transferred down to Blenheim and Major Comyns Carr complained he had not received the file. The secretary was eventually contacted but she insisted she had followed her orders and safely delivered the file in question. A serious alert was started because it began to look as though a sensitive document had gone missing. Eventually the mystery was solved when Malcolm Cumming reported that he had found a secret file on the back seat of his car which he had left parked in the prison courtyard.

At the same time as the move to the Scrubs took place, Kell also saw to the completion of the arrangements made by Stimson at Latchmere House, the large ugly Victorian Mansion chosen to be MI5's interrogation camp. The property was set in its own wooded grounds near the Surrey village of Ham Common. The house was ideal because it was already owned by the War Office. It had been used as an asylum and recuperation centre for officers shell-shocked in the Great War. Two perimeter fences were constructed around the establishment's extensive garden and beyond that a wicket fence was built to cut off visual contact with the outside world. Stimson then set about the design of a one-storey cell block to be added to the eastern wing of the main house. In all there were some two dozen cells laid out in parallel with a wide central corridor. Nissen huts were hastily placed in the grounds for the Intelligence Corps guards and the garden divided up into exercise areas. Altogether the new compound approached ten acres of woodland and was as remote as any site so close to the centre of London could be.

The three-storey mansion itself was converted into a series of interrogation rooms on the ground floor with office accommodation above. When the project was completed Latchmere House was given the military designation of Camp 020 (Camp 001 being the hospital wing of Dartmoor where sensitive internees who could not mix with other prisoners were housed), but it was omitted from the lists of camps submitted to the International Red Cross and Protecting Power for neutral inspections.

Although Stimson had supervised the construction of the building, Kell appointed another officer to be its first commandant. His choice was Colonel R.W.G. ('Tin-eye') Stephens, a fearsome, monacled Indian Army veteran. Stephens was half German and could speak several languages fluently, including German. He was disliked by most of the people he came into contact with because of his almost Nazi behaviour and vile temper. He would stand no nonsense from anyone and did not hesitate to reprimand MI5 colleagues (including Guy Liddell and Tar Robertson) if they were unpunctual. He was also a fine horseman and a generous entertainer. Invitations to his mess were much sought after because of the plentiful supplies of food and especially drink on offer. He retained his old Peshawar Rifles uniform throughout the war and was always immaculately dressed.

Although it is jumping ahead slightly to write about Stephens' immediate post-war activities, it is perhaps apposite, for what happened later gives some indication of the man.

At the end of hostilities Stephens was transferred to the No 74 Combined Services Detailed Interrogation Centre at Bad Nenndorf near Hanover (CSDIC) where many of the important surviving Nazis were interned. Amongst those questioned there was General Erwin von Lahousen, the former Austrian Secret Service director who was recruited by Canaris to run Abwehr II, the sabotage section, in 1939. He headed the organization until August 1943 and was therefore in a better position than most to describe the German side of operations that MI5 had attempted to counter and frustrate. The debriefing sessions carried out on all Abwehr personnel were designed to establish once and for all just how genuine certain of the MI5 cases had been.

The Bad Nenndorf camp eventually came in for criticism following allegations of brutal treatment. In June 1948 Colonel Stephens as Camp Commandant was charged with (1) conduct to the prejudice of good order and military discipline in that, in June 1946 he 'ordered the handcuffing in an empty cell of a prisoner, whereby he was subjected to undue hardship', (2) disgraceful conduct of a cruel kind by causing a prisoner on two dates in December 1946 to be confined in an empty and unheated cell in freezing weather, and (3) that he failed in his duty as Camp Commandant. The final charge listed eight separate instances of alleged negligence. These were: water was thrown into the cells of prisoners; prisoners were required to scrub their cells for excessive periods; they were confined in unheated cells; they had their clothing or part of it removed; they were handcuffed back to back; they were made to stand naked in front of an open window; they were subjected to physical violence; they were supplied with food inadequate to maintain physical health, causing undue suffering and hardship.

The proceedings were held *in camera* at the request of the Director of Military Intelligence, Major-General Packard, and on the first day several of the charges were withdrawn. The witness against Stephens was his deputy, Lieutenant-Colonel Short, an officer who had served in both 020 and CSDIC. The President of the Court Martial, Major-General Calvert-Jones, ordered that further proceedings should take place in London and found Stephens not guilty on all counts on 20 July, 1948.

By implication, Colonel Short's testimony related more to his own behaviour than his commanding officer's, and he was disgraced.

When 020 opened for business in July 1940 the senior interrogator was the veteran MI5 officer Colonel Edward Hinchley-Cooke, on whom, as has already been seen, Kell always relied to give evidence for MI5 at the various inter-war spy trials. However, in spite of his long counter-intelligence experience and his fluent German Hinchley-Cooke did occasionally experience defeat.

He had failed to crack Walter Simon, who had been imprisoned for a minor breach of the registration order for aliens in 1939. Simon was repeatedly interviewed by Hinchley-Cooke but the German never admitted that he had come to Britain to spy. When Simon had served his brief sentence, he was deported home from Grimsby. On the dock to see him off was Hinchley-Cooke, who warned him: 'Don't come back … you won't be so lucky next time.'

The other important figure at 020 was Dr Harold Dearden, a distinguished psychiatrist and author of many books on the criminal mind, including *A New Way With The Insane* and *Medicine and Duty*. In

1939 Dearden had tried to join his old regiment, the Grenadiers, but had been rejected on grounds of age. He was fifty-eight. Kell, however, was quick to appoint him Medical Officer at 020 so he could advise on interrogation techniques. Dearden found it impossible to get on with Colonel Stephens and eventually, in 1943, resigned his post after a major row. The problem arose because before the war Dr Dearden had filed his own bankruptcy after receiving several tax demands for royalties on some of his successful books. Stephens was appalled when he learnt of this and accused Dearden of making a fraudulent petition for bankruptcy to evade taxes properly due. The charge was in fact unfounded but as Stephens had made the allegation in the mess in front of a number of colleagues Dearden pressed for a retraction and an apology. Stephens refused and the matter was reluctantly referred by Dearden to the then Director-General, Sir David Petrie, who investigated and then ordered Stephens to apologize. Stephens grudgingly withdrew his remarks and peace, of a sort, reigned at 020.

In 1941 a further 92-cell block known as 'B' Wing was built in the south-east corner of the 020 compound so as to accommodate the growing number of suspects who were being processed by MI5. At the same time some elaborate listening devices were wired into the ceilings of all the original cells. Even the provision of this new, two-storey block was insufficient to cope with the 'refugees' being referred to 020 and a special, long-term detention centre was hastily sited at a quiet spot on Lord Nuffield's estate, Huntercombe Place, Nettlebed, near Henley. This new purpose-built camp consisted of four single-storey cell blocks, each with twenty-four single cells, arranged in a square around a central compound.

In spite of the ghastly reputation that 'Tin-eye' Stephens earned for himself, there were few allegations of bad treatment. On the whole there was a very good reason for the suspects to be sent to 020 and spies were specifically exempted from the protection provided by the Geneva Convention. There was in fact one case of serious assault that nearly resulted in death. A non-permanent member of the 020 staff (who shall, for obvious reasons, remain unnamed) lost his temper with a prisoner and beat him up very severely. This event became known as 'the deplorable incident' and an enquiry was held. The officer concerned was reprimanded and transferred to other duties.

The case, however, did not rest there; the relevant papers were passed to the Home Office and the Home Secretary, Herbert Morrison, decided that 020 should pass to a stricter, civilian control. The Director-General intervened and, on his undertaking that there would never be a repetition of the affair, 020 survived within the domain of the Security Service.

The interrogation methods used at 020 were subtler than the crude use of physical force. A variety of sophisticated techniques were employed but all concentrated on the mental balance of the suspect rather than the short-term advantage. To have used obvious torture would have undermined the stability of those experiencing the turning process, and, indeed, affected the confidence of the individual case officers, who were generally not professional intelligence officers and would have resented the use of violence on persons for whom they later had to take a responsibility, quite apart from any humanitarian considerations.

Camp 020 really proved its value in the case of TATE, who arrived in England by parachute on 19 September, 1940. He was a committed member of the Nazi Party and seemed quite prepared to die for the cause. Indeed, he boasted to the staff at 020 (to their discomfort) that in a matter of days *they* would be *his* prisoners, so convinced was he of the imminent invasion of Britain by the Wehrmacht. TATE received the standard treatment in 020 and it must be a measure of its success that he still lives in the Home Counties and has nothing but praise for the behaviour of his captors, except, perhaps, of Colonel Stephens whom he regarded as 'frightening, but a little stupid'. Within three weeks of entering the 020 compound as a determined Nazi, TATE was sending bogus messages to his Abwehr controllers – with genuine enthusiasm.

As soon as any snspect arrived at 020 he was treated to the reception committee which welcomed the newcomer, in his real name, to a sort of cocktail party at which the British revealed just how much they knew about their captive – which was generally disconcertingly much – and offered their somewhat shaken victim the opportunity to co-operate. This approach was generally adopted with agents who had been betrayed by decrypted Abwehr signals or earlier 'turned' spies. The method also served to prove, to those agents who had already taken the decision to surrender themselves, the soundness of their chosen course of action. The objective of a 'soft' approach was to undermine the confidence of a spy, who would still be suffering the trauma of capture, and instil in him a sense of 'Well, they know so much already, why not help them?' The first few hours after interception were unsuitable for questioning because the Abwehr habitually gave their parachute agents a shot of benzedrine just before the mission. This kept them alert for twenty-four hours but after that they succumbed to exhaustion. In practice this meant the 020 interrogators began their interviews at their subjects' lowest ebb.

The alternative treatment was a harder regime. The newcomer would be thrown into his cell and left alone for a matter of hours. He would then be given the mandatory medical examination by Dr Dearden and possibly a dental search to detect false bridge work with poison concealed inside before being served with a fairly inedible plate of food. Finally, the interrogations would take place, which involved the prisoner being led into the main house and forced to stand before what was known as 'the Board'. Some eight or nine officers, headed by Stephens, would bark questions at the subject and accuse him of being a spy and working for the Nazis. He would then be invited to write a full statement which, it was explained, would be the document used to decide whether or not he should be hanged. The spy's sense of isolation would be developed by being told over and over again that he was beyond the reach of the civil authorities and at any moment might be taken out and executed without any further warning and certainly without any trial.

The real 'torture' at 020 came from the NCOs in charge of the cells who tormented their prisoners with rough behaviour and the odd throw-away line such as 'The chap next door has just been shot; I gather you are next', which understandably crushed what morale the prisoner had left. A harrowing plea from a detainee was found hidden in one of the cable ducts above a cell in 1979. A workman found the letter, written in Flemish, as he was modernizing the cell. The name of the author and his fate are unknown.

The double agent TATE remembered that some of the other ranks had little idea of the individual status of their charges and occasionally misunderstood situations. When TATE was collected by Russell Lee for his first wireless transmission his guard thought he was being transferred to a civil prison for execution and casually asked whether he could have TATE's watch as 'You won't be needing it any more.'

* * * *

Sometimes the 020 process backfired on MI5. Double agent ZIGZAG (Eddie Chapman, see Chapter VIII) was so angry about being locked up and treated as a spy that he threatened not to co-operate unless he was released immediately. Chapman was no stranger to prisons, having served several sentences before the war for cracking safes. Another agent who failed to be intimidated by Colonel Stephens was MUTT (John Moe) who was merely irritated by the attitude of his captors. He too protested about Stephens' accusations and spent only a minimum of time at 020.

Because of the secrecy surrounding 020 it acquired a very sinister reputation after the war. Many who had experienced the sharp end of the regime told hair-raising stories about executions at midnight and dummy firing squads, the latter apparently designed to give the prisoner one final opportunity 'to save himself'.

Some of Britain's other secret organizations also maintained their own detention camps. SOE, for example, kept a 'cooler' at Inverlair Lodge in the west of Scotland for agents who, for one reason or another, could not be allowed their liberty.

A few of the MI5 detainees did succumb and suffer breakdowns. There were several suicide attempts at 020 and Huntercombe Place, but there was only one actual fatality throughout the war. An elderly German suspect collapsed and died of a heart attack in his cell during an air raid. One of the bombs was a near miss and left a large crater between the perimeter fences. William Boyd, a South African detainee, unsuccessfully tried to slash his wrists in Latchmere House and a Norwegian Merchant Navy Captain, Axel Coll, went mad at Huntercombe Place. Coll was subsequently transferred to Camp 001 on Dartmoor, which was better equipped to deal with such cases.

Perhaps the worst feature of 020 was the system of selecting detainees for trial. The 1940 Treachery Act provided only one sentence for those found guilty – execution. Of all those appearing on such a charge at the Old Bailey only Sjoerd Pons escaped the hangman. He was acquitted by the jury and then promptly rearrested by Special Branch detectives as he left the dock. Having failed to obtain a conviction on a capital charge MI5 interned him under 18B for the duration. After the war he was deported to Holland where he served a further gaol term.

With this single exception a conviction was obtained in every one of the Treachery cases. This in effect meant that whoever was deciding to prosecute was also deciding on who should live and who should die. Certainly, prosecutions were desirable and had considerable impact when they were publicized. The government rarely lost an opportunity to make the appropriate press announcement. When Duncan Scott-Ford was hanged on 3 November, 1942, *The Times* commented:

> 'The moral to be drawn from this case is that British and Allied Seamen when visiting neutral ports should be constantly on their guard against strangers who may frequently approach them for apparently innocent purposes. Such strangers are apt to be enemy agents who lure their unsuspecting victims into a course of conduct which may expose them to blackmailing attempts by the enemy, and induce them to betray their country and the allied cause.'

Rather than leave the selection of Treachery defendants to one man a special panel was formed which became known as the 'Hanging Committee', in practice a sub-committee of the 020 interrogating 'Board'. Once a case had been deemed suitable the papers were handed by the Legal section to the civil authorities for prosecution.

The appointment of Winston Churchill as Prime Minister on the evening of 10 May, 1940 heralded all sorts of changes in the war effort, and MI5 was certainly not excluded from the new Prime Minister's plans. On the same day Germany began its offensive against France, Belgium and Holland. German troops poured across the neutral frontiers, causing the Cabinet to meet the following day in sombre mood.

But even before Churchill's first National Coalition Cabinet initial moves had been made in a strategy which was to end in the dismissal of Kell as Director-General of the Security Service. The previous day, some hours prior to Churchill's audience with the King, the Chiefs of Staff obtained Churchill's consent to the formation of a Home Defence Executive, a co-ordinating body to supervise preparations for the worst – invasion. The Executive itself was to consist of the Commander-in-Chief, Home Forces, General Sir Walter Kirke, and the three Chiefs of Staff. Later, on 28 May, the Cabinet created a special sub-committee specifically to deal with security matters, the Security Executive. This secret group's role was to oversee MI5 and give political guidance to those departments coping with the many difficulties involved in the wholesale internment of aliens. The origins of this sub-committee dated back to December 1939 when Chamberlain commissioned his Minister Without Portfolio, Lord Hankey, to undertake a study of MI5 and SIS. This remarkable assignment was in part due to a welter of complaints from the Services concerning the quality of the intelligence they were being given by SIS. Hankey had vast experience in the field and was ideally qualified for the investigation, even if 'C' and the D-G felt the exercise to be superfluous. Hankey had served in the NID under Admiral Ottley, and for twenty-six years had been Secretary to the Committee of Imperial Defence. Indeed, he had been Ottley's assistant when the retired DNI became the CID Secretary and created the forerunner of MI5, MO5, in 1909.

On 11 May, 1940 Lord Hankey informed Churchill of his interim findings, which were mainly concerned with SIS and the GC & CS. He also reported on the various other sabotage organizations that had sprung up since September 1939, such as Section 'D', but had yet to embark on MI5 in any detail. Churchill, characteristically, was unwilling to accept any delay and went to work on MI5 immediately.

He enjoyed a poor relationship with Kell, who was almost exactly a year older.

The reason for the friction is almost impossible to fathom but Kell undoubtedly mistrusted Churchill, perhaps it went back to Churchill's attempts to merge MI5 and SIS in the Twenties. Kell once claimed to have refused a pre-war request for intelligence information from Churchill but that is unsubstantiated. It could, however, be argued that because Desmond Morton had had to rely on Maxwell Knight for 'situation reports' he was obviously not obtaining them from the horse's mouth.

Certainly, it had been a bad twelve months for MI5 and they had come in for more than their fair share of criticism. Two particular incidents had attracted an embarrassing amount of adverse press coverage even though, like the sabotage of *Oleander, War Afridi*, HMS *Cumberland* and *L-54* before the war, described in Chapter I, they had nothing to do with MI5. As before they were concerned with the Royal Navy but some felt that Churchill might have marked them all down as Security Service blunders and as further examples of their inefficiency.

The first incident thought to have broken Churchill's patience was the audacious German attack on Scapa Flow on 14 October, 1939. The loss of the *Royal Oak* with 834 hands was a savage blow to the morale of the country and the Navy. For quite unjustified reasons MI5 were blamed for much of the Admiralty's incompetence. A U-boat captain named Günther Prien succeeded in picking his way through the anti-submarine defences around the Navy's refuge in the Orkneys and proceeded to select an enviable target. The Admiralty held an enquiry and NID sent sleuths, up to Kirkwall to investigate rumours of German spies, but failed to get any evidence. The results of the official enquiry were eventually published and it was obvious that the local precautions against an underwater attack were negligently inadequate.

On the day after the disaster a blockship arrived at Scapa Flow. It was to have been sunk in the narrow channel negotiated by *U-47* the previous afternoon. A long delay occurred before the Admiralty were even sure that the *Royal Oak* had been sunk by a submarine. Sabotage was a popular theory. No one ever denied that espionage was at the bottom of it all so journalists had a field-day. After the war several accounts were published of a mysterious Nazi watchmaker who had vanished from his shop in the Orkneys the day of the attack! It was, of course, all eye-wash, though to their credit MI5 did turn up a suspicious Italian photographer who ran a camera shop in Inverness. There was nothing to suggest that he was in any way connected with the disaster at Scapa Flow but he was interned anyway.

The second incident that gave MI5 a bad press was an explosion in Churchill's constituency at the Royal Gunpowder factory at Waltham Abbey in January 1940. Sabotage was rumoured and Chief Inspector William Salisbury, later of the Murder Squad, launched an investigation. His conclusion, with which the MI5 counter-sabotage unit and Detective Chief Inspector Williams of Special Branch agreed, was that none of the three explosions which occurred on 18 January and killed five workers were caused by sabotage. The announcement of their findings received very little coverage compared to the headlines that the incident provoked at first. The investigation left the First Lord of the Admiralty unimpressed.

Whatever the background, the circumstances of Kell's abrupt dismissal are clear. He was summoned to Sir Horace Wilson's office on Monday, 10 June, and left, a broken man, a short time later. Kell broke the news to his Deputy D-G Eric Holt-Wilson, the same evening at his club, and promptly received his resignation. That night Kell made this bitter entry in his personal diary: 'I get the sack from Horace Wilson, 1909-1945.'

Kell was stunned by his dismissal, and it took MI5 by surprise. The following day Lady Kell, who managed the canteen at Wormwood Scrubs, gathered the staff together and told them bitterly, 'Your precious Winston has sacked the General.' She accepted a few sympathetic comments from the old-timers. Only Kell's closest confederates were aware of his clash with Churchill.

Officially retired in 1923 and confirmed in that year by the *London Gazette*, Kell now genuinely relinquished a post he had held since 1909. There was no obvious successor so Brigadier Harker, the Director of 'B' Division, was promoted Deputy D-G with the rank of Acting Director-General. In his place Guy Liddell was appointed Director of 'B' a post he was to hold until 1947.

In fact, the real power of MI5 was soon to be invested in the Security Executive, the recently formed Home Defence Executive off-shoot. Churchill's choice for Chairman was Lord Swinton, previously Sir Philip Cunliffe-Lister and Chamberlain's Air Minister. His powerful committee was established in great secrecy in Kinnaird House, Pall Mall, and Sir Joseph Ball, another senior figure in the Conservative Party, was appointed Deputy Chairman. The Security Executive was also served by two Joint Secretaries, William Armstrong (later Lord Armstrong), a civil servant from the Board of Education, and Kenneth Diplock (now Lord Diplock), an Oxford-educated barrister. Other members included Harker as the new Acting D-G, Valentine Vivian ('C's ACSS), Colonel Roger Reynolds from the War Office, Sir Alan

Hunter, the head of the War Office's POW Department, Arthur Rucker (later Sir Arthur Rucker) a Ministry of Health civil servant who had served as Chamberlain's Principal Private Secretary, Arthur (later Sir Arthur) Hutchinson from the Home Office, Alf Wall, a trade unionist to give the Executive 'political balance', Edwin Herbert (knighted in 1943), the Director of Postal Censorship, Malcolm Frost from the BBC and Isaac Foot, the ex-Liberal MP and father of the future Labour Party Leader. The Prime Minister was determined to keep the existence of the Security Executive, and especially its membership, a State secret, but gradually word leaked out, and several MPs began pestering to discover more about this mysterious body. In August the speculation resulted in a Parliamentary Question which elicited the retort that the matter was 'not fitted for public discussion', and with that further pressure on the subject was deemed to be unpatriotic.

The Swinton Committee, as the Security Executive came to be known, quickly exercised control over MI5 and Brigadier Harker acquiesced without dispute. In truth the fifty-year-old Gunner had no desire to be involved in the distasteful political controversies surrounding wartime internment and certainly was not personally ambitious. The situation, however, was unprecedented because of the overall grasp Kell had previously kept on the organization.

The Secret Intelligence Service too had been undergoing a period of transformation at much the same time, though perhaps in not quite such a dramatic manner. On 4 November, 1939 Admiral Sinclair died from a combination of a malignant tumour and sheer exhaustion. The retirement or death of a SIS Chief had only occurred twice since the Great War and the appointment of each successor had been preceded by intense lobbying, so much so that an informal agreement had originally been reached between the three Armed Services allowing each to provide a 'C' in rotation. Admiral Sinclair, formerly DNI, had become 'C' after Sir Mansfield Cumming so it was now the turn of the Army or the RAF. When the post came up in November 1939 it was widely believed that Chamberlain, the Prime Minister, would ignore the inter-Service agreement on the grounds of wartime expediency. The favourite for the job was the DNI, Rear-Admiral John Godfrey, who himself had only been appointed in March 1939 in succession to Vice-Admiral James Troup.

The manoeuvrings in support of Sinclair's eventual successor were positively Byzantine and, in the end, Chamberlain bowed to the advice of Lord Halifax and David Margesson MP, his Chief Whip and close confidant, and selected Stewart Menzies, Sinclair's Deputy and Head of Section IV, the Military Intelligence (Army) branch. Menzies was a popular choice with at least the Palace (if not the rest of SIS) because of his strong royal connections and in theory at least the post of 'C' was in the King's gift. Stewart Menzies was forty-nine years old at the time, and the son of Lady Holford, whose second husband, Sir George, had been, until his death in 1926, an intimate friend of the King's.

SIS may have had a strong tradition of mobilizing political influence in the Chief's selection, but the Security Service certainly did not. This was solely due to Kell's long reign from MO5's inception in 1909. The sacking of the Director-General was unique and no one pretended his departure was due to chronic ill-health. After all, he had lived with illness most of his life.

Gradually the news filtered through the office. For the newcomers it had little significance. Many of them had never met the D-G and had only come into contact with the Director of their Division, or, in the case of the women, Miss Dicker, who ran the female personnel section. That Kell was too old at sixty-seven and should have stepped down gracefully was a widely held view but everyone privy to the details of his departure was loyal to Kell and sympathetic. This was especially true of the 'old guard', the thirty or so officers who had served him in the Twenties and through the crises of Invergordon, the IRA internments of 1922, the uproar over the Arcos raid and other memorable incidents. Kell died broken-hearted at his tiny rented cottage in Emberton, Buckinghamshire on 27 March, 1942.

However unjustified Kell's dismissal, the deed was done and Brigadier Harker stepped into his shoes for a few months. The office underwent a major reshuffle and a transfer to St James's Street. Guy Liddell was promoted Director of 'B' Division in Harker's place and the role of his department altered slightly from counter-espionage to counter-intelligence, a subtle transformation but not an insignificant one. Tar Robertson, the Head of B1(a), now hoped that he would be allowed the opportunity to develop his ambitious plan to run a whole network of double agents. With Liddell in control he was confident his proposals would be forcefully advocated in the Joint Intelligence Committee and the CIGS.

It was not long before Swinton's informants were telling the Security Executive that Harker was proving a less than adequate guardian of MI5. The Security Executive then decided to appoint a Director-General over the head of Harker and the matter was passed to the Prime Minister for approval. Churchill immediately became the target of some considerable lobbying from Stewart Menzies, the new SIS Chief, who undoubtedly saw the opportunity to bring MI5 within his own sphere of influence. His man for the job was David Petrie, a man close to his own ACSS, Valentine Vivian. In November 1940 'C's arguments prevailed and Petrie was installed as the new Director-General of the Security Service, Harker stepping into the post of Deputy D-G.

When Petrie took over as D-G he was determined to make changes in the structure of his new department. At sixty-one years old he was certainly not new to intelligence work. He had joined the Indian Political Intelligence Bureau from the Indian Police and headed the organization for seven years before being posted to Palestine. One of his first decisions was to hire a business efficiency expert, for Swinton wanted a detailed study of the work being done in every MI5 section. The services of a Mr Horrocks were obtained from a large City firm and over a period of six months he and his assistant Mr Potter paid a visit to each office and interviewed every employee, from the Director of 'B' Division down to the lowliest typist. Petrie studied Horrocks's final report (it was considered so secret that no copies were circulated outside the office) and then reorganized the system of Divisions and doubled the pay (then £3 10s a week) for all secretaries. Since Horrocks had learned more about MI5 than anyone else living Petrie felt obliged to find a niche for him within his own Secretariat, the D-G's immediate office. He was later joined by Mrs Elsie Abbot, who was transferred from the Post Office to help him. The loyalty of Mr Potter was secured by his marriage to a girl from Registry.

The most serious criticism in the Horrocks Report was a query against the method of recruitment into MI5, or rather the lack of any over-all policy. When Kell had started to expand his service in 1936 there had been fewer than thirty officers, all of them very badly paid. There had been an urgent need to build up strength but the elderly D-G was reluctant to open the doors to people who were not known to either him or his friends. He had felt very deeply that he had been entrusted with the security of the nation and he would be betraying the trust placed in him if he failed to employ staff from less than completely reliable backgrounds. After Kell's departure MI5 underwent a further transformation and was infused with a mass of new talent, under the aegis of the Security Executive and its Chairman. Swinton, anxious to shake up the organization, had sent two Security Executive members to carry out his wishes: Malcolm Frost, the BBC representative, and William Charles Crocker, an immensely successful solicitor who, as well as serving on the Security Executive, was a platoon sergeant in the Seal (Kent) Local Defence Volunteers.

As might be expected these two were regarded with suspicion by the 'regulars', as were some of their recruits. Frost was inserted into 'B' Division with Assistant Director rank in July 1940, alongside Dick White and Roger Hollis, who had recently succeeded Colonel Alexander on the latter's retirement. Frost was given charge of 'W', a new unit (the 'W' standing for wireless) which was to be the origin of B1(a), the section controlling most of the German double agents.

William Charles Crocker, a man destined to be knighted and become President of the Law Society, was Swinton's other principal hatchet man, but he was also something of an embarrassment to 'B' Division. Before the war he had built up a unique reputation as a sleuth extraordinaire and had been credited with the detection of a gang of arsonists who had defrauded several London insurance companies out of very large sums. The arsonists were sent to prison, as was the Chief of the London Salvage Corps whom Crocker unmasked as a conspirator. Through this and other successes Crocker established the very best of contacts in the City (particularly with the grateful insurance companies), the police and the underworld. When rationing was introduced and the Black Market began to flourish it was to him that Lord Woolton, the Food Minister, appealed for help. Once again Crocker triumphed and an illicit meat distribution network was eliminated.

This remarkable solicitor's chief contribution to MI5 was his recommendation that a police unit be created within 'B' Division. The Security Service had never enjoyed the powers of arrest and had therefore always relied on the civil authorities to take suspects into custody; invariably this had meant Special Branch, with whom MI5 liaised closely. Crocker was very friendly with a number of senior police officers, and his idea was to incorporate a limited number of Metropolitan Police detectives into MI5 so that at least some members of the Security Service could exercise a legal power of arrest. There were obvious political considerations to be taken into account, but in the end the Assistant Commissioner for the CID, Sir Norman Kendal, and his deputy Ronald Howe approved the plan. In August, 1940 six policemen, led by Leonard Burt, were commissioned into the Intelligence Corps and became regular attenders at 'B' Division meetings. In the spring of 1939 the Special Branch, headed by Albert Canning, had consisted of 156 detectives and administrative staff. Within a year that number had grown to 800. Burt, assisted by Donald Fish and Reg Spooner, became a very successful interrogator, as did another young member of his unit, Jim Skardon, who was to remain in MI5 after the war.

The Special Branch policemen participated in several of the important MI5 investigations, and after the war led enquiries into the British renegades, which resulted in the prosecutions of Joyce, Amery, Baillie-Stewart and the members of the British Free Corps (known also as the Legion of St George).

Crocker was undoubtedly an excellent choice in the eyes of Lord Swinton, but his appearance in MI5 was not welcomed by the Director of 'B' Division, who had private reasons for his reservation. Before the war Liddell's wife Calypso had deserted him and taken their children to the United States, where she set up home with her half-brother. In Britain this behaviour was regarded as bizarre and Liddell made strenuous efforts to have his children returned. His solicitor in the unsuccessful case was William Charles Crocker.

At the time of this close examination by the Security Executive a number of distinguished solicitors and barristers were drafted in with the title of 'Civil Assistant, War Office'. They included 'Buster' Milmo (later Sir Helenus Milmo and a judge), who was to head B1(b) and Henry ('Toby') Pilcher (later a judge), who headed the Legal section in 'A' Division wiih the assistance of another barrister, Jim Hale. Liaising with the Director of Public Prosecutions over internments and prosecutions were Patrick Barry, KC (later a judge) and Edward Cussen (also later a judge). Other recruits included E.B. Stamp (later Sir Blanshard Stamp and an Appeal judge), John Senter (later a QC), Ashton Roskill (later Sir Ashton and Chairman of the Monopolies Commission), Alex Kellar from the Middle Temple, John Stephenson (later Sir John and an Appeal judge) from the Inner Temple. The large crop of solicitors included John Marriott, Christopher Harmer, Ian Wilson and Ronnie Haylor; Rupert Speir (later Sir Rupert and a Conservative MP) and Martin Furnival Jones (later Director-General of the Security Service from 1967-1972).

The influx from the law integrated surprisingly well with those from the universities, the Indian Police, the MI5 regulars and those who had no qualifications whatever. Nevertheless, Swinton's two reorganizers failed to achieve any measure of popularity with their colleagues, in spite of some valuable innovations. Frost was responsible for recruiting Roland Bird from the *Economist*, who successfully introduced a Hollerith punch-card sorter into Registry, thus revolutionizing the filing system. Frost also managed to begin the co-ordination of the intelligence being fed to the double agents, a development that ultimately led to the formation of the 'W' Board and the Twenty Committee.

While MI5 were coping with the Swinton-inspired reorganization they also received massive new funding, and special support from other related intelligence groups. Principal amongst these was the Radio Security Service, a technical unit operating with the military designation MI8(c). MI8 itself came under the jurisdiction of the War Office and the DMI. Shortly before the war Kell had voiced concern about possible dangers from a well-established network of enemy agents equipped with transmitters to signal raiding aircraft on to their targets. It was not a far-fetched idea. The Germans actually did use radio beams to guide their bombers, but the transmission originated from tail beacons rather than illicit stations hidden in Britain. A high priority had been placed in 1939 on the formation of a Radio Security Service under the command of Colonel J.P.G. Worlledge. He had gathered around him a collection of amateur wireless enthusiasts who had scanned the air waves for illegal broadcasting. The RSS had worked closely with the GPO who for some years had monitored British radio hams and developed direction-finding equipment to seek out those operating without a Home Office licence. Kell had envisaged that the RSS would be able to clamp down on any signals not accounted for.

As it turned out, the RSS were to play quite a different role. At first the only 'illegal' signals originated from within the United Kingdom were from Tar Robertson's double agent SNOW. However, they did make an important discovery during the course of their twenty-four-hour watches. Early in 1940 the RSS Voluntary Interceptors pinpointed a vessel in the North Sea as a source of transmissions received by SNOW. The cypher was easy to break because SNOW was already 'in harness'. The ship was a floating Abwehr radio station, communicating both with SNOW and a number of agents in Norway. The VIs duly homed in on the messages and sent the intercepted groups of letters for analysis to GC & CS, who had now moved to Bletchley. Here the intercepts were received by Oliver Strachey, Lytton Strachey's brother, and Dillwyn ('Dilly') Knox, brother of Monsignor Ronald Knox, the Catholic writer. These two eminent scholars set to work on the Abwehr cyphers and divided them into those based on hand cyphers and those intercepted from the special Abwehr version of the Enigma machine. Constant surveillance of the Abwehr signal traffic revealed that the Germans used the Enigma for messages passing between the secure Abstelles, but relied on the hand cyphers for communicating with more vulnerable bases and their individual agents in the field. The German occupation of Norway provided a wealth of information about the Abwehr's radio drill, which in turn led the RSS to reconsider their role.

The breakthroughs into the enemy's communication system occurred over Christmas 1939, and Strachey and Knox reported to the RSS the likelihood of providing a constant flow of Abwehr intercepts. The news was overwhelming, and was certainly not lost on two RSS officers in particular, Major E.W. Gill and Hugh Trevor-Roper (now Lord Dacre and Master of Peterhouse College, Cambridge). Gill had long been absorbed by radio transmitters and had written *War, Wireless and Wrangles* based on his experiences during the Great War. Trevor-Roper too saw the possibilities of eavesdropping on the Abwehr and began circulating learned reports on the subject to other departments who he thought would encourage this new venture. The work on the decrypts was considered sufficiently important for two further scholars to be assigned to the work. They were Denys Page (later Sir Denys and Master of Jesus College, Cambridge) and Professor Leonard Palmer (later Professor of Comparative Philology at Oxford). Unfortunately, Trevor-Roper's efforts also served to alert the Head of the SIS Section V, Major Felix Cowgill, to the new pre-occupation of the RSS. As Head of SIS Counter-Intelligence Cowgill naturally liaised with 'B' Division of MI5, but he felt strongly that Colonel Worlledge and his men had strayed dangerously from their brief and had encroached on an area which was undoubtedly in the parish of SIS. There now began a battle of personalities between Section V and the RSS which was to last for eighteen months, until May 1941, when SIS finally triumphed and took over the RSS, absorbing it into GC & CS. There the raw intelligence was decyphered and translated, becoming ISOS (Intelligence Services Oliver Strachey) for the hand cyphers, and ISK (Intelligence Services Knox) for the Enigma-based messages. From Bletchley dispatch riders delivered the summaries to the RSS at Arkley, a tiny village on the outskirts of Barnet. The RSS analysts quickly increased their number to cope with the traffic. Originally the RSS consisted of Worlledge, his Adjutant, Colonel Sclater, Gill and Trevor-Roper. New recruits included Charles Stuart from Oxford, Gilbert Ryle (the Oxford philosopher) from the Welsh Guards, Stuart Hampshire who transferred from the Western Desert (later Warden of Wadham College, Oxford), and two liaison officers, Kenneth Morton Evans, the link with 'B' Division, and R.L. Hughes, who negotiated with Section V.

The problems with Section V, with whom MI5 generally succeeded in getting on well, eventually boiled down to a matter of security. At first the RSS depended almost entirely on GPO personnel for technical expertise, which was a far from ideal situation. After several wrangles concerning overtime pay all the Post Office staff were called up and put into uniform. This removed one of SIS's objections but they still clung to the belief that the RSS was dabbling in a field which should be left to the 'professionals', ie themselves. Section V was particularly sensitive about intercepts which named British agents, and at one point a directive went out from the St Albans Section V headquarters banning anyone outside SIS from glimpsing so-called ISBA intercepts –

Intelligence Service British Agents. This was exactly the information needed so desperately by MI5's B1(a) so the order was quietly ignored (at some peril) by the GC & CS decrypters.

The first blow in the Section V/RSS battle was struck when the RSS began to lose their Voluntary Interceptors. They had become so skilled in such a short period that other 'Y' services requested transfers to improve their own methods. At one stage in 1940 it appeared that GC & CS had been successful enough to request more material from the radio operators, who themselves were too understaffed to cope with the demand. The crisis reached the Prime Minister through 'C', and Lord Hankey was asked to supervise the distribution of the VIs. Worse, however, was to come. Section V continued to apply pressure to the RSS and eventually made a case for a complete take-over of the organization. This plan was strenuously opposed by Colonel Worlledge and his new Adjutant, Cole-Adams, but the SIS view prevailed. The RSS were brought under the formal control of Colonel Gambier-Parry, the Head of Section VIII – the SIS Communications department, and an SIS nominee named Maltby who moved into Hanslope Park to oversee operations.

This change-over was, in effect, 'C's final consolidation of his grasp on signals interception, and was only achieved after a closely-fought struggle with MI5's 'old guard'. The recently appointed D-G, Sir David Petrie, was in no position to obstruct Menzies' wishes. By this date SIS had established a liaison section within MI5 and the flow of ISOS material from Bletchley to 'B' Division was unimpeded. The new decrypts were received in St James's Street by Herbert Hart, now working in B1(b). Hart in turn passed the ISOS summaries on to the other B1(b) analysts and the B1(a) officers when the intercepts concerned their agents.

The RSS, as MI5's principal technical support organization, were responsible for the investigation of all forms of illicit communication with the enemy and at one stage early in the war created a special MI8 unit to monitor the movements of carrier pigeons. The section consisted of Lord Tredegar and Wing-Commander Walker, both keen falconers, whose birds of prey were sent in pursuit of suspected spy pigeons. The question of Nazi pigeons was taken sufficiently seriously to launch a pigeon deception plan over the English Channel during the German advance into Belgium and France. The object of the exercise was to confuse the enemy by filling the sky with pigeons which, in theory, were to fill the Abwehr pigeon lofts, if indeed there were any. The first attempt failed when the RAF flew a pigeon dropping flight along the south coast of England. Unfortunately, most of the birds were sucked into the plane's slipstream and 'defeathered'. The solution dreamed up by Walker was to place the pigeons in paper bags before tossing them out of the aircraft. This plan apparently worked well and for some days it was thought that the Germans had been engulfed with pigeons. A few days later however it became obvious the pigeons were homers and the scheme was hastily dropped. The operations of Falcon (Interceptor) Unit were curtailed further with the arrest and imprisonment in the Tower of London of Lord Tredegar. Apparently, the old Etonian Welshman had been somewhat indiscreet after lunching with Lady Baden-Powell and actually gave her a guided tour of his office as well as describing how he was engaged in the destruction of Nazi carrier pigeons. When word leaked of Tredegar's lapse he was taken into custody at the Tower but was released soon afterwards when MI5 intervened.

This, however, was not the last of the affair. Tredegar was outraged by his arrest and threatened dire consequences. He retired to his country seat, Tredegar Park in South Wales, and invited Aleister Crowley, the renowned occultist and magician, to prepare a spell. Coincidentally or otherwise, Tredegar's arresting officer fell painfully ill shortly afterwards and nearly died.

The Security Executive continued to exercise their influence over MI5 until Lord Swinton was posted to West Africa by Churchill in June 1942. His successor as Chairman was Duff Cooper, the Minister of Information. By this date Petrie had completed his own internal changes and was in a position to confirm MI5's independence of both SIS and the politicians.

Swinton's departure marked the end of an extraordinary phase in the history of the Security Service. Kell had battled for permission to expand in time for the war he was convinced would come. He failed, and then was obliged to watch his old organization being swamped by an intake that undoubtedly did not conform with his own rigid standards. As the new recruits were being absorbed, so the new Prime Minister removed the longest-serving officers and imposed a measure of political control through that most terrible of all weapons, the committee. Predictably the politicians found fault and provided bureaucrats and mavericks to execute the changes deemed so necessary. Still not satisfied the Cabinet appointed an experienced professional to take command, but he too demanded organizational changes. It says much for MI5's morale that in the midst of all this confusion and relocation they were able to continue their work and expand, with untried staff, into new fields.

The Regional Commissioners

Northern	Sir Arthur Lambert
North East	Lord Harlech (until March 1941), General Sir William Bartholomew
North Midland	Lord Trent
Eastern	Sir Will Spens
London Senior Commissioner:	Capt Euan Wallace MP (until January 1941), Sir Ernest Gowers MP
London Joint Commissioners:	Sir Ernest Gowers MP (until January 1941), Admiral Sir Edward Evans, Charles Key MP (from January 1941)
Southern	Harold Butler (until January 1942)
South-West	General Sir Hugh Elles, Sir Geoffrey Peto (April-September 1940)
Wales Senior Commissioner:	Lord Portal
Wales Joint Commissioners:	Colonel Gerald Bruce, Prof Robert Richards MP
Midland	Lord Dudley
North-West	Sir Warren Fisher (until April 1940), Sir Harry Haig (until January 1942), Lord Geddes (until July 1942), Hartley Shawcross KC
Scotland	Thomas Johnston MP (until February 1941), Lord Rosebery
South-East	Lord Geddes (until July 1941), Lord Monsell

PART THREE:

WAR

VII

The Double Agents of 'B' Division

'It seems incredible, but we do not have a single informant in Great Britain. On the other hand, the Germans have many. In London itself there is a German agent who makes radio transmissions up to twenty-nine times a day. At least, so it is stated by Admiral Canaris.'

Ciano's Diary. 11 September 1940

Under the leadership of Brigadier Harker and his second-in-command, Guy Liddell, 'B' Division had held over-all responsibility for counter-espionage in the United Kingdom in 1939. Their range of operations had been free of statutory limitation so it covered a very wide area. Its prime role had been that of investigation, involving physical surveillance, telephone and postal interception and the use of informants. On occasions other methods, such as burglary and illicit search, had been employed as necessary with a measure of immunity from the police.

In spite of its heavy weight of responsibility 'B' Division had had to rely on a very small staff. As the transition from peace to war took place the numbers increased tenfold but they were still comparatively tiny. Right at the centre of operations were the extraordinarily talented Guy Liddell and Max Knight. As the war progressed these two men ran any number of informants and confidential sources, only sometimes referring to them as 'agents' for they were not all agents in the true sense. The overwhelming majority were part-time, occasional sources who knew their information would be acted on by the proper authority. They were also safe in the knowledge they would never be asked to appear before a court or Internment Appeal Tribunal in person. Indeed, it can be said that as counter-intelligence officers Liddell's and Knight's empire depended almost exclusively on the reliability of their informants.

Certainly 'B' Division was an empire. It was run on a need-to-know and no-questions-asked basis with a latitude that encompassed such activities as the recruitment of 'stooges' for infiltration into POW camps and the surveillance of political undesirables. Knight veered towards the counter-subversion end of this spectrum, leaving the more general counter-espionage duties to Liddell and his men.

Understandably, cloaked as it was with its own secrecy, 'B' Division was rather slower to expand than some other departments. It was all very well to admit a newcomer into Registry or the transport section, but entrusting an outsider, or even a Special Branch man, with MI5's essential knowledge was a very different matter. Thus, early in the war Liddell looked to his pre-war hands, Dick White, Tar Robertson and Jack Curry to cope with the problems of German espionage. It fell to them to investigate rumours, follow up denunciations, deal with agents and guide their Special Branch contacts. Once an investigation had been completed and perhaps an arrest made the matter could be left to others. Skilled interrogators were on hand and 'A' Division's legal section had a small army of trusted barristers and solicitors to prepare cases and draft internment or detention orders. This division of labour worked well in the cut-and-dried cases but the management of German agents who had been 'turned' round to work for Britain was extremely time-consuming and called for an altogether more sophisticated approach which Dick White and Tar Robertson were the first to recognize.

So, whether they liked it or not, they were just going to have to increase the personnel available for the sensitive task of running double agents. Robertson was assigned John Marriott, a young solicitor and Cambridge graduate as his deputy, Cyril Mills from the circus family and William Luke, a young industrialist from Glasgow. Luke had originally intended joining the Navy but was prevailed upon to volunteer for 'secret work of national importance' instead. Later recruits were Christopher Harmer (another solicitor and friend from Cambridge of John Marriott), Ian Wilson (another solicitor), and finally Hugh Astor, an Oxford graduate whose lameness precluded regular military service. Since the first contacts with the Abwehr depended on illicit wireless transmissions several reliable 'ham' operators were seconded to MI5 to supervise the radio and cypher aspects of the cases.

If you 'turn' a German agent and make him work for you, he still has to continue to supply secret, highly confidential information to the enemy or he will become suspect. But equally the enemy may check up on this information or even act upon it, so what is sent has to be carefully vetted, yet useful, true and sufficiently high-powered to be believed and accepted as beyond suspicion. This particular aspect of counter-intelligence had not previously been a serious snag for 'B' Division because it was rather out of their province, but with the ever-growing number of agents and Abwehr questionnaires it became a problem. At first Air Commodore Archie Boyle, Director of the Intelligence Section of Air Ministry and a keen supporter of 'B' Division's efforts had personally provided, at not inconsiderable risk to his career, various useful pieces of true air intelligence with which to spice the bogus and innocuous. Now something more centralized and controlled was needed if this dangerous game was to be played with any success.

A new Wireless Branch was therefore created in July 1940, partly a result of post-Kell reorganization and partly due to the increasing need for MI5 and MI6 to co-ordinate their activities. This was felt to be a rather sensitive but nevertheless increasingly critical area, with MI5 double agents holding meetings or 'treffs' in neutral countries abroad, and the Abwehr pressing with detailed questionnaires for more information.

The Director of Military Intelligence, Major-General F.C. ('Paddy') Beaumont-Nesbitt, was particularly anxious to see some centralized control of the material being channelled to the Abwehr and at his suggestion the Wireless Board consisted of Guy Liddell (now Director of 'B' Division), Stewart Menzies ('C'), John Godfrey (DNI), Archie Boyle and the DMI. This lofty group were sufficiently highly placed to clear the information needed for the double agents and agree general policy but they proved to be rather too far removed from the field. The day-to-day requirements of 'B' Division argued for a more representative body able to meet regularly and cut through military red tape. The Wireless Board therefore agreed to delegate much of its work to a special sub-committee which became known as the Twenty Committee, a suitable 'cover' derived from the Roman numerals of a double cross, XX. Its Chairman was an MI5 nominee, J.C. Masterman, a Christ Church don who had been interned during the Great War in Germany at the notorious Ruhleben Camp. 'B' Division also provided John Marriott as co-ordinator and permanent Secretary. The Committee of course rarely came into contact with individual double agents, or for that matter, knew their real identities, but remained a brilliant and necessary innovation. Matters were decided by the Committee with a marked degree of unanimity.

The first meeting of the Twenty Committee included representatives from MI5, MI6, NID, HDE, War Office, Air Ministry Intelligence, Air Ministry Deception and GHQ Home Forces and took place on 2 January, 1941. The actual membership changed later during the war to reflect intelligence development.

The establishment of the Twenty Committee allowed the 'positive counter-intelligence' lobby to demonstrate the extent of their newly-acquired expertise. B1(a) continued to manage the agents on a day-to-day basis but their efforts were now combined with B1(b), a hybrid unit devoted to the art of assessment of the enemy. B1(b) was headed by Helenus ('Buster') Milmo. He gathered around him an extraordinary galaxy of brain-power, drawn from the law and from the universities. They included Anthony Blunt, a transfer from 'D' Division, Herbert Hart, the left-wing barrister, Patrick Day, the philosopher from New College, Oxford, and E.B. Stamp.

B1(b) were given over-all responsibility for combining all the available sources of intelligence concerning the Abwehr and SD and developing a strategy for the double cross agents. Herbert Hart was granted unlimited access to the intercepts concerning the German intelligence services (code-named ISOS) and analysed them for material pertinent to MI5's operations. Other staff examined captured documents while Milmo prepared questionnaires for the Latchmere House 020 people and Royal Victoria Patriotic School refugee processing centre interrogators. Meanwhile John Gwyer and Patrick Day, who transferred to MI5 from the Gunners, began composing a picture of the various different branches of the German intelligence system.

As B1(a) and B1(b) got down to work they were joined by Victor Rothschild, another Trinity, Cambridge graduate, whose anti-sabotage unit was designated B1(c).

The potentially combustible mixture of regular officers, academics and lawyers worked and the B1 sections quickly became the hub of MI5's counter-intelligence activities. Information gleaned from the ULTRA decrypts (courtesy of MI6), the interrogators at 020 and 001, and the double agents proved its worth without delay and the terrible gamble of providing the enemy with deceptive intelligence was won.

The Twenty Committee succeeded in co-ordinating all the interested parties and by the end of the war had met (usually on Wednesday afternoons) 226 times. Through its influence with the other services MI5 was able to refine the practice of strategic deception into a practical weapon.

It could perhaps be argued that the double cross system was a natural development of the cunning, guile and desperation of MI5 at the end of

Top Right: Lt-Colonel Edward Hinchley-Cooke the half-German MI5 officer who began his thirty-year career in counter-espionage by acting as a stool-pigeon in British POW camps. Hinchley-Cooke became a well-known face at pre-war spy trials and occasionally gave evidence as a representative for MI5. *(After the Battle magazine)*

Centre Right: Maxwell Knight, possibly the most mysterious man in MI5. He ran dozens of agents throughout the Twenties and Thirties and successfully penetrated the Fascists and the Communists. His investigations culminated in the Woolwich Arsenal case in 1938 and the conviction of Anna Wolkoff in 1940 the first major espionage trial of the war. He is pictured here wearing a military uniform to which he was not entitled. He joined MI5 in 1924 after serving in the Royal Navy.

Bottom Right: Joan Miller: a portrait study by Harlip the society photographer who as a Hungarian refugee was investigated and cleared by MI5. Miss Miller joined MI5 in 1939 and was one of Max Knight s principal agents penetrating the Communist Party the Indian Nationalist movement and the Fascists. Her successful penetration of the Right Club led to the conviction of Anna Wolkoff in November 1940. This photograph was damaged by a jealous woman.

WAR OFFICE,

WHITEHALL,

S.W.1.

Officer in Charge,
Room 055,

To whom it may concern

The Bearer ....*Joan P. Miller*...................

Holder of Official Pass and Identity Card No. **A.F.C.B.82/1**
is employed on special duties, and for this reason is supplied
with supplementary Petrol Coupons.

    Any enquiries as to the nature or place of work, or the
reason for the journey, should not be made of the bearer, but
should be referred to the above address.

                                      Moore

12.5.43.   *for* Lt.Col. M.E. Cumming.

Above: Joan Miller's MI5 pass signed by the Assistant Director of 'A' Division Lt-Col Malcolm Cumming directing all enquiries to 'Room 055 the War Office'.

Right: Anna Wolkoff in her Auxiliary Fire Service uniform prior to her arrest on Official Secrets charges in May 1940. Evidence against her was given by 'Miss X', Joan Miller, one of MI5's most successful agents. Wolkoff received ten years' imprisonment and swore from the dock to kill Joan Miller. *(Keystone)*

90

Dem Admiral Sinclair sollen folgende Abteilungen unterstanden haben:
1. Administration Section,
2. Military Section,
3. Naval Section,
4. Air Section,
5. Communication Section (Verbindungsabteilung) = Fernmeldedienst.
6. Political Section,
7. Cifre Section (Chiffrier-Abteilung),
8. Financial Section,
9. Press Section,
10. Industrial Section.

Aufgaben der Abteilungen

1. Administration Section:

Leiter: Captain Howard (R. N. = Royal Navy); unter ihm die Commanders der Marine Slocum und Bowlbey (Schreibweise nicht sicher).

Aufgabe: Prüfung des Personals, sowohl der Offiziere und Angestellten wie auch der von den PCO's gemeldeten Agenten, die die Abteilung annimmt oder ablehnt. Die Organisation des ganzen Dienstes liegt bei Abteilung I. Sie verteilte die eingehenden Nachrichten.

Sitz: Im 5. Stock des Broadway Building.

2. Military Section:

Leiter: Major Hatton-Hall. Keine Offiziere als Mitarbeiter.

Aufgabe: Alle Nachrichten, die von den Nachrichtenoffizieren der Länder-Außenstellen kommen, werden ihm zugeleitet, soweit sie das Heer angehen. Stevens gibt folgendes Beispiel: „Ich melde, daß die Deutschen über Holland angreifen werden. Abteilung I gibt das als Verteilungsstelle an Abteilung 2. Sie vergleicht diese Meldung mit denen anderer PCO's, nimmt Stellung und gibt diese weiter an das Kriegsministerium, „wahrscheinlich" an die Intelligence Branch. (Stevens meint das Int.-Department.)

Sitz: von Hatton-Hall und seiner Abteilung im 5. Stock.

3. Naval Section:

Leiter: Captain Russel. Ohne Mitarbeiter, d. h. ohne Offiziere.

Aufgabe: Die gleichen wie bei 2, abgewandelt auf Marinefragen. Nachrichten gehen weiter an die Admiralty: Naval Intelligence-Division.

Sitz: Im 6. Stock.

4. Air Section:

Leiter: Winter-Bottom (Whing-commander?). Er hat zwei Offiziere als Mitarbeiter: Adams und ?.

Aufgabe: Wie bei 2 und 3, abgewandelt auf Angelegenheiten der Luftwaffe. Bearbeitete Nachrichten gingen am Air-Ministry, zum Air-Intelligence-Department.

Sitz: Im 6. Stock. Die Abteilungen 2, 3 und 4 sind Auswertungsabteilungen in erster Linie. Sie geben aber auch Aufträge, d. h. sie äußern Wünsche, stellen Fragen, die an die PCO's weitergeleitet werden. Sie tun das entweder aus eigener Initiative oder als Mittelinstanzen für Wünsche der drei Intelligence-Abteilungen.

91

5. Communication Section:

Leiter: Perry, Vorname: Gambler, nennt sich Colonel, ist es aber nicht. Stevens weiß nicht sehr viel davon; will die Abteilung nie besucht haben. Sie soll jetzt in Bletchley sein.

Aufgabe: Wireless = Radio und Funkverbindungen, Telephon, Brieftauben usw.

Sitz: Bis dahin im Broadway Building, Stockwerk nicht bekannt.

6. Political Section:

Leiter: Major Vivien und Polizeioffizier Mills (Vivien nennt sich Major; auch er ist Polizeioffizier).

Aufgabe: „Konterspionage" (siehe unten) in Verbindung mit MJ 5 (siehe unten). Außerdem Bearbeitung der „subversive movements": Kommunisten, Faschisten usw. Bekämpfung staatsfeindlicher Bewegungen in England. Stevens und Best machten keinen Unterschied zwischen Gegenspionage und Abwehr. Stevens sagte: „Das überschneidet sich so stark, daß da keine Cäsur gemacht werden kann". Die Abteilung 6 hält Verbindung mit kommunistischen und anderen politischen Organisationen für Nachrichtenzwecke. Stevens weiß angeblich nicht, wie diese Unterabteilung der Abteilung 6 heißt.

Die Nachrichten von „101 B." (Agent von Hendricks in Antwerpen, Gegner von Pötzsch), wurden von der Abteilung 1 der Abteilung 6 zugeteilt.

Sitz: Im 5. Stockwerk.

7. Cifre Section = Chiffrier- und Dechiffrier-Abteilung:

Leiter: Ein pensionierter Oberst namens Geffreys arbeitete dort. Leiter ist nicht bekannt.

Aufgabe: Brechung fremder Codes, Vorbereitung eigener Codes, auch für die PCO's.

Sitz: Stevens kennt ihn nicht.

8. Financial Section:

Leiter: Commander Sykes.

Aufgabe: Anweisung der Gelder für Nachrichtenfonds, der Gehälter usw. an die PCO's und die Zentrale.

Sitz: Im 4. Stock.

9. Press Section:

Leiter: Wahrscheinlich Hennecker-Heaton, kein Offizier.

Aufgabe: Lesedienst, Überwachung von Inseraten, Verkehr mit der Presse, soweit dienstlich erforderlich.

Sitz: Im 4. Stock.

10. Industrial Section (Ökonomische Nachrichten):

Leiter: Pensionierter Admiral Limpenny.

Aufgabe: Sammlung aller Nachrichten über die wirtschaftliche Lage des fremden Landes: Wieviel Flugzeuge im Monat hergestellt werden, Kohlenförderung, Rohstoffversorgung usw., Auswertung und Weitergabe, möglicherweise an Board of Trade. — Sitz unbekannt.

Im Erdgeschoß des Broadway-Building habe es — so sagt Stevens — noch ein Büro gegeben, das nach außen hin der Propaganda-Abteilung gehörte. Im April

Im übrigen mag die special branch wirklich mit MJ 5 so eng zusammenarbeiten, daß die Abgrenzung nach außen hin nicht leicht ist. Richtig wird sein, daß MJ 5 in Thames-House Verbindungsglied ist zwischen special branch und Geheimdienst — wobei MJ 5 und special branch in gewissem Umfang auch zusammenarbeiten. — Dadurch ist gewährleistet, daß der „Dienst" geheim bleibt. Die Außenwelt lernt durch Amtshandlungen nur die Spezialbeamten kennen.

Die special branch hat ihren Sitz in New Scotland Yard am Victoria Embankment. (Vgl. unter „Aufbau der britischen Polizei" zu III B.)

Stevens erklärte, daß MJ 5 eng mit der politischen Sektion (6) des Majors Vivien zusammengearbeitet habe. (Siehe oben.)

Hinchley-Cook trägt eine Brille, ist kräftig, von frischem Aussehen, macht einen gutmütigen Eindruck und spricht „fließend deutsch in einer Mischung von sächsischer und Hamburger Mundart.

Eine Deckfirma bzw. ein Tarnbüro von MJ 5 ist das Büro des Captain King in London, Delphin Square, Hood House, Flat 308, bei Coplestone. Hier fertigte MJ 5 V.-Leute ab. Captain King selbst wohnte Whitehall Mansion. Im War-Office hatte er seinen Dienstsitz.

Quellen des britischen Nachrichtendienstes

Auf die Frage, ob er auch auf die deutsche Öl- und Treibstoffversorgung angesetzt habe, antwortete Stevens: „Nein. Das hielt ich nicht für nötig; was Shell weiß, erfahre auch der SIS."

Das führt auf die bereits gestreifte Frage nach den Informationsquellen des britischen Nachrichtendienstes zurück.

Ihre Erörterung gibt zugleich in gewissem Umfange Aufschluß über die Arbeitsweise des britischen ND.

Bedingungen und Voraussetzungen sind für die Briten außerordentlich günstig — sie waren es zumindest noch vor nicht allzulanger Zeit. Kapitalistische internationale Verflechtungen, die Weltweite des Empires, eine jahrhundertelange Tradition und Übung sind die Ursachen, die dem britischen ND. eine ideale Basis geschaffen haben. Wirtschaftlich, industriell und im Hinblick auf Handel, Finanzen, Rohstoffversorgung usw. mit allem, was damit zusammenhängt und Rückschlüsse auf Militärisches und Politik zuläßt, hat der Service einen billigen und zuverlässigen vielgestaltigen Apparat zur Verfügung, der es ihm vielfach erspart, hochbezahlte Agenten oder kleine fragwürdige Zuträger anzusetzen. Es sei nur auf die Ölkonzerne verwiesen, deren Berichte an ihre Muttergesellschaften in Groß-Britannien und USA. immer unter der Tarnung des Geschäftsberichts eine genaue Übersicht über die Feindlage (von England aus gesehen) auf diesem Gebiete geben und damit auch militärische Dispositionen ermöglichen. Nicht viel anders ist es in den übrigen Zweigen der Industrie, des Handels und der Finanz, wo Konzerne ausschlaggebende Rollen spielen, in deren Aufsichtsrat oder Geschäftsführung neben angehörigen des britischen Landes Briten oder andere englandhörige Ausländer sitzen. Die Folgen ergeben sich aus der Wichtigkeit, die man auf britischer Seite dieser „Economic War-Information" beilegte. Major Stevens hat darüber Aufschluß gegeben, soweit er es aus seinem Wirkungskreis übersehen konnte. Die schwarzen Listen waren von untergeordneter Bedeutung für den ökonomischen Krieg. Sie führte das Handelsattaché Laming in Den Haag. Man veröffentlichte sie laufend in niederländischen Zeitungen. Geheim waren sie nicht.

Three pages extracted from 'Der Britische Nachrichtendienst', the fourteen-page chapter of *Informationsheft Grossbritannien* written by the Nazi Security Service in 1940 in preparation for the invasion of England. The two pages reproduced above detail the internal organisation of SIS and correctly identify their headquarters and senior officers. The principal source quoted for the information is Major R. H. Stevens, the SIS Head of Station in The Hague, kidnapped in November 1939 at Venlo. (Left) The page shown on the right deals with MI5 and suggests Thames House is the headquarters of the Security Service; it is slightly out of date on this point. 'Captain King' was the nom-de-guerre used by Max Knight, the head of MI5's B5 (b) section.

A unique photographic record of Karel Richter's return to the spot in Hertfordshire where he had hidden his parachute on 14 May 1941. Richter is accompanied by Colonel 'Tin-eye' Stephens (in forage cap) the Deputy Commandant of Camp 020 and Major 'Stimmy' Stimson. In civilian clothes are Doctor Harold Dearden the 020 psychiatrist, and Superintendent Albert Foster from Special Branch. Also present are Major Samson an MI5 investigator whose scruffy military appearance frequently got him into trouble, Captain Eric Goodacre one of the interrogators at 020, and Major Short, who was later to give evidence against Stephens at a court martial, alleging maltreatment of prisoners. Stephens was acquitted. Richter was escorte to Camp 020 immediately after these pictures were taken and remained there until his trial at the Old Bailey in October 1941. *(Martin Dearden)*

The wireless transmitter deposited by Robert Petter at the left luggage office of Waverley Station Edinburgh in September 1940. This photograph was taken by the Edinburgh CID before passing the radio on to MI5. Petter was arrested as he tried to reclaim his suitcase. *(After the Battle magazine).* Below: A notebook filled with Abwehr transmitting instructions and cardboard code disc recovered from Petter's luggage. *(After the Battle magazine)*

Left: The British identity card found on Robert Petter. It gave the name of the bearer as Werner Wilti, a Swiss subject, of 23 Sussex Gardens London W2. *(After the Battle magazine)*

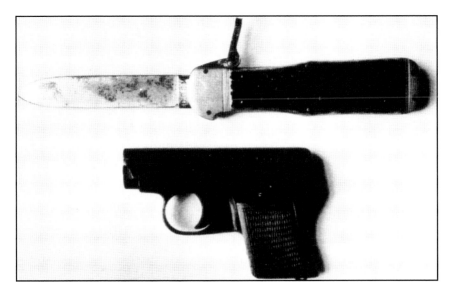

Abovve: The loaded 6.35 Mauser automatic No. 20074 taken from Karl Drueke by Inspector John Simpson after a struggle and the flick-knife found when his suitcase was seached at Buckie police station. *(After the Battle magazine)* Below: Colonel T. A. Robertson *(right)*, pictured with William Luke outside the old MI5 office in St. Jame's Street in 1979. Robertson led the highly successful B1 (a) section which turned and ran Abwehr agents in Britain. Luke was the case officer responsible for handling such cases as TATE, TRICYCLE and GELATINE and later became Secretary of the Twenty Committee. *(Sunday Telegraph)*

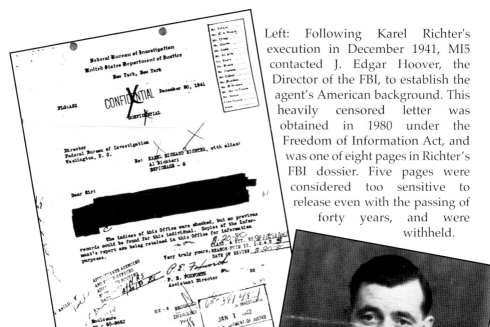

Left: Following Karel Richter's execution in December 1941, MI5 contacted J. Edgar Hoover, the Director of the FBI, to establish the agent's American background. This heavily censored letter was obtained in 1980 under the Freedom of Information Act, and was one of eight pages in Richter's FBI dossier. Five pages were considered too sensitive to release even with the passing of forty years, and were withheld.

Right: Pierre Neukennans a Belgian army officer who claimed to have engineered his own escape from Occupied Europe and was initially believed when he landed by flying-boat at Poole in July 1943. He re-enlisted with the Belgian government-in-exile but was arrested six months later. He was hanged at Pentonville shortly after D-Day.

Left: Inspector Bill Adamson of the Gibraltar Security Police having arrested Luis Cordon-Guenca, is taking him to the MI5 office in the Irish Town police headquarters - 23 June 1943. In the agent's breast pocket can just be seen the pen-like detonator with which he intended to blow up the Ragged Staff Magazine *(Imperial War Museum)*

the Phoney War, but true or otherwise, the grand plan had started with just one man – Arthur George Owens.

The Welsh Ring

Owens was a Welshman, born in 1899, who had emigrated to Canada. In 1933 he returned to live in London as an electrical engineer and succeeded in forming the Owens Battery Company Limited which built accumulators and sold them to, amongst others, the Royal Navy. He was helped to set up his own firm by G.C. Hans Hamilton, a director of the Expanded Metal Company who had links with the Deputy Director of Naval Intelligence at the Admiralty, and it was at his suggestion that Owens started to take an interest in intelligence. In due course he was taken on by SIS as a part-time agent, specializing in Naval matters. He made frequent visits to several north German shipyards on his business tours of the Continent, and his observations were considered very useful. Owens was an enthusiastic volunteer.

His SIS case officer at Broadway, however, Lt Col Edward Peal, was to have second thoughts about his new recruit at the end of 1936, when Hinchley-Cooke reported that Owens (who was later given the MI5 code name SNOW) had been communicating with a known Abwehr cover address in Germany. The LIU routinely inspected all the mail for 'PO Box 629, Hamburg' and traced any correspondents. One letter made it clear that SNOW had been in contact with the Germans for some time and that he wanted to arrange a meeting shortly in Cologne.

SIS decided to await events and allowed SNOW to keep his appointment. When he returned their patience paid off. Without being challenged SNOW admitted that one of his German sources, an engineer named Konrad Pieper, had made overtures to him about switching sides and joining the Abwehr. SNOW agreed with the plan to infiltrate the Abwehr but SIS were not so sure. At any rate SNOW subsequently was put in touch with 'Herr Müller' of Hillermann AG in Hamburg, an Abwehr cover.[24] He also met 'Dr Rantzau' who ran an import-export firm named Reinhold & Co and doubled as the head of the Hamburg Abstelle's Air Intelligence section.[25]

Although SIS mistrusted their Welshman and forbade him to continue contact with the Germans, Owens carried on sending and receiving messages via the cover address. His case was passed on to MI5, and Tar Robertson managed to develop a slightly better relationship with Owens than Colonel Peal had achieved. Most of his letters were photographed by the LIU and for a time prosecution was considered. It was SNOW himself who pointed out what a counter-productive exercise this might prove, given the amount of information he had accumulated about SIS and MI5 and given the general reluctance of judges to hear cases *in camera*. Very wisely MI5 concluded that it would be better to allow the persuasive Welshman a certain amount of rein, safe in the knowledge that he could be arrested under Emergency Regulations if and when the time ever came. In this way SNOW operated for a further three years, constantly in touch with 'Dr Rantzau' at his Hamburg cover address. By this time Robertson realized he was involved in a very complex and dangerous game.

In January 1939 SNOW told his Special Branch contact, Detective Inspector Gagen, that the Germans had offered him a wireless. This caused considerable excitement and it was agreed that he should take delivery and then hand it over to Special Branch. They would pass it on to MI5 and the SIS scientists who were working on high-powered compact suitcase transmitters. SNOW was instructed to retrieve the set from the left luggage office of Victoria Station. He was sent the ticket in the post and handed over the set to Inspector Gagen. The Abwehr asked their agent, whom they called JOHNNY and numbered A3504, to store it 'until an appropriate time'.

Unfortunately, the SIS boffins were rather caught off guard by SNOW's equipment and having dismantled it were unable to get it to work again. Eventually it was repaired and returned to SNOW who expressed his lack of confidence in the Secret Service in his usual terms. By this time SNOW had abandoned his wife and house in Hampstead and moved in with a Mrs Funnell, an English lady of German extraction who lived in Kingston. In August he took Mrs Funnell and a new recruit, Alexander Myner, off to Germany on holiday. The three were abroad for two weeks and returned at the end of August, when SNOW went to ground. He surfaced on the morning of 4 September 1939, telephoning Inspector Gagen at Scotland Yard. He asked for a meeting that day at Waterloo Station and the Special Branch detective agreed. When they met, though, he served Owens with a detention order under 18B and took him straight to Wandsworth. As soon as he was in his cell SNOW demanded to see Colonel Peal and Tar Robertson. He claimed he had something of vital importance to offer. When Robertson arrived, SNOW outlined the deal. In return for his freedom he would show MI5 where he had hidden his Abwehr transmitter and their latest instructions. He would contact Hamburg under control. This indeed was a prize. Robertson agreed and the wireless set was quickly brought to the prison cell. SNOW then rigged up the aerial and promptly made contact with Germany. The message he sent, though, was something of a mystery to the MI5 observers. It was:

MUST MEET YOU IN HOLLAND AT ONCE. BRING
WEATHER CODE.
RADIO TOWN AND HOTEL WALES READY.

SNOW's explanation for this rather bizarre signal was that the Germans expected him to transmit weather reports and he needed the special shortened code to reduce the length of his transmissions now that war had been declared. The reference to Wales concerned his efforts to recruit saboteurs amongst the ranks of the Welsh Nationalist Party and the meeting in Holland was required to make further arrangements for his work in the future. Robertson was both amused and impressed. SNOW was offering him a ready-made network of double agents who had already established their bona fides with the Abwehr. From the enthusiastic replies from Hamburg it was clear that the agent JOHNNY, alias SNOW, had successfully talked his way into the Germans' confidence. The opportunity was too good to miss.

SNOW's first operation was to renew personal contact with 'Dr Rantzau' and receive instructions and money for the largely fictitious Welsh network. On 28 September SNOW was allowed to cross over to Rotterdam and keep an appointment with his Abwehr masters in neutral Antwerp. A safe house had been arranged, the apartment of a German shipping broker living in Belgium. 'Dr Rantzau' was waiting for him with a young assistant who was later identified as Karl-Heinz Kraemer and the three men got down to business. The meeting lasted all afternoon and then SNOW returned to England – and to Tar Robertson.

SNOW reported that he had been accepted as genuine by the Germans and that his cover story had gone down well. In order to explain how he had been able to travel abroad so easily Robertson had suggested he say that permission was not hard to come by for someone like Arthur Owens, a businessman engaged in trade vital to the war effort. A second meeting a fortnight later had been arranged when SNOW was to return to the Continent with his chief agent. This 'chief agent' was Gwilym Williams, a retired police inspector from Swansea, and an activist in the Welsh Nationalist movement. Williams had all the right qualifications for the Germans and for MI5. He had retired aged fifty-three from the Swansea Borough Police in January 1939 on a pension after twenty-five years in the force. A big man – six foot two, eighteen stone and an expert swimmer – he joined the police in Salford in 1908 and then served in the Royal Garrison Artillery from 1914 to 1919. Although he could neither read nor write when he left school he taught himself in the Army and discovered he had a gift for languages.

Eventually he spoke no less than seventeen languages and dialects. On retirement he had taken a job with the Ministry of Food and had then become a court interpreter, where he first came into contact with MI5.

Williams became SNOW's chief agent and was code-named GW by Robertson. He was presented to the Germans as an ardent Welsh Nationalist and they enrolled him as agent A3551. Another meeting was arranged for 21 October, 1939 in Antwerp and this time GW went as well to meet 'Dr Rantzau'. Williams met the Abwehr controller in a suite in the Hotel London along with two other men. One was introduced as 'The Commander', later identified as Kapitaenleutnant Witzke, and the other was an older man, Major Brasser, the head of the Air Intelligence section at the Hamburg Abstelle. Williams was readily accepted and the following day the party moved to Brussels where they held a long meeting at the Hotel Metropole. The fervent Nationalist explained he was an explosives expert and was willing to start sabotage operations as soon as the Abwehr provided the necessary materials, an offer that delighted the Germans. When the two spies were ready to return to Britain they were given the name and address of agent 3725 and some instructions for him in the form of a reduced photograph the size of a postage stamp. Apparently, the internment procedure had failed to scoop up all the Abwehr spies in Britain. Apart from 3725 there was U3529, a German woman living near Bournemouth who had escaped the round-up and would act as a post-box, forwarding money to SNOW. SNOW was also given a new cypher which was to prove extremely useful to the decrypters at Bletchley. It consisted of a series of five-figure groups and was later recognized as the basis for a number of Abwehr codes.

At the same time Williams was given a cover address in Brussels (which was duly added to the LIU stop-list) and some detonators hidden in a slab of wood. These prizes were promptly handed over to Tar Robertson who informed SNOW that in his absence in Antwerp he had received two envelopes post-marked London W1 each containing a £20 note. SNOW revealed that these must have been sent by U3529 and after the brilliant detective work of Richmond Stopford, Robertson's assistant, they were traced to Mrs Mathilde Krafft who was arrested and sent to Holloway's 'E' Wing. This left only 3725 to pick up, though SNOW was instructed to visit his address and behave as if he had not informed MI5. In the meantime, Robertson interviewed 3725 who turned out to be a very reluctant Abwehr agent.

Robertson enrolled him and dubbed him CHARLIE, as has already been explained. He was not told of SNOW's double work, as a check on them both, though in time each guessed that the other was operating under control if only because each was still at liberty after numerous reports to MI5. CHARLIE was an expert photographer and the plan was that he should process SNOW's lengthy reports to Hamburg by reducing them in size.

By the end of 1939 the Welsh ring was functioning, but not quite as the Abwehr had intended. SNOW was making almost daily transmissions to Hamburg with the help of his Voluntary Interceptor Russell Lee, while GW was busy recruiting fictitious agents and preparing PLAN GUY FAWKES, an elaborate plot to poison the reservoirs in Wales which provided water for the industrial Midlands.

1940 became a year of dramatic change for Robertson. His stable of double agents to date had been necessarily limited. SNOW was the star of the pack who had introduced GW and helped intercept Mathilde Krafft and CHARLIE. CHARLIE's less co-operative brother agent 3528 had been classified Category 'A'. Several useful cover addresses had been identified and registered with the LIU. In short, the Abwehr were setting off at a marked disadvantage.

At the same time as operating the Welsh ring, Robertson and his small staff were handling a variety of other investigations and other less significant agents. In January 1940 a young Portuguese named Pierce reported to the police that he was being recruited as a spy by the Germans. The case was quickly passed on to Special Branch, who arranged an interview. Pierce explained that he had lived and worked in Germany until his return in 1938 when he had found lodgings with Mr and Mrs Evans at 41 Webster Gardens in west London. While there he had become friendly with another lodger, a young German student named Gunther Schütz who was attending the German Commercial School in nearby Eaton Rise. He admitted having spent several weekends helping Schühtz with 'industrial espionage' which involved taking pictures of various factories up and down the country. Robertson was put in touch with Pierce and RAINBOW was added to the list of double agents. Schütz had written to RAINBOW suggesting he take over Schütz's 'position' in Britain and had proposed a meeting in Antwerp. MI5 agreed to the visit and in due course RAINBOW was recruited by Captain Dierks in Antwerp. His tasks included air raid damage reports, observations on internal transport within the UK and a questionnaire about air defence and air developments. He was given a cover address in Antwerp and the official English agency of a Belgian firm which the Germans considered would provide suitable cover. RAINBOW returned to 41 Webster Gardens, reporting to Robertson all that had taken place. He also surrendered his invisible ink and a quantity of money. In future his instructions were to come in microdot form in mail from his new Belgian employers. The full stop at the end of the date in his letters would conceal a photographically reduced message which could be read with a microscope. Three months later, in April 1940, RAINBOW made a further trip to Antwerp where he received another questionnaire and three more cover addresses (two in Switzerland and one in Yugoslavia for use in emergencies) which were recorded on the LIU stop-list.

In December 1939 the Welshman SNOW had made another trip to Antwerp for new instructions and this was followed by a five-day visit in February 1940 when he was warned that he would be 'unwise to be caught on the Continent during April'. A major offensive was planned during that month which would involve Holland and Belgium. This intriguing piece of intelligence was followed up by MI5 who insisted 'Dr Rantzau' should be available for a rendezvous in Brussels on 6 April 1940. A hurried meeting took place during which 'Dr Rantzau' confided that this might be the last 'treff' for a long time. A big offensive was expected to start at any moment. SNOW made a note of this and in exchange offered a damaging titbit to the Abwehr man: he had found a London businessman with close links to MI5 who was desperately short of money. This man, William Rolph, was apparently willing to disclose (for a sum) secrets of the Security Service. This was a real breakthrough for the Germans and they suggested another meeting at which SNOW would have the opportunity of introducing yet another recruit, a small-time smuggler using the alias Sam McCarthy. MI5 were at this stage quite unaware of Rolph's duplicity and had come to the conclusion, somewhat prematurely, that SNOW was to be trusted. GW had been accepted and SNOW's Voluntary Interceptor reported that the radio transmissions were going smoothly. It was therefore somewhat alarming for MI5 to hear that the next meeting with 'Dr Rantzau' was to take place at sea. The Germans were so impressed with the ease with which GW could apparently set up illicit routes to Britain using smugglers that they reckoned it must be possible for the Welshman to get hold of a boat and hold a 'treff' at sea. SNOW was to meet a U-boat in the North Sea and hand over a further sub-agent for training in Germany.

Sam McCarthy was actually MI5's nominee, a convicted smuggler and confidence trickster who had proved himself a useful source in the past, both for the police and MI5. He was introduced to SNOW and arrangements were made for McCarthy (now known as BISCUIT) and SNOW to join a trawler at Grimsby. The Fisheries Board contacted the firm of Sir T. Robinson & Son who kindly lent a suitable vessel for the

The Welsh Ring

CODE NAME	REAL IDENTITY	HISTORY / CONCLUSION
BISCUIT	(alias Sam McCarthy)	MI5 nominee
Calvo	Luis Calvo Spanish journalist	Interned Feb '42
CELERY	(alias Jack Brown) Walter Dicketts	MI5 nominee
CHARLIE	MI5 nominee	Briton of German background
Del Pozo	Del Pozo	Recalled to Spain
GANDER	Hans Reysen	Interned Oct '40
G.W.	Gwilym Williams	Network collapsed Feb '42
Krafft	Mrs Mathilde Krafft	Interned Oct '39
Richter	(alias Fred Snyder) Karel Richter	Executed Dec '41
Rolph	William Mair Holph	Committed suicide May '40
SNOW	Arthur Owens	Interned Mar '41
SUMMER	Goesta Caroli	Interned Sept '40
TATE	(alias Harry Johnson) Wulf Schmidt	Arrested Sept '40
Yosii	Mitinory Yosii Japanese diplomat	Recalled to Japan

This table shows the links that existed between the founding member of the Welsh Ring, SNOW, and later Abwehr agents, including members of the Spanish Ring.

operation. The Master, Captain Walker, agreed the mission and on 19 May, 1940 both agents boarded the *Barbados*, a trawler built in 1905, and headed out towards 53° 40′ N, 3° 10′ E, a position just south of the Dogger Bank.

Two days after the trawler left Grimsby BISCUIT locked SNOW in his cabin and ordered the skipper to turn round and head back to England. The accounts the two men gave of the events leading up to this change in plan differed wildly. BISCUIT said that after a day on the bottle SNOW hinted he was working completely for the Germans and had duped MI5 into believing he was a double agent. SNOW denied the claim that he was a 'triple cross' and said that he got the impression from BISCUIT that *he* was the one faithful to the Abwehr. Whatever the truth, utter confusion prevailed when the trawler sailed into Grimsby having abandoned the rendezvous. However, in the midst of the accusations and counter-accusations SNOW was searched and found to be carrying several documents which most definitely had not come from his case officer even though they were actually about MI5. The source of this secret information was William Rolph. Rolph was a sixty-four-year-old electrical engineer who had been employed from time to time by the Security Service. In 1940 he was running a restaurant, Hatchetts of Piccadilly.

Rolph had been secretly recruited by SNOW and given the Abwehr number A3554. He had served in the Great War and had been presented with the Order of the *Chevalier de l'Ordre de la Couronne* by the King of the Belgians. He lived at 95 Cromwell Road, a matter of yards away from the old MI5 headquarters, and had an office in Dover Street behind Hatchetts. Tar Robertson and Richmond Stopford went round to Dover Street and interviewed Rolph about the various papers he had written for SNOW and demanded an explanation. Rolph admitted he was the author but begged to be allowed to help. He pleaded poverty and said that he would co-operate fully with MI5 if a way out could be found for him. Robertson and Stopford accepted his explanation and decided to consult Liddell on what further action MI5 should take. To bring in Special Branch and prosecute Rolph would be awkward and might well tip off the Germans that SNOW was operating 'in harness'. Later that same day though, MI5's dilemma was solved for them by Rolph. After Robertson and Stopford had left Rolph put his head into the gas oven in his office and committed suicide. He was found the next day and a post-mortem was carried out. Unfortunately, MI5 had to intervene again because any whisper of suicide might be correctly interpreted by the Abwehr as meaning discovery and exposure. The Coroner for London,

W. Bentley Purchase, certified the Cause of Death was 'Rupture of Aorta atheromatous ulceration of Aorta' – a heart attack. Rolph left £201 6s 4d in his will to his widow and son.

The whole episode had jeopardized the credibility of SNOW in the eyes of both MI5 and the Germans. 'B' Division carried out a painful session with their double agent to determine his real loyalties. As usual he was a persuasive talker and commented that no harm had been done since Rolph's offerings had failed to reach the Germans. This view was not fully accepted by MI5 who reluctantly interned SNOW but the Abwehr undoubtedly were suspicious about SNOW's failure to turn up at the rendezvous. SNOW explained he was at the agreed spot but that fog had made contact impossible.

BISCUIT's report was perhaps the one reliable source on the fiasco. He said that on the evening of 21 May a German plane had flown over their vessel and flashed the correct recognition signal. This convinced him of SNOW's treachery because the rendezvous was not supposed to take place until midnight on 23 May, 1940. This created panic. BISCUIT ordered the captain to switch off all the ship's lights and head for home.

Misunderstanding had compounded misunderstanding but it was decided to risk another attempt at contacting the Germans. On this occasion BISCUIT would travel to Lisbon for the meeting.

More signals were exchanged with Hamburg and BISCUIT set off to Lisbon in the guise of an importer of Portuguese wine. He was joined by 'Dr Rantzau' and the subsequent meetings went well. On his return to Britain BISCUIT handed over a new wireless set, an Abwehr questionnaire and $3,000 to his case officer. He also brought news that 'Dr Rantzau' was about to send an agent by parachute to England. A South African was waiting in Belgium to undertake a mission. In fact, Major Ritter had two South Africans waiting in the wings: Dieter Gaertner and Herbert Tributh. Their route to England took them to Ireland where they were arrested in July 1940. (See Chapter XII.)

Meanwhile, the other member of the Welsh ring, GW, had been relatively inactive during these hectic weeks and complained to Hamburg about the lack of support. In September 1940 these complaints paid off. He received a postcard from a man named Del Pozo in London requesting a meeting. SNOW was quickly able to confirm with Hamburg that Del Pozo was indeed a messenger from 'The Commander', code named PIKE. A rendezvous was set up and Del Pozo, a Spanish Falangist, handed over £4,000 in a tin of talcum powder and collected GW's latest reports for dispatch to Germany. The appearance of a Spaniard on the scene complicated matters for MI5 and an investigation into Del Pozo was organized.

The Spanish Ring

Del Pozo turned out to be a Spanish Embassy employee working for the Press Attaché, Alcazar de Velasco. Velasco was known to be the London representative of General Vigon's Spanish Secret Intelligence Service, which in turn made him an Abwehr agent. The ISK intercepts referred to him as GUILLERMO but nevertheless he was allowed to continue his activities in Britain until late in 1941 when MI6 broke into his Madrid apartment. This effectively tipped off Alcazar de Velasco who promptly returned to Spain. His replacement was Luis Calvo, the long-serving London correspondent of *ABC*, the big Madrid daily. Calvo was a rather reluctant recruit for the Abwehr, but an interview with Ramon Serrano Suner, the Spanish Foreign Minister and, incidentally, Franco's brother-in-law, helped to persuade him to send reports to a cover address in Madrid.

Meanwhile MI5 had made further progress in penetrating the Spanish Embassy. An office clerk and interpreter in the Press Attaché's office, a Briton named William Jackson, was recruited into the double cross system as SWEET WILLIAM. He had worked in the Embassy since 1936 and in August 1941 joined B1(a)'s growing list of agents. His role was to pass specially prepared (allegedly top secret) documents to the Attaché for inclusion in the Madrid diplomatic bag.

Also active was GW, who had continued his activities in spite of the loss of his personal contact at the Embassy, Del Pozo, who was recalled to Spain in February, and the collapse of the SNOW network the following month. In spite of these setbacks GW made contact with a porter at the Embassy who in turn introduced him to Calvo. Calvo in fact worked from an office in the *Observer* building and did not have diplomatic status, but nevertheless, as General Vigon's man in London, did have access to the Spanish diplomatic pouch, thus giving B1(a) a further channel for documents

In December 1941 the penetration of the Spanish Embassy was completed by the recruitment of Jose ('Pepé') Brugada Wood, a courier being used 'legally' by the Press Attaché's office. This Spaniard from Catalonia (with a British mother) was code-named PEPPERMINT, and successfully sent secret ink letters to Spain for sixteen months, long after Calvo's arrest and the end of GW's case. His information concentrated on aircraft production and general civilian morale.

Calvo was picked up at London airport immediately on his return from Madrid and driven straight to 020 Latchmere House for interrogation. B1(a) took the view that Calvo's arrest might well jeopardize other double agents, and indeed in February 1941 GW was forced to close down. At Latchmere Calvo was confronted with the evidence of a bottle of pills, thought by MI5's Stephens and the rest of the 'Board' to contain the ingredients for secret ink. Much to their embarrassment Dr Dearden analysed the suspect substance and declared them to be genuine pills – for the treatment of Calvo's VD! In spite of the Spaniard's protests MI5 decided to detain him and duly served him with an 18B Order. Calvo remained at 020 until August 1945 when he was shipped to Gibraltar and deported across the frontier. He spent most of his thirty months in captivity as the Latchmere librarian, and later became editor of *ABC*.

Surprisingly this did not spell the end of the Spanish network. The ring's best agent, GARBO, was proving to be one of MI5's greatest weapons, and was certainly the most complicated case of the war.

Britain's first intelligence contact with this extraordinary Spaniard took place in January 1941 when SIS refused his offer to spy on either the Germans or the Italians on the grounds that he was a self-confessed Communist, and therefore unreliable. At his initial interview at the British Embassy in Madrid his offer to assist the Allies was rejected, politely but firmly.

Juan Pujol was a Catalan businessman who had fought on both sides during the Civil War and was virulently anti-Nazi. Quite undeterred by his rejection Pujol proceeded to offer his services to the Abwehr, apparently in the hope that once recruited the British would change their mind. His plan worked. He was eagerly taken on by Karl-Erich Kühlenthal,[26] an Abwehr officer based at the German Embassy in Madrid. Code-named ALARIC, Pujol was equipped with secret ink and cover addresses and sent off to Britain in July 1941. Although ALARIC reported a safe arrival in London, he had in fact only got as far as the Portuguese capital. He began manufacturing elaborate reports, all purporting to have come from his newly-recruited network in Britain. Again, he approached the British, and again he was shown the door. However, seven months after commencing his imaginative operation his activities started to create a stir in London. ISK intercepts testified to his high standing within the Abwehr, so Tomas Harris, from 'B' Division's Iberian section, B21, went to Lisbon to open negotiations with ARABEL. Harris made contact with the German agent and his wife and arranged to bring them to London with forged Spanish travel papers, known within the Security Service as RED DOCUMENTATION. Pujol arrived in Britain in April 1942 and was dubbed GARBO. He continued his reports, and those from CHAMILUS, BENEDICT and DAGOBERT, his fictitious sub-agents.

In Lisbon GARBO had relied on out-of-date travel guides for his information but nevertheless his reports had in some respects been uncannily accurate. The second of his three 'assistants' had been placed by him in Liverpool which, in the autumn of 1942, was teeming with troops destined for TORCH, the invasion of North Africa. The agent conveniently succumbed to a sudden illness and an appropriate notice was placed in the *Liverpool Daily Post's* obituary column.

Harris, supported by his wife Hilda, proved to be a brilliant case officer, ideally suited to GARBO's temperament and character. Both men spent hours every day encyphering messages and manufacturing reports from sub-agents. In March 1942 one of these imaginary assistants (actually one of Ronnie Reed's Voluntary Interceptors) purportedly bought a transmitter, opening up another line of communication with GARBO's controller. The GARBO network thus stretched across the whole country and was to become by far the most important contributor to the FORTITUDE deceptions for D-Day. In April 1941 Churchill had formed the London Controlling Section under Col The Hon Oliver Stanley MP to oversee deception strategy, and now at Ops B (in SHAEF) Roger Hesketh and David Strangeways, co-ordinated by John Bevan of the London Controlling Section, created fictitious troop movements which indicated that the long-expected invasion would be centred on the Pas-de-Calais and Norway.

In spite of the great care that went into the preparation of the deception material, not all of GARBO's schemes worked as expected. On one occasion, while trying to give his reports of V1 rocket damage authenticity, GARBO, who was using the cover name Garcia, was arrested by a plainclothes policeman. GARBO aroused his suspicions by trying to discover the exact time of a particular explosion. Harris was unable to secure his release until news of an espionage incident in east London had leaked out. To reassure the Abwehr GARBO reported to Madrid that he had sent an indignant letter to the Home Secretary complaining of his 'unlawful detention'. Much to the amusement of the Germans, GARBO received a (forged) apology! GARBO's duplicity remained undetected by the Abwehr who, by May 1945, had supplied him with some £20,000 to finance his operations. He was also awarded the Iron Cross (Second Class), and for their part the British decorated him with the King's Medal For Service In The Cause Of Freedom. The award was made shortly after the war by the Foreign Secretary, Ernest Bevin, in the presence of the new Director-General of MI5 Sir Percy Sillitoe.

Not all the members of the Spanish ring proved as reliable as GARBO. One late-comer to the double cross scene was a Catalan separatist named Josef Terradellas, dubbed LIPSTICK. He had asked the German Embassy in Madrid to assist his passage to Britain in the belief that they had ways of obtaining the necessary Portuguese transit visas. The price for this help was espionage, so the Spaniard reported the deal to the British Embassy, who in turn made the necessary arrangements with MI5 in London. LIPSTICK survived under B1(a)'s control for sixteen months, but the agent himself showed very little interest in working for either the British or the Abwehr. All he really cared about was the separatist movement of Catalonia, and the task entrusted to him by his father-in-law Cornella, its leader in Barcelona. He was told to link up with Catalonian activists in London and this took so much of his time that B1(a) had to abandon the case in March 1944, in spite of the good results which had been obtained via the six cover-addresses thoughtfully provided by the Abwehr.

The Summer Ring

Between April and September 1940, a total of six Abwehr spies were intercepted by the Irish Secret Service (G2), as described in Chapter XII. Even though Guy's brother, Cecil Liddell, who also worked for MI5 was prevented from sitting in on their interrogations, word filtered through that at least two of these agents, Deiter Gaertner and Herbert Tributh, were destined for Britain and the SNOW network. Apart from these two, there was very little evidence of the Germans wanting to link further agents to SNOW. The obvious conclusion was a pessimistic one: SNOW's erratic behaviour on the Continent had warned his controllers of his unreliability and they had turned to other routes for infiltrating agents into the United Kingdom.

The results during the year seemed to bear out this judgment. Other sources revealed no reduction in the Abwehr's activities. An MI6 double agent in Lisbon, SWEETIE, was acting as a talent spotter for the local Abstelle. By the end of August, he had persuaded the Germans to take on two Czechs who had been serving in the French army. They became GIRAFFE and SPANEHL and were passed on to London but unfortunately their controllers in Lisbon lost interest in the low-grade intelligence they were able to offer.

The major breakthrough for the SNOW ring came during the first few days of September 1940, at the height of the 'espionage offensive' timed to coincide with SEALION, the possible German invasion of Britain. Waldberg, Meier, Pons and van den Kieboom were picked up on the invasion beaches of Kent (see Chapter IX) and SNOW was warned to expect the imminent arrival of 3719, a neutral subject, by parachute.

Regrettably the Abwehr were somewhat vague about the precise location of 3719's dropping zone but in one of SNOW's wireless messages the general area of Oxford was mentioned. MI5's RSLO for the Army Districts covering the area, Michael Ryde, paid visits to the two Chief Constables involved, Eric St Johnston in Oxfordshire and Colonel Tom Warren in Buckinghamshire. They were warned about the parachutist and instructed to put their men on a discreet alert.

In the event 3719 dropped into Northamptonshire, close to the village of Denton. Late in the afternoon of 4 September, 1940 an Irish farmhand named Paddy Daly made his way back to The Elms Farm after a day of cutting barley. As he passed through a field known as the Twenty Acre Meadow he noticed a pair of yellow shoes protruding from under a hedge. He got closer and saw the figure of a man fast asleep under the bushes. This was not such an unusual sight as it might at first seem because there were plenty of London evacuees living in the district. Very often their families would travel up on the train for a visit and then, if the weather was good, spend a night out in the open before returning to London. Nevertheless, Daly reported what he had seen to Cliff Beechner, the tenant farmer of the Elms and a Lance-Corporal in the LDV (later the Home Guard). Cliff Beechner decided to investigate further and rounded up two London University undergraduates named Brett and Slade to escort him down to the Twenty Acre Meadow. The students were working at the farm during their vacation and enthusiastically joined in the search, even though they were armed with only one elderly shotgun between them.

The four men approached the hedge at the bottom of the meadow and woke up the man Paddy Daly had found. He was undoubtedly a foreigner, in his mid thirties. He was wearing grey flannels and a good quality sports coat. His necktie had a curiously large knot which struck the four inquisitors as decidedly Continental in style. The slightly startled stranger answered their questions in good English and identified himself as Gösta Caroli, a Swedish citizen. He explained, to the astonishment of Beechner and his companions, that he had arrived the previous night by parachute from Hamburg. He then produced a loaded automatic and his wallet containing £300. At this point the little group returned to the farmhouse and Cliff Beechner started alerting the authorities. His first call was to Sergeant Smart, the commander of the Local Defence Volunteers. It was received with disbelief. Nevertheless, Beechner insisted he had arrested a German spy and advised Smart to get over to The Elms as soon as possible!

His next call was to Lord Northampton, his landlord, at his home at nearby Castle Ashby, who promised to motor over immediately. His final call was to the County Police Station at Angel Lane, Northampton, where Superintendent John Frost was in charge. He too promised to motor over to Denton and investigate.

By half-past six in the evening Caroli had settled down in the dining-room at The Elms and had started answering the questions put to him by his assembled inquisitors. The Marquis of Northampton ruled he should be allowed to listen to the BBC Radio News and the prisoner seemed mildly upset when the broadcaster, Stuart Hibbert, announced that Hamburg had been bombed by the RAF. The two undergraduates meanwhile were employed collecting Caroli's parachute, suitcase and wireless set which had been left temporarily in the hedge. He had also been equipped with a compass, a bottle of brandy and some maps which had been marked in pencil, indicating that the spy thought he had landed in the area between Stratford-upon-Avon and Banbury. All of these items were handed over to Superintendent Frost when he arrived, along with the contents of Caroli's wallet.

Lance-Corporal Beechner later made a claim for Caroli's cash from the government under a 1748 statute but to date his attempts have failed.

Caroli was calm throughout these proceedings and offered his Swedish Passport (No 2676) as proof of his nationality. He was also able to produce a genuine Alien's Registration Certificate (No 729544) dated 15 May, 1939 and issued in Birmingham by a Sgt Reginald Rowley. This document was to cause considerable problems for MI5 for at this stage the police decided the matter was a civil case and nearly ruined the SNOW ring, albeit unwittingly.

Superintendent Frost escorted Caroli back to Police county headquarters in Northampton and reported the matter to his Chief Constable, who in turn telephoned Colonel Tom Warren for advice. Caroli was undoubtedly a neutral and his papers proved that only the previous year he had been living in Birmingham at addresses in Soho Road, Handsworth, and Alcester Road South. At this stage Caroli had been in England thirty-six hours and MI5 were still unaware of his arrival. Colonel Warren suggested Caroli spend the night in Angel Lane and then be brought over to his headquarters in the morning for interrogation. There had been several spy scares in the region during the past three months and it seemed premature to stir up a hornet's nest at this point. The Chief Constable concurred and the following morning Caroli was driven to Aylesbury, where Colonel Warren was quickly convinced Caroli was telling the truth. He rang Major Ryde, the RSLO, at his office in Reading and passed on the news to Eric St Johnston in Oxford. Ryde and St Johnston both motored over to Aylesbury to see their colleague's prisoner. They found him in good spirits, sitting alone in a cell (although Caroli later stated he had been badly injured on landing. A strap on his radio had broken, hitting him sharply on the chin. Before his death in Sweden in 1975 he applied unsuccessfully to the German government for a disability pension). He willingly confirmed that he was a German spy and explained that before the war he had taught English in Birmingham. He even boasted two examination passes in English and German at the London-based Institute of Linguists. By an extraordinary coincidence, Eric St Johnston recognized one of his Birmingham addresses, a hostel in Alcester Road South, as being only yards from All Saints Road, where he had been born, which helped to establish Caroli's credibility. Caroli had been born in November 1902 at Norra Vram, a small community in the south of Sweden. He was the son of the local parson and had travelled widely in Europe and the United States. He had crossed the Canadian Rockies on foot and in 1935 had walked from Holland to Italy, where he worked for a time in a market garden. The thirty-eight-year-old Swede was perfectly candid about his past but pointed out that his sister Gerda was married to a German cleric and that to some extent his actions had been governed by concern for her safety.

Ryde reported Caroli's arrest to London in a coded telegram and meanwhile arranged for him to spend the night in Aylesbury Gaol, a prison largely housing women. It was thus not until 6 September, 1940 that Gösta Caroli officially became MI5's responsibility. He was driven under escort to 020 and interrogated to establish what links he had with the spies arrested in Kent: Waldberg, Meier, Pons and van den Kieboom. As it turned out, he had no knowledge of these other 'Espionage Offensive' agents.

At 020 Caroli disclosed his background and gave details of his mission. He was supposed to radio reports of the area bordered by Oxford, Northampton and Birmingham and assess air damage in Birmingham.

Apparently Caroli had been engaged to a German girl at some time during 1938, and while living with her in Germany had been approached by an Abwehr representative. The subsequent offer made to him was to visit Coventry and Birmingham under 'travel journalist' cover and correspond with an Abwehr address. Caroli agreed and made two trips to the Midlands before the outbreak of war.

The Abwehr then asked him to make a third trip to England, this time by boat from Narvik, in German-occupied Norway. Caroli again agreed, only on this occasion the mission had to be abandoned after his vessel was torpedoed in the North Sea. He duly returned to Hamburg and was sent on a wireless training course.

Having graduated from the radio school Caroli travelled to Rennes in Brittany for a Luftwaffe flight to England. On the evening of 30 August, 1940 Caroli boarded an aircraft bound for the Bristol area but again the mission had to be abandoned. Bad weather closed in over the English coast and the pilot was unwilling to risk a parachute drop.

A week later, however, Caroli successfully landed in Northamptonshire. Caroli said that his emergency contact in Britain was none other than SNOW – news greeted with delight by B1(a); but Caroli's real value was in the information he could provide about future German intentions. According to him, at least two other agents were preparing to land in Britain directly by parachute, and both men were known to him. They were Hans Reysen and Wulf Schmidt.

This intelligence was, of course, immensely valuable but it also presented a few problems. Caroli had not contacted Hamburg since his arrival, an oversight which contravened his instructions. There had been a delay in handing him over to MI5, thanks partly to police enthusiasm and their raids on the two addresses in Birmingham – which, incidently, revealed nothing, and the 020 interrogations too had been time-consuming because they coincided with those of the four south coast spies.

B1(a) decided the best course was to invent a story which would fill in the time-gap and in due course persuaded Caroli to radio Hamburg. In his first message he reported being injured on landing and was therefore being obliged to live rough, somewhat east of Oxford. The weather, he said, had deteriorated, and he proposed to make his way to London posing as a refugee. As expected, this idea filled his Abwehr controllers with alarm. They ignored 3719's delay in making contact and ordered him to stay put. The Germans would make all the necessary arrangements! In fact, SNOW was sent a message explaining the situation and ordering him to rescue 3719, a task which he duly agreed to undertake. Of course, SNOW at this stage was firmly under B1(a)'s control and an elaborate plan was made for SNOW to meet Caroli and bring him up to London in safety. A notional rendezvous was agreed via Hamburg at High Wycombe railway station. Caroli was to hobble on to the London-bound platform where he would be met, on 17 September, by an emissary from SNOW (BISCUIT). By this means Caroli was reportedly conveyed to BISCUIT's flat where he fell ill as a result of all the time he had spent sleeping rough.

This explanation seemed to satisfy the Abwehr and allowed the 020 interrogators to continue their sessions with Caroli who, by this time, was co-operating well and operating his wireless under the new MI5 code name of SUMMER. Robertson struck a bargain with the Swede. If he disclosed all he knew about the German agents who were to follow, MI5 would arrange for him and the others to escape a civil trial. Such a trial automatically meant the death sentence since the passing of the Treachery Act. SUMMER agreed to this arrangement and told his inquisitors about Hans Reysen, a middle-aged married man from Bremen and Wulf Schmidt, a twenty-six-year-old Dane from Schleswig-Holstein. SUMMER's crucial week at 020 persuaded Robertson that SNOW was still highly regarded by Hamburg and encouraged him to pursue the double cross game with the next arrival.

In fact, they did not have to wait long, although a flight planned for 13 September was cancelled at the last minute. Just before 11 PM on 19 September Wulf Schmidt dropped from a matt black Heinkel 111 and drifted down perilously close to RAF Oakington's AA Battery near the Cambridgeshire village of Willingham. As he jumped from the aircraft his wrist hit a strut and smashed his watch, so the following morning he walked into the village nearby and bought a new pocket watch in Wilfred Searle's barber shop. He washed a slightly swollen ankle in the village pump and bought a copy of *The Times* from Mrs Field the newsagent. He then had breakfast in a small café and started to retrace his way back to the field near Half Moon Bridge where he had hidden his wireless and suitcase. At 10 AM, just as he was crossing the village green, he was challenged by Private Tom Cousins of the local Home Guard and escorted to their headquarters, the Three Tuns public house. Here he was interrogated by Colonel Langton, the commander of the Home Guard detachment. Schmidt carried papers in the name of 'Harry Johnson'[27] and claimed to be a refugee. The explanation was considered unsatisfactory and a telephone call was made to the County Police in Cambridge. Shortly before lunchtime on 20 September Schmidt was collected from the Three Tuns and driven into Cambridge, where he submitted to further questioning. By this time there was little doubt in anyone's mind that 'Harry Johnson' was a German spy. Chief Constable Pearson of Cambridge called in the RLSO, Captain Dixon, who, at the time, was lodging in the University. They decided to keep their prisoner in Cambridge overnight and then send him down to Camp 020 by car the following day.

On the morning of 21 September, 1940 Schmidt was taken out of his cell and put in the back of an unmarked MI5 saloon next to a silent MI5 escort. He was then driven down to 020 but the route chosen by the MI5 driver had a profound effect on the German spy. Jock Horsfall drove straight through the centre of London into Trafalgar Square and Parliament Square. The young German had been told by his controllers in Hamburg that he would find London in chaos and the country generally in a state of imminent collapse. Clearly, their information was inaccurate and this point was not lost on Schmidt.

The MI5 car arrived at 020 shortly before lunch and Schmidt was welcomed to his new prison by the Commandant, Colonel Stephens, who showed him to a room upstairs. His interrogation started without delay but it was clear to the MI5 team from the outset that Schmidt was going to be far tougher than Caroli. Their prisoner was impressed by the extent of MI5's knowledge of Abwehr training techniques and various Hamburg Abstelle personalities but he consistently refused to co-operate. He was questioned about the identities of other agents he had met and was challenged on points of detail concerning his previous history, which had been provided by Caroli. Nevertheless, Schmidt steadfastly maintained his silence. At times he was even arrogant. On one occasion he told his interrogator, Alan Shanks, that the German invasion was only days away and it was 'only a matter of time' before the Commandant and his staff were prisoners themselves!

At the end of thirteen days of interviews, just when the 020 staff were beginning to despair of Schmidt's ever giving in, he suddenly announced a change of heart. He agreed to be 'turned' and offered to play his transmitter back to Germany. The transformation was dramatic. An apparently died-in-the-wool Nazi was now offering to defect. 'B' Division made no effort to determine his motive but immediately set him to work with SNOW's Voluntary Interceptor, Russell Lee, a rather pimply young radio ham enthusiast. For his first transmission to Germany Schmidt was released from 020 and driven into the Home Counties. Shortly before midnight on 13 October contact was made with Hamburg without incident. MI5 then dubbed him TATE because of his likeness to Harry Tate, the popular music-hall comedian, and the SUMMER ring was well under way.

Some years later Schmidt reflected on his dramatic switch of allegiance. 'Nobody ever asked me why I changed my mind, but the reason was really very straightforward. It was simply a matter of survival. Self-preservation must be the strongest instinct in man.'

TATE's decision to join the double cross system was a turning point for Robertson and 'B' Division. On 27 September SUMMER sent a message to Hamburg explaining that he had now recovered from his illness and had found lodgings just south of Cambridge. In reality he was under MI5 supervision at a safe house at Hinxton Grange.

Within days of this historic transmission there was a newcomer to the system. Hans Reysen landed in Northamptonshire in the same area as Caroli, but spent four full days at liberty before being arrested by a farmer named Percy Keggin in Yardley Hastings. Reysen had dropped into a copse known locally as Hollow Well Planting and had buried his wireless in a rabbit warren. For two nights he slept in the open but then took refuge in the barn of Len Smith, a local farmer. Mr Smith discovered Reysen late in the afternoon of his fourth day at liberty and accused the well-dressed young man of stealing his eggs. Reysen protested innocence, saying he was merely a visitor to the area staying with a friend, another Yardley Hastings farmer named Walter Penn. Reluctantly, Mr Smith let Reysen go but minutes later related the incident to Percy Keggin who happened to drive past on the way to his farm.

Mr Keggin then caught up with Reysen on the Yardley Hastings-Grendon road and offered him a lift. Reysen said he was on his way to Kettering. When Mr Keggin reached his home, the Lodge Farm, he invited Reysen inside and immediately telephoned Farmer Penn to check Reysen's story. When Penn denied all knowledge of the stranger Percy Keggin was convinced he had caught a German spy. Penn promised to drive over with a couple of men from the Home Guard and take Reysen into custody.

Meanwhile Reysen was growing impatient and said he was anxious to continue his journey. As proof of his bona fides he offered an identity card in the name of 'Frank Phillips', a waiter with an address in Southampton. Keggin was unimpressed and his wife noted that the stranger sometimes had difficulty in pronouncing certain phrases. He seemed to put emphasis on the wrong parts of words, such as the last syllable of Bedford. When Walter Penn arrived with Bob Ingram they too were suspicious and decided to take their reluctant captive to Bozeat Police Station. The German gave no resistance and was driven into Bozeat, some five miles away.

In the end, Reysen admitted he was a German parachutist. By 7 PM Reysen was leading Walter Penn and Sergeant Rogers of the Northamptonshire Constabulary back to Hollow Well Planting to unearth his transmitter. They also found £500 in sterling and various provisions he had brought from Mrs Harrotti's shop in Yardley Hastings over the previous three days. When all his espionage equipment had been recovered Reysen was driven to Wellingborough Police Station and later Northampton from whence he was collected by MI5 for a journey to 020. Faced with the MI5 interrogators he collapsed and agreed to transmit under control. When his equipment was examined it was discovered that Reysen's transmitter had no facility to receive signals. Nevertheless, he was given the code-name GANDER and for a few weeks he obeyed his instructions to report on morale and defences in the north-west of England. There was a limit to how much he could reasonably be expected to comment on these subjects so in the absence of further orders he went off the air the following month, November 1940.

By November 1940 the SUMMER ring consisted of SUMMER, TATE and GANDER, with SNOW on the periphery. Even at this relatively early date it was becoming clear that TATE, the agent who had resisted MI5 most, was destined to become a great weapon in their hands against the Abwehr.

From the moment TATE decided to work 'under control' he co-operated fully. His written statement to his MI5 inquisitors made fascinating reading. He completed a comprehensive history of his background and revealed he had a sister and two brothers, both the latter being in the German armed services, one in the Luftwaffe before the war. Schmidt had gone to work for a German fruit company in the Cameroons and had met his first Englishman there, a District Commissioner named Johnson. When he had been asked later by the Abwehr what name he would like to use on his mission, he had chosen Johnson. It was the only English name he knew!

He was a small, slightly built young man and certainly not unlikeable. He got on well with Russell Lee (who was about the same age) and his superior in the RSS, Ronnie Reed, and his two case officers, Ian Wilson and Bill Luke. In the months to follow he also spent a great deal of time with Tar Robertson and his wife Joan. Both found him a thoughtful, intelligent fellow. At first, he was kept under strict supervision, sharing quarters with SUMMER at Hinxton, but gradually he gained the confidence of his captors and was allowed more freedom. He was later moved to Roundbush House, near Radlett in Hertfordshire, and for a time shared the safe house with Colonel Robertson and his wife. The environment helped him prepare messages and transmit with Russell Lee in peace, away from the bombing. He was rapidly becoming the ideal double agent.

Unfortunately, the same could not be said of the Swede SUMMER. He had started off well and of course was partly responsible for delivering up TATE, but shortly after Christmas 1940, which he spent at Hinxton with TATE, he began suffering serious bouts of depression. Most of his family had become pastors and this had originally been Caroli's intention before roaming Europe and Canada without a regular job. He felt his betrayal deeply, even though he was not himself a German. He constantly launched into long conversations with his captors on the subject of duplicity. In one of his rambling discourses he let slip that his pre-war role as a language student had actually been a cover for a mission for the Hamburg Abstelle, a fact he had not previously mentioned to MI5. When this information reached his case officers he was whisked back to 020 for further interrogation to establish the truth. During his second visit to 020 Caroli slashed his wrists in a vain suicide attempt. It was then decided to allow him once again to leave 020 for a softer regime. He was transferred to Hinxton, which improved his spirits, but on 13 January, 1941 he made an escape attempt. He half throttled one of his Intelligence Corps guards, apologizing while he did so, and made his way east towards the coast on the motor-cycle of one of his other guards. An alert was sounded throughout the east of England and eventually the motor-cycle was found abandoned near Ely. Shortly afterwards Caroli was spotted and shot in the legs when he tried to evade capture. He was returned to 020 and later sent down to Nettlebed where he tended the kitchen garden. He did not, however, stay there long. He later claimed that he agreed to undertake a mission to Stockholm. He successfully contacted the Abwehr and returned to Britain and MI5 custody.

During 1941 TATE continued to make valuable progress and was apparently equally highly regarded by the Germans, who were to present him with the Iron Cross, First and Second Class, later in the war. To enable him to receive these awards he was given a special citizenship of the Third Reich by wireless!

Meanwhile, with TATE's star in the ascendant, SNOW's seemed to be in decline. In January 1941 arrangements were made for SNOW to travel to Lisbon for a meeting with his Abwehr controller, 'Dr Rantzau' (now identified by MI5 as Major Nicolaus Ritter). On this occasion SNOW was to introduce his latest recruit, an ex-Royal Naval Air Service Flight Sub-Lieutenant named Dicketts who had been refused a commission when war broke out because of a criminal conviction for deception. SNOW informed Hamburg that 'Jack Brown' bore a grudge against the RAF because of this rebuttal and was willing to betray his country. The real story was somewhat different. Born in Luxembourg, Dicketts served in Air Intelligence in the Great War. He had indeed been refused a commission in 1939 but he certainly had no intention of betraying his country. The reverse was actually true. When he met Owens in 1940 he thought his behaviour so suspicious that he decided to investigate him privately. He spotted one of Owens' routine meetings with Tar Robertson, another character he considered suspicious, and came to the conclusion there was a German spy-ring at work! Dicketts reported the two men to the police and found himself recruited as an MI5 nominee with the cover name CELERY!

The plan was for CELERY to be introduced to the Germans in much the same way as BISCUIT eight months earlier.

SNOW flew to Lisbon and made contact with 'Dr Rantzau'. A few days later 'Jack Brown of the RAF' arrived by ship and was introduced to the Abwehr. CELERY then underwent a thorough interrogation but managed to convince the Germans of his sincerity. Indeed, they were so impressed that they invited him to undergo a more detailed debriefing in Hamburg. After first extracting a promise from 'Dr Rantzau' that he would be able to return to Lisbon, Dicketts bravely agreed and spent the next three weeks at the Vier Jahreszeiten hotel in Hamburg as 'Werner Denker' answering questions about the RAF from Luftwaffe intelligence officers. Incredibly, CELERY survived the ordeal and was flown back to join SNOW in Lisbon. There they were issued with some sabotage material for the Welsh ring and about £10,000 in cash.

Both men returned safely to London and underwent a thorough debriefing during which SNOW confessed to MI5 that the Germans had challenged him in Lisbon and forced the truth out of him. Now the situation was bizarre. If indeed SNOW had revealed all, then why did they entertain CELERY? Why had SNOW not tried to warn CELERY that he had been betrayed and why did the Abwehr pass over £10,000? Were the Abwehr playing a complicated triple game?

Whatever the explanation, SNOW had had enough. Reluctantly it was decided to 'run down' his case, even though this meant abandoning the other agents who relied on SNOW for communication with Hamburg. Wireless messages were sent reporting SNOW to be in the grips of a serious illness and, a little later, his decision to close down altogether. By March 1941 SNOW was safely lodged at Camp 001, the hospital wing of Dartmoor Prison. Simultaneously the cases of CELERY, BISCUIT and CHARLIE came to an end.

Although the Welsh ring effectively collapsed with SNOW's removal from active operations, B1(a) did at least manage to retain GW who was unaffected, thanks to his link with the Spanish Embassy. Even more encouraging was the progress being made by TATE.

After some four months, apparently at liberty, TATE informed Hamburg that he was running short of funds. Special arrangements were made to supply him with cash. After his first demand SNOW had been instructed to send TATE £100 but this proved to be only a stop-gap measure. The Gemans suggested he receive further supplies through RAINBOW who by this time had moved from Webster Gardens down to Weston-super-Mare where he was working as a pianist in a dance band. Instead of following up this line of communication the Abwehr then suggested a parachute drop, before finally settling on the employment of a courier. The first two attempts failed badly. On 29 January, 1941 Josef Jakobs landed by parachute, breaking his ankle (see Chapter IX) and in the middle of May Karel Richter was also arrested soon after landing. On one occasion the Abwehr arranged for a Japanese diplomat, Mitinory Yosii, to make a delivery to TATE on a London bus. The event was duly recorded by Special Branch cameras, and the Assistant Naval Attaché was trailed back to his Embassy.

Eventually it seemed to be up to MI5 to devise a suitable method to pay TATE. They dubbed the system PLAN MIDAS and obtained the eager consent of the Germans, even though it endangered the latest of the Abwehr's networks in London, the Yugoslav ring.

VIII

The Double Agent Networks

The Yugoslav Ring

Fours days before Christmas 1940 a young Yugoslav arrived at Bristol from Lisbon, was met by Jock Horsfall of 'A' Division's transport section and driven to the Savoy Hotel in London. Most refugees from Occupied Europe received quite different treatment when they landed in Britain but Dusko Popov was armed with the best kind of wartime introduction: sponsorship from MI6.

Popov had been recruited into the Abwehr in the summer of 1940 in Yugoslavia by a university friend, Johann Jebsen, the son of a wealthy shipowning family from Schleswig-Holstein, and had immediately reported the event to the British Passport Control Officer in Belgrade, the local SIS representative. After consultations with Queen Anne's Gate it was agreed that Popov should follow the instructions given to him by the Germans and make his way to Britain via Lisbon, where the SIS Head of Station would arrange a flight for him to Bristol and send a signal for MI5.

Once installed at the Savoy, Popov was introduced to Tar Robertson and given a thorough debriefing to log all his contacts with the Abwehr and discover the Abwehr's future intentions. Popov had brought some interesting information. Jebsen, his Abwehr recruiter, was undoubtedly anti-Nazi, and reasonably pro-British; his mother had been English. Later he was to guess the reason for Popov's apparent enthusiasm for his mission to Britain and would eventually be willing to become a double agent himself. Furthermore, Popov was able to produce the name of the top Abwehr agent in Britain, GIRAFFE, a Czech already known to MI5.

Popov's appearance was considered a godsend by MI5. He had been vouched for by none other than Stewart Menzies and had delivered an agent placed high in the Abwehr's organization. Without delay MI5 set

155

about exploiting their new network. Popov was given the code name SCOUT and introduced to Bill Luke (using the name Bill Matthews) who was to be his case officer. An import-export business, Tarlair Limited, was set up as a cover for SCOUT and he was assigned a 'B' Division employee, Gisela Ashley, to act as his secretary.

Within a month SCOUT was on his way back to Lisbon to report to his Abwehr contact, Major Ludovico von Karstoff (the cover name of von Auenrode, the Abwehr Chief of Station operating under diplomatic cover at the Lisbon Embassy). The German greeted Popov without suspicion and was impressed by the progress he had made. Before going on to Madrid to meet Jebsen, 'von Karstoff' suggested that Popov try to recruit some assistants in London, in case Berlin needed to send him to the United States. SCOUT agreed to investigate the matter and in due course passed on this proposal to MI5 in London who naturally were delighted at the prospect of developing a ring to take over from SNOW.

SCOUT travelled on to Madrid for his 'treff' with Jebsen, who was later dubbed ARTIST, and then made his way back to London via Lisbon. The news he brought to MI5 could hardly have been better. He was authorized to recruit two MI5 nominees, an ex-British Army officer named Dickie Metcalfe and his current girlfriend, Friedle Gaertner. Popov's value had tripled overnight and his code name was changed from SCOUT to TRICYCLE.

Both his new recruits had remarkable qualifications that made them attractive to the Germans. Metcalfe had resigned his commission following financial problems involving a business deal in Central America. He now worked for a small arms company based in Piccadilly and was well placed to gather technical intelligence. Being rather stoutly built he was dubbed BALLOON. The second recruit, Friedle Gaertner, was a young Austrian, whose sister was well connected, in that she was on close terms with the family of Ian Menzies, 'C's younger brother and confidant. Under normal circumstances Miss Gaertner would have been interned as an enemy alien but 'C' had intervened on her behalf, as did Dennis Wheatley who gave her a cover-job as a secretary. She also had another sponsor – Max Knight of MI5's 'B' Division. In the months leading up to the war Friedle Gaertner, then aged twenty-seven, had posed in London as a pro-Nazi and had participated in Knight's operations against the Nazi front organizations (see Chapter III). When the Anschluss had happened in her native Austria she went straight round to the German Embassy in Cornwall Gardens to congratulate the regime and change her passport. The diplomats there immediately registered her as a Nazi sympathizer. She also became a regular visitor to the German Ausland organization in Eastbourne Terrace as an *agent provocateur*. On the outbreak of war, she was able to identify several candidates suitable for 18B detention.

Miss Gaertner joined the Yugoslav ring as GELATINE (because she was thought within 'B' Division to be a 'a jolly little thing') and began supplying political gossip to the Abwehr via cover addresses in Lisbon.

TRICYCLE's network had now grown to a strength of five, when ARTIST and Popov's elder brother Ivo, a doctor who remained in Yugoslavia, are taken into account. He was operating under the code name DREADNOUGHT, giving advance warning of Abwehr intentions against Britain. Tarlair Ltd thrived under the guidance of Gisela Ashley, importing manufactured goods and food from Spain and Portugal, and in Imperial House, 80 Regent Street, Mrs Brander supervised the preparation of the letters destined for the Abwehr in Lisbon. The one outstanding problem was the transfer of funds to finance TRICYCLE's agents and it was to overcome this difficulty that Plan MIDAS was created.

When TRICYCLE next met von Karstoff in Lisbon in February 1941 he pretended that he had become acquainted with a Jewish theatrical agent, who, he alleged, was anxious to export some large sums of cash and might even perhaps pay some commission into the bargain. As expected the Germans seized upon the idea. The arrangement was made perfectly simple. Whatever sum the agent wanted to export would be paid into a New York bank account in his name by the Abwehr, less a percentage cut. For his part the agent was to hand over the cash in London on receipt of a pre-arranged password which confirmed that the money had been lodged. The first attempt was for £20,000. By mistake TRICYCLE gave the wrong name for the agent but the scheme worked anyway. The money was deposited in America and TATE received instructions to collect the badly needed funds from the agent's offices at 15 Haymarket, where 'B' Division had temporarily established a receptionist. The agent himself was unaware of the operation and had not even been consulted!

Plan MIDAS was considered a success by all concerned, Abwehr and MI5. The Germans congratulated themselves on initiating a new route into Britain and MI5 had the satisfaction of taking £20,000 off the enemy and confirming the continued high standing in Berlin of TATE and TRICYCLE.

TRICYCLE made a further visit to his Abwehr contact in Lisbon in March 1941 and received new instructions. He was to fly to the United States and obtain the answers to a long and detailed questionnaire, much of which related to a US Navy installation located at Pearl Harbor in the Pacific. In his absence BALLOON and GELATINE were to continue their good work. In due course in August 1941 TRICYCLE flew via Lisbon to Bermuda where he collected an SIS escort, John Pepper, and arrived safely at Port Washington, the Pan Am flying-boat terminal. Here he was met by an FBI representative, Charles Lehrman, and driven into Manhattan.

TRICYCLE had now passed from MI5 into the control of the FBI and British Security Co-ordination. To put it mildly, his mission was not a success. He clashed with the FBI Director, who chose to remind his staff baldly that, whatever the British might think, Popov was a self-confessed Nazi spy, and after some twelve months of womanizing and night clubbing at the expense of BSC, Ian Wilson was sent to New York to retrieve the Yugoslav ring's chief agent. TRICYCLE then returned to Lisbon in October 1942 and successfully persuaded his Abwehr contact that his failure in America had in part been their fault for not financing him properly!

The Germans apparently accepted TRICYCLE's version of events because a week later he was back in Britain with several thousand more dollars and a scheme to free various Yugoslav patriots identified by his brother DREADNOUGHT as potential agents.

The project involved DREADNOUGHT recommending certain Yugoslavs to ARTIST as suitable recruits for missions to Britain. The agents would be instructed to report to TRICYCLE and in this way the Allied cause would be furthered. The first along this route was Eugn Sostaric, an ADC to the King of Yugoslavia who had failed to escape the Nazi take-over of Belgrade. He had trained as a Naval pilot before the war at Farnborough and sought Ivo Popov's help in joining the Allies. Unfortunately, his first attempt to escape from occupied Yugoslavia collapsed when he was betrayed by a friend and he had to be rescued from prison. Sostaric later learnt that DREADNOUGHT had decided to kill him in prison to save him from the inevitable torture, poisoned cigarettes were sent in to Sostaric who, being of a generous nature, gave most of them away to some Greek fellow prisoners. He was mystified when his new friends started dying. When DREADNOUGHT admitted his plan to his friend, Sostaric agreed he would have done the same in his place. ARTIST managed to devise a cunning scheme to get him out of prison and to persuade his Abwehr masters to take on such an obviously risky case, he was to become a triple cross. The Germans instructed him to confess his espionage mission to the British and then use a cover address in Lisbon which he was to keep secret.

The idea was accepted by the Abwehr, confident that Sostaric's mother and brother would be remaining in Zagreb. ARTIST gave him a Danish passport and Sostaric travelled by train to Berlin via Belgrade and was put up for a month at the Hotel Adler as a guest of the Abwehr. Finally, he got permission to continue on to Paris and then Madrid, where he reported to the British Embassy. The Security Officer there arranged for him to stay with the Yugoslav Chargé D'Affaires until space could be found for him on a refugee train to Gibraltar.

In April 1943 Sostaric got to Gibraltar and after a further delay of two weeks obtained a seat on an aircraft going to England. He then had to spend three days of interrogation at the Royal Victoria Patriotic School before being released, and free at last to contact TRICYCLE. Popov introduced Sostaric to Tar Robertson and Ian Wilson over lunch in a St James's Street club and by the end of the meal Sostaric had become METEOR and was the latest recruit into the Yugoslav ring.

His recruitment, though, was not without a hitch. METEOR came from an aristocratic Croatian background and disapproved of espionage. At first, he was quite adamant about joining the RAF as a pilot, but at thirty-seven he was considered too old. He made the strongest of protests and only accepted his MI5 role with the greatest reluctance. He was a brave officer, determined to fight in the open with his compatriots. His job in the Yugoslav ring was a cruel disappointment to him even though his reports on Naval matters were highly considered by the Abwehr. Ian Wilson was appointed his case officer and after finding him a flat in Nell Gwynne House in Sloane Avenue he started a correspondence with his 'withheld' address in Lisbon. When his case came to an end in May 1944 he was delighted to serve with the regular forces in the Mediterranean as a Yugoslav Liaison Officer under Admiral Sir John Cunningham the Naval C-in-C.

TRICYCLE's fifth recruit was again a candidate spotted by DREADNOUGHT and enlisted into the Abwehr by ARTIST. The Marquis Frano de Bona had been to school with TRICYCLE and was just a year older than DREADNOUGHT. His family had been living in Dubrovnik since AD 1023 and were a part of the region's history. He was a Lieutenant-Commander in the Yugoslav navy and had cautiously agreed to go to Britain on behalf of the Germans when asked to do so by DREADNOUGHT. In the summer of 1943 he travelled to Belgrade and received a new identity – Guttman – and instructions to report to the Hotel Lutetia on the Boulevard Raspail in Paris, the Abwehr headquarters for the whole of France.

Intriguingly, Herr Guttman was warned that if he fell into the hands of the Sicherheitsdienst or the Gestapo on his way to Paris the Abwehr would be powerless to protect him. In the event he arrived in Paris without incident and began an intensive wireless course. He then went down to San Sebastian on the Franco-Spanish border and was met by ARTIST who smuggled him over into Spain and drove him to Madrid to meet TRICYCLE. After a successful rendezvous TRICYCLE escorted the Marquis to the British Embassy and introduced him to the MI6 representative, Kenneth Benton. From there he was taken to a small pensione in the suburbs of Madrid which doubled as an MI6 safe house.

Unfortunately, the accommodation was far from satisfactory in the eyes of the aristocratic Yugoslav, and the following day he appeared at Benton's office, causing much consternation. He announced he would arrange his own affairs but would report to the Embassy every couple of days until his travel arrangements had been finalized. Benton was appalled by this astonishing lack of security from someone so vulnerable to arrest by the Spanish, but nevertheless agreed to the plan. He later discovered that the Marquis had checked into Madrid's leading brothel and never left its confines for four days. He had to agree that the cathouse had good security.

When the Marquis did emerge from the brothel he had a new identity. MI5 had dubbed him FREAK and the Madrid Passport Control Office had cooked up travel documents in the name of 'Peter Benwin', a young Canadian farmer. He was now permitted to start the first leg of his journey to Britain on a refugee train to Gibraltar. Benton sent word ahead of FREAK's arrival and Lord Gort's 'Chief of Staff' (actually the SIS Head of Station, Colonel Codrington) was discreetly dispatched over the frontier to free the Yugoslav from the awkward questions the Gibraltar Security Police would ask.

The guise of 'Peter Benwin' was dropped and the Marquis became a temporary VIP guest. The weather on the Rock prevented him from flying out immediately so he spent four days in the fortress waiting for a flight. During this period, he underwent the customary medical examination given to all newly-arrived refugees. The doctor in charge of the examination discovered that FREAK was suffering from an unpleasant by-product of his stay at the Madrid brothel – he was covered in crabs. His clothes were removed for fumigation and in their place, he was issued with a Lieutenant-Commander's naval uniform. Once this ordeal was over the weather lifted and FREAK started the second part of his journey, the ten-and-a-half-hour flight to Bristol.

On his arrival at Bristol FREAK was driven to the Royal Victoria Patriotic School, Wandsworth for detailed debriefing by MI5. Here he was introduced to his case officer, Ian Wilson, and after a stay of nearly two weeks was released on Christmas Eve 1943. He moved into TRICYCLE's home at The Clock House in Hyde Park Gate and immediately started transmitting on a wireless smuggled into Britain

The Yugoslav Ring

CODE NAME	REAL IDENTITY	DURATION
ARTIST	Johann Jebsen*	Sep '43 – May '44
BALLOON	Dickie Metcalfe	May '41 – Nov '43
DREADNOUGHT	Dr Ivo Popov*	Apr '43 – May '44
FREAK	Marquis de Ruda	Dec '43 – May '44
GELATINE	Friedle Gaertner	May '41 – May '45
JUNIOR	Hans Ruser*	Jun '43 – Nov '43
METEOR	Eugn Sostaric	Apr '43 – May '44
TRICYCLE	Dusko Popov	Dec '40 – May '44
THE WORM	Stefan Zeis	Jul '43 – Jan '44

*Asterisk indicates Abwehr officers

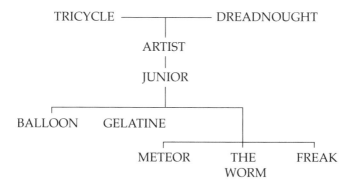

This table shows the links that existed between members of the Yugoslav Ring and some other double agents.

by TRICYCLE. Each day he conferred with either Wilson or BALLOON and then transmitted a signal to the Abwehr which had carefully been prepared by the deception staff. Within weeks of arrival FREAK had scored several successes and was highly regarded by his German masters. Indeed, he was passing some of the best grade intelligence the Germans had ever received. TATE and BRUTUS were still supplying the information but neither had access to the quality of material offered by TRICYCLE's network.

Soon after his arrival in Britain King Peter of Yugoslavia appointed FREAK his ADC, which brought the German agent into contact with some of the top Allied decision makers. Each Friday he visited 10 Downing Street with King Peter and attended the regular Cabinet briefings for Allied heads of state, and became a frequent guest at diplomatic receptions and parties in London. The Prime Minister enjoyed his company and the two men often discussed Yugoslavia's post-war future at these gatherings. The Abwehr could hardly have hoped for a more highly placed agent. Indeed, as the Normandy invasion approached it was thought that FREAK's messages were becoming too sensitive and it was decided to remove him from the scene of operations for a while. King Peter of Yugoslavia was asked by the British Ambassador to his Court in exile, Sir Ralph Stevenson, to post his ADC temporarily to the United States. The King was aware of only a part of his ADC's extra-mural activities but nevertheless agreed to Stevenson's proposal without pressing for details. Urgent needs therefore sent FREAK to New York for his monarch in May 1944, thus removing him from the increasingly detailed Abwehr questionnaires.

Although FREAK was handling much of the radio traffic for GELATINE, METEOR and TRICYCLE he rarely knew the contents of their messages, or even the identities of all his fellow agents. He had known TRICYCLE and METEOR for many years but none of them ever discussed the details of their MI5 work amongst themselves. He had been introduced to BALLOON by Ian Wilson but was never aware of GELATINE's true identity (known to the Abwehr as LADYMAY) even though he had met her several times with TRICYCLE. The purpose of all this was security but occasionally the precautions themselves became dangerous. On one occasion TRICYCLE returned from one of his frequent visits to Lisbon and congratulated FREAK on his high standing with the Germans. Apparently, they were most impressed by his reports. This made FREAK slightly nervous as his messages were produced by MI5 and he rarely had knowledge of their contents. When

TRICYCLE informed him his description of the Flying Fortress had particularly impressed the Germans he became even more anxious. He knew nothing about them and was not even aware he had sent such a report. However, before he could voice his concern he was ordered to New York.

Generally, MI5 went to elaborate lengths to preserve the authenticity of their double agents. In the early days of TRICYCLE's operations, he was escorted around the country by his case officer, inspecting all the various installations he was including in his reports. On one occasion he and Bill Luke travelled up to Scotland to spy on some Naval bases. They booked into the Caledonian in Edinburgh but during dinner the police arrived to question them. TRICYCLE had neglected to include his Aliens number in the hotel register and an observant hall porter had spotted the omission. Luke quickly intervened and explained to the Edinburgh detective that Mr Popov was in his custody and was engaged on important war work. This failed to impress the policeman who pointed out that Luke had himself registered in a false name – Bill Matthews.

Eventually Luke proffered his 'DR 1' identity card but this had little impact. The detective had never seen such a pass before (understandably, for few people ever had) and seemed determined to arrest both suspects. Luke was aghast and tried to contact the Edinburgh Chief Constable but he was unavailable. Finally, Luke managed to get through to Percy Sillitoe, Glasgow's Chief Constable, who persuaded the enthusiastic CID man to drop the case. Luke returned to London to receive a lecture on good security. TRICYCLE was assured that the police had arrived at the hotel because reports had been received from Leith that Popov's questions in pubs concerning Naval matters were suspicious, thus leaving him with the impression that no real German spy could survive long in the vigilant British Isles.

By the time FREAK returned from New York the Yugoslav network had virtually collapsed. ARTIST had been arrested by the Gestapo in the German Embassy in Madrid and sent back to Germany. The MI6 Station in Madrid reported that there could be no doubt that he was well and truly blown. He had been bundled into the boot of an Embassy car and driven over the frontier to Biarritz where he had been transferred to a military aircraft bound for Berlin. There was little chance of his escaping a very rigorous interrogation in the cellars of Prinzalbrechtstrasse. Even if he refused to talk it would still mean all his agents would come under suspicion. MI5 felt it was too dangerous so close to D-Day to allow continued contact with the Abwehr.

Effectively this spelled the end for TRICYCLE, METEOR and FREAK, all valuable conduits for deception. The sole survivor was GELATINE who continued her secret writing on political matters. She had such close contacts with the top of MI6 that it was felt to be wiser to allow her alone to maintain her role.

The collapse of the network was a particularly disappointing blow to 'B' Division because the ULTRA intercepts showed that until ARTIST's arrest its information was very highly regarded. The Abwehr had felt sufficiently confident about the ring's security to discard one of its members and allow another to fade out. BALLOON's case had actually come to an end in November 1943, perhaps due to FREAK's impending arrival but in any event, it allowed him to share some of Ian Wilson's duties as case officer for the ring. He gave up his secret writing and concentrated on supervising FREAK's activities. The only unsatisfactory member of the ring had been Stefan Zeis, a wealthy young engineer dubbed THE WORM by MI5, whose constant fights in clubs and pubs threatened to jeopardize his case. In one incident he unwisely picked a fight in a pub with two Canadian Commandos who all but killed him. THE WORM had also been recruited by DREADNOUGHT in tandem with ARTIST but his loss was not greatly felt. He had finally arrived in Britain in September 1943, shortly before FREAK, but his correspondence with neutral post-boxes was terminated in January 1944 once FREAK had started operations.

Fortunately, ARTIST's arrest and subsequent interrogation did not put any lives in danger because his link with the Yugoslav ring, DREADNOUGHT, had been arrested by the Gestapo in Belgrade just a month beforehand.

ARTIST, TRICYCLE and DREADNOUGHT had all met together in Lisbon in March 1944 under the protection of the SIS Head of Station. The two brothers had decided to keep the ring operating but ARTIST declared that he would remain in Portugal because of an intense Gestapo investigation into his recent activities. On his way back to Belgrade DREADNOUGHT received word from an SIS contact that it would be dangerous for him to complete his journey to Yugoslavia. The information had been obtained through an extraordinary route. As well as operating as DREADNOUGHT for MI5, Ivo Popov was also a senior functionary in the Serbian Mihailovic's partisan army, with the code name of LALA. To complicate matters further he was known to the Abwehr by yet another code name and had been given papers identifying him as Sonderführer Hans Pahle. Incredibly Popov was, like his younger brother, a master of duplicity, and fulfilled all three roles more or less independently, although only TRICYCLE and his case officer, Ian Wilson, were fully aware of all his activities. DREADNOUGHT had always had to rely on Mihailovic's radio link with the British and it was via this connection that London received word of his impending arrest as LALA.

DREADNOUGHT ignored the advice he was given and decided to risk his return because he had no other way of warning his partisan networks. He got as far as Belgrade and was able to spend three days at liberty contacting his Serbian networks before the Gestapo hauled him off to Glavnyaca Prison. It then became apparent that his arrest was unconnected with activities either as DREADNOUGHT or as LALA. The Germans accused him of illegal currency dealings, a crime of which he was completely guilty. He had financed a large part of his partisan network by purchasing gold in France and then selling it in Yugoslavia where the price ensured a profit of some 300 per cent. His Abwehr papers enabled him to cross frontiers without having to endure the usual rigorous searches.

DREADNOUGHT remained in prison for several weeks before escaping to join Mihailovic's army in the mountains. Meanwhile, early in May, ARTIST had been lured over the border from Portugal and kidnapped by the Gestapo in Madrid.

DREADNOUGHT immediately contrived to get news to TRICYCLE of his escape but his message was misrouted. Instead of being received by Ian Wilson at the War Office, a name given to DREADNOUGHT for use in extreme emergencies, the message landed on General Sir Henry Maitland Wilson's desk in Cairo. It was several frustrating weeks before MI5 realized that their agent was free although still behind enemy lines. Urgent telegrams were hastily dispatched to the DSO in Cairo and arrangements were made for an RAF Dakota from 267 Squadron to fly Popov out of Yugoslavia. The operation went according to plan and DREADNOUGHT was duly delivered to Bari in the heel of Italy, the SOE, SIS and OSS base of operations for the region.

However, before Wilson could get a seat on a London-bound aircraft for his charge, Popov was back in a cell. On this occasion he had been thrown into a British military guardroom for assault. Instructions had been issued to the Bari SIS to welcome DREADNOUGHT when he arrived and to treat him like a VIP. When the RAF transport landed, SIS personnel took him to a local hotel and installed him in some comfort. Coincidentally there was a visiting delegation from the British Ministry of Information in the area and DREADNOUGHT was invited to have dinner with them. All went well until one of the delegates, Konni Zilliacus,[28] made a speech denouncing Mihailovic as a Nazi collaborator. DREADNOUGHT was incensed and amongst other things, threw a bottle of wine at the future left-wing Labour MP. Before the incident could deteriorate further the raging Yugoslav was grabbed and locked up in the guardroom on a charge of assault. Ian Wilson stepped in shortly before his agent came before a court and arranged a flight for him to Algiers on 17 August, 1944, the day of the Allied landings in the South of France. He arrived at Swindon on 24 August and was put on a train to Paddington where he was greeted by his brother and Ian Wilson. DREADNOUGHT was now given papers in the name of Pedrag Ivanovitch and accommodated temporarily in the Savoy Hotel. Through METEOR employment was found for him as King Peter's private physician.

The repatriation of DREADNOUGHT to London allowed the 'B' Division organizers of the Yugoslav ring to conduct an extensive post-mortem on their operations to date. All the double agents had now ceased contact with the Abwehr and it seemed likely that ARTIST had been executed. In any event there were no more agents at risk still in the field. For two men in particular the cessation of activities meant freedom. Two Yugoslav patriots recruited by DREADNOUGHT and sent to Britain, Bogdan-Boda Mihailovic and Dragos Pavlicevic, failed various hurdles at their Royal Victoria Patriotic School interrogations and were interned on the Isle of Man. Pavlicevic was arrested in Cairo as he reported to Security Intelligence Middle East after his 'escape' from occupied Yugoslavia and had to endure a particularly gruelling journey as a detainee back to Britain. Both men were in a sense the innocent victims of the double cross system. It was thought that even the sympathetic Abwehr would have difficulty in explaining the phenomenal success of their Yugoslav ring if, uniquely, it succeeded in getting all its agents to Britain without any losses. Two token arrests enabled the ring to preserve its integrity with the German controllers.

The Yugoslav network came to a disappointing conclusion but it was undoubtedly one of the stars of 'B' Division. It had enjoyed considerable trust from the Germans for over forty months and had extracted considerable sums from the Abwehr. If the cases of TATE and SUMMER had not already been 'harnessed' the Yugoslav ring would have revealed them and perhaps a few others. Certainly, the Abwehr must have felt that the information it was getting was unrivalled – an agent close to the family of the head of the British Secret Service and a frequent visitor to 10 Downing Street who sometimes conversed with Mr Churchill. Certainly, MI6 could not boast an agent in Admiral Canaris' family or a spy occasionally close to Hitler.

The Norwegian Ring

Just before dawn on 7 April, 1941 a small inflatable rubber dinghy was rowed ashore by two men on the Banffshire coast of Scotland not far from the tiny hamlet of Crovie on the Moray Firth. Both men were carrying suitcases and were in their early twenties. They walked up the beach from their dinghy and knocked on the door of a small fisherman's cottage.

At first there was no reply so the shorter of the two men produced a revolver and tried to raise the occupants by hammering on the door with its butt. Eventually the door was opened by an astonished fisherman who was still getting into his clothes. The two strangers announced that they had just arrived from Norway and asked directions to the nearest military camp. Their English was good although one spoke with a broad Lancashire accent. The fisherman pointed the way up to the main road to Crovie and watched them return to their dinghy and remove two bicycles from the craft. They then trudged off up the hillside towards the metalled road. As soon as they were out of sight the fisherman ran along the beach to a telephone kiosk and alerted the local police who promised to dispatch a patrol car to investigate the two young men.

Nearly two hours later a patrol car found the strangers riding their bicycles on the wrong side of the road in the direction of Crovie. The taller of the two introduced himself as Tor Glad, a Norwegian subject from Oslo, while his companion explained that his name was John Moe and that he had British nationality. The two policemen listened with amazement to their story; they claimed to be German spies and offered as proof a wireless transmitter in one of the suitcases. Glad fished a loaded revolver from his pocket and surrendered it. One of the police constables recorded the details in his notebook, while the other strapped the bicycles on to the roof of the car. All four men then piled in and set off for Banff.

At Banff police station Glad and Moe were given breakfast and various authorities were telephoned by the Sergeant in Charge. One call went to the Chief Constable, George Strath, who rushed over to the station to interview the two men. Gradually word spread through the town that two German agents had been arrested and by the time Peter Perfect, the MI5 RSLO, arrived from Aberdeen that evening the spies had become local celebrities. The Mayor of Banff had come to inspect them, as had most of the local ARP wardens. When Perfect took charge, he ordered a crowd of spectators away from the station and began interrogating his captives.

It was not long before he accepted their story and he immediately contacted St James's Street to break the news. His orders were brief. Both spies were to be kept in isolation and brought down to London the next day under guard. Moe and Glad were transferred to the local prison (which had less than half a dozen cells) and given a large supper by the only warder and his wide-eyed teenage daughter.

Early the next day they caught the express to London in the company of two policemen, one of whom, Inspector Slatterer of the Aberdeen City Police, took some delight in explaining that he was an expert in unarmed combat. Unfortunately, the specially reserved carriage attracted several inquisitive glances and the ticket collector could only be got rid of after he had obtained autographs from the wicked Nazi spies. At Euston Station the four men got into a cab and duly arrived at Scotland Yard. At the sergeant's desk the two policemen were mistaken for the prisoners, because Moe and Glad were so smartly dressed, but when this initial confusion had been sorted out the party went up to the canteen to have a cup of tea and wait for transport to 020. As they queued for their much-needed refreshments word spread that there were two German spies in the room and the waitress on duty refused to serve them; eventually the Special Branch officer escorting them made the necessary threats and the party completed their meal without further incident.

An Army truck duly arrived from Ham Common and the two spies climbed into the back, guarded by an Intelligence Corps sergeant and a corporal who sported a cauliflower ear. On arrival they were ordered out of the truck by Captain Nunn in uniform and shown to their cells. After half an hour Tor Glad was led off to an examination by the Medical Officer, Dr Dearden, and a dentist. Moe was then taken for his first interrogation into one of the large ground floor rooms where Colonel Stephens presided over an 020 'Board'. This consisted of the Commandant sitting behind a large trestle table at one end of the room flanked on either side by various uniformed officers and one civilian observer at the end.

Moe stood before them and answered the hundreds of questions that were fired at him. He explained that he had been born in London and that his grandfather, Colonel P.H. Wade, was still alive and on the Retired List. He had served with the 9th Manchester Regiment. As soon as one of the officers at the trestle table confirmed this by reference to the Army List the questions became a little more civil and a chair was provided for the prisoner to sit on. Moe continued to explain that before the war he had been a regular visitor to England and had worked for a time learning about film make-up at Denham Studios. He also claimed that Trygve Lie, the Norwegian Foreign Minister, at that time in London with the Government in exile, would be able to vouch for his bona fides. At this Colonel Stephens became a little more friendly.

Eventually the interrogation came to an end and Charles Cholmondeley took both men to stay at the Argyll Mansions safe house that 'B' Division had prepared for just such occasions. The small party were then joined by a Danish-speaking intelligence officer from 'D' Division's Dutch liaison unit and the group went out to dinner at the Ecu de France in Jermyn Street. After a somewhat heavy evening they returned to the Earls Court flat and Moe bedded down in the living room on a sofa and was provided with a German pornographic book to go to sleep with.

For several days informal interrogations continued and the two men, especially the Norwegian, were pumped for Military information and questioned about the German presence in Norway. The debriefings were constantly disturbed by air raids, which had a particularly bad effect on Moe, so the two men were moved into a second safe house at 35 Crespigny Road, near Hendon Central Station. There they were introduced to their two Intelligence Corps watchdogs, Andrew Corcoran and Philip Rea.[29] Next door in No 33 were Edward Poulton, the MI5 radio expert, his wife Muriel and their son Jimmy. At first the pair were not allowed out on their own and wherever they went they were accompanied by one of the watchdogs.

The only unhappy moment here was when a new housekeeper was appointed to look after them. Miss Titoff also brought her mother and the resultant disruption led the two Russian emigré ladies to be transferred.

After Moe and Glad had settled in they were brought into London for a meeting at the Regent Street sub-office run by the formidable Mrs Brander. It was on this occasion that Christopher Harmer was introduced to the duo. This young solicitor had been up at Cambridge with John Marriott, the deputy head of B1(a), and had so far spent the war as an NCO on an Ack-Ack battery. He had been refused a commission because of his bad eyesight and one day in 1941 he had been sent to London to report to Marriott, who promptly enrolled him into MI5. MUTT and JEFF, as they had now been dubbed, were to be his first cases. After much debate it was eventually decided that radio contact with the Germans should be allowed and a small party motored down to Winchester to set up the equipment. An aerial was erected in the attic of Inspector Walters' house in Quarry Road by Mr Poulton, but unfortunately Hamburg could not be raised.

It took a visit back to Aberdeen to make a successful transmission. Arrangements were made for MUTT and Mr Poulton to lodge with a

Scottish police inspector, Jock Westland. The spy, the radio expert and occasionally Christopher Harmer took up residence in Buckland Avenue, Aberdeen, with the Westland family, which included three teenage daughters. A radio receiver was set up in the communications room of the Aberdeen police station and a direct link established with the Abwehr.

One of the major difficulties involved in sending messages to the Germans was that MUTT had to transmit for both himself and JEFF because the tall Norwegian had fallen foul of MI5.

Tor Glad had become very depressed by the constant supervision and lack of freedom at Crespigny Road although MI5 had tried their best. MUTT and JEFF had been given a clothes allowance and sent off to the Army & Navy Stores in the company of one of the guardians, a Field Security Wing officer using the alias 'Townsend' who in fact was a friend of Christopher Harmer's who was waiting to join a regular unit. They had also been given an allowance of £2 or £3 a week. After some representations this amount had been doubled but JEFF was still anxious to be given something useful to do. Unfortunately, he never got his chance, owing to a series of incidents that did nothing to impress B1(a).

The first had happened early on at Crespigny Road. JEFF had been invited on what became a pub crawl around the West End by Philip Rea. The object of the exercise had been to fill JEFF with alcohol and perhaps extract one or two indiscreet pieces of information from him that he had neglected to mention to his debriefers. In fact, the reverse had happened. JEFF had held his drink and his tongue but Rea had got very tight. Eventually JEFF had carried him home to Crespigny Road and put him to bed, but not before Rea had told some remarkable stories about his exploits abroad for the SIS. Shortly after this performance, when word spread, Rea was transferred out of MI5.

Another embarrassing incident took place in Glasgow in June 1941 when JEFF had gone to stay for a short time with another of his guardians, Andrew Corcoran, at his home in Carlisle. JEFF was instructed to go through the motions of collecting intelligence so his accounts would ring true to the Germans but the operation was misinterpreted by JEFF as a possible MI5 trap. To be on the safe side he decided to be as obvious as possible, thus proving to the British he had no aptitude for espionage. He spent a morning touring pubs in Glasgow, pumping seamen for information. Within a matter of two hours he had been arrested and the telephone wires buzzed between Percy Sillitoe, the Chief Constable of Glasgow and St James's Street.

The final straw came after JEFF had spent the night away from Crespigny Road with his girlfriend, Joan, a nurse. He broke his curfew and panic set in. After this incident JEFF was given a last chance, but then there was a further security scare. JEFF had landed in Scotland with a brand-new Leica camera, unavailable in wartime Britain. One afternoon in August 1941 JEFF took it into the local camera shop near the station at Hendon Central and offered it for sale to the shopkeeper who understandably became suspicious. He made arrangements for JEFF to return the following day and immediately telephoned the police. In due course the message arrived in St James's Street that there was a suspect in the Hendon area. The flap that ensued was far-reaching. On 16 August, 1941 JEFF was taken up to the Regent Street sub-office by Christopher Harmer and given a rocket by John Marriott. He was also informed that to ensure there would be no further incidents he was being interned.

JEFF was appalled and pleaded not to be sent back to 020. MI5 agreed and packed him off to Camp WX, an internment camp near Peel on the Isle of Man. JEFF remained there until 1943 when he was transferred, via Stafford Gaol, to Dartmoor Prison, a part of which had become Camp 001.

It was later discovered that an Abwehr agent, Erich Carl of the German War Graves Commission, had been interned in a neighbouring camp to JEFF and according to an informer messages had been exchanged between the two inmates. An investigating team was sent down to 001 to establish how much had been put at risk and the worst was soon discovered. Details of JEFF's case had probably leaked out and it seemed likely that TATE's case had also been compromised as TATE had visited Crespigny Road to see Mr Poulton.

Despite the strict regime at Dartmoor where some sixteen internees were isolated on the third floor of the hospital wing there were some further leaks. One of the regular prisoners, named Coxley, who had worked for a while in the hospital wing, had made contact with a Spanish internee who had been picked up in Trinidad with four colleagues and offered to give a message to the internee's wife, who was in London working at the Mexican Embassy. When Coxley was released he found the internee's wife and persuaded her to part with a sum of money that he promised would reach her husband. Needless to say, Coxley kept the money but he did not count on the wife informing the police of what had taken place. Coxley was charged with theft and in Court started to enlarge on what MI5 were doing in the hospital wing. The proceedings were brought to an abrupt end but it resulted in the

Camp Commandant, Major Pennell, being replaced. This prompted MI5 to send all the internees including JEFF to the WX camp near Peel on the Isle of Man.

JEFF took a long time to come to terms with his internment and frequently demanded his release so that he could fight in a regular unit, but his knowledge of the double cross system made this impossible. Shortly before he was transferred to 001 he sent appeals to the Director of Military Intelligence and even the King of Norway, but his letters never arrived. He did however communicate with MUTT, who kept him supplied with records and books. JEFF would address his letters to Crespigny Road and they would be intercepted, read at St James's Street and then passed on to MUTT. Occasionally he would request a particular item and an MI5 officer would add a line or two of permission, with his initials, at the end of the letter.

The other internees at 001 and WX were cosmopolitan. They included a Dutchman who had been connected with the Nazis before the war and had served in the Dutch navy; a Gibraltarian named Wrexler; a South African, William Boyd, who had tried to commit suicide at 020; a Welshman, Arthur Owens, who regaled everyone with his enterprises as SNOW; several Spaniards including Lecoube, who was a Jesuit priest and another who was the son of General Gonzales; two Belgians who had been arrested before Dunkirk; a Dane, Jorgen Borresson, the son of a prominent businessman who had been captured on Jan Mayen Island; a German, Otto With, who had defected in Sweden; and two Norwegians including Axel Coll, a Merchant Navy captain who later had a breakdown at the camp at Nettlebed.

JEFF's internment left MI5 with a difficult problem. The Germans would have to be told that he was no longer available but at the same time they should not be allowed to suspect the truth. In the end MUTT radioed from Aberdeen that his companion had 'joined the army' and was incommunicado in Iceland. On the few occasions JEFF supposedly returned to Britain he made wireless contact with the Abwehr but in reality his role was taken over by MUTT who devised an ingenious method of creating and maintaining a difference in style of communication between the two agents.

His own messages were translated into German from English while JEFF's messages were encoded from Norwegian. This scheme worked well and prevented the Abwehr from ever discovering that MUTT was transmitting for both men.

The Abwehr had expected the duo to carry out sabotage so several operations were skilfully executed, resulting in impressive reports in the newspapers. The first was PLAN BROCK which involved the destruction of some Nissen huts in Hampshire. Elaborate clues were left on the scene to persuade local investigators that saboteurs had been at work, but unfortunately too much explosive was used and the evidence was destroyed along with the huts. A Norwegian compass was also planted nearby to guide the police but someone took a liking to it and this valuable item was stolen! Finally, after a local soldier had been accused of the deed, Len Burt was dispatched down to Southern Command to put the police on the right track and in due course MI5 achieved the newspaper reports they had worked so hard for.

MUTT and JEFF enjoyed only a tenuous relationship with the Abwehr because, so often, their information on military matters was far from accurate. During the build-up to the TORCH Allied landings in North Africa in November 1942, they participated in PLAN SOLO 1, a deception intended to suggest an Allied invasion of Norway, an operation repeated again early in 1944 to cover the Normandy landings.

Perhaps MUTT's finest achievement occurred in February 1943 when he and his partner reported they were running out of cash. A previous request for money had resulted in a letter arriving at MUTT's grandfather's house in Rosham Gardens, Manchester, containing £400 in £5 notes. Special Branch, at the request of Len Burt, launched an investigation to determine the source but they had few clues to follow. The envelope was a common English product and the postmark showed that it had been posted in Piccadilly. The search was called off finally because it was assumed the package had originated from one of the 'neutral' embassies.

MUTT now suggested that he should purchase an isolated cottage in Scotland and then give it to the Germans as a centre for sabotage operations. The prospect of an organized group of saboteurs descending on Scotland filled the War Office with horror and the plan was quickly dropped. Nevertheless, it was decided to try and persuade the Abwehr to arrange a parachute drop so that MUTT and JEFF's dwindling supplies could be replenished. A suitable dropping zone was chosen approximately halfway between Peterhead and Fraserburgh in Aberdeenshire. By February 1943 all the arrangements were completed and a small MI5 team went up to Scotland to witness the event. They included MUTT, his case officer Christopher Harmer, Victor Rothschild from the sabotage Section of 'B' Division and a visitor from the American G2, Captain Fisher, who remained doubtful of the operation until the very last minute.

This event was dubbed Operation OATMEAL. MUTT and Mr Poulton agreed a date and details of the drop with the Abwehr from the radio room of the Aberdeen Central Police Station. The target area was to be some distance from the main road and close to a small lake. At midnight on the appointed evening the MI5 reception committee drove up to the lake in the Aberdeenshire Chief Constable's car. A large camouflage net was spread over Mr McConnoch's car and Jock Westland took up a covering position with a rifle in case the Luftwaffe decided to send an escort with the parachute. Shortly before one o'clock the party detected the sound of aircraft. MUTT immediately started flashing a prearranged signal with his torch and moments later a bomber flew low overhead and dropped a parachute. It then banked high over the horizon and, to the horror of the reception committee, proceeded to bomb Fraserburgh. This incident was most unfortunate because the RAF had been asked not to send any fighters up that night. The German aircraft was therefore completely unopposed as it made its bomb runs over the town before disappearing across the North Sea.

The parachute canister was recovered and found to contain a new wireless set, some £400 and a considerable amount of sabotage material which had originated from another British intelligence unit, SOE, which had been set up to aid and encourage partisans and guerrilla warfare in occupied countries. The party then returned to Aberdeen without incident but the following day MUTT learned that an eleven-year-old boy had been killed in the air raid on Fraserburgh. He felt partly responsible for his death and so wrote a brief letter of condolence, anonymously, to the Mayor of Fraserburgh.

MI5 considered OATMEAL a success and preparations were made again two months later for another supply drop but on this occasion the Germans promised MUTT they would refrain from covering the sortie with a bombing raid. MUTT's excuse was that he had been unable to leave the dropping zone for two days after their last raid because of police activity on the roads and had nearly frozen to death. The Luftwaffe radioed their apologies and assured the spy the incident would not be allowed to happen again.

The parachute drop happened in the same place but this time MUTT pretended not to have received the delivery, which again was found to contain £400 and more SOE sabotage materials. The Germans apologised for not getting the exact location and made another drop with another £400 and yet more SOE equipment!

Eventually, in February 1944, after nearly thirty-three months of contact with Abwehr, the cases of MUTT and JEFF were abandoned and MUTT was allowed to join a regular Norwegian unit. The sabotage duo had seemingly achieved some remarkable *coups*, including the 'destruction' of a food store in Wealdstone in November 1941 and the 'bombing' of a disued power station in Bury St Edmunds in August 1943.

For the first twelve months of his internment JEFF had been extremely angry and bitter and at one point, in April 1942, had threatened to go on a hunger strike until he was released but MI5 considered JEFF too temperamental to be allowed to leave the Isle of Man.

Slowly he settled down in his internment camp and concentrated on learning languages.

The Women Double Cross Agents

Generally speaking the Germans were rather reluctant to introduce women to the game of espionage and, according to some sources, thoroughly disapproved of the use made of women agents by SOE. Apparently, they considered SOE's persistence in infiltrating women most ungentlemanly.

In any event, the Abwehr themselves did not miss an opportunity to recruit a woman when they themselves made the initial offer. Mrs Jordan and Mrs Krafft had been eliminated from the game in the early days, but four other agents achieved prominence in the double cross system. Vera Erikson provided evidence in the trial of Karl Drücke and 'Werner Wälti' but her liaison with MI5 before the war had severely compromised her usefulness. When the decision came to be made MI5 opted for her to be interned in Holloway's 'E' Wing as a potential security risk. GELATINE of course had impeccable connections with MI6 which made her a thoroughly suitable candidate for recruitment. Her relationship with TRICYCLE so soon after arriving in England made the Yugoslav ring an obvious choice and certainly the Germans raised no objections to her recruitment.

Another Yugoslav, operating independently on TRICYCLE, was THE SNARK, a domestic servant working in London for an English family. She had arrived as a refugee in July 1941 and for the next twenty months answered Abwehr questions concerning morale and food supplies. The Germans found her particularly well placed to detail food shortages and the difficulties experienced by Londoners queuing with their ration books.

Another source of political gossip for the Abwehr was the brave and beautiful divorced wife of a South American diplomat based in London. She was in fact an MI6 agent who had done valuable work in France during 1941 and 1942. Her friend Felipe Benavides (a Peruvian diplomat, and now Ambassador to London) introduced her to Dick

Brooman-White head of MI5's Iberian Section, B21. She was accepted as an MI5 source, but was to develop further. After one particularly hazardous mission to France she revealed to her MI6 case officer that the Germans had approached her with an offer of work. She had been supplied with a letter-box address and her case was immediately passed on to MI5. Christopher Harmer was assigned as her case officer in London and he dubbed her BRONX after the fashionable cocktail because he thought her so sophisticated! BRONX, a friend of many influential figures including Lord Mountbatten, continued supplying her cover addresses with information until shortly before D-Day.

Perhaps the most remarkable of all the women double agents was TREASURE, who, as her name suggests, was a highly valued member of the game. Lily Sergueiev first became known to MI5 when she applied for a visa from the British Embassy in Madrid in June 1943, giving the name of a cousin in Cambridge as a reference. A routine check with the cousin, Elizabeth, revealed she was less than happy about being used as a reference. Apparently, Lily had been born in Russia in 1915 but had spent most of her life living in Paris as an artist and journalist. Before the war she had obtained an interview with Hermann Goering and had published an article which received plenty of publicity. For someone trying to enter Britain in the middle of the war this qualification was less than desirable. It also transpired that her uncle was General Miller, the Russian emigré leader who had been kidnapped in a Paris street in September 1937. Miss Sergueiev's case was thought to merit further attention and she was called to a meeting with Kenneth Benton, the SIS Head of Station in Madrid.

Almost as soon as the interview began, on 17 July, 1943, Lily volunteered a mass of valuable intelligence. She claimed to have been recruited in Paris by the Abwehr to spy in Britain. She was equipped with cover addresses and secret ink and gave a detailed description of her German case officer, Emile Kliemann, whom she had known for two years.

When this news was received in St James's Street there was much debate. Major Kliemann was already well known to MI5 as DRAGONFLY's controller. It was agreed that Lily should come to London and see if the Germans intended to develop their Paris-based operations against Britain. Accordingly, SIS were asked to arrange for Lily's journey but this turned out to be no easy matter. The original plan was for Lily to stay in Madrid, keeping in contact with the local Abwehr staff until travel documents had been issued for her to fly to Britain from Lisbon. The Portuguese authorities, however, were somewhat chary of

Russian names and at the end of August 1943 refused Lily a transit visa. The Portuguese Secret Police, PIDE, suspected everyone with a Russian name of being a Soviet spy!

After much delay, arrangements were made for Lily to go by train to Gibraltar and she duly arrived at the frontier at La Linea on 8 October, 1943. There was then another complication. Lily had only agreed to co-operate with the British if her dog Babs, whom she adored, was allowed to accompany her. Benton had somewhat unwisely agreed that the Secret Intelligence Service could circumvent the quarantine regulations and promised that Babs would be allowed into Britain. News of this promise had not reached Gibraltar and Babs had to be left in the care of a Gibraltar Security Policeman who accepted the dog into the frontier kennel. Once Codrington's assistant, Captain O'Shagar, had wrenched Lily away from Babs he installed her in the Grand Hotel and sent a coded telegram to London.

After further delay on the Rock arrangements were made for Lily to fly to London with papers identifying her as 'Dorothy Tremaine'. Early in the morning of 5 November, 1943 she landed in Bristol – without Babs. The wretched dog was left at the Spanish frontier in the care of the GSP on the understanding that an American pilot had agreed to smuggle the animal into Britain. The promise was never kept, a failure which later created tremendous problems for MI5.

'Dorothy Tremaine' was met at Bristol by a uniformed police-woman and escorted to London on the train. At Paddington she was driven to Holloway and placed in the care of Mrs Maud, the very capable Governor who supervised MI5's more sensitive women internees. Five days of detailed interrogations followed during which time there was a development in DRAGONFLY's case. He had received a wireless message from the Abwehr informing him of Oscar Job's imminent arrival from Lisbon with funds. (Job was arrested on 22 November, 1943. See Chapter IX.) To the men of 'B' Division this was as clear an indication as the Abwehr were likely to give that a new lease of life for their double agent DRAGONFLY was under way. This story is told in Chapter IX.

Lily successfully negotiated her way through the minefield of her interrogation and was released, under close supervision, on 12 November, 1943. She was installed at a safe house in Rugby Mansions, a large block of flats opposite Olympia, and was interviewed by Tar Robertson. He formed a cautiously good opinion of her and approved her recruitment as TREASURE. She was then visited by Ronnie Reed who debriefed her to learn more of the latest German wireless techniques. By the end of a morning's questions Reed had discovered the type of set used by TREASURE and her instructors in Paris. She had been presented with a selection of photographs of radio sets and eventually found one identical to her original set. She had been instructed to wait for her transmitter which was to be delivered via some unnamed Portuguese courier. In the meantime, she had to rely on secret writing to two addresses, one in Spain, the other Sweden.

After a weekend visit to Cambridge to see her cousins, TREASURE settled down with friends in the village of Wraxall, near Bristol. From MI5's point of view this was ideal because the D-Day deceptions hinged on an informant in the West of England who could tell the Germans that there was no noticeable build-up of troops in the region. Naturally, an invasion centred in Normandy would involve sizeable troop movements to the ports of Dorset, Devon and Cornwall. TREASURE had been asked by the Abwehr to log such details of the military as she could find and then send them to her neutral cover addresses. With the aid of 'B' Division personnel she started this correspondence and received coded replies on regular German broadcasts on a household radio. However, after just two weeks' work in Bristol she returned to London and had a stormy interview with her MI5 contact[30] Mary Shearer who, understandably, had put her dog Babs rather low on the list of wartime priorities. TREASURE announced that unless she was assured that Babs was on his way, she would stop sending her MI5-instructed letters to the Abwehr. The B1(a) staff were aghast at this ultimatum but before they could make TREASURE see reason she was admitted to St Mary's Hospital, Paddington, with a serious kidney complaint.

TREASURE spent Christmas 1943 in hospital and was discharged early in the New Year. The spell in bed, combined with visits from Tar Robertson bearing bunches of flowers, seemed to have a marked effect on the young woman. She wrote to Kliemann via a cover address informing him that she had now bought an American Halicrafter radio (actually supplied by Ronnie Reed) and on 23 January, 1944 was rewarded with a brief message from Paris which simply stated:

INFORMATION VERY INTERESTING-
LETTERS ARRIVE WELL
CONTINUE - YOU ARE VERY CHARMING:

The final comment raised some eyebrows in St James's Street but TREASURE insisted it had no hidden meaning. It was, she claimed, typical of Kliemann to have given her that sort of encouragement. This explanation was accepted and over the following month TREASURE worked well without any further demonstrations of temperament. The American pilot to whom she had entrusted Babs had cabled from Gibraltar with the news that the wretched animal had been passed into the care of TREASURE's sister who lived in Casablanca. This apparently satisfactory compromise was spoiled some days later by the arrival of a letter from the sister breaking the news that Babs had been accidentally run over.

By the end of February 1944 TREASURE had become one of the most important double agents. Her reports from Bristol held the greatest significance for the Germans. If she could not detect any massive troop movements then messages from other sources indicating build-ups in the east of England were given more credence. The inescapable conclusion would be that the invasion was destined for the Pas-de-Calais area.

TREASURE had also grown in stature because of the dwindling number of reliable double agents in contact with the Abwehr left in Britain. Reluctantly MI5 had taken DRAGONFLY (see Chapter IX) out of circulation in January because his continued unfunded service might have tipped off Kliemann, his controller. MUTT and JEFF closed down in February when it seemed likely that the Germans had begun to suspect their reports. The vital D-Day FORTITUDE deceptions relied on a variety of informants all contributing to the same picture but few were strategically placed to observe military preparations first hand, thus giving the messages the authentic ring the Abwehr set so much store by. GARBO was permanently in London but TATE at least was able to notice First United States Army Group units on his visits to a farm near Wye in Kent. In fact, TATE was now based in Hertfordshire, notionally employed on a farm in Radlett. His employer allegedly had a friend living near Wye who needed extra help. By this rather flimsy excuse TATE was put in a position to overhear conversations and watch American infantry massing for the D-Day assault.

In fact, TATE never made most of these visits. A transmitter was set up in Kent by the RSS and a direct GPO telephone line was used to operate the set remotely. This ploy ensured that if the Abwehr took direction-finding fixes on their agent they would find that he was in fact where he claimed to be.

With all this activity in the east of England it was essential to reassure the Germans that all was relatively quiet in the west. TREASURE was the only suitable conduit because her Paris controller knew of her friends at Wraxall. The drawback to TREASURE, apart from her tempestuous nature, was the time lapse before her letters finally reached the Abwehr. She had been fully trained in wireless technique but to date the Germans had failed to deliver a set to her. Whilst this was a source of some self-congratulation in St James's Street it left the deception planners with a serious problem.

The solution was for TREASURE to return to Lisbon and persuade Major Kliemann to give her a set there and then. TREASURE would have to satisfy him that she had a good way of avoiding the British controls on her return with the contraband.

On 2 March, 1944, TREASURE flew to Lisbon in a desperate attempt to improve her method of communication. Her cover was dreadfully inadequte. She claimed to be working for Sidney Bernstein, the film producer, in the Ministry of Information and had come to Portugal to recruit professionals from the Continent who would add some realism to the Ministry of Information documentaries.

Very little preparation had been given to her story. Ronnie Reed had conducted a final briefing and she was driven past the MOI so that at least she knew where her supposed office was. She had been told to say that her job had been obtained for her by her influential cousin in Cambridge and that she had been chosen to go to Lisbon because, being French, she was thought to have the qualities necessary for persuading French and Belgian refugees to participate in a propaganda film. Obviously, the story was full of holes but TREASURE was given a rousing send-off by Tar Robertson and duly arrived in Lisbon early in the morning of 3 March, 1944.

TREASURE checked in at the British Embassy Press Office and the local SIS Station. She also contacted the Abwehr but discovered that her Paris controller had not yet arrived in Lisbon. TREASURE endured more than two weeks of frustration waiting for Kliemann before he finally turned up with a converted American radio on 20 March. He seemed quite unaware of the ease with which his agent had obtained a much sought-after position in the MOI or her apparent freedom to travel to a neutral country. TREASURE assured him that her MOI pass would allow her to avoid a Customs search on her return. He appeared satisfied by this and four days later she flew to Bristol with her transmitter, a valuable bracelet and £1,500 in notes stuffed in a shoe box.

As a reward for a successful mission TREASURE was given new quarters, this time at Flat 83, 39 Hill Street in the heart of Mayfair. Ronnie Reed and Russell Lee were on hand to debrief her – and relieve her of the £1,500. Sir Edward Reid Bt, a director of Baring Bros, the City Bankers, was Guy Liddell's first cousin by marriage, and was recruited by him as 'B' Division's expert on financial matters. He looked at the money and found that unfortunately, some thirty-nine of the £10 notes were forgeries, which sparked off another debate in St James's Street about TREASURE's standing with the Abwehr. D-Day was now only weeks away and B1(a) decided to take the risk and allow TREASURE to make radio contact, though only under the supervision of Russell Lee.

The first transmission took place late in the evening of 14 April, 1944 but the attempt ended in failure. A house high up in Hampstead had been chosen as a base but the Germans failed to acknowledge. After nearly a month of fruitless effort Reid and Lee moved the transmitter to a borrowed house in Palace Gardens Terrace, just north of Hyde Park. On 10 May, 1944, their signal was answered and TREASURE was able to start a regular schedule of transmissions.

By this date the RSS had accumulated a considerable amount of knowledge about German radio techniques and had little difficulty in reproducing the so-called fingerprint of operators. When TATE went into hospital for an ulcer operation. Russell Lee had taken control of his transmissions. The regular Abwehr operator appeared not to notice the change so it was decided to continue the arrangement even after TATE had been discharged and was fit to resume his duties. B1(a) considered a second change-over unnecessarily risky and thereafter had TATE supervising Lee in much the same way as MUTT had imitated JEFF's signals for more than two years.

TREASURE must have sensed that B1(a) had almost got to the point where the RSS could take over completely because she suddenly mentioned two days before D-Day that while in Lisbon Kliemann had given her a security check which only she knew. MI5 were appalled, but TREASURE absolutely refused to reveal how the check worked. She merely warned that MI5 would be unwise to discard her or try and operate her set alone. Naturally Robertson was furious at this breach of faith but TREASURE retorted that she owed the British nothing. After all, she said, they had failed to keep their promise about Babs! The head of B1(a) had no choice but to end her case, or so he told her. She was informed that as of 14 June, 1944 she was no longer employed by the British War Office. Unknown to her, the RSS operated her set for a further five months. This was made possible by TREASURE herself, who confessed the security check to her MI5 contact the following day, perhaps after an attack of conscience. It turned out to be a positive check, one which involved an addition to her message if she was sending under duress. If she inserted two dashes between her call sign and the beginning of her message the Germans would understand that she had been arrested. The message was only to be considered genuine if certain omissions were made in the text. Thus, a perfect message spelt correctly throughout would indicate enemy control over the operator. Most British operators were trained to use a negative security check.

By the end of June 1944 TREASURE had joined the French army and shortly after the liberation of Paris was reunited with her parents, who had lived in the capital throughout the occupation. By a curious irony, Major Kliemann was arrested in France in August and brought to Camp 020 for interrogation. Thus, TREASURE was in France while her Abwehr controller was in custody in England.

The Polish Ring

The first of the Polish double agents was CARELESS, an air force pilot shot down by the Germans in 1939. He went underground in France and made his way across the frontier to Spain. By July 1941 he had succeeded in getting to England but during his sea voyage he had confided details of his Abwehr spying mission to three fellow Polish refugees who denounced him to the British authorities at their first opportunity.

The patriotic Poles were assured their companion would be dealt with and encouraged to forget the incident. Subsequently CARELESS wrote under supervision to his post-box and received an encouraging reply from the Abwehr. Clearly news of his MI5 interception had not leaked to the Germans. His task was to report on RAF matters and a job was invented for him in an anti-aircraft battery. His letters were filled with details in secret writing of British defences against airborne attack.

Unfortunately, CARELESS proved a less than satisfactory double agent and MI5 were obliged to intern him at the end of 1942. Nevertheless, his correspondence was maintained until in January 1943 he refused to co-operate further. A promising case was thus abandoned but luckily a newcomer arrived in October 1942 who became a tremendous asset to 'B' Division and was eventually awarded the OBE.

In one sense BRUTUS was no newcomer to the world of intelligence. He was Roman Garby-Czerniawski, a Polish air force pilot who had been attending a French staff course when war broke out and had been unable to return to Poland. Instead of making his way to Britain he remained in Paris with false civilian papers and began organizing an embryonic resistance network. On 10 May, 1941 he made contact with London on an SIS transmitter. Using the code name ARMAND Garby-Czerniawski became the chief organizer of the INTERALLIE resistance network. INTERALLIE was phenomenally successful and operated branches throughout France until the whole network was betrayed to the Germans on 18 November, 1941.

Garby-Czerniawski's arrest in fact paved the way for his new role as a double agent for MI5. The Abwehr were anxious to send agents to

Britain and the chief of INTERALLIE was desperate to save the members of his network who had been betrayed. Eventually a deal was struck. The Pole would be allowed to make a dramatic escape in Paris and he would then make his way to Britain where, the Germans thought, his previous credentials would ensure an important position in the Allied intelligence hierarchy. For their part the Abwehr guaranteed to save the lives of the INTERALLIE personnel and treat them as POWs. If Garby-Czerniawski failed to deliver the required information his helpers would all be executed.

The elaborate escape plan in fact did not take place for reasons that were never made clear by the Paris Abwehr; instead the chief of INTERALLIE was released from Fresnes Prison through the front door. He was allowed to make his way to Madrid where he reported in October 1942 to Kenneth Benton, who immediately contacted London.

MI5 headquarters had been in contact with INTERALLIE almost every day until its betrayal; now they arranged for Garby-Czerniawski to come to London via Gibraltar.

Once in London he was housed by the exiled Polish intelligence service and SIS at a safe house in Church Street, Putney and underwent a thorough debriefing at the hands of MI6 and Colonel Gano, the Chief of Polish Intelligence in London. After several days he was released although at this stage he had not admitted his deal with the Abwehr. His reason for this omission was one of security. He was reluctant to explain his phoney escape immediately because he could not be sure news of his confession would not reach the Germans. He would confess all in due course.

Once passed by SIS and his own security inquisitors he took Colonel Gano out to lunch in Piccadilly and told him the full story. At first the Polish Deuxième Bureau were unsure what to do and Garby-Czerniawski's case was handed back to MI6 who in turn passed the file to MI5's 'B' Division. To them the solution was obvious. The Pole was a bona-fide double agent who had kept the best possible security. The Polish airman was dubbed BRUTUS in January 1943 and began transmitting military information to the Germans under the guidance of his case officer, Hugh Astor.

MI5 faced several problems in developing the Polish ring which were brand new and originated from within the circle of Allies. The Poles themselves were perfectly content to leave matters in the hands of MI5 and probably were rather relieved not to have to deal with the BRUTUS case. In any event they were never allowed to learn the full details. The Russians, though, posed almost insurmountable difficulties. They were at the best of times suspicious of British relations with the Nazis and the prolonged use of a Polish conduit was quite unacceptable to them, according to the Foreign Office. In normal circumstances these objections would have been ignored by MI5 on operational grounds but in the case of BRUTUS the Russians had some justification for their unease. He was violently anti-Soviet and was very active in the internal politics of the Polish government in exile. At one point in June 1943 he was involved in court martial proceedings instituted by the Poles but fortunately survived. The other fact that 'B' Division could not ignore was the attitude of the Germans in the case. BRUTUS had been under their care for nearly nine months after the betrayal of the INTERALLIE network and there was every chance they had been able to assess his character in that time. Might they not have realized he would never sell out the Allies? If they had come to that conclusion, might they not be reading his reports with an educated eye? Taking this into account it was decided to use BRUTUS but restrict his information to military intelligence of a non-operational nature. Gradually it was realized that MI5's initial fears had been groundless. The Germans welcomed his reports and, according to ISK decrypts, acted on them.

BRUTUS operated successfully for the following two years; it was then decided to lift the restriction on him concerning the operational value of his messages. As D-Day approached he became increasingly involved in the deception plans for OVERLORD and, with TREASURE, became the principal source of intelligence for the Paris Abstelle. His case finally had to be wound up when the French authorities began examining the betrayal of INTERALLIE and placing those responsible on trial. MI5 felt that any public disclosures concerning the leader of INTERALLIE would make his role as a credible double agent untenable. Reluctantly, as the trial of Mathilde Carré began, BRUTUS faded out.

The third Pole to be recruited to spy in Britain was ROVER, a professional boxer who joined the Polish navy early in 1939. He was taken prisoner the same year by the Germans and eventually, in June 1942, recruited into the Abwehr after many harrowing experiences as a forced labourer. He finally made his way to Spain and arrived in England in May 1944. In spite of all the morse training the Germans had obviously given him there was no response to his letters and in September 1944 B1(a) reluctantly sent him back to the Polish navy. Almost as soon as this was done MI5 regretted it. ROVER had not been provided with a transmitter by the Abwehr but had been taught how to build one. While he was in London the Germans failed to communicate, but once he was returned to his duties in October the Voluntary Interceptor picked up and acknowledged signals meant for him. The VI, Mr Reason, seemingly convinced the Abwehr operator he was in touch with ROVER and the deception worked well until November when the VI went into hospital. Unfortunately, the VI died in hospital, which forced MI5 to appoint a third ROVER. The changeover went unnoticed and the new ROVER explained in January 1945 that he had been hit by a lorry two months earlier and therefore had been unable to make contact. The Germans accepted this explanation of ROVER's absence during the preceding two months and remained in touch until the end of the war.

The French Ring

The most successful contacts with the Abwehr based in France were achieved through BRUTUS and TREASURE but they were not entirely alone. In June 1942 a Luxembourger arrived in Britain with instructions to send reports back to the French Vichy government which co-operated with the Nazis. Essentially this case was an internal French affair although MI5 were keen to discover if the Vichy intelligence organs had infiltrated other agents into Britain. He was code-named CARROT but was only able to operate for five months until December 1942 when his case was abandoned. His appearance in England had attracted the attention of the Deuxième Bureau, which complicated matters. Apart from the American OSS most foreign intelligence services based in London were treated with caution by MI5, partly because this was the province of SIS and partly because most were thought to have low standards of security. The French however were particularly troublesome and de Gaulle's own intelligence organization, BCRA, were a constant thorn in the side of 'E' Division. B1(a) allowed CARROT's case to collapse because to continue with him would have meant unacceptable political run-ins with the French as well as revealing to them something of 'B' Division's activities, a prospect the Twenty Committee categorically refused to contemplate.

Only two French double agents were run by B1(a). FIDO was a French air force pilot who made his way to Britain in July 1943 with instructions to send his military observations to a cover address in secret writing and eventually to steal an aeroplane and fly it to the Germans. Naturally the latter part could not be allowed but he did communicate via a neutral country for seven months. His case was abandoned because of the lack of any methods of return communication from the Abwehr and a few doubts about FIDO's reliability.

In SHEPHERD MI5 had a curious case. The SIS station in Madrid had previously obtained the services of an Abwehr talent-spotter whom they code-named NETTLE. Unfortunately, NETTLE's standing was not particularly high and it was thought that if he managed to recruit a really successful agent he might become an important figure and therefore get access to further German secrets. Thus, at SIS's request SHEPHERD was established in London in March 1944. Like FIDO his case was difficult to develop because he had only been equipped with cover addresses and therefore had no way of receiving messages from the Abwehr. After six months the RSS took over the task of preparing the letters in the hope of improving NETTLE's fortunes.

CARROT, FIDO and SHEPHERD contributed little to either Allied deception strategy or the double cross system but B1(a) was optimistic about one particular Abwehr agent long before he even arrived on British soil.

From May 1942 ISK intercepts of Abwehr messages in France revealed the existence of an apparent English renegade willing to return to the British Isles and execute various acts of sabotage. Little was known of him apart from the barest clues to his background. According to the Germans he had an authentic grudge against the British establishment. He was himself a young British subject from Sunderland, based in London. He had been selected for training from the internment camp at St Denis and previously had been imprisoned in Jersey. MI5 were able to follow FRITZCHEN's progress through Abwehr establishments at Nantes, Paris and Berlin. He was considered a star performer by the Germans and underwent a thorough training in sabotage, wireless techniques and parachuting. By December 1942 a clearer picture had emerged. FRITZCHEN was using the name of Fritz Graumann and was being prepared for a sabotage mission to England. He had apparently signed a contract with the Nantes Abstelle which gave him a regular salary of 450 Reichmarks a month with a special bonus of 100,000 Reichmarks (£15,000) if he succeeded in completing his mission in England. The mission involved the destruction of the de Havilland Mosquito factory near Hatfield.

All of this information was gleaned from ULTRA sources but MI5 were unaware of either the exact date of FRITZCHEN's mission or the location of the dropping zone beyond the general area of East Anglia. To be on the safe side Michael Ryde was dispatched to Cambridge in the middle of December 1942 to await FRITZCHEN's arrival. The German agent was due to depart to Paris on 17 December, 1942 in preparation for a flight from Le Bourget.

FRITZCHEN landed by parachute late in the night of 20 December, 1942 near the Isle of Ely in Cambridgeshire. He was equipped with a wireless, loaded automatic, 'L' pill and £1,000 in cash. As soon as he was on the ground he gathered up his espionage paraphernalia and walked to the nearest farmhouse. Having woken the occupants FRITZCHEN identified himself as a downed Allied flier and asked to use the telephone. He dialled 999 and asked the police for transport. When eventually a police car arrived FRITZCHEN ordered a bewildered constable out into the nearby field to collect parachute, overall and jump-boots.

Some four hours later in Littleport Police Station FRITZCHEN identified himself to the Chief Constable of Cambridgeshire and Major Ryde as Edward Chapman, a London safe-breaker with a considerable police record. He volunteered the information that he had been sent to England by the Germans to spy. Chapman was the man MI5 had been so eagerly waiting for. He was driven straight down to London and was received at 020 after a brief interrogation by Len Burt. The Germans, he claimed, had recruited him in Jersey, where he was awaiting trial for burglary. Apparently, he had cracked a safe in Glasgow before the war and had finally been caught by the police in St Helier.

At 020 Chapman underwent further questioning at the hands of Colonel Stephens, during which a misunderstanding arose over Chapman's use of an alias 'Edward Arnold'. His police record was in that name while his Army records showed that Edward Chapman had been discharged from the Coldstream Guards in June 1933. For a while it seemed that FRITZCHEN was a highly-trained triple cross agent out to dupe his captors. For that reason, Chapman spent forty-eight unpleasant hours at Camp 020. And all that time he was offering to transmit back to Baron von Grunen, his Abwehr controller. Eventually Chapman was allowed to use his set and under supervision sent a brief message to the Germans:

WELL – AM WITH FRIENDS – GOOD LANDING – FRITZ

The following day an acknowledgment was received and FRITZCHEN was wished good luck. MI5 now dubbed him ZIGZAG and his debriefing continued. This however was not what Chapman had in mind and in a tempestuous meeting with the Camp Commandant on Christmas Eve he demanded his release from 020 – or else.

Unknown to ZIGZAG, B1(a) had already arranged for his departure. Tar Robertson billeted him at 35 Crespigny Road, the safe house next door to Edward Poulton, now vacated by MUTT and JEFF.

Having established contact with the Abwehr ZIGZAG began planning his mischief at the de Havilland factory. He and Michael Ryde drove up to Hatfield in the New Year to reconnoitre the target and decided to blow up the power plant. The next problem was the sabotage material itself but again ZIGZAG offered unorthodox help. Before the war he had robbed a stone quarry near Sevenoaks for explosives and MI5 were quickly able to confirm that the quarry was still in business. ZIGZAG therefore notionally burgled its stores and seized enough gelignite to deal with de Havillands.

On 29 January, 1943 ZIGZAG and Michael Ryde went through the motions of laying charges around the power plant while Jasper Maskelyne, the camouflage expert, and famous magician, scattered debris in the area. Later that night ZIGZAG returned to London and reported a successful explosion. B1(a) arranged for several newspapers to report the sabotage and officially announced the arrest of a suspicious character, supposedly ZIGZAG's accomplice, on a charge of possession of gelignite in the neighbourhood of the de Havilland factory. The Germans apparently swallowed the story whole and sent ZIGZAG their congratulations. They also informed him that it was no longer possible to send a U-boat to collect him, as had originally been planned, so he would have to make his own way back to German occupied territory.

Naturally, this caused some consternation in MI5. The damage done to the de Havilland works looked fairly convincing from the air but it was by no means certain that ZIGZAG would be warmly received by his Abwehr controllers. ZIGZAG himself was quite willing to take the risk and even proffered assorted plans to assassinate Hitler if he managed to get back to Berlin. Like any other double cross agent, he had been prevented from learning too much about MI5's activities and of course had no knowledge of MI5's most valuable counter-espionage weapon – the ISK and ISOS summaries.

By the middle of February 1943, the Twenty Committee had given its approval to the second phase of ZIGZAG's career, his return to the Abwehr. His best route was judged to be via Lisbon where at least he had the address of a German contact. In order to get to the neutral capital, he had to sign on a ship as a seaman so arrangements were made for him to impersonate a friend, Philip Anson, who at the time was languishing in one of His Majesty's prisons. With an identity card in Anson's name he was granted a seaman's book and thus became available for service in the Merchant Navy.

Robertson had one final meeting with ZIGZAG to satisfy himself that his agent was fully aware of all the dangers and then the operation was set in motion. ZIGZAG believed the Germans would offer him another mission, this time to America, so arrangements were made with the FBI to provide an emergency telephone number where ZIGZAG could make his presence known if he was unable to signal his intentions from an Abwehr radio. MI5 agreed for their part not to try to make contact with him while he was in enemy hands. With all the preparations completed 'Philip Anson' joined the *City of Lancaster*, one of Sir John Ellerman's fleet, as a steward and started his journey to Lisbon.

The voyage turned out to be far from uneventful. The convoy was attacked by the Luftwaffe and then later by a submarine pack but fortunately the *City of Lancaster*, though superficially damaged, escaped serious harm and berthed in Lisbon on 12 March, 1943.

ZIGZAG had to wait two days on board before the Portuguese authorities cleared the crew for landing but as soon as he got ashore he made his way to the address supplied to him by his Abwehr controller Stephan von Grunen. Here ZIGZAG faced further difficulties. The German who met him had never heard of his password or of Eddie Chapman for that matter. In desperation the double agent went to the German Embassy the following day and eventually was put in touch with the local Abwehr representative who had received no word from Paris concerning FRITZCHEN's arrival. He was advised to return to his ship for the night so that further instructions could be sought and at the same time to place an explosive charge in the vessel's fuel bunker. This surprise order placed ZIGZAG in a dangerous situation. The sabotage device had the appearance of a lump of coal and was apparently safe until it came into contact with fire. Then, he was assured, it would blow any ship out of the water.

ZIGZAG smuggled the special coal on board the *City of Lancaster* and then went to see the captain. Open-mouthed, Captain Reason listened to 'Philip Anson's' incredible story. He claimed to be an important agent working for British Intelligence who was about to desert ship. 'Anson' explained that under no circumstances should the captain visit the British Embassy because it was 'full of Nazi spies'. Amazed, Keason agreed to ZIGZAG's plan of silence and promised to telephone Michael Ryde as soon as he docked in Glasgow. With that, Chapman handed over the two lumps of 'coal' and went ashore for the last time.

Meanwhile in London the Abwehr's signals between Lisbon, Paris and Berlin were routinely being intercepted. In one, the Lisbon branch reported the reappearance of FRITZCHEN and disclosed the fact that he had sabotaged his own vessel. Aghast, Colonel Robertson dispatched a B1(a) officer by the next flight to Lisbon to warn the *City of Lancaster*. More than one voice in MI5 believed that ZIGZAG might well sink his own ship in the hope of ensuring a good reception from the Abwehr. Once Captain Keason had been interviewed these fears were scotched and the lumps of coal removed for inspection. MI5 experts later confirmed that the apparently harmless lumps were actually pieces of self-detonating explosive approximately six inches square.

The day before the ship was searched ZIGZAG was given a German passport in the name of Hans Christianssen, a Norwegian-American, and flown to Madrid where German Embassy officials met him and started six days of intensive interrogation. At the end of this period ZIGZAG travelled to Paris by train and for the next sixteen months MI5 had to rely on occasional ULTRA intercepts for news of their extraordinary agent. All this time ZIGZAG was in the hands of the Abwehr, which evidently developed a very high opinion of him.

He was closely cross-examined about his mission and about general conditions in Britain but he passed every test. His controller, Stephan von Grunen, was recalled from duty at the Russian Front and assigned to take care of FRITZCHEN until a new operation could be prepared for the Abwehr's star agent. ZIGZAG moved with relative freedom between Paris, Berlin, Brussels and Oslo, where he became adviser on intelligence methods and helped train other German spies for use in the occupied territories. In Oslo, ZIGZAG was put in charge of some Abwehr transmitters which allowed him to include some prearranged coded messages to B1(a) in his regular test transmission. The local Abstelle apparently suspected nothing and MI5 were later able to get confirmation from SIS that their agent was indeed at liberty and living well in the Norwegian capital.

Shortly after the Normandy landings ULTRA summaries revealed that ZIGZAG had moved to Brussels in preparation for a second flight to Britain but for reasons that were not disclosed the new mission was delayed and the Abwehr party returned to Paris. Two weeks later they were ordered back to Den Helden near Utrecht and on this occasion, ZIGZAG was able to complete his mission. He was dropped in the vicinity of Wisbech, less than twenty miles from the point of his first landing, and again telephoned the police from the home of an obliging Cambridgeshire farmer. On this occasion the local police station insisted on a mass of personal details of the 'downed flier' before they would commit any transport to him so instead ZIGZAG made a call to Littleport where he had previously received good service. The police there remembered him and immediately agreed to send a car to collect him. He then telephoned the War Office in London and alerted Michael Ryde of his arrival.

The following day ZIGZAG had lunch with Tar Robertson at the Naval and Military Club and recounted his remarkable experiences inside the enemy camp. No one in B1(a) had any doubt but that ZIGZAG was an enterprising, resourceful and extremely brave man. He brought back a veritable gold mine of intelligence and gave some useful insights into current Abwehr operations. He reported that the U-boat losses in the Atlantic were causing grave concern in Berlin. One of his tasks was to discover exactly how the RAF could pinpoint German submarines so accurately. Various theories had been presented, ranging from the use of magic beams to the introduction of sophisticated heat detection equipment, but the Kriegsmarine experts, were themselves unsure what was causing the Allied successes and never suspected their signals were being intercepted.

ZIGZAG also had much to offer on Hitler's secret weapons. His bomb damage reports would be important, or so he was told, for the future control and guidance of the Germans' new VI doodlebug rockets. He was also to gather information about new wireless frequencies because German scientists suspected the Allies of having developed a special valve which would interfere with the systems of the V2. His questionnaire of subjects confirmed the Abwehr's apparent concern over Allied technical innovations and reflected one particularly baffling misapprehension. It seemed the Luftwaffe believed each airfield in Britain had been assigned a specific target in Germany on a regular basis. One of ZIGZAG's tasks was to position himself near different airfields in East Anglia and signal the departures of squadrons so the German air defences could be alerted in good time.

ZIGZAG was welcomed home by MI5 and established in a flat in Kensington from where he could prepare and send his messages. His case seemed certain of further exploitation until various sources indicated that ZIGZAG had been less than discreet when looking up old friends. Rumours about Eddie Chapman and his new-found wealth circulated amongst his associates and B1(a) had little choice but to abandon the case. ZIGZAG's last broadcast to Hamburg, where his controller had moved to on the fall of Paris, took place in November 1944.

After the war Chapman wrote an account of his experience with the help of Sir Compton Mackenzie and Wilfred Macartney. The story was brought by a French newspaper, *Etoile du Soir*, in 1946 which resulted in Chapman and Macartney being convicted under the Official Secrets Act at Bow Street on 29 March, 1946. A further attempt to publish in 1952 resulted in the *News of the World* having an edition pulped after representations by the Security Service. Shortly afterwards Chapman re-established contact with von Grunen and was forgiven for his duplicity. Von Grunen then flew to England and attended the wedding of Eddie Chapman's daughter.

The Belgian Ring

The Brussels Abstelle was one of the more active branches of German Intelligence in the espionage offensive against Britain. Four of their recruits were executed in London and as a result a much larger number of Belgian refugees were considered too unreliable to be given their liberty.

The first of the Belgian double agents was FATHER, a very distinguished Belgian air force pilot who arrived in England in June 1943 via Lisbon. He had actually sought out the Abwehr in Brussels and volunteered to go to Britain as a means of escape even though this meant separation from his wife and children, who were left behind. His German instructions were to send technical information to cover addresses and finally to steal an RAF fighter and return to Occupied France.

B1(a) had every reason to accept FATHER's sincerity but the fact that his family were almost hostages mitigated against him being allowed anywhere near an operational posting in the Belgian air force until his complete reliability had been proved. His case progressed well but not exactly in the direction the Germans had intended. His original earlier task had been to travel to America and buy a transmitter there but this was scotched when the US Embassy in Lisbon refused him a visa. He reported his new destination as Britain but complained that he had no effective way of communicating with his controller. The Abwehr solved his problem by sending a wireless message to DRAGONFLY. He was to telephone FATHER in London and give him a set of frequencies and schedules so that FATHER could at least get his messages direct. FATHER was told to continue using his cover addresses and only in an emergency to contact DRAGONFLY.

This arrangement worked well but FATHER's expertise in aeronautical matters made him a valuable and well-thought-of source for the Germans. Gradually the questions received from Brussels became more and more embarrassing to answer and it was decided to abandon the case. This move had to be made without arousing German suspicions. The best solution was found to be an overseas posting and in June 1943 FATHER was sent abroad.

Within three months of FATHER starting to send messages a second, less suitable, Belgian candidate arrived who was dubbed SCRUFFY. SCRUFFY was a seaman who had been provided with a cover address in Lisbon. As a rule, B1(a) avoided recruiting seamen because of the obvious difficulties involved in keeping their case officers informed of developments. Frequent visits to neutral ports also had to be carefully controlled and again this was difficult to do effectively. Only JOSEF's case was developed. This Russian seaman arrived in Britain in August 1942 and subsequently made contact with the Japanese Embassy in Lisbon. He continued to write letters to their cover address until December 1944 when his case was abandoned.

SCRUFFY's case therefore could be lost without much hardship to the system and B1(a) opted to seize the opportunity of demonstrating to the Abwehr just how ineptly MI5 handled an agent 'in harness'. In theory SCRUFFY had joined a vessel coasting in British waters but in fact he was being impersonated by an MI5 nominee. His letters to Lisbon were written in an overtly bogus manner but incredibly the Germans apparently failed to notice that SCRUFFY had come under MI5 control. To have British inefficiency compounded by German inefficiency was just too much for the Twenty Committee and SCRUFFY's case was quickly terminated.

MI5's next recruit from Belgium promised to be far more rewarding. He had spent most of his life in Belgium but had had a British father. His birth had been registered with the British Embassy in Brussels so he had British citizenship. Before the war he had worked as a senior insurance executive. In late 1941 he managed to get to Lisbon, on the way back to England and was there introduced to an Austrian Jew named Koessler who appeared to take an undue interest in the British insurance man.

Dr Koessler was an extraordinary figure, but in wartime Lisbon he blended in well with all the other hundreds of refugees and displaced persons trying to salvage their lives. Koessler had sent his two children to England before the war and was anxious to supply them with funds in the way of jewellery, or so he claimed. He explained that he had served as a cavalry officer and was now engaged in marketing various pharmaceutical products which he had patented. Of more interest was his assertion that he was in touch with anti-Nazi elements who were interested to hear Allied peace terms.

When MI5 learned of all this early in 1942 the insurance executive was recruited and given the code name MULLET. In August of that year he returned to Lisbon and confirmed what MI5 suspected: Dr Koessler, Jewish though he was, held a position in the Abwehr. He was also the head of the Kolberg Organization which in effect was a business cover in Portugal for the Brussels Abstelle. MULLET recruited Dr Koessler with the code name HAMLET while MULLET was entered in the Abwehr's books as FAMULUS. It was a bizarre exchange but prior to this date 'B' Division had never succeeded in netting a senior Abwehr staff officer. (ARTIST only began to co-operate fully late in 1943. At about the same time PRECIOUS – Dr Erich Vermehren – defected from the Abwehr's Istanbul office and was received by Nicholas Elliott, the local SIS man.) The principle of developing enemy intelligence officers as double agents was considered only superficially attractive for several reasons. Very little control could be exercised over their activities and as a matter of course they would be subject to snap investigations at the hands of other, rival organizations such as the Gestapo. In the event of exposure, a double-dealing controller would place the credibility of all his agents in danger, as was later to happen with ARTIST. Another disadvantage was the ever-present risk that an apparent defection was in reality an elaborate effort by the opposition to gain information about operating techniques. Therefore, such recruitments were generally avoided by B1(a) who remained acutely aware that one defector could destroy the entire double cross system simply by acting in good faith and offering the British details of Germany's best agents abroad. In HAMLET's case the motivation was clear. He was a committed anti-Nazi who wished to improve the political standing of those opposed to Hitler by building up the reported strength of the Allies. The Twenty Committee vetoed this strategy but nevertheless approved of MULLET posting reports to HAMLET for onward transmission to Brussels and Berlin. They also consented to the recruitment of another acquaintance of Dr Koessler, a Colgate-Palmolive executive named Fanto. He came to Britain in April 1943 as a representative for Dr Koessler's business interests. Together MULLET, HAMLET and PUPPET (as Panto was now code-named) formed the backbone of the ring even though they were all operating through Portugal. It is interesting to note that the ULTRA intercepts revealed some strong internal rivalries at work in the Abwehr. It seems the Lisbon Abstelle resented the intrusion of the Brussels Abstelle in what they regarded as their territory.

HAMLET informed MI5 late in April 1944 that he had 'retired' from the Abwehr which of necessity meant the end of MULLET and PUPPET but by this date the network had been able to make their contribution to the D-Day deceptions.

PLAN PREMIUM centred on MULLET and the knowledge the Brussels Abstelle had of his earlier commercial activities insuring industrial properties in Belgium, Holland and northern France. It suggested that MULLET had been appointed to a special position by his new employers who were according to PUPPET, one of the larger London-based insurance companies. The new job consisted of gathering together all available information from the company's files relating to the Pas-de-Calais region. MULLET claimed to have obtained a mass of intelligence on the area which was to be handed over to the government. Naturally MULLET had no idea why the information was needed – but it was hoped the Brussels Abstelle would draw their own conclusions.

With the demise of HAMLET's ring only one double agent was left in the Belgian ring. This was SNIPER, a Belgian air force sergeant pilot who arrived in Britain from Spain in November 1943. He came equipped with a cover address and secret writing materials but, more importantly, had a lengthy questionnaire which reflected German concern over their submarine losses. He was to report technical developments made by the RAF and try to discover all he could about the latest anti-U-boat tactics practised by the Allies.

SNIPER's case developed well but the Germans failed to send him a wireless transmitter as promised so a unique method of delivery was arranged. SNIPER informed his Brussels controllers late in 1944 that he was due shortly to return to Belgium with the advancing Allied troops. As expected, the Abwehr seized the opportunity to leave a radio behind in their retreat. Thus, in January 1945 SNIPER, now with Montgomery's 21st Army Group, confirmed that he had found his buried treasure at Turnhout. Retaining his same MI5 case officer, SNIPER continued to keep contact until the very last days of the war in Europe.

ARTIST was reported to have been executed at the Oranienberg concentration camp in 1945.

BALLOON returned to commerce after the war and became a successful businessman and director of Tarlair Limited, the Yugoslav ring's original 'cover' company. He now lives in retirement near Maidenhead.

BRUTUS remained in London after the war and started a small printing business which he still runs. He maintains his Polish nationality and is active in the government-in-exile.

CELERY continued to have difficulties with the police after the war but MI5 decided not to offer evidence on his behalf. He eventually retired to run a pub in Surrey.

DREADNOUGHT obtained a British passport after the war and now runs a medical clinic in the Bahamas.

FREAK moved to the United States after the war and opened a hotel on Long Island. He now lives in retirement in Italy.

GARBO took his wife and children to Venezuela after the war and remained there until his death in October 1988.

GELATINE married an American after the war and now lives in Italy.

GW returned to Wales after the war and died in 1949, having kept silent about his wartime work for MI5.

JEFF was deported back to Norway on an American Flying Fortress in 1946 and narrowly escaped being tried for collaborating with the Germans before his mission to Britain. MI5 intervened through the offices of Special Branch, and secured his release from custody. He now works in Oslo as a translator for Norwegian television.

METEOR was granted a British passport after the war and remained in London, suffering from bad health. He died in Switzerland 1981.

MUTT went to live in Sweden after being demobbed. He now works near Malmö and has become friendly with the Caroli family. At the invitation of his friend Detective Inspector Jock Westland he returned to Scotland in November 1958. On his arrival he was warned by MI5 not to discuss his wartime experiences and as a result a Rotary Club lunch was cancelled.

SNOW the Welshman, was released from Dartmoor after the war and returned to Canada where he became 'Mr Brown'. While in Canada he approached the British High Commission in Ottawa and demanded compensation for his 'wrongful arrest' in 1941. He threatened to publish his wartime memoirs and apparently received several substantial payments from the British government. He retired to Eire and lived in Harristown, near Dublin, using the name 'Mr White'. He died in 1976.

SUMMER was deported to Sweden at the end of hostilities and found a job in an agricultural seed firm near Malmö. His health deteriorated gradually and he died in 1975, having spent his final ten years in a wheelchair. He made one attempt to secure a disability pension from the German government but his claim was rejected.

SWEET WILLIAM continued to work in the Spanish Embassy in London until his death in 1973.

TATE now lives in the Home Counties, his identity still protected by the Security Service.

TREASURE married an American army officer after the war and went to live in the United States. In 1966, shortly before she died, she wrote *Secret Service Rendered*.

TRICYCLE retired to the South of France and in 1974 published *Spy Counterspy*, an account of his wartime adventures, thoughtfully altering the names of many of those involved.

ZIGZAG became the subject of a film and several books and now runs a health hydro in Hertfordshire.

MI5 Double Agents

CODE NAME	REAL IDENTITY	DURATION OF CASE
ARTIST	Johann Jebsen	Sep '43-May '44
BALLOON	Dickie Metcalfe	May '41-Nov '43
BASKET	Lenihan	Jul '41-Dec '41
BISCUIT	(alias Sam McCarthy)	May '40-Aug '41
BRONX	Diplomat's ex-wife	Oct '42-May '45
BRUTUS	Roman Garby-Czerniawski	Oct '42-Jan '45
CARELESS	Polish airman	Jul '41-Jan '43
CARROT	Luxembourger	Jun '42-Dec '42

CELERY	Walter Dicketts	Jan '41-Aug '41
CHARLIE	Briton of German descent	Sep '39-Aug '41
DRAGONFLY	Briton of German descent	Apr '40-Jan '41
DREADNOUGHT	Dr Ivi Popov	Apr '43-May '44
FATHER	Pilot Capt Henri Arents	Jun '41-Jun '43
FIDO	French air force pilot	Jul '43-Feb '44
FREAK	Marquis Frano de Bona	Dec '43-May '44
GANDER	Carl Grosse	Oct '40-Nov '40
GELATINE	Friedle Gaertner	May '41-May '45
GIRAFFE	Czech in French Army	Sep '40-Sep '40
GW	Gwilym Williams	Oct '39-Feb '42
HAMLET	Dr Koessler	Dec '41-May '44
JEFF	Tor Glad	Apr '41-Feb '44
JOSEF	Russian seaman	Aug '42-Dec '44
JUNIOR	Hans Ruser	(Defected Nov '43)
LIPSTICK	Josef Terradellas	Nov '42-Mar '44
METEOR	Eugn Sostaric	Apr '43-May '44
MULLET	British businessman	Dec '41-May '44
MUTT	John Moe	Apr '41-Feb '44
PEPPERMINT	Jose Brugada Wood	Dec '41-Apr '43
PUPPET	Fanto	Apr '43-May '44
RAINBOW	Pierce	Feb '40-Jun '43
ROVER	Polish seaman	May '44-May '45
SCRUFFY	Belgian seaman	Sep '41-Nov '41
SHEPHERD	Frenchman	Mar '44-May '45
THE SNARK	Yugoslav domestic servant	Jul '41-Mar '43
SNIPER	Belgian Sgt Pilot	Nov '43-May '45
SNOW	Arthur George Owens	Sep '39-March '41
SUMMER	Gösta Caroli	Sep '40-Jan '41
SWEET WILLIAM	William Jackson	Aug '41-Aug '42
TATE	Wulf Schmidt	Sep '40-May '45
TEAPOT	(triple cross agent)	Jan '43-May '45
TREASURE	Lily Sergueiev	Aug '43-Dec '44
TRICYCLE (SCOUT)	Dusko Popov	Dec '40-May '44
WASHOUT	Ernesto Simoes	Jun '42-Dec '42
WATCHDOG	(based in Canada)	Nov '42-Jan '43
WEASEL	Belgian doctor	May '42-Dec '42
THE WORM	Stefan Zeis	Jul '43-Jan '44
ZIGZAG	Edward Chapman	Dec '42-Nov '44

IX
The Unlucky Sixteen:
Pour Encourager les Autres

'I want to speak to you tonight about the form of warfare which the Germans have been employing so extensively against Holland and Belgium – namely, the dropping of troops by parachute behind the main defensive lines. Let me say at once that the danger to us from this particular menace, although it undoubtedly exists, should not be exaggerated. We have made preparations to meet it already.'

Anthony Eden, Secretary of State for War, broadcasting to the nation on the evening of 14 May, 1940.

Between 3 September, 1939 and 7 May, 1945 fifteen spies working for the Germans were hanged in Britain and one man was shot by firing squad. Of these unlucky sixteen only four are definitely known to have held German nationality.

The first man to be hanged was Charles van den Kieboom, a twenty-six-year-old Dutch Eurasian born in Japan. He was arrested shortly before dawn on 3 September, 1940 near Dymchurch on the south coast of Kent.

Second Lieutenant E.A. Batten of the 6th Battalion, Somerset Light Infantry, was making his usual 'stand to' patrol along the sea wall some two miles south of Dymchurch when one of the members of his platoon on sentry duty noticed a small rowing boat on the beach. The oars (preserved in the SLI Museum, Taunton) were still in their rowlocks but the beach was deserted. Batten ordered an immediate search because the coastline was designated a Prohibited Area. His orders were to arrest any unauthorized person – if they were not shot first by the invasion-wary sentries. The platoon fanned out and began moving inland on to

Romney Marsh. They had walked only a matter of two hundred yards when Private Tollervey of 'D' Company discovered a slightly-built young man crouching in some reeds.

The figure emerged and explained in good English that he was a Dutch refugee who had just rowed ashore. Batten accepted his story and escorted van den Kieboom the mile or so back to battalion headquarters, which was housed in a requisitioned seaside villa on the main road to Dymchurch.

There the refugee was searched by Major D.I.L. Beath who discovered a loaded Colt automatic, a pair of field glasses and a quantity of tinned food. Major Beath retained the field glasses (because his own pair had been recently 'borrowed' by a visitor from the Royal Signals) and sent the young Eurasian off for breakfast in the mess.

After breakfast Major Beath began questioning van den Kieboom and heard how the refugee had paid a French fisherman four hundred francs to take him from Cap Griz Nez to the English coast. Apparently, he intended to travel up to Liverpool where he hoped to obtain a passage to Canada. All of this was duly reported to the Intelligence Officer at Brigade headquarters, Captain Harrap, a 10th Hussars officer on temporary attachment. He advised Major Beath to turn van den Kieboom over to the civil authorities and a telephone call was made to the police at Dymchurch. A short time later Sergeant Robertson and a constable arrived on the scene to take charge of the prisoner, and took away the field glasses and Colt pistol.

Meanwhile, the neighbouring 5th and 7th Somerset Light Infantry Battalions were alerted and Lieutenant Batten deployed the men of 'D' Company through Romney Marsh. Before long Private Chappell of No 16 Platoon found a sack and a suitcase, and Corporal Goody of No 10 Platoon discovered a man changing his trousers in a clump of reeds.

This second man identified himself as Sjoerd Pons, a twenty-eight-year-old Dutch refugee. He too was escorted back to battalion headquarters where he explained how he had made his way across the Channel with a second man who, he feared, had been shot by sentries. The soldiers accepted Pons' story, but a little later in the morning the situation changed dramatically. Major Beath's men found a suitcase wireless on the Marsh, together with some dry cell batteries. There could be little doubt but that the 'refugees' were spies.

Some miles further down the coast at Lydd a third arrest took place at ten o'clock. A young man in his mid-twenties, speaking good English, knocked on the door of the Rising Sun public house in New Street. Mrs Mabel Cole, the publican's wife, was asked for a bottle of sparkling cider. The foreigner, who was obviously ignorant of England's licensing laws, pointed to a poster on the wall of the pub advertising the drink. Mrs Cole tried to explain that she was unable to sell the stranger any liquor, and suggested he return later. The man then asked for a packet of cigarettes so Mrs Cole directed him over the road to Tilbey's Stores. As he turned to follow her suggestion his head collided with a light fitting on the low ceiling. Mrs Cole was now very suspicious of her nervous visitor and sent a message down to the butcher's shop a hundred yards away (which was also owned by Mr Cole), telling her husband of her strange encounter. Mr Cole shared his wife's suspicions and consulted an RAF officer billeted in a neighbouring house.

When the stranger returned to the pub the RAF officer challenged him for his permit which would allow him access to a Prohibited Area. No pass was forthcoming, the foreigner explaining that he was a refugee recently landed in England from France. He gave his name as Carl Meier.

Meier was quickly marched down to Lydd police station where Sergeant Tye listened to the story of the 'Dutch refugee'. Tye found it difficult to believe his story and suggested Meier point out to him the exact spot where he claimed to have landed and come with him to recover the sack of food Meier said he had left hidden on the beach.

While Sergeant Tye was questioning Meier a local labourer named Hayles had noticed the sack protruding from under the wreckage of an old lifeboat. To his delight the contents turned out to be cans of foods so he took it home to his coastguard cottage. When Sergeant Tye eventually tracked down Hayles he was able to confirm at least part of Meier's story. The policeman then returned to the station and telephoned for assistance.

There was however a fourth member of the Abwehr team who was to remain undetected until the following day. He was Jose Waldberg, a twenty-five-year-old German from Mainz. He was challenged by a patrolling police constable on the main Lydd-Dungeness road. He replied, in French, that he spoke no English but would like to see an officer. The constable was mystified but nevertheless accompanied the man to a nearby pumping station. Waldberg indicated that he had spent the night there, and then pointed out two suitcases hidden in a tree. One contained a radio transmitter, the other five batteries and a morse key. There were also two other bags close by, a raincoat and an aerial strung out between a bush and a tree.

Waldberg was taken to join his comrades for MI5 interrogation at 020. Colonel Stephens quickly discovered that all four were 'short term' agents, provided with only the barest essentials to sustain them until the SEALION assault on the south coast of England had begun. Their task was to reconnoitre the invasion area and report beaches free of mines and suitable glider landing areas free of obstacles.

Exactly why these four men were sent across the Channel was to remain a mystery to MI5. The SEALION operation was due for cancellation and these agents appeared to have no further instructions beyond reporting on such matters as local tank traps and the weather. Nevertheless, they yielded useful information concerning Abwehr personalities and training techniques. All made long statements.

Van den Kieboom claimed he had acted for the Germans out of fear. He had apparently been threatened with a prison sentence for currency smuggling. He had originally met Pons while serving in the Dutch army. Before the war he had worked as a book-keeper and receptionist in the Amsterdam YMCA. Both men had been drafted into an ambulance unit and had been demobbed in June 1940. Now, they claimed, they wanted to join Prince Bernhard's army in exile and be given the chance to fight for their country. They identified their Abwehr Conducting Officer as Captain Jules Boeckel and recounted how they had been put up in great style at the Hotel Metropole in Brussels. Having received their rather rudimentary training they had been moved to a villa just outside Boulogne where all four met for the first time. The day before their departure they had been driven to Le Touquet for a celebration lunch. After this they boarded an Abwehr trawler in the port area of Boulogne and then kept a rendezvous with two German escort minesweepers off the Cap d'Albrecht. All three vessels waited for darkness to fall and then made their way to the English coast in convoy.

Shortly after midnight the escorts peeled off, leaving the fishing vessel to continue the journey to the Kentish coast alone. The first to disembark were Waldberg and 'Meier', who climbed into an inflatable rubber dinghy with their transmitter and a sack of meat, cigarettes and chocolate. They were also handed two small spades to bury the evidence of their arrival.

Some twenty minutes later van den Kieboom and Pons rowed another small boat towards the beach a couple of miles further along the coast.

When Waldberg was facing his MI5 interrogators he was presented with a notebook which had been found amongst his possessions. It appeared to contain three messages in French, ready to be encoded. The first read:

ARRIVED SAFELY DOCUMENT DESTROYED
ENGLISH PATROL 200 METRES FROM
COAST BEACH WITH BROWN NETS AND

RAILWAY SLEEPERS AT A DISTANCE OF
50 METRES NO MINES FEW SOLDIERS
UNFINISHED BLOCKHOUSE NEW ROAD
WALDBERG

The second message was sent some hours later:

MEIER PRISONER ENGLISH POLICE
SEARCHING FOR ME AM CORNERED
SITUATION DIFFICULT I CAN RESIST
THIRST UNTIL SATURDAY IF I AM TO
RESIST SEND AEROPLANES WEDNESDAY
EVENING 11 O'CLOCK AM 3 KM NORTH
ARRIVAL LONG LIVE GERMANY
WALDBERG

The final text read:

THIS IS EXACT POSITION YESTERDAY
EVENING 6 O'CLOCK 3 MESSERSCHMITT
FIRED MACHINE GUNS IN MY
DIRECTION 300 METRES SOUTH WATER
RESERVOIR PAINTED RED MEIER
PRISONER

These three messages precluded any idea of 'turning' any of the spies. In any event none of them showed any inclination to be co-operative. Waldberg, just the older of the first pair, had been in the service of the Abwehr since 1938 and had taken part in the Blitzkrieg through Belgium and France earlier that year. He had been born in Mainz during the Great War and his French mother had taught him to speak her native language fluently. Before the war he had studied at Oxford on an exchange programme and had then 'graduated' from an Abwehr spy school near Wiesbaden. After a spell processing Allied POWs at a camp near Mainz he had been transferred to the Hamburg Abstelle in preparation for LENA, the code name for the Abwehr's part in the invasion of Britain.

His partner, Carl Meier, was a Dutchman born in the German town of Coblenz. He was twenty-four years old and before the war had been active in Mussert's National Socialist Party in The Hague. After the German occupation he had accepted an Abwehr offer of a 'risky job'.

All four men were selected for prosecution under the Treachery Act and appeared at the Old Bailey on 22 November, 1940. The Solicitor-

General, Sir William Jowitt, led for the Crown and the case lasted most of the week as all four pleaded Not Guilty. Waldberg declined to take part in the proceedings at all while Meier's defence was undermined by his initial silence on the subject of a companion. Pons and van den Kieboom offered a vigorous defence, claiming that they had only participated in the scheme to escape the Germans and join the Allies.

Waldberg, Meier and van den Kieboom were all found guilty but much to the embarrassment of Edward Hinchley-Cooke, who sat in on the trial on behalf of MI5, Pons was acquitted by the jury. Hasty arrangements were made to arrest Pons as he left the dock and serve him with an 18B Internment Order.

Mr Justice Wrottesley sentenced the remaining three to death and the executions were set for 10 December, 1940 at Pentonville. The two Germans declined to appeal against their sentences but van den Kieboom did make an application to the Appeal Court which at least served to delay matters.

However, the Dutchman changed his mind before the Appeal could be heard and he walked to the scaffold on 17 December, 1940, exactly a week after Waldberg and Meier.

This prosecution was the first of its kind in Britain and it was decided to turn the event into a major occasion for Fleet Street. The object of the exercise was to reassure the public and Parliament that the security authorities were on their toes. A press conference was organized by Derek Tangye's MI5 Press Liaison section and photographers were given the opportunity to take pictures of the contraband the three agents had brought ashore. No mention was made of the fourth defendant in the case.

Picture Post managed to extract some humour from the press exhibition by comparing the illustrations of the other newspapers but in general the affair was a sombre one. *The Times* commented the next day:

> 'In official quarter it is suggested that the capture of these enemy agents emphasizes still more the need that the public exercise the greatest care when talking among strangers.'

MI5 could not of course gauge the public's reaction to the publicity but it did at least serve to quell some of the criticism MI5 had experienced following the 18B internments.

Two MPs in particular, Victor Cazalet, the Unionist Member for Chippenham, and Richard Stokes, the Labour Member for Ipswich, were active on behalf of all internees. Cazalet had previously served as

Lord Swinton's Private Secretary and was now Chairman of the Parliamentary Committee on Refugees, a position from which he fired frequent broadsides at the War Office and Home Office. Stokes too held strong views on the question of wholesale internment and kept tabling awkward questions for the government. Atone point in the summer of 1940 he learnt of the existence of 020 and demanded an end to the solitary confinement of internees there. His request was turned down, as was a request from Herr Preisswerk, the Swiss Protecting Power liaison officer to visit Latchmere House. The capture and prosecution of genuine German agents (called 'spies' for the benefit of the press) gave point to MI5's actions and fulfilled what was judged to be the public's need for reassurance. The security authorities were thus able to demonstrate and publicize their expertise.

On 30 September, 1940, while the four visitors from Boulogne were preparing to undergo further interrogation, there was a second alert. The RSLO in Edinburgh, Peter Perfect, received a telephone call from George Strath, the Chief Constable of Banffshire in the north of Scotland. He passed on the message that two possible German agents had been detained at Buckie, a tiny fishing community on the Moray Firth. The names of the two suspects were given as François de Deeker, a French refugee from Belgium, and Miss Vera Erikson, an attractive young Danish lady. They had first been spotted in Portgordon, where the stationmaster, John Donald, and a porter, John Geddes, had noticed the rather damp appearance of the couple. They had called the local constable, Robert Grieve, to the station and he too was dissatisfied with the strangers. Both were now being taken under escort to Edinburgh.

In their first statement to Inspector John Simpson at Portgordon police station the two 'refugees' said that they had come ashore the previous day from the *Norstar*, a vessel based in Bergen in Norway. They claimed to have spent the night at a hotel in Banff, and then to have taken a taxi most of the way to Portgordon station. Simpson searched the couple and made several interesting discoveries, including a loaded 6.35 Mauser automatic, a wireless set, coding equipment and two National Registration Cards giving their addresses as 18 Sussex Place, London W11 (No CNFX/141/2) and 15 Sussex Gardens, London W2 (No CNFQ/141/1).

Simpson and Constable Grieve were now quite certain they had caught a pair of spies and escorted them to Buckie police station from where they telephoned the Chief Constable at Banff.

Strath's first reaction was to discover if the couple were operating alone, or if they had arrived with other companions. He quickly organized a search of the area which revealed a pair of rubber boots bearing a foreign name on the beach at Gollachy Burn. A farmer nearby reported his dog barking furiously in the night, and as the morning wore on evidence grew of a third German agent. The staff at Buckpool railway station reported a stranger shortly before seven the same morning, enquiring about the times of trains to Aberdeen. He had been informed that the next train would leave Buckie, a mile to the east, at two minutes to ten. The booking-office clerk in Buckie confirmed a youngish man in his early thirties buying a single ticket to Edinburgh and getting on the connecting train to Aberdeen.

An alert was sounded for the missing third agent in Aberdeen but meanwhile Inspector Simpson was having more success with the two spies already in custody. The twenty-seven-year-old Danish woman revealed that her real name was 'Vera de Cottani-Chalbur'. She claimed to be a widow, born in Siberia. According to her she had someone of importance in London who would vouch for her. His name was Captain King and he worked in the War Office.

'Captain King' turned out to be Max Knight of MI5's B5(b) and accordingly special instructions were sent in a coded telegram to Peter Perfect.

Before the war Vera de Cottani-Chalbur had acted as a part-time informant for Knight. She had worked in London for a while in a Mayfair salon and from time to time had passed on interesting pieces of gossip. Now, she revealed to Peter Perfect, she was in the pay of the Abwehr and was supposed to accompany two of their agents, Karl Drücke and a man known to her only as Werner Wälti, to London. Apparently Wälti was going to make his own way to Euston so Perfect quickly telephoned the Chief Constable in Edinburgh, William Merrilees, to meet the Aberdeen train. Unfortunately, his men reached Waverley Station too late to intercept the passengers and a major search operation was started in Edinburgh.

The Edinburgh police did have one further clue. The staff at the left luggage office recalled a particularly damp suitcase being deposited with them, and when it was examined it was found to contain a wireless. The office was quickly 'staked out' with Edinburgh CID officers but it was more than three hours before Wälti returned from the direction of Princes Street to reclaim his suitcase. As soon as he approached the office William Merrilees stepped forward and pinned his arms. Wälti was found to be carrying a loaded Mauser automatic, and once this was removed he suddenly produced a flick-knife. When he had been disarmed for the second time he was taken by ambulance to police headqurters in Edinburgh for interrogation by the RSLO and his deputy, Lieutenant Mair. Wälti had a mass of incriminating documents on him, including a list of thirty-four airfields in the east of England and a wireless code but he strenuously denied being either German or a spy. He claimed to be a Swiss and as proof offered a passport issued in Zurich, a traveller's ration book and a National Registration card bearing the address 23 Sussex Gardens, London W2. He also denied knowing either 'Miss Erikson' or 'François de Deeker'.

The following day Detective Inspector Alexander Sutherland escorted Wälti down to Scotland Yard and banded him over to Inspector Bridge of Special Branch. De Deeker was also conveyed to Camp 020 while Vera Erikson was lodged in Holloway's 'E' Wing.

The MI5 interrogations revealed a fascinating background to the case. De Deeker's real name was confirmed to be Karl Drücke, a thirty-four-year-old German merchant in the service of the Abwehr. Wälti declined to give his genuine identity, but described his peacetime occupation as 'chauffeur'. Miss Erikson remained in Holloway in spite of her previous association with MI5 but nevertheless contributed some valuable details concerning the Hamburg Abstelle.

After more than nine months in detention Wälti and Drücke were sent for trial at the Old Bailey before Mr Justice Asquith. At the end of a two-day hearing both men were found guilty and sentenced to death.

Both men appealed to the Court of Criminal Appeal on 21 July, 1941, but their plea was rejected. They were hanged at Wandsworth Prison on 6 August, 1941, and details of the case were released for publication the following day. Not surprisingly, no mention was made of Miss de Cottani-Chalbur's contribution to the event.

There was however a sequel. One of the overseas newspapers carrying the story and photographs of the rubber dinghy found by the coastguard off the Banffshire coast was the big Zurich daily, the *Neue Zurcher Zeitung*. Their article centred around the Swiss nationality claimed by Wälti, and mentioned the Home Office statement announcing his execution. It caught the eye of Brigadier Roger Masson, the Head of the Bundespolizei, the Swiss State security organization. He ordered an independent Swiss enquiry on 19 August, 1941 only to learn from the Zurich City Police that there was no trace of 'Werner Heinricn Wälti', born in 1915 or, for that matter, in any other year. Masson then contacted the Swiss Legation in London and suggested they obtain further details of the executed man. A photograph of Wälti's passport was delivered to the Legation and arrived at BUPO headquarters in Berne on 1 October, 1941. The passport bore the number 636723 and the Cantonal number 26435 and had first been issued on 5

January, 1937. Twelve months later the passport had been renewed but the validating stamp shown was not in fact in use in 1938.

The more BUPO investigated the details of the passport the more certain they grew that it was a forgery. The passport number had been allocated to a Swiss woman in 1936 and did not correspond with the Cantonal number, which had been issued to a Herr Robert Spiller. The renewal number related to an Alma Olga Kiener, and a reference to the Zurich suburb of Horgen in the passport failed to satisfy the local officials who (in theory) were shown to have originally endorsed it, for in the Swiss Federation passports are issued by the local Canton rather than by the central government.

Brigadier Masson advised the federal government in Berne that the document was a forgery and the identity of 'Werner Wälti' a reasonable fabrication although BUPO would welcome the opportunity to examine the original. MI5 refused to part with it but changed their records to show Wälti as merely 'thought to be of German nationality'. It was however too late to alter the death certificate which had been signed by the Coroner, Mr R.B. Wyatt, after an Inquest held the day following the execution.

After the war new evidence was obtained suggesting that Wälti's real name was Robert Petter, a German rather than a Swiss.

The first Briton of the war to be tried for spying was George Armstrong, a thirty-nine-year-old merchant seaman and son of a Newcastle tripe dealer.

Armstrong was a member of the Communist Party of Great Britain and came to the notice of Britain's wartime intelligence apparatus in the United States. In October 1940 Bill Stephenson, the head of British Security Co-ordination in New York, reported to London that Armstrong had been spotted making contact with a German diplomat and Abwehr representative in New York. Armstrong had deserted his ship in Boston and had made his way south to New York, apparently motivated by a speech made by Molotov, the Soviet Foreign Minister, to the seventh session of the Supreme Council. Molotov, who had been the driving force behind Stalin's pact with Ribbentrop, denounced the war as a capitalist plot and an exploitation of the working class. He urged all workers engaged in making munitions to strike and suggested that dockers stop loading ships with war materials. To all Allied merchant seamen, he had a special message: desert your ship as soon as you reach a neutral port.

Although the United States were not to join the war for a further fourteen months Stephenson was operating BSC in conditions of relative freedom. The FBI reluctantly tolerated his activities which, they believed, were restricted to the dissemination of anti-Nazi propaganda and a degree of political arm-twisting to rally support for the beleaguered British Isles. As Hoover was later to discover, BSC's brief went far beyond this. The BSC office in New York incorporated the responsibilities in the Western Hemisphere of both SIS and the Security Service and inevitably became the hub of a major counter-intelligence effort directed against the Abwehr. Any person identified by BSC as a German agent became the target of a comprehensive surveillance and terror operation. Stephenson had no qualms about sending his men with sandbags into the American waterfront districts to wage war against the Germans, even if the territory was supposed to be neutral. The Abwehr scouts engaged in sabotaging Allied vessels and suborning their crews found the decks dangerous places to operate. Further to protect British interests, BSC established a network of well-paid informers who reported to Stephenson any suspicious approaches or behaviour.

When Armstrong came ashore in Boston he made straight for the Germans and, under the alias George William Hope, offered to supply information concerning Atlantic convoys. BSC however tipped off the American Immigration Department, who arrested 'Hope' in Boston on 16 October, 1940.

Armstrong remained in American custody until the following year when deportation proceedings were brought against him by the US Department of State.

On 21 February, 1941 Armstrong arrived in Cardiff on board a Californian oil tanker, the SS *La Brea* and was met on the quay by Detective-Superintendent Lowden Roberts of the Cardiff City Police. He was arrested and taken under police escort to London where he was transferred into the care of MI5. Less than three months later, on 8 May, 1941, Armstrong was sent for trial *in camera* at the Old Bailey. He appeared before Mr Justice Lewis, was found guilty and sentenced to death. His appeal was dismissed on 23 June, 1941 and he climbed the scaffold at Wandsworth Prison on 10 July, 1941.

Between the end of Armstrong's brief trial and his appeal Hitler launched BARBAROSSA, his massive offensive against the Soviet Union. News of the attack reached London on the morning of 22 June, 1941, a Sunday, and caught the CPGB completely off guard. A meeting of their 'Political Bureau' was hastily called to reverse the CPGB's war policy (which had been one of support for the Nazis) and later the same day the Bureau issued a statement condemning Hitler. Douglas Hyde, then a senior CPGB official, described the event as 'the Party's most spectacular somersault'.[31] Overnight an unjust war had been transformed into a righteous one. It must have been bitter news for Armstrong.

By early 1941 the Bl staff had created an impressive picture of the Abwehr's structure and with the aid of the Bletchley decrypters were beginning to speculate with considerable accuracy on the intention of the enemy. Many of the principal opposition personalities had been identified and the ISOS and ISK intercepts enabled the Bl analysts to monitor the standing of their double cross agents. One example of their cross-referencing activity occurred shortly after Christmas 1940 when the name 'George Rymer' was spotted on a routine ISK summary. The name had previously been given to SNOW by MI5 as a suitable fictitious identity for him to pass on to Hamburg, should they ask him for an inconspicuous name. Now apparently, the Germans intended to make use of the details provided by B1(a).

The agent using the name George Rymer dropped by parachute in to a field near Ramsey in Huntingdonshire on the night of 31 January / 1 February, 1941. His arrival was first noted by two farm labourers, Charlie Baldock and his brother-in-law Harry Coulson, who were walking to work across their small holding, Dove House Farm, at around half-past seven in the morning. They were discussing the sound of a low-flying aircraft they had heard the previous night, and both agreed that it had been a German bomber. Suddenly a shot rang out and both men dropped to the ground in surprise. Another shot was fired and almost immediately they spotted the source – someone lying in a potato field a few hundred yards away. They cautiously approached the figure, who began to wave his arms in the air. He was evidently injured and needed their help.

The man on the ground was middle-aged, and introduced himself as a parachutist from Germany. When the two farm labourers had recovered from their surprise they examined the leg of the injured man. It was badly broken and all three agreed he could not be moved without help. Coulson elected to stay with the distressed figure while Baldock ran over to Shelton's Farm to raise the alarm. The foreman at Shelton's promptly telephoned Ramsey police station and also warned his son. Harry Godfrey, of Baldock's discovery. Harry Godfrey held the rank of Lance-Corporal in the local Home Guard so he quickly slipped on his uniform, armed himself with a rifle and went to arrest the German parachutist.

In the meantime, Coulson had taken the opportunity to talk to his immoblized captive who started to explain that he was not in fact a

German. He was, he claimed, a Luxembourger by birth. He had spent a miserable night in great pain and had smoked only a part of his cigarette supply before his lighter had run out of fuel. Underneath his Luftwaffe regulation flying tunic he wore a grey pin-striped suit with spats. Beside him was a smart brown trilby, a steel helmet with some pieces of chocolate in it and a flask of brandy. A few feet away lay a small military-issue shovel and a partly concealed fibre suitcase. When this was eventually dug up and opened, a five-valve radio transmitter was found inside. Coulson also searched his prisoner's pockets and recovered a forged identity card in the name of George Rymer and an unused ration book.

At nine o'clock a single policeman from Ramsey arrived on his bicycle to take command of the situation. He borrowed a horse and cart from Shelton's Farm and transported the wretched German spy to Ramsey police station in the back of it. Once safely in his cell he was given a thorough search and relieved of some five hundred one-pound notes in two bundles. There was little doubt in anyone's mind that the prisoner was a spy so he was driven the same day down to Scotland Yard, and finally 020. There he underwent the usual intensive interrogation by Colonel Stephens and 'the Board'. The parachutist gave his name as Josef Jakobs, born in Luxembourg on 30 June, 1898. In civilian life he had been a dentist, typewriter salesman, mortgage broker, bookseller and in a variety of other trades. When war broke out he was a Reservist and had been called up for service in the Wehrmacht before transferring to the Abwehr in Hamburg in September 1940. For three months he had undergone wireless training until he could achieve sixteen words per minute in morse. On 8 January, 1941 he moved to The Hague for instruction in weather reporting and when this was completed he was dispatched on his mission.

Jakobs also claimed to have joined the Abwehr in an attempt to escape Germany and sabotage the war effort. A mysterious Dr Burgos had asked him to join the Abwehr as an agent of a secret Jewish society. His aim was to make contact with Jews in Britain and resist the Nazis. None of this impressed 'the Board' much and it was decided to place Jakobs on trial.

As a bona fide member of the German armed forces Jakobs was entitled to be kept in military custody and be tried by court martial. This involved considerable preparation and was to be a unique case for the legal section of 'A' Division. Under usual circumstances espionage prosecutions were handled by the Director of Public Prosecutions's staff who liaised closely with Toby Pilcher, Jim Hale and Edward Cussen. In this case however the prosecution for the Crown was to be brought by the Judge Advocate-General's office, in the person of Major A. Marlowe. Jakobs himself was transferred from 020 to Brixton Prison, and as the latter was a civilian establishment Anthony Eden, then Secretary of State for War, signed a special Order placing Jakobs' cell under military authority.

On 4 August, 1941 Jakobs was driven from Brixton to the Duke of York's Headquarters in Chelsea where Major-General Bevil Wilson DSO, a Royal Engineers officer, was to preside over the court martial. Captain Eric White, a barrister from Lincoln's Inn, was appointed for the defence, and an Intelligence Corps officer, Lieutenant W.J. Thomas acted as interpreter.

The proceedings lasted two days, all were *in camera*, and were attended by, amongst others, those who had initially found the prisoner, Harry Coulson, Harry Godfrey and Charlie Baldock. At one point Jakobs nodded his recognition to the three men and when the verdict of guilty was announced, tried to give them his silver cigarette case and lighter. Jakobs' defence rested solely on the mysterious Dr Burgos and was not well received by the tribunal. He also denied being a member of the Nazi Party, and pleaded with the Court to remember his wife and three children.

When the death sentence was pronounced Jakobs was taken straight to the Tower of London where a cell had been prepared for him on the top floor of Waterloo Barracks, at the east end of 'E' Block. He was in the custody of the Holding Battalion, the Scots Guards, while a fruitless appeal against sentence was heard by the King. When the appeal was refused a German-born priest, Father Josef Simmil, from St Boniface Church in Aldgate, was made available for the prisoner. In the event Jakobs declined the opportunity to have his confession heard.

On Thursday, 14 August, 1941, Jakobs was escorted limping from his cell to the indoor miniature firing range at the eastern end of the Tower's perimeter wall. A firing squad was waiting, consisting of eight men, two from each of the Companies, under the command of Major P.D.J. Waters MC. Jakobs was seated in an ordinary brown Windsor chair with a circular piece of white lint pinned over his heart as target.

At exactly twelve minutes past twelve noon Major Waters gave the signal to fire and Jakobs was executed. Five bullets pierced the lint.

Jakob's body was then carried to the Tower mortuary in the moat where Sir Bernard Spilsbury carried out a postmortem. He certified the cause of death as 'injuries to the heart due to the passage of bullets'. When the examination was over the corpse was driven across London in conditions of secrecy and buried in a common grave (No 1734G) in St Mary's Roman Catholic Cemetery, Kensal Green. The damaged chair is now in the Tower of London; the lint has been retained by the Scots Guards HQ.

The following day the national newspapers reported the finding of the spy and his execution and for a while the farm workers Baldock, Coulson and Godfrey became the centre of attention 'somewhere in the Home Counties'. The censors prevented many details of the case from being published but this did not stop a few Fleet Street journalists from following up the story. The sequel however was unfortunate. A small celebration was held in the local pub, The Farmer's Boy, at the expense of one of the interested newspapers. The ensuing revelry was interrupted by the police, who put a stop to the after-hours drinking. Mr Townsend, the landlord, and Charlie Baldock were fined 2s 6d and 5s respectively the following day in the Magistrate's Court.

On 14 May, 1941 MI5 entrapped yet another German parachutist through the efforts of B1(a). TATE had for some time been pestering his Hamburg controllers for a new valve for his radio. After much delay the Abwehr agreed to send one. The agent chosen for this task was Karel Richard Richter, a twenty-nine-year-old Sudeten Czech, born in Kraslice. He was instructed to contact TATE in the lobby of the Regent Palace Hotel in Piccadilly, and failing that, the Tate Gallery on the Embankment. In the event of the spies missing each other at these rendezvous they were to meet at the British Museum. These directions were received by TATE's Voluntary Interceptor, Russell Lee, who made the appropriate arrangements with B1(a).

When the time came there was no need for the elaborate surveillance operation that had been prepared. Richter landed by parachute early in the morning of 14 May in a field near Tyttenhanger Park, London Colney, Hertfordshire. He hid his parachute in a dense hedge and spent the rest of the day in hiding. The following evening, he started walking west along the A405 towards the A6 main road to London. He had not gone far when a lorry pulled up beside him. The driver leaned over and asked Richter for directions, which he was unable to give. His somewhat incoherent reply mystified the man in the cab, who drove on. As luck would have it the driver spotted a policeman soon afterwards and obtained the directions he needed from him.

During the course of their conversation the driver mentioned the suspicious character who had been so unhelpful a few minutes earlier. Constable Alec Scott promised to investigate and climbed on his bicycle in pursuit of Richter. He found the German agent in a telephone box at the A6 crossroads. Scott challenged him for his papers and was offered an Alien's Registration Card in the name of 'Fred Snyder'. The card was in order but Scott realized that the alien before him would soon be breaking the law. There was less than an hour until 11 PM, the curfew limit when all aliens were obliged to be at their registered addresses. The address on the card was in London and it would be impossible for 'Snyder' to comply with the regulation. Scott suggested Snyder should accompany him to the police station, at which the German said he felt unwell and needed a drink. Scott knocked on the door of a house nearby to get a glass of water, but there was no reply. Richter then watched as Scott telephoned the Fleetville police station for a patrol car.

Sergeant Palmer and Constable Clark were soon on the scene to take charge of Richter and drive him to Tess Road police station. Once there he was searched and found to have a Swedish passport in the name of Karel Richter. The following morning, he was driven to Hatfield police station where he was interviewed by a delegation from 020 – Colonel Stephens, Major Stimson, Major Samson, Dr Dearden, Superintendent Foster of Special Branch, and Captains Short and Goodacre.

Richter quickly admitted his true identity and agreed to take the party back to the field where his parachute was concealed. The MI5 team also took possession of his wireless, his genuine Czech passport (No 109/39), his loaded automatic and his money ($1,000 and £300). The operation in London was called off and Richter was driven back to 020.

A tall, thin, red-haired individual, Richter declined to join B1(a)'s double cross system but agreed to make a full statement documenting his background. He described his education and air force service in Czechoslovakia, and how he had joined the Hamburg-Amerika Line in 1936 as a marine engineer. For three years he worked on the trans-Atlantic run, fathering a child in Long Island during one period in the United States. When the war broke out he was on the SS *Hansa* bound for Southampton from Hamburg. The liner was ordered back to Germany, and as soon as it docked Richter headed for his home in Kraslice, Czechoslovakia. Called up for industrial war duty when he arrived, he travelled across Poland and Latvia during November 1939 in an effort to reach neutral Sweden. His intention was to go to the United States but he never got further than Stockholm, where he was arrested as an illegal alien by the police on 2 February, 1940. He was interned for the following five months and then deported back to Germany.

Once in Germany Richter was evidently arrested by the Gestapo and eventually recruited in November 1940 by the Abwehr as a courier for TATE. Richter appeared at the Old Bailey before Mr Justice Tucker and was sentenced to death on 21 October, 1941. He was led to the scaffold on 10 December, 1941, but to the dismay of those gathered to watch the proceedings the prisoner went berserk when he reached the trapdoor.

The hangman, Albert Pierrepoint, and four warders struggled for some minutes to pin Richter down so that a leather strap could be secured around his wrists. After an extraordinary free-for-all he was forced into position and Pierrepoint pulled the lever. To his horror though, the noose slipped over Richter's chin as he dropped, and then caught him under his nose. The noose held and the first and second vertebrae of the prisoner's spinal column were dislocated, causing an almost instantaneous death.[32]

The grisly scene had a profound effect on all those present and, indirectly, on some other Abwehr agents. Several months later Pierrepoint and his chief assistant, Steve Wade, carried out an execution at Mountjoy in Dublin. News of Richter's final moments reached Gunther Schütz and his fellow internees (some of whom were bound for England before their arrest). The Irish warders gleefully recounted the details of the struggle on the scaffold, sending Richter's former colleagues into a deep depression.

No sooner had the Richter case been closed in Britain by MI5 than it was opened on the other side of the Atlantic. A memorandum was sent by the Director-General to the FBI in Washington because of Richter's American connections. Richter's wife was living in California although the rest of his family, including his mother, Martha was in Kraslice. The FBI investigation that followed was instituted by J. Edgar Hoover, and centred on Richter's last known address in New York. In his statement to MI5 Richter admitted arriving in the United States in July 1938, although the Immigration authorities on Ellis Island could find no record of his entry. He had apparently lived at 3727 79th Street, in Jackson Heights, New York, a predominantly German and Irish neighbourhood, but again the FBI could find no trace of anyone in the ten apartments who remembered the young Sudeten. After three months the FBI came to the conclusion that 'Karel Richard Richter, alias Al Richter' was of no further interest, except as an unusual case history.

The speed with which the parachute agents were intercepted proved the degree of vigilance maintained by the population in Britain, especially in rural areas. The parachutists themselves had helped by being conspicuous in their initial contacts with the local residents, but the large number of refugees still pouring in from the Continent during the autumn of 1940 and on into 1941 worried MI5 for such crowds offered plenty of cover for the infiltration of agents. After the evacuation of Dunkirk, Poles, Danes, Belgians, Dutch and French continued to flood in. Each one had to be individually screened at one of the refugee reception centres: few were allowed to escape the examination which sometimes took several weeks to complete. Even agents under the sponsorship of another intelligence organization, such as SIS or SOE, were obliged to undergo the treatment.

The first confirmed German agent to be intercepted at the RVPS was Alphons Timmerman, a twenty-eight-year-old Belgian ship's steward who landed at Rothesay Dock, Glasgow, on 1 September, 1941. Timmerman had joined the SS *Ulea* in Gibraltar, having allegedly trekked across France and been arrested by the Spanish authorities in Vitoria. The local Belgian Consul had, he claimed, negotiated his release from the Nancleres Internment Camp, and Timmerman had been allowed to continue his journey. In Gibraltar, he had found a passage on the *Ulea*, a Glen Line vessel carrying a cargo of iron ore from Seville to Glasgow. The journey had passed without incident, although some damage was suffered when Captain Ambrose docked his ship at Rothesay.[33]

Timmerman was given a routine interview on the dock at which he expressed a desire to join the Free Belgian Merchant Navy. His army service had been limited to less than a year in the 1st Medical Unit, from which he had been discharged in May 1925 for general ill-health and 'lack of strength'. The diminutive Belgian had very few possessions with him, as might be expected, but he was extraordinarily well funded. His wallet contained $475, £97 10s, and a small envelope.

The envelope attracted the attention of the examining officer and his suspicions were justified when the white powder inside was analysed. It was an ingredient for secret writing and was apparently to be used with a small bunch of orange sticks and a ball of cotton wool, also found on the 'refugee'.

Timmerman was sent for trial at the Old Bailey before Mr Justice Humphreys on 20 May, 1942. He was found guilty of Treachery. His appeal was dismissed on 22 June, 1942, and he was hanged with Jose Key on 7 July.

This date had a particular significance for Franciscus Winter, the next Abwehr agent to use the same route to Britain, for he had arrived in Gibraltar just two days earlier and was thus already beyond recall. Winter was also a Belgian seaman and had started his 'refugee' trek from Antwerp in May 1942. He had travelled by car to Paris, and having stayed there a week, motored on to Hendaye, near the Spanish frontier. A Basque guide had taken him to San Sebastian where he had caught a train to Madrid, only to be arrested by the police in Vitoria, just as Timmerman had been. He was taken to the Nancleres Internment Camp, but was released before the end of the month. Winter, by now established as a refugee, carried on to Madrid by train and had finally arrived in Gibraltar on 5 July, via Seville and Huelva. Three days later the newspapers carried the story of the execution of Timmerman and

Key, news that received plenty of attention on the Rock because Key, a Gibraltarian, had been arrested earlier in the year (see Chapter XI).

If the Abwehr had even wanted to warn their agent, it was too late. Winter was in British territory and arrangements had been made to send the thirty-nine-year-old deck-steward to England. He joined the SS *Llanstephan Castle* with a group of other refugees and arrived at Gourock in Scotland on 31 July, 1942. All were routinely taken into custody and escorted down to the RVPS by the police.

Winter spent the next three months at the RVPS demanding his right to join the Free Belgian Forces but he had difficulty in explaining how he came to possess over £100 in francs, pesetas, dollars and sterling. Eventually in November Winter signed a confession and was charged with Treachery. He was tried the following month at the Old Bailey before Mr Justice Humphreys and found guilty on 4 December, 1942. He was hanged in Wandsworth Prison on 26 January, 1943.

The interrogators at the RVPS centre, who were a mixture of MI9 and MI5, claimed Timmerman and Winter as their first successes, but as these cases were being examined another German agent was being cornered by the Dutch section of the RVPS.

On 18 May, 1942 His Majesty's Trawler *Corena*, on patrol in the North Sea, spotted a small craft bobbing in the water. Three men were on board, all refugees from Nazi-occupied Holland – or so they claimed. They gave their names as Mulder, Dronkers and de Langen and were ferried into Harwich, where they were met on Parkstone Quay by Detective Constable Len Chaplin. Chaplin led the three to 'Fairhaven', a seaside villa on Marine Parade which had been requisitioned by the Field Security Wing.

This was the first contact with the British Security Service for the three Dutchmen. They were segregated and then interviewed by Captain de Vries and Sergeant Jock Morrison. Mulder and de Langen, the two younger men, seemed genuine enough, but Dronkers, a forty-six-year-old post office clerk demonstrated an exaggerated gratitude for his salvation. His first act was to kneel down and kiss the ground. His behaviour was suspicious as well as ridiculous, so the Field Security Wing delivered all three separately to Harwich police station for onward transmission to the RVPS in the company of Constable Knock.

At the RVPS Dronkers was interrogated by Colonel Oreste Pinto, the head of the Dutch section, and Adrianus Vrinten, a former private detective.

When Dronkers was confronted with Vrinten his pose as a resistance activist collapsed. Before the war Vrinten had investigated the activities of the National Socialistische Beweging, Mussert's Dutch Nazis, for the Justice Department and he recognized Dronkers as a leading Party member. Dronkers admitted being in the pay of the Germans and surrendered his cover addresses. He further gave up the message of 'safe arrival' he was supposed to broadcast over Radio Oranje to Holland. He was sent for trial at the Old Bailey on 13 November, 1942 and was hanged on New Year's Eve at Wandsworth.

The youngest of all the spies to be executed during the war was a Briton, Duncan Scott-Ford, a twenty-one-year-old seaman from Plymouth. He was recruited by the Abwehr following an encounter in a Lisbon bar in 1941.

Scott-Ford was the son of Edwin Ford and Mary Scott of 3 Pym Street, Plymouth. He joined the Royal Navy at Devonport on 9 March, 1937 with the rank of 'Boy 2nd Class'. His Naval career was far from distinguished. After a period of training ashore Scott-Ford joined his first ship, HMS *Cornwall*, in April 1938. This modern county class cruiser was at the time on station with the Home Fleet and in June 1938 took part in the Fleet Review before King George VI. The following year *Cornwall* was sent to the Far East, so Scott-Ford transferred to shore establishment before joining the newly commissioned HMS *Gloucester*. Again, when *Gloucester* was ordered to the East Indies in March 1939 Scott-Ford remained in England at a shore base.

Scott-Ford was dismissed from the Navy on 3 March, 1941 in Alexandria, following disciplinary proceedings for theft. The pay-book of one of his ship-mates disappeared and when it was recovered Scott-Ford was found guilty of the offence.

After his dismissal Scott-Ford made his way back to England from Egypt and got a job on the *Medway*, a cargo vessel plying on the river between Bristol and the Avonmouth Docks.

In September 1941 he travelled up to Glasgow to join the Merchant Navy, and on 12 September found a berth as an Able Seaman on the SS *Almenara*. He spent three and a half months on the *Almenara*, leaving her in January the following year to sign on with the SS *Finland* in Greenock on 2 February, 1942. This vessel's first voyage with Scott-Ford aboard ended without incident in Liverpool in April, but a second voyage to Lisbon to collect a cargo of tungsten ended in Scott-Ford's arrest.

According to Scott-Ford's statement to MI5, he was approached in a bar, the 'Las Quandierras', by a girl who kept ordering drinks. He was unable to pay the bill at the end of the evening and gratefully accepted a loan of 1,800 escudos (about £18) from a man who inevitably turned out to be working for the Germans. Scott-Ford foolishly signed an IOU, but instead of repaying the money agreed to give information about Allied convoys. Scott-Ford claimed that initially he had objected to the proposal but later collapsed when the Abwehr agent threatened to send his IOU to Sir Ronald Campbell, the British Ambassador in Lisbon.

Scott-Ford's recruitment did not, however, go unnoticed by the Bletchley decrypters who followed the affair on the ISK intercepts between Portugal and Germany. When the *Finland* docked in Salford on 19 August, 1942 Detective Sergeant John Brown of the Salford City Police was waiting for him.

The *Finland's* skipper, Captain Archibald Lockie, gave permission for the seaman's quarters to be given a thorough search and amongst his belongings were found some incriminating notes concerning the speed, course and composition of the convoy from Lisbon. Scott-Ford was taken into custody under Regulation 18B of the 1939 Defence Regulations and then transferred to 020 for interrogation by MI5.

Scott-Ford made a full confession and admitted collecting information for the Germans. He was charged with Treachery at the Old Bailey on 16 October, 1942 before Mr Justice Birkett. The senior prosecuting counsel in the DPP's office, Mr George McClure, led for the Crown while his deputy at the Old Bailey since 1932, Mr Anthony Hawke (later Sir Anthony Hawke, and a judge) appeared for the defence. In spite of his genuine remorse Scott-Ford was found guilty of aiding the enemy on his last voyage on the SS *Finland* and was sentenced to death. He refused to appeal against his conviction and was hanged at Wandsworth on 3 November, 1942.

Until the arrival of Oswald Job in the autumn of 1943 the infiltration of agents into the United Kingdom had not presented major difficulties. Each of the cases to go for trial had been identified without any danger of compromising MI5's two chief sources on enemy intentions, the ULTRA intercepts and the double cross agent. Job, however, created considerable problems because of his link with DRAGONFLY, a 'double' dating back to the end of April 1940 who had declared himself to MI5 as soon as he arrived in Britain from Holland. DRAGONFLY had collected a wireless disguised as a record player from Lisbon in January 1941 and had kept in radio contact with the Abwehr ever since. A large part of his messages was devoted to the subject of money and it was Job's mission to deliver the badly-needed funds from the Abwehr. B1(a)'s dilemma was two-fold. An arrest of Job, a British subject, would inevitably raise doubts about DRAGONFLY, and unless Job volunteered that he was working as a spy there would be little excuse to arrest him.

This debate continued in St James's Street while Job presented himself at the British Embassy in Madrid, apparently an exhausted refugee from occupied France. His story combined fact with fiction. He had been born Oswald John Job at 4 Chadbourn Street, Bromley, on 4 July, 1885, the son of John and Christina Job, both German bakers. He had been educated privately in England and had gone to live in France in 1911. There he married his wife Marcelle, and had set up a business manufacturing artificial eyes. Whe Paris fell to the Germans in June 1940 Job was arrested at his home at 1 rue Rossini, and taken to the St Denis Internment Camp in the north of the capital. Job was to spend the next three years in the camp before succumbing to an offer from the Abwehr to spy in England. Aged fifty-eight and a non-combatant, Job was able to get a Portuguese transit visa without much difficulty and was passed from the Madrid Embassy to the British Repatriation Office in Lisbon. Here he admitted to having only £81 so a message was sent to his brother in Lewisham who agreed to act as guarantor for the cost of the air ticket from Lisbon to Bristol.

Meanwhile the Refugee Department of the Foreign Office were being discreetly warned of MI5's interest in Job. A seat was found for him on one of the scheduled flights and he duly arrived in Britain on 1 November, 1943. At Bristol airport he was subjected to a routine search and was allowed to continue his journey to London where, according to the ULTRA summaries and DRAGONFLY, he was supposed to deliver a valuable diamond tie-pin from the Abwehr. Job had been offered three opportunities to confess all to the British authorities but he had kept silent. Now he was kept under surveillance but he made no attempt to hand over the tie-pin.

Reluctantly MI5 decided that their only course was to maintain permanent observation on Job, who had settled into his brother William's house at 37 Rhyme Road. Suddenly though, on 22 November, matters came unexpectedly to a head. Job was crossing Piccadilly just a matter of yards from MI5's headquarters and stepped on to a 'refuge' in the middle of the road. The heavy traffic forced his Special Branch tail to do the same thing, and Job angrily turned on him and accused him of following him. Astonished, the policeman arrested Job and took him to Vine Street police station where frantic telephone calls were made.

B1(a) were furious, but it was too late to recover the situation. The only option left was to find evidence against Job which could be publicized, thus informing the Germans of his demise and reassuring them of DRAGONFLY's continued industry. The flaw in the scheme was the lack of proof against Job. The tie-pin itself was unimportant and MI5 were reluctant to reveal their special information to the prisoner. As expected Job protested his innocence but his story collapsed when his 020 interrogator produced the name of his Abwehr contact in London, Edith Agnes May. Special Branch detectives then went to Rhyme Road and ransacked his brother's house. The search turned up a bunch of keys which on examination were found to be hollow. The barrels of each key had been skilfully drilled out, leaving a cavity for secret ink crystals. This evidence was enough to get Job to admit his guilt. He made a full statement to his interrogators and was charged before a magistrate four days before Christmas. His trial took place over three days at the Old Bailey, commencing on 24 January, 1944. He was found guilty of Treachery and sentenced to death by Mr Justice Stable.[34]

Job's appeal was dismissed on 28 February and he was hanged at Pentonville Prison on 16 March, 1944. The following day the newspapers reported the execution and described how Job had been instructed by the German Secret Service to send messages in secret ink to the St Denis Internment Camp. The letters were to be intercepted en route, but, as the *Daily Telegraph* stated, Job 'was caught before he had any opportunity of spying'. The article was sub-titled 'HID SECRET INK IN KEY HOLLOWS' and gave the impression Job had been intercepted at the airport where his special keys had been spotted. No mention was made of DRAGONFLY or Job's three weeks at liberty in London!

There were several sequels to the case, not least of which was Mrs Marcelle Job's letters from Paris to the Foreign Office requesting information. Job's brother William was asked by the Foreign Office's Refugee Department to repay the £35 owing for the Lisbon air ticket. And, perhaps the greatest irony of all, DRAGONFLY was obliged to cease operations in January because the Abwehr had not paid him.

The route taken by Job to England had in fact already been used successfully some months earlier by yet another Abwehr agent, Pierre Neukermans, a twenty-eight-year-old Belgian officer from Waarbeeke who presented himself in Spain as an escapee from the Nazis.

Neukermans had entered the Belgian military Ecole des Cadets shortly after his sixteenth birthday and graduated in July 1935 with a respectable overall assessment mark of 7.5 out of a possible 10. During his three years' training he had attended a course at the Belgian Aeronautics School and was attached from the 7th (Infantry) Division to the Air Force with the rank of Second Lieutenant in December 1937. The following year he was transferred back to the army on undisclosed medical grounds, and discharged on 28 September, 1938.

Neukerman's journey to England began in the middle of June 1943 when he left his wife, Mariette, at home in and travelled to Lille, Paris,

Perpignan, Barcelona, Zaragossa, Valladolid and Lisbon, where he flew by flying-boat to Poole on 16 July. The following month he was cleared as a genuine refugee and re-enlisted in the Compagnie Administrative with the rank of Sergeant-Major. He was assigned to the Belgian War Office-in-exile at their headquarters in Belgrave Square and was working in the Congolese affairs department when he was arrested on 5 February, 1944. His six months at liberty came to an end because two of the 'Resistance workers' he had claimed as friends had been unmasked in Brussels as collaborators. As soon as word reached London Neukermans was interviewed. He admitted sending letters in secret ink and was charged with Treachery. He was found guilty on 1 May 1944, and was hanged at Pentonville on 24 June, 1944.

The last German agent to be executed in Britain was a twenty-seven-year-old Belgian waiter from Deurne named Joseph Vanhove who arrived in Scotland via Sweden, a novel route.

Before the war Vanhove had volunteered for the Belgian army, but had been discharged after suffering a double hernia. He then went to live in France, but returned to Antwerp after the German occupation in 1940. He had only been back in Belgium a matter of weeks before he was in trouble with the police for black marketeering. He had to leave the country quickly so he obtained the help of the Germans through a collaborator friend. Vanhove was offered employment as an informer in northern France. His job was to betray any of the Belgian and French labour building Luftwaffe airfields who were sympathetic to the Resistance. Vanhove apparently executed his duties on behalf of the Germans so well that he was selected to go to England. In the middle of 1942 he set off on his mission to England, via neutral Switzerland, with a Belgian companion. The attempt failed when they were turned back at the frontier. The Abwehr then decided to infiltrate him to England via Sweden. In April 1943 he joined a German merchant vessel, the *Saar*, in Hamburg as steward, and jumped ship on arrival in Gothenburg. On 28 April Vanhove reported to the Belgian Legation in Stockholm and informed the Chargé d'Affaires, Prince Reginald de Croÿ, that he wished to travel to England and re-enlist. De Croÿ was impressed by the deserter's patriotism and arranged for him to stay at a hostel in the Stockholm suburb of Spomanshen, at Peter Myndes Racka 3. On 5 May, 1943 de Croÿ wrote to Henri Spaak, the Belgian Foreign Minister in London, and recounted some of the adventures Vanhove had described, including an incident when 'Vanhove was arrested by the Germans in Antwerp earlier this year on suspicion of keeping a hidden store of revolvers, but was released for lack of proof.'

The Sixteen Spies Executed in Britain During World War II

Name and (Alias) Of Spy	Age	Date of Birth	Nationality	Place of Birth	Date of Formal Arrest	Place of Original Arrest	Date of Trial	Date of Execution	Place of Execution
Jose Waldberg	25	15.7.15	German	Mainz	4.9.40	Dungeness, Kent	22.11.40	10.12.40	Pentonville
Carl Meier	24	18.10.16	Dutch	Coblenz	3.9.40	Lydd, Kent	22.11.40	10.12.40	Pentonville
Charles van den Kieboom	26	6.9.14	Dutch	Takarazuka Japan	3.9.40	Dymchurch, Kent	22.11.40	17.12.40	Pentonville
Robert Petter (Werner Wälti)	25	14.12.15	German (Swiss)	(Zurich)	30.9.40	Edinburgh	12.6.41	6.8.41	Wandsworth
Karl Drücke (François de Deeker)	34	20.3.06	German Hessen	Grebenstein,	30.9.40	Portgordon, Scotland	12.6.41	6.8.41	Wandsworth
Josef Jakobs (Gerorge Rymer)	43	30.6.1898	German	Luxembourg	1.2.41	Ramsey, Hunts	4.8.41	14.8.71	Tower of London
George Armstrong (George Hope)	39	4.2.02	British	Newcastle	21.2.41	Boston USA then Cardiff	8.5.41	10.7.41	Wandsworth

Jose Key	33	1.7.08	British	Gibraltar	5.2.42	Gibraltar	15.5.42	7.7.42	Wandsworth
Alphons Timmerman	28	1.8.04	Belgian	Ostend	1.9.41	Glasgow	20.5.42	7.7.42	Wandsworth
Karel Richter (Fred Snyder)	29	29.1.12	German	Kraslice	14.5.41	London Colney, Herts	21.10.41	10.12.41	Wandsworth
Johannes Dronkers	46	3.4.1896	Dutch	Nigtevecht	18.5.42	Harwich	13.11.42	31.12.42	Wandsworth
Franciscus Winter	39	17.1.03	Belgian	Antwerp	31.7.42	Gourock, Scotland	4.12.42	26.1.43	Wandsworth
Duncan Scott-Ford	21	4.9.21	British	Plymouth	19.8.42	Salford Docks	16.10.42	3.11.42	Wandsworth
Oswald Job	58	4.7.1885	British	London	22.11.43	London	24.1.44	16.3.44	Pentonville
Pierre Neukermans	28	1.5.16	Belgian	Waarbeeke	2.2.44	London	28.4.44	24.6.44	Pentonville
Joseph Vanhove	27	2.3.17	Belgian	Antwerp	5.5.44	Leuchars	23.5.44	12.7.44	Pentonville

Spies Executed in Gibraltar

Luis Cordon-Cuenca	23	27.8.20	Spanish	La Linea	23.6.43	Gibraltar	19.8.43	11.1.44	Gibraltar
Jose Munoz	19	28.7.24	Spanish	La Linea	1.7.43	Gibraltar	11.10.43	11.1.44	Gibraltar

In spite of de Croÿ's letter to London Vanhove remained in Stockholm for eight months, usually working in restaurants as a dishwasher. The Swedish authorities granted him four temporary residence and work permits, but finally a flight to Britain was arranged, just days after he had obtained a further three-month extension. Vanhove arrived at Leuchars Airport on the east coast of Scotland on 11 February, 1944. The Port Security staff routinely took him into custody for questioning and then had him taken down to London for more detailed interrogation.

Vanhove was formally arrested in London on 5 May, 1944, and appeared at the Old Bailey *in camera* on 23 May. The following day he was found guilty of Treachery and sentenced to death by Mr Justice Hallett. His appeal was dismissed on 27 June and he was hanged at Pentonville on 12 July, 1944.

The sixteen men executed in London during the war have sometimes been referred to as 'the unlucky sixteen'. One further German agent, who nearly became the seventeenth, can be described however as very lucky indeed. He holds the unique distinction of being the only wartime spy to be sentenced to death for espionage, and be reprieved.

Rogerio de Magalhaes Peixoto de Menezes was twenty-six years old at the time of his conviction in April 1943. He had worked for the Germans since coming to London in June the previous year to take up a junior post in the Portuguese Embassy. His mail was routinely examined by the LIU when the Lisbon address he wrote to turned out to be a known Nazi Security Service 'post-box'. In spite of his diplomatic status he was arrested on 22 February, 1943 and taken by Special Branch detectives to Scotland Yard where he was questioned in the presence of an Embassy official. Confronted with evidence taken from his flat de Menezes admitted his guilt.

When the Ambassador, Dr Armindo Monteiro, learnt of the confession he fired the clerk, thus depriving him of his diplomatic status. He was tried *in camera* at the Old Bailey and sentenced to death. His appeal was rejected on 13 May, 1943 but the following month the Home Secretary, Herbert Morrison, recommended a reprieve to the King and the sentence was reduced to one of life imprisonment.

Only one man is known to have spied in the United Kingdom during World War II and evaded capture. At least two men claim to have parachuted into Britain between 1939 and 1945 and successfully returned to Germany without being detected, but their stories cannot be checked. The case of Jan Willem Ter Braak was the only one to be investigated by MI5 – because his body was found on the morning of April Fool's Day 1941.

Ter Braak's real identity has never been established, but enquiries made by the Cambridge RSLO and a representative from B1(b), Herbert Hart, confirmed that the dead man had indeed been a spy. His body was found by the Air Raid Shelter Marshal for Christ's Pieces, Mrs Alice Stutley, shortly after 9 AM in a partly completed shelter. He wore a dark overcoat and a homberg hat, and had been shot in the head. The Chief Constable, Mr R.G. Pearson, immediately contacted Richard Dixon, the RSLO, and a major search was put in motion.

There was little doubt that Ter Braak had committed suicide but MI5 had to establish that he was an independent agent, and not a part of an established network operating outside the double cross system. The address on his Registration Card, 7 Oxford Road, was examined, as was his 'office' in Rose Crescent.

Very little, however, could be discovered about Ter Braak. He had first turned up in Cambridge in November the previous year, and had found lodgings at 58 Barnabas Road, claiming to be a Dutch refugee. Shortly afterwards he moved to Montague Road, before finally settling in Oxford Road. His Registration Card was a poor forgery although the Coroner, Walter Wallis, confirmed that his age was approximately twenty-seven, as stated in his papers. His remaining possessions included a wireless transmitter and a number of bus tickets. His journeys were meticulously reconstructed and found to take in several of the important airfields in the county. Hart's final report to MI5 was inconclusive, but suggested that Ter Braak had shot himself because he had run out of funds and ration books. It was impossible to judge the value of the intelligence he had managed to send back to Germany. He was indeed a unique spy.

Somewhat luckier was Lilian Smith, a nineteen-year-old daughter of a British father and Dutch mother. She was arrested by Canadian troops on the morning of 11 November, 1944, having crossed the River Maas from the enemy lines opposite. Miss Smith admitted that she was a German agent and was passed into British custody. Her father had moved to the United States in 1940 and had left his wife and daughter to fend for themselves near Utrecht.

Three months later she was tried by a British military court in Brussels and sentenced to twelve years' imprisonment on a charge of espionage. After four months in a Belgian prison the General Officer Commanding ordered her release. She had the dubious distinction of being the last British subject of the war to be charged with spying.

X

11 and 16 King Street, WC

'The Comintern Is Not Dead'

The title of Max Knight's report on Soviet infiltration of the United Kingdom. The report was rejected by Roger Hollis but was later read by Churchill, having been passed to him secretly by the Prime Minister's Personal Assistant, Major Desmond Morton.

In May 1935 Stalin addressed the Red Army academies and inspired the creation worldwide of 'cadres', Party enthusiasts willing to promote covertly the interest of the Seventh Communist International. Like most of the other Communist Parties, the Communist Party of Great Britain had long debated the issue of preparing for an underground war. Various reliable activists had already dropped from view, their former political allies instructed to forget that their 'comrades' had ever been members of the Party. The CPGB's motive for the recruitment of 'closed members' was eminently practical. The Party could not fail to be aware of the interest of the authorities and most of the Central Committee believed that sooner or later the Party would be banned by the government. It was therefore expedient to plan for that event. In King Street a secret Cadres Department was set up and the names of its members passed to the NKVD representative in the Soviet Embassy for safe-keeping.

As war approached the CPGB became increasingly convinced that the organization would be closed down. The system of 'closed members' was reinforced by the dispersal of several Party printing presses to the homes of reliable sympathizers, thus establishing the infrastructure of an illicit network.

The CPGB's fears were realized to the extent that the *Daily Worker* was banned for a period of twenty months in January 1941 under Emergency

Regulation 2D. The Party itself though was never banned, even during the Molotov/Ribbentrop pact when trade unionists were encouraged to foment strikes, thus sabotaging the 'capitalists' war'. Throughout this period the CPGB advised its members to resist the call-up and lent considerable support to a variety of anti-war groups. One particularly vocal front organization was the Peace Pledge Union, founded by the Reverend Hugh Sheppard, Canon of St Paul's, and publicized by George Lansbury, the editor of the *Daily Herald* and ex-Labour MP for Bow. They produced a *Peace Service Handbook* for conscientious objectors, and even promoted the pro-Nazi organization the Link.

The *Daily Worker* also took precautions against a government crackdown. A number of CPGB and Young Communist League officials had been arrested at rallies during the first year of the war and convicted of such offences as 'using insulting language'. Among those who had been charged was Douglas Hyde, the *Daily Worker*'s new editor, who found a loop-hole when his paper was closed down in January 1941. Hyde promply created a new agency named Industrial & General Information and continued his work.

One of the direct results of the CPGB's opposition to the war, and Molotov's command to the working classes, was the arrest in October 1940 in the United States of George Armstrong, a CPGB member. Armstrong was subsequently executed for Treachery (see Chapter IX).

Quite suddenly in June 1941 the CPGB made a dramatic U-turn in policy. As soon as news of the Nazi invasion of Russia filtered into London the Central Committee decreed that the 'capitalist conspiracy against the working class' had become a 'struggle for the survival of the masses'. Factory strikes, previously encouraged by leftist shop stewards, were now banned by the Party in an effort to keep the Red Army supplied with war material. The fact that Stalin had denounced Churchill's warnings of an impending Nazi invasion as 'inflammatory lies' was conveniently forgotten.

For their part MI5 were unimpressed by the CPGB's policy reversal or their new calls for Hitler's defeat. Max Knight continued his penetration of King Street while Roger Hollis, newly promoted after Colonel Alexander's retirement, concentrated on the covert links between the NKVD detachment now established in Bush House, the Soviet Embassy and the CPGB.

If the CPGB were not sure their mail was being read by MI5 they received confirmation when an envelope turned up in the post in September 1940. Inside was a letter clearly intended for John Beckett, Secretary of the British People's Party. The LIU had mixed up two intercepted letters and replaced them in the wrong envelopes. Much to the embarrassment of the Post Office's security staff an exchange took place, again via the mail, as Beckett forwarded the letter he received to King Street with a covering note.

The anti-Communist section MI5 moved into one of the Nissen huts in Blenheim after the transfer from the Scrubs and retained two of Liddell's stalwarts, Bunty Saunders and Miss McCulloch. The relative inactivity that followed took its toll however, and Nigel Watson, who had been brought into the office for the Arcos operation, requested a transfer to an active unit. He managed to organize a move to SOE but was injured on his first operational parachute drop, a mission into Yugoslavia. He spent much of the rest of the war recuperating under arduous circumstances behind the enemy lines.

Hollis was promoted to Assistant Director rank in 1940, after two years in 'F' Division, and was also appointed to serve on one of Lord Swinton's sub-committees, the Committee on Communist Activities, a Whitehall inter-departmental group formed to monitor CPGB sympathizers and the growing Soviet diplomatic presence in London.

Throughout 1940 Liddell, Knight and Hollis were all aware of the large number of pro-Soviet recruits that had been drafted into the services, including their own. Prior to Kell's dismissal the Security Service had chiefly been concerned with the threat to the armed forces from internally-organized subversion. The War Office was understandably determined not to endure a military version of Invergordon. The threat of a Fascist-inspired disaffection plot had come to nothing and as described in Chapter V Oswald Mosley for his part had ordered his British Union followers to serve their country once war had been declared. Nevertheless, the enemy remained Nazi Germany, so many people regarded left-of-centre politics as acceptable credentials for the Security Service. In theory Communists were barred from MI5, as they were from SIS and SOE. In practice all three organizations took on covert CPGB members.

For the Security Service the dangers from Soviet penetration were not all that great. Their operations were compartmentalized into three separate 'boxes'. The agents rarely visited MI5's headquarters and generally only knew their case officer and possibly one of his colleagues; very few of MI5's agents were ever allowed to learn 'office' business or even the name of the MI5 department that ran them. The agents ranged from the sophisticated informants who merely passed on pieces of cocktail party gossip, like Tom Driberg, to the long-term professionals like Olga Gray. The MI5 case officers made up the second 'box'. These were the men actually on the inside of St James's Street and the other offices who ran individual agents. They were frequently responsible for all the day-to-day handling of their 'case' and in all probability had recruited him (or her) originally. A case officer jealously guarded the identity of his case and only referred to him or her to others or in paperwork by a chosen code name. Usually the agent never learnt his own code name. The third 'box' which included a number of officers with either leftist political leanings or who had past associations with anti-Fascist organizations, was that of the intelligence analysts. These were the staff members who assessed the information which was passed up from the sections running agents, and they recommended what further action should be taken, or where the intelligence should next be routed. The academic and legal brains that existed on this level inside MI5 included several with leftist tendencies but only two were ever thought to have actively provided the Soviets with details of their work.

There has been much speculation about the extent of the undoubted Soviet wartime penetration of MI5. To read some of it might make one conclude that there were no successful anti-Soviet operations while the Russian agents were in place. This of course was not the case. Very often, as happened with the Springhall prosecution, MI5 staff would learn of a successful operation at the same time as the general public, by the same means – the newspapers. Only a very few in the office would be 'in the know' throughout.

Douglas Springhall, known as 'Dave' to his comrades, had been a member of the CPGB's Central Committee since 1932, and had first earned a dossier in MI5's Registry when he had been dismissed from the Royal Navy for causing dissension. He had been a delegate to the 1924 Communist International in Moscow and had been convicted during the 1926 General Strike of possession of seditious material. He was the first political Commissar of the XIth (British) International Brigade during the Spanish Civil War and had been appointed CPGB National Organizer on his return from Spain.

Springhall was routinely kept under surveillance by MI5 'watchers', which was a fairly simple exercise because he lived in a flat owned by the CPGB in King Street, a matter of yards from the Party's headquarters. In October 1942 Springhall was followed to the home of Mrs Olive Sheehan, a Customs and Excise clerk working in the Air Ministry. By this date Springhall had already extracted a promise from the woman that she would assist the Soviet Union in every way she could, and he had convinced her that any information she could lay her hands on would be sent straight to Moscow. Mrs Sheehan could not actually extract files from the Air Ministry but she did verbally report on the progress being made by the British in their development of jet propulsion.

Mrs Sheehan was visited by Special Branch and she immediately told of how Springhall had 'wormed' the secret information out of her. Mrs Sheehan was arrested and charged under the Defence Regulations. She appeared before magistrates and, without any publicity, was sentenced to three months' imprisonment. She also agreed to give evidence against Springhall should he be brought to trial.

He was, in due course, but not before he had unwittingly implicated another Soviet agent, Mrs Sheehan explained that Springhall had convinced her that the government intended to cheat their Russian allies and prevent important strategic information from reaching Stalin. His evidence, apparently, came from a 'Secret Service source'.

In fact, Springhall's source was a twenty-four-year-old Cambridge linguist, Captain Ormond Uren, who hadjoined the Hungarian section of SOE in May 1942, transferring from his regiment, the Highland Light Infantry. He was fluent in Hungarian, and had been selected for a blind drop into Hungary by his SOE Commanding Officer, Colonel Perkins. Between May 1942 and his detention on 24 September, 1943 Uren had lived in an SOE safe house in Dorset Square, and had worked in Norgeby House, the SOE headquarters in Baker Street. He had constant access to all the Eastern European country sections, which were housed in the same building and was on close terms with many of the senior SOE personnel.

Uren's first meeting with Springhall took place on 9 April, 1943 in a street just off the Charing Cross Road not far from King Street. He was able to provide details of SOE policy in the Balkans, Poland and Czechoslovakia. At the subsequent court martial the material he handed over was described *in camera* as being 'highly secret'.

In total Uren and Springhall had five illicit meetings, all in the area of St Martin's Lane and the Tottenham Court Road. A sixth rendezvous had been arranged for the evening of 17 June, 1943 but Special Branch detectives raided 11 and 16 King Street that morning, arresting Springhall at his flat in No 11. By this date Uren had spent more than twelve months in 'the racket' and had been able to give Springhall a substantial amount of intelligence, including a floorplan of Norgeby House and secret SOE communications information. The CPGB National Organizer had turned it all over to his contact at the Soviet Embassy, Anatoli Gorski.

Douglas Springhall was tried *in camera* at the Old Bailey in June 1943 for offences against the Official Secrets Act. Mrs Sheehan gave evidence against him, as did an RAF officer who confirmed the value of jet engine research. Springhall declined to give any evidence in his own defence and was sentenced to seven years' imprisonment. Springhall was promptly expelled from the CPGB and his wife sacked from her job on the *Daily Worker*. On his release he went to live in China, and later died in Moscow.

The Russians were furious at the conviction and lodged strong protests when, contrary to Foreign Office advice, news of the trial was made public. Reprisals were threatened against Britons in Moscow, but the storm passed with only the arrest of a Russian secretary at the British Embassy in the Soviet capital. Once the fuss had died down Uren was arrested on 24 September and court-martialled at the Duke of York's Headquarters in Chelsea on 21 October, 1943, for passing secret information to Springhall. Colonel J.S. Fitzgerald MBE MC presided and a solicitor serving in the RASC, Lieutenant C.V. Ford, defended. The prosecutor was Major J.R. Willis of the Judge Advocate-General's office.

Uren admitted to holding covert meetings with the Communist National Organizer and passing secret information on these occasions but claimed his motive was merely 'to show Springhall that I had complete faith in him and that he could have complete trust in me as a sincere believer in Communism'. He was duly cashiered and sentenced to seven years. The announcement in the press stated that 'War substantive Lieutenant (Temporary Captain) Ormond Leyton Uren' had been convicted of passing highly secret information to Springhall. He was described as 'an army officer on special duty' but there was no elaboration of what kind of special duties he was undertaking at the time of his arrest. Nor was there any mention of Special Operations Executive which, of course, was a top-secret organization.

The Springhall case was a considerable *coup* for MI5 but it did highlight the security problems facing SOE. The Director of Security there was John Senter QC, an MI5 nominee who liaised closely with 'B' Division and conducted investigations into charges of treachery against SOE personnel. Senter's task was virtually impossible because he could only be brought into cases long after they had developed. MI5 had already proved that good security depended on being 'in on the ground floor', as they were with the CPGB. SOE also suffered from a problem of jurisdiction. If collaboration had taken place abroad it was extremely difficult to fly in witnesses from Occupied Territory, although on occasion this did happen. Inevitably SOE had to plan many of their operations with foreign nationals, or the secret intelligence organizations of other countries. This too led to difficulties. The French boasted several different secret services, including de Gaulle's Bureau

Central de Renseignments et d'Action, and none of them apparently trusted the others. They had their own methods of establishing the loyalty of their nationals and deeply resented any interference from the British. French interrogations took place either in the basement of their London headquarters at 10 Duke Street or at their notorious camp outside Camberley.

An illustration of these problems arose in December 1942 when a French agent named Dufour was imprisoned in Camberley Camp. Dufour had previously been employed by SIS in France and on his return to Britain had declined to give the BCRA any details concerning his activities. The BCRA responded with torture and even threatened to have his girlfriend raped. Incredibly, Dufour managed to escape and turned up at the High Court in London where he issued writs against de Gaulle, Colonel Passy (the alias of the BCRA Chief Dewavrin) and several other senior French officers. De Gaulle protested that Dufour was a deserter and therefore could only seek justice from a French military court. In the end Dufour was persuaded to withdraw his writs, in exchange for £3,000 compensation.

SOE was constantly bedevilled by security problems and ultimately relied on a 'cooler' at Inverlair, in Scotland, to isolate their failures. By contrast Britain's other intelligence services fared better. MI5 suffered only one leak to the Germans, William Rolph, and the other possible unreliable (or 'triple') agents were interned. The Soviets managed to penetrate virtually every corner of Britain's secret organizations, including MI5. The degree to which they succeeded in respect of MI5 is discussed in detail in the Postscript. Anthony Blunt passed details of his work to his Soviet case officer verbally throughout the war, very occasionally committing to memory the complete texts of ISOS messages. Perhaps surprisingly the Soviets concentrated their questions on MI5's anti-Nazi operations rather than their meagre anti-Soviet operations. Philby for his part made his now well documented penetration of SIS while Burgess gained brief employment with SOE and Cairncross reported on Bletchley's decrypting activities.

There were of course several other wartime Soviet agents who remained undetected during the 1939-1945 period. Alan Nunn May offered his services to the Russians early in 1945 in Canada while he was working near Ottawa on the Chalk River heavy water project. Nunn May never spied in Britain even though the Russians tried to contact him in London after he had returned from Canada in September 1945. He was arrested in January 1946 by Len Burt after he had been identified as a KGB agent (ALEK) by Igor Gouzenko. He pleaded Guilty at his trial on 1 May, 1946 and was sentenced to ten years' imprisonment.

Klaus Fuchs escaped detection until December 1949 even though he had been in regular contact with the Russians since 1941 and had been denounced to the authorities as a Communist long before the war. This is not quite as surprising as it might at first seem. Fuchs arrived in Britain as a twenty-two-year-old refugee in September 1933 and was soon afterwards the subject of a police enquiry when the German Consul in Bristol named him as an extremist left-wing agitator. Not a great deal of credence was given to the allegation because such denunciations were fairly frequent and anyway the young physicist was just one of thousands of Germans who fled their homeland for ideological reasons. An accusation by a representative of the Nazi-controlled German Foreign Office against a member of its political opposition certainly did not mean that the British government would or should take punitive measures. In fact, though, that is almost exactly what did happen. Fuchs applied to become a naturalized British subject in 1939 but his papers were not processed by the Home Office when war broke out. Fuchs found himself categorized as an enemy alien and sent to an internment camp on the Isle of Man. He was then transferred to Sherbrooke Camp in Canada where he came into contact with a number of Category 'A' and 'B' detainees who undoubtedly influenced him. One of those was Hans Kahle, a Great War veteran, radical journalist and long-time member of the German Communist Party. He had served with distinction in the XIth International Brigade in Spain and had commanded the Thaelmann Battalion before coming to Britain as a refugee. He arrived armed with the addresses of a number of Republican sympathizers who gave him accommodation. One of those he stayed with in Cambridge was Charlotte Haldane, fiery left-wing wife of Professor J.B.S. Haldane. Kahle too was interned as an enemy alien. He later returned to Britain and eventually to Germany. He became Chief of Police in Mecklenburg and died in 1951.

Fuchs was allowed to return to Britain after the war following representations from many distinguished scientists, protesting that his skills were going to waste. A prominent leader of the lobby to have the 'reliable' scientists released was C.P. Snow, who wrote numerous memos to his Whitehall superiors and distinguished British scientists pointing out the talents that were being ignored. The brilliant young German physicist was posted to Birmingham University to work on the TUBE ALLOYS project under Professor Rudolf Peierls, himself a refugee from Nazi Germany. By November 1943, when he transferred to Los Alamos to work on the MANHATTAN project he had held regular covert meetings with Simon Kremer, secretary to the Russian Military Attaché, and other London-based Soviet intelligence officers. The

Russians were of course under a certain amount of scrutiny from MI5 but these secret meetings, held mainly in Banbury, went unnoticed.

The Lord Chief Justice, Lord Goddard, sentenced Fuchs to fourteen years' imprisonment on 1 March, 1950. At the time of his arrest on 2 February, 1950 he was working at the Atomic Energy Research Establishment at Harwell where, ironically, Guy Liddell was to be appointed Chief Security Officer on his retirement from MI5 in 1953, having risen to the rank of Deputy D-G. Fuchs made a full statement to Jim Skardon and was instrumental in trapping the American atomic spies Harry Gold and David Greenglass.

Fuchs served nine years of his sentence and was deprived of his British citizenship. On his release on 24 June, 1959 he was deported to East Germany where he took up a post at the Central Institute of Nuclear Research at Rossendorf, near Dresden.

It was the unscheduled flight of Burgess and Maclean in May 1951 which sparked off the historic investigation destined to last for more than thirteen years. That Maclean was to be questioned in connection with the Washington Embassy leaks (the culprit identified only as HOMER at that stage) was knowledge possessed by a very limited circle. The 'warning trail' led from Maclean to Burgess, as later confirmed by Burgess's defection. But who warned Burgess? The trail went dead beyond Blunt, who declined to confess, and Philby, who also underwent (and survived) investigation. MI5 did track down several vintage Soviet sources, but none had been active for years, and none was in a position to know of the intention to question Maclean on that particular Monday morning. It was this terrible uncertainty, linked to the continuous flow of intelligence from defectors, that plagued the Security Service until 1964 and led, somewhat belatedly, to the final post-mortem on Soviet espionage in Britain during the Second World War.

Under the pre-war 'amateur' management, MI5 had dealt the Comintern some real body blows. With the 'professionals' in control things had not been so easy. The Arcos raid in 1927, masterminded by Kell and Liddell, had sent Moscow reeling. The consequences were felt all over Europe, in every capital where the local security services followed up the MI5 lead. Had the successors of the NKVD learnt their lesson too well?

XI

Overseas Control

Overseas Control was the organization responsible for co-ordinating the London end of the Defence Security Officer network.

To be posted abroad was sometimes a pleasure but the system could also be used for other purposes. Billy Luke, the B1(a) case officer who at various times handled TATE, TRICYCLE and GELATINE found himself pursuing his sometimes amorous adventures in South Africa and then, after further distractions, was transferred to Honduras, where the previous DSO had incurred the wrath of the Governor by serving 18B Detention Orders on several relatively harmless local smugglers. Luke was later called back to St James's Street to become the Twenty Committee's Secretary in succession to John Marriott.

SIS maintained their pre-war Passport Control Offices worldwide and whenever necessary staffed some of the more vital overseas posts with officers from Section V, the counter-intelligence branch. The main purpose of Section V was to combat the Abwehr and therefore they maintained close links with their MI5 counterparts. This relationship between the two separate intelligence organizations has in the past been widely misunderstood, with Philby invariably being described as 'head of the SIS Iberian section'. This is of course incorrect. While MI5 based some of its departmental structure on sections devoted to particular countries or regions, SIS had its basis in the intelligence product. SIS related their system and their structure to the dissemination of the intelligence they were gleaning. In any given place, SIS would have officers from different departments each looking after their sectional interests. Whereas MI5 organized themselves according to the source of their intelligence information, not its type; their structure was more geographically based. Thus MI5 'B' Division's Iberian section B21 (run by Dick Brooman-White and Tommy Harris) concentrated all its Iberian affairs in Britain, whereas MI6 had several sections interested in Spanish and Portuguese matters. Amongst those was Section V which recruited Philby from SOE in September 1941.

Inevitably there was overlapping between Section V and MI5, but in general the division of responsibility worked well. In particular theatres the intelligence efforts were combined to create unified umbrella organizations. In December 1939 MI5 collaborated with SIS to create SIME, Security Intelligence Middle East, based in Cairo and headed by Raymund Maunsell, a thirty-six-year-old Royal Tank Corps officer with ten years' experience of the Middle East. SIME staff were drawn from a number of sources, including MI5, who provided several experienced personnel.

Another combined unit was created in New York in June 1940 to liaise with the American authorities and supervise intelligence operations in a territory which included North and South America, the Caribbean and Bermuda, and was presided over by William ('Little Bill') Stephenson, a friend of the new Prime Minister. The precedent for this special office had been established during the Great War when Sir William Wiseman, a prominent New York banker, had been asked by 'C' to look after British interests in the Western Hemisphere. His successor was a Canadian millionaire who had served in the Royal Flying Corps with distinction. His new organization absorbed the staff of the Passport Control Office in Manhattan (headed by Colonel Dick Ellis, a veteran SIS officer) and opened a headquarters entitled British Security Co-ordination in the Rockefeller Center on Fifth Avenue. The BSC role was one of liaison with the FBI on the one hand and SOE, MI6 and MI5 on the other, but the dynamic Stephenson took it upon himself to deal directly with President Roosevelt and advise him on a range of political and security matters. Unfortunately, this did not impress the Director of the FBI, J. Edgar Hoover, who disapproved of BSC's activities and gave only limited co-operation with Stephenson. MI5 therefore had to rely on its usual channel of communication with Hoover, which was through the Legal Attaché at the London Embassy, via Scotland Yard's Special Branch. Eventually MI5 posted an officer to Washington because BSC's operations on the North American continent were attracting too much attention and Stephenson was losing his political protection. The representatives picked generally had American connections but there was no great volume of business.

Further south, MI5 established a presence in the person of Colonel W.T. ('Freckles') Wren, who before the war had been managing director of Aga Cookers. He was based in Trinidad as Defence Security Officer and was assisted by Lord (Harry) Tennyson. Together they covered an area bounded to the north by Bermuda and to the south by the coast of

Venezuela. One part of their duties was the protection of the Duke of Windsor, who had taken up residence in Nassau as Governor of the Bahamas. The threat of an attempt to kidnap the Duke was taken very seriously and a warning that a German U-boat might land a team of commandos was passed on by Wren.

The DSO in Trinidad had a busy war searching neutral shipping and intercepting passengers who had come to the attention of counter-espionage colleagues in London. Several German agents bound for South America were detained by Wren and sent back to Britain and Camp 020. Amongst the Abwehr arrested were Leopold Hirsch, Gilinski and even a Jesuit priest named Father Lecoube. The DSO also supervised the 18B internments ordered by the Governors of the various Caribbean possessions.

In Bermuda H. Montgomery Hyde, the distinguished barrister and author, took on the job of liaising with MI5 and MI6 and maintaining a watching brief for Contraband Control. Even before America came into the war this tiny group of islands in the Atlantic had achieved a special significance as a stepping-stone between the United States and Europe. The Royal Navy dockyards in Somerset were strategically very important and became part of the Lend-Lease deals organized by Roosevelt and Churchill. Montgomery Hyde was also responsible for overseeing the transit passengers travelling by flying-boat on the Clipper service between Lisbon and New York. As well as interviewing those of interest to London who were using the route[35] he also intercepted the diplomatic pouches of various embassies. By the end of the war the Hamilton Princess Hotel had become the hub of a massive mail surveillance operation designed to isolate letters posted in the United States to cover addresses in Europe in neutral cities that the LIU in London had already identified as suspicious. The Bermuda censorship section was headed by Peter Wilson, a young arts graduate from New College, Oxford, later Chairman of Sotheby's.

MI5 in Gibraltar

On 13 July, 1713 the Treaty of Utrecht was signed bringing an end to the War of Spanish Succession. Article X yielded Gibraltar to the Crown of Great Britain. The Rock remained British in spite of numerous assaults, sieges and negotiations. In 1721 and 1748 the Colony's status was confirmed and in 1869 the opening of the Suez Canal increased its strategic value.

In 1939 the British Crown were no less anxious to retain Gibraltar as an important base for the Royal Navy and the strategic key to the

Mediterranean. This significance was not lost on MI5 who carried responsibility for local security. Between 1939 and 1945 MI5 maintained their largest overseas office on the Rock and succeeded in convicting no less than three Abwehr agents of Treachery. All three were eventually hanged.

In the early days of 1939 MI5 boasted just one part-time representative in Gibraltar, Captain Airey of the Buffs. The previous year he had presided over the formation of an entirely new unit, the Gibraltar Security Police (GSP), which consisted of a dozen locally recruited policemen. They were given the responsibility of overseeing the docks and port, the airfield, policing the Spanish frontier and processing the movements of individuals in and out of the Colony. The sudden creation of an élite police force caused offence and friction and for time it looked as though this division of authority would completely disrupt the flow of travellers using the Rock. There were numerous incidents of passengers being waved through by the civil police at the Three Corners crossing point, only to be searched by the GSP. The resentment which built up caused headaches until the GSP took over complete control of the international movements to and from the Rock. An additional nightmare for the GSP was the proximity of La Linea, whose population largely depended on Gibraltar for employment. Over 6,000 Spanish neutrals filed through the frontier gates every day to go to work and made their way directly across the airfield's single runway, which until recently had been the racetrack. This airfield had not been fully completed until the invasion of North Africa, Operation TORCH, in November 1942, although it had first been discussed in 1936 when the Secretary of State for the Colonies, Lord Harlech, had suggested the idea to the Governor, General Harington.

The constant flow of civilian traffic across the runway was a major worry for MI5 and the GSP, who were well aware that the Spanish took a great interest in everthing that went on in 'their' Gibraltar. They also knew that the Germans kept the Rock under constant visual surveillance, maintaining a permanent twenty-four-hour-a-day watch from neutral Spain. To the west, across the Bay of Algeciras was 'Spy Row' where the intelligence services of several countries were known to keep observation posts in luxurious shore-side villas. Gradually most were identified. The Hotel Reina Cristina became famous because of its popularity with the Abwehr. The Villa Leon, Villa Isabel and Haus Keller also proved to be under Abwehr management, as was the Villa Luis, which came as particularly uncomfortable news; it had previously been owned by the Air Attaché at the British Embassy in Madrid.

Understandably, the atmosphere in Gibraltar at this time was that of a fortress under siege, even though the residents were perfectly free to travel across the frontier into 'neutral' Spain. Surrounded by the enemy MI5 and MI6 hoisted their covert battle colours. The SIS Head of Station was Colonel John Codrington, code-named FISHPASTE, grandson of a previous Governor of the Rock and scion of a family with a long naval and military history. His brother William Codrington had been drafted back into the Foreign Office's Security Department on the outbreak of war. (Both Codringtons were distant relatives of Norman Baillie-Stewart, mentioned in Chapter III.) The SIS base of operations was housed in the top two floors of the central police station, known as the Irish Town headquarters. During the course of the war most of the northern part of the building and its annexe were taken over by various intelligence outfits. The MI9 Escape Officer, code-named SUNDAY, had an office in the same block. From January 1942 until late 1943 SUNDAY was Major Donald Darling, a young recruit from MI6 who had previously been acting for MI9 in Lisbon. MI5 were assigned space in the same building as the SIS, on the upper floors at the northern end. Kell's man on the Rock was Major H.G. ('Tito') Medlam, an ex-Coldstream Guards officer who had the difficult task of making Gibraltar secure from sabotage and infiltrating Axis agents.

The neighbouring MI5 and MI6 offices illustrate how closely the two organizations were obliged to work in the field. The SIS Iberian networks had a chain of command originating in London with Section V(Counter-intelligence). The next link was the Madrid SIS Head of Station, Kenneth Benton, who was the senior intelligence officer in the Embassy. The NID were represented by Commander Alan Hillgarth,[36] while MI9 had (Sir) Michael Creswell operating as MONDAY. In Lisbon the SIS Station was staffed by Colonel Ralph Jarvis, Philip Johns and Cecil Gledhill. The chain was completed by Neil Whitelaw, Paddy Turnbull, Colonel Malcolm Henderson and Colonel Toby Ellis in North Africa.

The Head of MI5's Iberian Section in 'B' Division was Dick Brooman-White, a twenty-seven-year-old graduate of Trinity, Cambridge, who had political aspirations. Before the war he had been Sir Archibald Cochrane's private secretary and in 1951 was to become the Conservative Member for Rutherglen. His deputy on the Iberian Section was a remarkable painter and art dealer who had been recruited from the fledgling SOE, Tomas ('Tommy') Harris, who had been running an art gallery business from his sumptuous home in Mayfair's Chesterfield Gardens. Harris had an English father and Spanish mother and won a scholarship to the Slade. When he joined his father as a director of the Spanish Art Gallery he was recognized as perhaps the world's leading expert on Goya and El Greco. Apparently, his work at SOE had consisted of cooking for the trainees at Brickendonbury Hall, the SOE school of sabotage near Hertford. Harris was a natural intelligence officer and proved his worth when he was given the case of GARBO in April 1942 (see Chapter VII). It had often been rumoured that his first experience of under-cover work had been in Spain during the Civil War when the Harris family had acquired many of their fabulous works of art.

MI5 relied heavily on SIS for information about the Abwehr's activities in the neutral Iberian countries and the business of effective counter-intelligence depended on a close relationship between the two organizations in the field. Gibraltar became a key MI5/MI6 station and Bertram Ede, the Director of 'F' Division sent Medlam out to reinforce the office operated on the Rock by Captain Airey. Medlam was recommended by Joe Spencer, Ede's Assistant (ADF). Medlam was a tall, somewhat aloof bachelor, fluent in Spanish, who was more than a little appalled by what he found in his new post. The town and dockyards were filled with Spanish 'neutrals' who came through the frontier gates each day to their jobs. The RAF airfield's perimeter fence was yards away from the neutral ground that separated the two borders. Nothing in the area could move without being logged by the watchful eyes beyond the wire. Another major security problem was the number of merchant vessels arriving and leaving. Their indiscreet crews always came ashore determined to enjoy what might perhaps be their last night and there seemed no way of controlling the rumours and gossip about routes of convoys and their destinations, if that was not enough to cope with, the GSP staff were unpopular locally and two of its members had been masterminding illegal activities. One was caught redhanded smuggling cigarettes across the frontier and another was discovered to be the owner of a brothel in the town.

Medlam was well briefed on the current situation by Codrington and knew that he would have his hands full just trying to identify and eliminate German agents and saboteurs. Some of the agents were practically overt. The Italian Consul on the Rock used to throw cocktail parties timed to coincide with air raids so his guests could enjoy the spectacular view. It was agreed that Codrington and his Section V team of David Bristow, and an ex-monk named O'Shagar would concentrate on the area of counter-intelligence and the daily running of agents. MI6 had already developed a sizeable stable of paid agents who monitored the activities of the Abwehr but it was a constant worry to be permanently observed by the telescopes on 'Spy Row'. The geographical limitations of the Rock would inevitably reduce MI5's role. At Wormwood Scrubs the daily routine for 'B' Division officers included the skilful handling of agents and double agents but in Gibraltar the opportunities looked bleak. In Britain the Special Branch were a vital arm in the business of dealing with and following suspects but the GSP had practically no training and were anyway of doubtful reliability, at least to start off with. In the event of an agent offering his services the possibilities of fooling the enemy were few. In the UK a 'B' Division case officer could arrange an elaborate deception and get away with it because in all probability the Abwehr could only check his reports by cross-referring with other, controlled agents, by the interception of signals, which were easily faked, and by aerial observation, which again could be misled. There was little point in an agent overhearing that a particular convoy was bound for Alexandria on a certain date. The fact that a group of ships were in the area would already be well known to the sophisticated coastal observation teams and undoubtedly reports would be sent to the Abwehr in Madrid as soon as they left Gibraltar. This ability to double check information virtually ruled out major deceptions but two particular schemes dreamed up in London actually relied on the efficiency with which the Abwehr carried out their surveillance.

The first was Operation MINCEMEAT, a bizarre deception dreamed up by Charles Cholmondeley, a 'B' Division officer. He originally suggested the idea of planting a corpse on the Germans bearing authentic-looking documents specially prepared to dupe the Abwehr. At first the scheme was code-named Plan TROJAN HORSE and later, as the project developed, it was dubbed MINCEMEAT.

On the face of it the suggestion assumed a high degree of credulity on the part of the Germans but an incident shortly before TORCH, the invasion of North Africa in November 1942, indicated the ruse might work. An aeroplane carrying a Free French courier had crashed on a flight from Lisbon to Tangiers and the body of the Frenchman had been washed up on the beach near Tarifa. Fortunately, TORCH was not compromised but the Germans had obviously been passed various documents by the Spanish police before the body was surrendered to the Allies. The letters carried by the courier were not of vital importance but the behaviour of the Spanish suggested that MINCEMEAT might well achieve its purpose.

The plan was given all the necessary approvals and MI5 set about getting hold of a suitable body. The invasion of Sicily, Operation HUSKY, was scheduled for July 1943 and the   deception cover target was to be Sardinia. The representative of the DNI, Commander Ewen Montagu liaised with MI5 to procure a cadaver. Sir Bernard Spilsbury, the Home Office pathologist, advised on what sort of body would be practical and Mr W. Bentley Purchase was approached to select an unclaimed body from the Westminster Mortuary. The Coroner had already proved co-operative over the falsification of William Rolph's death certificate (see Chapter VII), and on this occasion he was helpful again.

A suitable body was found and put on ice while Charles Cholmondeley and Ewen Montagu manufactured a plausible identity for 'Major Martin RM' and engineered some sensitive documents for him to carry. On 17 April, 1942 Jock Horsfall (who had by now recovered from his fall from the roof of Wormwood Scrubs), Ewen Montagu and Charles Cholmondeley loaded Major Martin into an MI5 30-cwt Ford and drove their charge up to Scotland to the submarine that was waiting to carry the body to the Spanish coast. The canister holding the body was packed with ice and bore the legend 'optical instruments' for the benefit of the curious. It also contained a standard issue black government briefcase into which had been placed several bogus letters. The important one was from Admiral Mountbatten and was addressed to the Naval C-in-C Mediterranean, Admiral Cunningham. This letter explained that Major Martin was to deliver a personal note from the VCIGS 'Archie Nye' to 'My dear Alex' (General Alexander). For good measure there was a further letter from Mountbatten to General Eisenhower concerning the preface to a pamphlet on joint operations that Eisenhower was to write.

On 9 April HMS *Seraph* sailed from Greenock and eleven days later it surfaced off Huelva in southern Spain to place Major Martin in the water. In due course Major Martin was found on the beach alongside his rubber dinghy and all the evidence suggested that he was indeed an Allied courier whose plane had crashed into the sea. His official briefcase was still chained to his wrist. The British Ambassador in Madrid, Sir Samuel Hoare, was duly informed of the discovery, though he was not let in on the deception, and indignantly demanded the return of the valuable letters. When eventually the Naval Attaché, Commander Hillgarth, did receive the briefcase from the Spanish Ministry of Marine it was only after the sensitive documents had been photographed and passed on to the Abwehr. The operation had been a success. ULTRA intercepts later showed that the MINCEMEAT documents had been accepted as genuine. The Berlin High Command (OKW) sent reinforcements to Sardinia and changed their appreciations of Allied intentions in the Mediterranean.[37]

The strategic gains achieved by this relatively simple and inexpensive deception did not go unnoticed. The following year MI5 launched an equally strange operation in the same theatre. If MINCEMEAT depended on the Abwehr having excellent contacts within the Spanish provincial police then the Montgomery deception assumed that the German agents in Spy Row had good eyesight or were still able to penetrate the Rock's defences.

The object of the exercise was to have the Abwehr believe that General Montgomery was headed for a command in the Mediterranean. In fact, he was due to spearhead the D-Day landings in Normandy, but SHAEF felt that if Berlin could definitely place him in Gibraltar or North Africa at about the time that OVERLORD was scheduled to be launched the Germans might be deceived. If the Abwehr fell for the bait it was hoped they would dismiss the initial Naval movements as yet another exercise.

The idea for COPPERHEAD originally came from the FORTITUDE D-Day deception planners. Roger Hesketh's father was approached to act the part of Monty's 'double' (in spite of a sixteen-year age difference) but he turned it down. Gilbert Lennox of MI5 was then asked by LCS to find a suitable candidate for the operation. He passed the task on to his assistant, Stephen Watts, a former newspaperman who traced an article published by the *News Chronicle* on 14 March, 1944. The story, complete with photograph, centred on a Lieutenant Clifton James of the Royal Army Pay Corps, who undoubtedly resembled Monty. Watts quickly found James, who in civilian life had spent twenty-five years on the stage. James was stationed in Leicester, and Watts arranged for him to come to London, apparently for an interview with David Niven of the Army Kinematograph Service. This enabled Lennox to 'view' him, and once he was satisfied Clifton James was sworn to secrecy and dispatched to join Montgomery's entourage for a couple of days of familiarization. When everyone was sure Clifton James had mastered his new role, he was transferred into the Intelligence Corps with the rank of sergeant. On 26 May, 1944 he was kitted out in a duplicate uniform, complete with the distinctive beret and its twin badges, and escorted to RAF Northolt in west London by Lennox, Watts, Hesketh and Major Marcus Haywood, who was dressed in the uniform of a Brigadier as 'Monty's' ADC.

James was virtually identical with Montgomery in every respect except one. In the Great War Lieutenant James had lost the middle finger of his right hand, and the real General was well known for his famous salute. A replacement finger was essential and overnight James was able to make one from papier mache and a little greasepaint.

Squadron-Leader Slee flew 'Montgomery' to Gibraltar where he was met by the Governor's ADC, Major Foley, who had been let in on the secret. He was welcomed with much ceremony and driven to the Convent, the Governor's residence on the Rock, where Sir Ralph Eastwood greeted him. The Governor had been at Sandhurst with Montgomery but even he was impressed by the deception. The purpose of the operation was to create a mythical top-level meeting between Monty, General Maitland Wilson and General Patch, thus diverting attention away from northwest Europe.

The following day 'Montgomery' returned to the airstrip in a suitably public fashion, waving and saluting to the onlookers, and stepped aboard his Liberator for the flight to Algiers. Earlier that morning he and the Governor had strolled through the Convent rose garden, indiscreetly mentioning 'Plan 303' in front of Spanish workmen who were busy repairing the left wing of the residence.

In Algiers Lieutenant James was met by General Maitland Wilson and a Guard of Honour. By the time 'Montgomery' reached the St George Hotel he had been spotted by hundreds of locals. The town was alive with stories about the famous visiting General. At this point Lieutenant James 'disappeared'. His mission was over and it was decided to remove him from the scene as quickly as possible before the deception was noticed by the Abwehr. He was bundled on a plane to Cairo and then kept under wraps until 7 June, when he was returned to Gibraltar. The following day he was flown back to Britain, (apparently) a mere Sergeant in the Intelligence Corps. After his return to his unit he reverted to his genuine rank.

COPPERHEAD did not achieve all that it was hoped to do. After the war evidence was obtained that Berlin had indeed been alerted to Montgomery's presence in the western Mediterranean but they suspected a trick. They never guessed that a 'double' had been employed but assumed that the real General had participated in a deception plot.

General Montgomery played little part in the operation except to give the idea his blessing. After James had returned to his unit some unfortunate remarks were made at a SHAEF lunch which made the General furious. A guest mentioned, tongue in cheek, that Monty had been seen in Gibraltar drunk as a lord smoking a huge cigar. Montgomery neither drank nor smoked and was not renowned for his sense of humour. He dispatched a series of furious telegrams to 'Room 055, the War Office'. This regrettable incident was also keenly felt by Lieutenant James who later recounted his experiences in an autobiography entitled *I Was Monty's Double*.[38]

Operations MINCEMEAT and COPPERHEAD were both MI5 Mediterranean counter-intelligence deceptions but they were devised by wartime recruits and certainly were not in the Kell tradition, which depended on slow, painstaking slog. The short, quick, risky, colourful project was utterly alien to the original D-G's methods.

However, 'Tito' Medlam was a counter-intelligence officer in exactly Kell's mould. His first action on arriving on the Rock had been to institute a card-index system based on Miss Paton-Smith's Registry. The name of every Spanish worker was entered in the files, as was every new work permit and every entry and exit pass. In time the completely comprehensive system was to employ over forty full-time clerks at the Irish Town headquarters. Medlam also supervised the enlargement of the GSP and made sure that they included a number of men who could speak Spanish. The GSP were divided into three sections which were given over-all responsibility for security in their areas. Captain Mundy dealt with the port and sea arrivals while Captain Milne screened the few lucky enough to travel by air. Captain Gubbins controlled town security with Bill Adamson, an ex-HM Dockyard Police Officer from Sunderland, who had been seconded from the regular civil police.

Medlam realized he faced a massive task if he was to make Gibraltar really secure and immediately began pressing for extra staff from London. At first, he was given Captain Chilcott, GSO (3) from the Fortress Garrison, but he continued to send telegrams asking for more help. Eventually he was sent Superintendent Philip Kirby Green who had previously served in Scotland Yard's Special Branch and had been brought up in Tangier. KG, as he came to be known, was the son of Sir William Kirby Green, the former British Ambassador to Morocco. He had joined the Metropolitan Police in 1931 and became one of the first cadets at Hendon Police College.

Sir William retained his North African links and later became a member of the International Legislative Assembly for the Tangier Zone.

KG was commissioned into the Intelligence Corps with the rank of Major – the DSO had in the meantime been promoted to Acting Colonel – and flown to the Rock in civvies. Shortly afterwards Captain David Thomson arrived to take up the post of Assistant DSO. He had spent a number of years in the Argentine and could speak Spanish faultlessly. He had been recommended for the job by Len Burt (the post-war Commander of Special Branch).

By the end of 1940 some order had been put into the various security units that safeguarded Gibraltar, but the Rock never managed to throw off the atmosphere of a town under siege. The civilian population had either been called up for military service or had been evacuated in June

1940 to Madeira, Jamaica or London. The Governor announced new Ordinances to improve the security of visiting ships. In future all crews were to report to their vessels a full twenty-four hours before sailing and were prohibited from discussing details of their voyages with anyone. Medlam was sure that important naval intelligence was slipping out of the town via the dance-hall and café hostesses who reportedly pumped sailors for information. The few bar-girls left on the Rock after the evacuation were prevented from sitting with their clients in order to curb gossip. The authorities thought that it was more difficult to pass information on the dance-floor. Medlam also interned the Maltese D'Amato brothers who owned the largest café on Main Street, the Universal. MI5's few informants indicated that the indiscreet conversations of young sailors were being reported to La Linea, across the border.

This local regulation caused a certain amount of inconvenience to the men serving on visiting ships and provoked some discontent among the MI5 staff. KG and Bill Adamson complained bitterly that they were safeguarding both the secrets and the morals of Gibraltar.

During the following eighteen months Medlam took on more administrative officers in the rabbit warren of the Irish Town police station, increasing the combined MI5 and MI6 contingent to just over two hundred.

When Italy joined the war in June 1940 the security of the Rock was threatened for the first time by frogmen operating from midget submarines. Under normal circumstances this would have been the province of the area NID representative, Commander (later Sir James) Grenville Pyke-Nott, but the resources of all the local covert services were pooled following the underwater attack on the battleship HMS *Barham* on 30 October, 1940. A special twenty-strong Field Security unit was created under the leadership of Harry Allen, a boatswain from the MacAndrew Line. All the men were experienced seamen and excelled at searching suspect vessels for contraband and their hulls for limpet mines. Eventually Gibraltar became a centre for training sub-aqua teams, a unique example of MI5, MI6, NID and SOE co-operating successfully.

The card-index at the Irish Town headquarters grew in its sophistication and a system of coded entries was introduced to increase security. Suspects who had been logged as having had contact with the Abwehr were given one-syllable code names such as SCUM, RED and ROB. If a suspect was considered a likely source of information for the Germans he would be summoned to Irish Town and informed that his entry permit had been withdrawn. This was considered the best course of action and preferable to a prosecution. The logic behind this lay in the massive unemployment that plagued post-Civil-War Spain. The loss of a job on the Rock was a punishment of some consequence because there was little chance of finding other work. There was also a deterrent value. Added to this was the extreme difficulty in accumulating evidence good enough to impress a court, which even in wartime would depend on a jury conviction.

The first major espionage case to be dealt with by the MI5 office in Gibraltar began in early 1942. Jose Key was a British subject of Spanish extraction born in Gibraltar. He was a thirty-three-year-old labourer working in the dockyard whose name had appeared in Medlam's card-index because of a 1936 police memo listing him as a possible subversive. MI5's suspicions were confirmed when he was logged making contact with a known Falangist in Spain. Key's case was pursued because Kirby Green, the DDSO, was confident that a simple search of the suspect would reveal papers and information amounting to evidence of espionage. A prosecution of the man was also politically feasible. The British government were initially reluctant during the early stages of the war to do anything that might provoke the Franco regime in Madrid. That the Germans failed to persuade the Caudillo to collaborate on a joint assault on the Rock was undoubtedly due in part to the skilled diplomacy being carried out by Sir Samuel Hoare, British Ambassador since May 1940.[39]

When he was arrested he did indeed have incriminating documents relating to port logistics, justifying a prosecution under the Treachery Act. Key was taken for questioning to Irish Town on 4 March, 1942 where he was also given a medical examination. The doctor concerned made the unpleasant discovery that MI5's suspect was riddled with syphilis.

Key's interrogation was a fairly straightforward affair except for the prisoner's ill-judged attempt to escape. He jumped out of an open window while waiting for Kirby Green and found himself in the central courtyard surrounded by surprised policemen. Once returned to his inquisitors Key signed a full statement. He said that he had been offered an important post in Madrid if he agreed to work as an Abwehr agent. He admitted that he had been recruited by a Falangist who was acting for 'Dr Hans Hoeberlein', a German of considerable influence. His instructions were to take notes of war supplies passing through Gibraltar bound for the Middle East. Len Burt was flown out from Britain to assist in the interrogation, and persuaded Lord Gort to allow Key to face trial in London. Key was duly escorted back by David

Thomson and went before Mr Justice Humphreys at the Old Bailey on 15 and 18 May, 1942. He was found guilty and sentenced to death. His appeal was rejected on 22 June by the Lord Chief Justice, Mr Justice Asquith, and Mr Justice Tucker, and he was hanged on 7 July at Wandsworth Prison. Mr Pierrepoint, the Official Executioner, hanged Alphons Timmerman the same day (see Chapter IX).

In June the following year Colonel Medlam and Major Kirby Green had to deal with what became Gibraltar's most serious and potentially most dangerous case of espionage of the war. The caves tunnelled deep into the Rock had become the Allied Command Headquarters for the invasion of North Africa. Eisenhower had taken up residence on 6 November, 1942 and following the success of TORCH the Rock became the most important staging area in the Mediterranean for Allied operations. Indeed, in November 1942 the Allies 'possessed not a single spot of ground in all the region of western Europe, and in the Mediterranean nothing west of Malta except the Gibraltar Fortress,' as General Eisenhower wrote in his memoirs.

It was therefore with some consternation that Kirby Green greeted the news that a Gibraltarian had approached the police with a story about German saboteurs who were already inside the town. A man of some standing named Charles Danino claimed that he had been asked to place a bomb in the main tunnel of the dockyard where he worked. The tunnel he described was better known as the Ragged Staff Magazine and was used as a munitions dump. The Rock is a virtual honeycomb of inter-connecting shelters and galleries which in total measure more than thirty miles in length. The original chambers were excavated on the Spanish side of the Rock as part of the Fortress's ancient defences. Over the years of British possession Gibraltar's underground accommodation had been hugely increased and extended from Forbes Shaft in the north to the Brewery Magazine in the south. In between were such places as The Great North Road, the Fosse Way, Harley Street North and The Beefsteak Magazine. The Army calculated that its protected facilities were sufficient to support the entire garrison for a twelve-month siege. The underground accommodation included hospitals, reservoirs, laundries, power stations, telephone exchanges, living areas and cold stores. The prospect of the Abwehr penetrating into Gibraltar's deepest defences was both appalling and astonishing. Certainly, they had chosen the right spot. The Ragged Staff Tunnel emerges into the daylight close to the Navy's dock area, which itself was packed with equipment and supplies in readiness for HUSKY, the invasion of Sicily scheduled to start on the night of 9 July, 1943. Even a minor explosion in such a sensitive area would be catastrophic. The Ragged Staff Tunnel led directly to the Green Lane Magazine, which lay under and some yards to the north of the famous Rock Hotel. A series of caves and chambers, all large enough to accommodate motor traffic, linked the Brigade headquarters, the Europa Road pumping station and several other important installations. The merest suggestion of sabotage was enough to turn seasoned campaigners grey.

Kirby Green immediately called Danino in for an interview and had the story repeated. The Abwehr had threatened the life of Danino's wife, who lived across the frontier in La Linea. His instructions were relayed to him by Luis Cordon-Cuenca, who worked as a clerk in the Empire fruit shop in Main Street. The worst news was that Cuenca had apparently already managed to smuggle a large bomb into the town and was now merely waiting for Danino to place it in the Magazine. A check with the card-index revealed that the Empire fruit shop at 114 Main Street did indeed have a Spanish national working there. He was twenty-seven years old and lived in La Linea, one of the many neutrals making the daily journey through the gates at Four Corners. KG was in a predicament. If the GSP arrested Cuenca without any evidence there could well be an ugly incident. Unless he was actually caught with the bomb or some other convincing proof he could deny the whole matter and walk out of the territory. While this would remove one German agent it would still leave the bomb somewhere on the Rock and no doubt the Abwehr had alternative agents willing to place the device where it would cause havoc. The dilemma was whether it was worth the risk to act quickly, perhaps before the plot developed into a disaster.

KG decided, in consultation with Colonel Medlam, to discover more before moving in and instructed Danino to co-operate with Cuenca, to establish the location of the bomb and report back to KG. A limited surveillance operation was then put into gear. A member of the town security section of the GSP, Bill Adamson, was to befriend Cuenca and carry out a survey of the fruit shop. From that day onwards, Adamson became a regular customer at the store, sometimes making two visits a day to satisfy his newfound craving for bananas. Unfortunately, Cuenca did not serve in the shop and usually kept to a small office in the rear. Nevertheless, Adamson made a point of calling on him from time to time to discuss when the next shipment of bananas was due to arrive. None of this seemed to arouse the young Spaniard's suspicions but MI5 were no closer to facing the location of the bomb. However, the first week of the investigation did yield some information: Cuenca might have used a consignment of fruit or vegetables to conceal the explosives, if indeed he really had got them into the town; the Hungarian owner of the shop seemed above suspicion; Adamson thought he saw swastikas doodled on a notepad on Cuenca's desk. None of this was hard enough evidence to justify an arrest with possible diplomatic repercussions, even at this stage in the war.

Adamson kept up his passion for bananas as the investigation seemed to be going nowhere until 22 June 1943, when Danino telephoned KG. Cuenca had contacted him and a rendezvous had been arranged for the following evening at six. Apparently, Cuenca had taken delivery of a special time fuse which would delay the detonation of the bomb until Danino had got clear of the area. Cuenca would hand over the fuse at the meeting. KG advised Danino to follow the Abwehr agent's instructions and explained that both men would be arrested by the GSP during the meeting. Linking Cuenca to a detonator was more than enough evidence to justify his arrest.

The following day Colonel Medlam, KG and Adamson all congregated at half-past five in the office of the Fortress Commandant, which conveniently overlooked the spot where the rendezvous was to take place. The place chosen by Cuenca was the Sir Herbert Miles Promenade, a raised pavement near the centre of the town which commanded a good view of the hockey pitches below. There were several park benches on the Promenade and it was a favourite meeting-place for Gibraltarians. Colonel Medlam had also drafted in some extra help in the shape of Captain John Ellis, the MI5 officer in charge of the card-index.

At five minutes to six Danino appeared and sat down on one of the empty benches to wait for Cuenca, but it was another fifteen minutes before the Abwehr agent rode into view on his bicycle. Cuenca dismounted and wheeled his bicycle up to the raised level of the Promenade, still wearing his cycle clips. The MI5 team looked on and allowed the two men a couple of minutes' conversation before signalling Adamson. The GSP policeman, unarmed and in uniform, approached Cuenca and Danino and asked what they were doing. Cuenca was more than a little surprised by this intervention and protested that he and his friend were spectators, watching the football match being played in the square below. Adamson pointed out that it was a hockey match that was in progress, and arrested the stunned Cuenca. He then took the German agent by the arm and led him down the street to the Irish Town headquarters only yards away. Meanwhile KG dealt with Danino, who was arrested for the sake of appearances, and Captain Ellis took charge, somewhat gingerly, of Cuenca's bicycle.

Cuenca was given a thorough search as soon as the party reached the police station and a detonator was found in his breast pocket. It had been constructed to look rather like a fountain pen and can be seen poking out of the top of Cuenca's pocket in the illustration. He immediately denied that it was his and claimed that it had been planted on him by his interrogators. The Spaniard also stubbornly denied any knowledge of a bomb.

It now seemed that MI5 had succeeded in catching Cuenca with the necessary incriminating evidence but the crucial bomb was yet to be found and clearly, they could expect no help from the prisoner. A GSP search team was sent up to Danino's house in case Cuenca had managed to hide it there without Danino's knowledge but it was a wasted effort: the policemen tore the house apart, but there was no trace of the elusive bomb. At the same time a second team was dispatched to the Empire fruit shop which was given similar treatment. Much to the relief of everyone concerned Inspector Ernest Gilbert found a cache of explosives hidden in the cistern of the shop's toilet.

The bundle of explosives was then brought over to the MI5 office and Cuenca was confronted with it. He immediately broke down and signed a full statement. He claimed that his father had been a staunch Republican during the Civil War and that he had been forced to watch him and the rest of his family being shot in cold blood by the Falange. Since that time, he had lived in fear of the Franco regime. Then early in 1943 he had been approached by a Falangist named Blas Castro who had suggested that he might carry out one or two missions for some German friends. In turn he was introduced to two Germans in Algeciras who promised him £500 if he smuggled a bomb past the frontier into Gibraltar hidden in a consignment of vegetables. All his actions, he claimed, were performed under duress.

Cuenca and Danino were taken separately to the military prison at Windmill Hill at the southern end of the Rock. Danino was quietly released later that night and rewarded for his loyalty to the Crown with a British Empire Medal.

Cuenca was charged with offences against the Defence Regulations and appeared before the Chief Justice of Gibraltar, His Honour John J.G. McDougall, at a Special Court on 19 August, 1943. Six days later he was sentenced to death. Cuenca's defence counsel argued that the British Defence Regulations were invalid in the Crown Colony and that therefore the Special Court had no jurisdiction over the prisoner. It was a fine technical point but lives had been saved with less. An appeal was lodged with the Privy Council in London and on 13 December, 1943 the submission was rejected.

The Lord Chancellor, Lord Atkin, sat with Lord Porter and Lord Clauson and upheld the sentence, and Cuenca was hanged in Gibraltar on 11 January, 1944.

Exactly a week after Cordon-Cuenca's arrest, just as the MI5 team were congratulating themselves on a thoroughly satisfactory investigation and conclusion, a major explosion ripped through the Naval fuel depot on Coaling Island, not far from Colonel Medlam's office. The incident happened at lunchtime on 30 June, 1943 and several of the MI5 staff were at lunch in the Intelligence Corps Mess in Main Street. They ran down to the dock area and found a fire raging in the diesel enclosure. Sabotage was the first thought that came to them and this was confirmed later in the day at a meeting held in the Admiralty Offices. The meeting took the form of a post-mortem on the incident and it was announced that the Naval explosives experts had established that a charge, possibly in the form of a limpet mine, had been set off close to one of the storage tanks. Detonation had been timed for the hour when most of the dockyard workers were at lunch. This clue was interpreted to mean that one of the workers employed on Coaling Island was responsible.

The following day the MI5 office started to check on the local workmen and one name in particular seemed likely: Jose Martin Munoz, a Spanish daily worker employed as a casual labourer on Coaling Island. The MI5 card-index revealed that a Field Security Wing sortie had spotted him in Algeciras earlier in the year with some known prostitutes. There was no obvious explanation as to how the labourer had acquired sufficient wealth to afford these expensive luxuries. A telephone call to Coaling Island confirmed that Munoz had not turned up for work after the explosion.

The case now became routine. The GSP were alerted to detain Munoz in the unlikely event of his using the entry permit again and MI5 turned to more pressing matters. Incredibly though, Munoz did turn up at Four Corners a short time later. He was immediately arrested by Sergeant Joseph Ferro of the GSP and driven up in the 'meat wagon' to Irish Town. Munoz readily admitted that he was responsible for the Coaling Island explosion and explained that he had returned to the Rock to place a second device which he had kept stored out of harm's way in the coal-hole under the Imperial Café in Main Street. A bomb disposal unit was quickly on the scene and the explosives were recovered intact. Munoz was brought to trial before

Chief Justice McDougall and defended by the Hon P.G. Russo, just as Cordon-Cuenca had been. The hearing lasted only fifteen minutes because Munoz pleaded Guilty and was summarily sentenced to death. The sentence was translated into Spanish for the prisoner, who took the news calmly and nodded. After the pronouncement Russo pointed out that the similar case of Cordon-Cuenca was awaiting an appeal hearing in London and that this case too might well be considered *ultra vires*. Execution of the sentence was delayed until the Privy Council had delivered their ruling on the matter.

No sooner had MI5 locked up Munoz than they were involved in yet another sabotage investigation. On 3 July, 1943 a Liberator on a flight from Cairo landed at Gibraltar and was met by the Governor, Lieutenant-General Sir Noel Mason-Macfarlane. The party on board was led by General Wladyslaw Sikorski, the Polish ex-Prime Minister and now head of the Polish government in exile. The other passengers included two British MPs, Brigadier Whiteley and Victor Cazalet, who was acting as the General's British liaison officer. The plane landed safely and after the formal greetings the new arrivals were escorted up to the Convent where they were entertained to dinner and accommodated for the night.

The following night after dinner General Sikorski was scheduled to continue his journey back to Britain. A cocktail party was given in the garden of the US Mission Library in honour of Gibraltar's distinguished visitor and then the Governor gave a dinner party before taking the party back to the airfield in time for the 11 PM departure.

Altogether seventeen people climbed on board the Liberator, including Sikorski, his daughter and two SIS men, Messrs Pinder and Lock. Minutes later all except the pilot were dead.

The crash was inexplicable. Flight-Lieutenant Prchal an experienced pilot who had been a peacetime airline captain, completed his-pre-flight checks and then taxied the aircraft to the western end of the single runway. As was customary the floodlights had been switched off on the field to reduce glare. The Liberator then rolled forward and reached 'rotation' perfectly normally. The plane lifted off the ground with more than five hundred yards to spare and climbed to around two hundred feet. Then the unexplained happened. The onlookers on the tarmac watched the Liberator's navigation lights gain altitude and then level off. Instead of continuing to climb the nose of the aircraft dipped gently and the plane flew straight into the sea some three-quarters of a mile offshore. Moments before impact some of the witnesses thought they heard the four engines cutting out.

A rescue operation was immediately launched but the only survivor was Flight-Lieutenant Prchal, who was picked up by the first boat on the scene. It also carried the bodies of General Sikorski and his Chief-of-Staff, Major-General Klimecki. By Monday the Germans were broadcasting news of the General's death throughout Europe and claiming that the crash had been engineered by the 'British Secret Service' because the Allies had found the Polish leader troublesome. The allegation was particularly mischievous because it linked what the British considered (after a formal Court of Enquiry) to be an accident with the assassination of General Darlan in Algiers seven months earlier.[40]

Whatever the Nazi propaganda machine churned out was automatically suspect but the deaths of two such important men within such a short space of time inevitably led to speculation.

Among those who found the Sikorski affair mystifying was the Governor of Gibraltar, who had seen the whole incident. He had been flown by the Czech pilot on two or three occasions and had a high opinion of him. The Governor was himself an ex-intelligence officer who had served in Berlin, Vienna, Berne and Budapest as Military Attaché and had even offered to shoot Hitler with a sniper's rifle from his apartment, which overlooked a reviewing stand frequently used by the Führer. The Foreign Office had turned his suggestions down. Sir Noel was well aware of the intrigues of European intelligence organizations and carefully considered the possibility of sabotage before ruling it out. Both the RAF and a Commando unit had posted sentries on the plane throughout the time it was on the ground which would have made sabotage by an enemy agent virtually impossible. The only alternative explanation apart from a verdict of accident was deliberate murder by the British or at the very least their complicity in a plot.

General Sikorski's political stand against the Russians made him an unlikely target for the Nazis. He was virulently anti-Communist and the Polish government had broken off diplomatic relations with Moscow. Undoubtedly, he was a thorn in the side of Stalin with his constant demands for the return of Polish POWs captured in 1939. Furthermore, he had been pressing the Soviet authorities about the discovery of a mass grave in the forest of Katyn near Smolensk. On 13 April Berlin radio announced that the bodies of 10,000 Polish officers had been found, and blamed the Russians for the massacre. The Russians countered with: 'This was yet another example of Nazi atrocities.' The Polish leader in exile had no love for either the Germans or the Russians but was inclined to believe the Berlin version. This attitude was not unhelpful to the Nazis who never lost an opportunity to try to drive wedges between the Allies, and it certainly made him a strange candidate for an Abwehr or Sicherheitsdienst assassination.

The Governor conferred with the DSO on the possibility of the crash having been caused by sabotage and they agreed that there was very little likelihood of the Germans being able to pull off the *coup*. They also dismissed the idea that SOE, MI6 or OSS would have attempted to engineer the crash. After all, if Churchill had ordered Sikorski's murder, as was later alleged in *The Soldiers* by the German playwright, Rolf Hochhuth, MI6 would have had far better opportunities to get the General alone and kill him. In any case SOE had only just scotched a Soviet-inspired plot to assassinate the General in Cairo.

The RAF Court of Enquiry into the incident opened on 7 July under Group Captain J.G. Elton, DFC AFC at Air Headquarters in Gibraltar and heard evidence from twenty-eight witnesses, including the pilot, who was recovering from his injuries.

Most of the Liberator was recovered from the sea and the vital cockpit flight controls were also salvaged and meticulously examined by the crash investigators. The Court of Enquiry ruled out sabotage as the cause of the crash but did leave a number of questions unanswered. Speculation continued for many years and several people suggested that Mason-Macfarlane's diaries of the time threw suspicion on the Czech pilot, but from Colonel Medlam's point of view the case was closed at the end of the Enquiry. No evidence was ever found to implicate MI6 or OSS, though the controversy was slow to die down. In February 1965 the whole episode was resurrected by an unnamed 'English Colonel who had been in charge of the sabotage team'. This alleged 'embittered intelligence officer' living in Switzerland was quoted as a mysterious source of secret information by Hochhuth. The 'Colonel' never came forward to substantiate the claims made on his behalf and he was certainly neither Colonel Medlam (who retired to Worcestershire), Colonel Codrington (who retired to a garden design business in Rutland), nor Colonel Kirby Green (who stayed on in the Security Service after the war and then retired in 1964 to Wells in Somerset).

Edward Prchal moved to the United States after the war but was not interviewed by David Irving for his book *Accident*. Carlos Thompson found him in 1967 in Los Altos in California and quoted from him at length in his account of the post-war wranglings over the crash, *The Assassination of Winston Churchill*. Irving, Prchal and Thompson were later brought together for a television programme by David Frost on 20 December, 1968. Also present were Randolph Churchill, defending his late father, and Kenneth Tynan, who had backed Hochhuth's play. In the aftermath of the Sikorski affair there was at least some good news for the DSO. Luis Cordon-Cuenca's appeal was heard on 13 December, which meant that Jose Martin Munoz's sentence could be carried out and publicized. A scaffold was constructed in the courtyard of the civil prison and at nine o'clock on 11 January, 1944, Cordon-Cuenca was executed. Three minutes later Munoz followed him.

Altogether three Abwehr agents were executed for their wartime activities in Gibraltar. Little had been achieved by their efforts, which had been so effectively frustrated by the staff of the local DSO. In February 1944 ULTRA intercepts of the telegrams destined for the German Embassy in Madrid made it clear that Berlin considered further sabotage attempts useless and possibly counter-productive. Even the favoured method of booby-trapping crates of oranges bound for Britain was abandoned, but not before Lord (Victor) Rothschild, the head of B1(c), had won the George Medal for defusing a bomb concealed in a consignment of Spanish onions. Rothschild bravely carried the suspect box away from the cookhouse of a Polish military camp in Leicestershire, and then dismantled the explosive device.

Malta also had a DSO, Brian Atkinson, who was based at the British Military headquarters in the Castile; he supervised the construction of a special internment camp in Rabat, the island's ancient capital, to house pro-Axis Maltese. Some forty-three detainees, thought by the DSO and the Acting Governor, Major-General Dobbie, to be particularly pro-Italian, were shipped to Uganda for the duration of hostilities.

Apart from SIME in Cairo, Colonel Medlam's department in Gibraltar was the largest MI5 offshoot in the Mediterranean theatre. These overseas arms were largely defensive in nature and so inevitably were restricted in their ability to contribute positive intelligence to MI5.

XII

The Irish Back Door

The one European capital to remain completely closed to all British intelligence services throughout the war was Dublin.

On 12 January, 1939 the IRA made their intentions known to Whitehall in a personal letter addressed to Lord Halifax, the Foreign Secretary. The letter took the form of an ultimatum and gave the British government four days to withdraw from Ulster. The alternative was war, warned the letter, which was signed by 'Patrick Fleming, Secretary of the Army Council'. The document was passed to Scotland Yard, who gave a reassuring reply to the Cabinet. The IRA had been all but destroyed by RUC arrests in Northern Ireland just before Christmas. The police had rounded up all the men who had survived an explosion on 28 November and had interned them under the Special Powers Act in the Crumlin Road Prison. Special Branch were confident that there was little to fear but they were proved wrong. On 16 January, 1939 there was an explosion just outside the control room of the Southwark power station. On the same morning a heavy-duty cable over the Grand Union Canal leading to Willesden power station was badly damaged. Other bombs went off in Birmingham, Manchester and Alnwick. More bombs went off the following day and responsibility was claimed by the IRA army council. Scotland Yard were acutely embarrassed by their misjudgment of the IRA's strength and took all the obvious measures without delay. Passengers bound for Ireland at Liverpool, Holyhead and Fishguard were closely examined and police descended in force on the homes of known IRA sympathizers in the Irish districts of the major cities, but the results were negligible. The police had been caught completely unprepared but to their relief the bombing campaign seemed to end as quickly as it had begun. Peace reigned until the beginning of the next month, although the calm was interrupted by one bizarre event.

On Thursday, 19 January, a small bomb exploded in the porch of Hawney's Hotel in Tralee. It would probably have been written off as a minor prank or even perhaps a gesture by a frustrated Republican on the wrong side of the water if Neville Chamberlain's son had not been staying in the building. Francis Chamberlain had quietly slipped over to County Kerry for a shooting holiday and was the hotel's principal guest. The IRA were quick to disclaim the affair but it was not long before the attacks in England started again.

On 4 February the government admitted that they had received advance warning of the 'war' and the Home Secretary, Sir Samuel Hoare, explained that the police had so far arrested thirty-three suspects. On the same day two time bombs went off in London underground stations. The devices had been deposited in the left-luggage offices of Tottenham Court Road station and Leicester Square station. Two people were seriously injured and the newspapers the next day demanded action. There were more explosions in London during the night and fires were started in Coventry.

Two days after Sir Samuel's statement to the House an unsuccessful attempt was made to blow up the walls of Walton Gaol in Liverpool and four London shops were damaged by incendiary bombs. The 'English Campaign' was being resumed but not everything was going the IRA's way. The police dragnet throughout the country had achieved several arrests and had one sinister and unexpected result. A search at the Harrow Weald home of a twenty-four-year-old labourer, Michael O'Shea, had uncovered a remarkable document which was to become known as the 'S-Plan'. It was found by Detective-Inspector Barnes amongst a collection of IRA papers and led to a dramatic rethink of British intelligence appreciations about the IRA. What made the S-Plan so important was the amount of careful thought that had so obviously gone into drawing it up. The plan gave a well-argued account of an urban bombing offensive and listed a variety of useful targets. It suggested acts of sabotage for propaganda and detailed how Britain's defences could be paralysed. The English Campaign, it concluded, should be aimed at public utilities – especially public transport and gasworks – industrial plants and various other commercial establishments. The document was devastatingly well prepared and was certainly a change from the usual low-quality material often seized by the police. Most of the documentary evidence the police managed to confiscate was handwritten instructions from 'GHQ, Dublin' to the IRA's various 'Active Service Units' in England. The S-Plan was passed on from Special Branch to Guy Liddell's 'B' Division, which prepared a report on its military implications.

When the S-Plan was eventually made public in March it caused considerable interest because for the first time for many years it demonstrated that the IRA were a potent force to be reckoned with. The plan was linked with the letter to Lord Halifax and was widely quoted at the trial of O'Shea and seventeen other bombers which opened at the Old Bailey on 22 March, 1939.

Meanwhile the attacks continued. On 2 March the aquaduct carrying the Grand Union Canal over the North Circular Road near Stonebridge Park in north London was unsuccessfully bombed. On the same day damage was done to the Birmingham Navigation Canal at Ball's Hill Bridge near Wednesbury in Staffordshire. The next day Henry West, an observant railwayman, saved a railway bridge in Willesden. The Old Bailey trial seemed to provoke more outrages. On 23 March five bombs went off in London wholesale food markets and the *News Chronicle* office in Fleet Street was badly damaged by an explosion. Other bombs went off in Birmingham, Liverpool and Coventry. On 29 March Hammersmith Bridge was rocked by two explosions.[41]

The attacks continued unabated. On 13 April no fewer than eleven bombs went off in public lavatories in London and Birmingham and every time convictions were obtained in the courts another series of attacks seemed to start. Tear-gas grenades were tossed into packed cinemas in London and Birmingham on 5 May and fifteen people went to hospital. Cinemas in Liverpool were similarly attacked and Coventry reported two bombs. On 19 May a total of four magnesium bombs went off in the Paramount Cinema in Birmingham. More cinemas were hit in London two days later, forcing the police to search every theatre in the capital.

The Special Branch were forced to admit that the IRA's activities had hardly been affected by the mass of arrests they had made. They seemed powerless to deal with all the incidents, which was exactly what had been planned. MI5 carefully examined the S-Plan and concluded that it had been written by someone with a military background who was perfectly up to date with sophisticated modern tactics. They did not rule out the strong possibility that it had been masterminded by the Abwehr.[42] They could offer little else of practical help becuase 'B' Division had absolutely no contacts within the Irish community. They had always left Irish affairs to Scotland Yard. Nevertheless, Liddell was sufficiently concerned about the situation to ask Cecil, his younger brother, to head an Irish section within 'B' Division, B11.

As a family the Liddells had excellent links in Ireland. Guy, Cecil and David all had Irish backgrounds, and Guy had married Calypso Baring, Lord Revelstoke's youngest daughter. Lord Revelstoke himself owned substantial estates in Ireland including Lambay Island near Dublin.

The beginning of June was marked by an increase in the number of IRA incidents. A secret transmitter in Ulster co-ordinated a massive demonstration in Belfast that ended in a night of violence during which thousands of IRA sympathizers built bonfires out of their government issue gasmasks. On 9 June the IRA switched their attention to the Post Office, as recommended in the S-Plan, and some twenty pillar boxes burst into flames, which forced the police to open and search all the rest in London. A Post Office van was destroyed and several   mail-sorting offices were damaged by fire in London, Manchester and Birmingham. All police leave was cancelled and a final drive against the IRA was organized. Boarding-houses throughout the country were raided and more suspects taken into custody. The government announced new measures to curb the terrorism. The Prevention of Violence Bill gave the authorities new powers of detention and required all Irish nationals to register with the police just as other aliens were obliged to do.

The Home Secretary introduced the Bill to the House and totted up the score so far: 127 terrorist incidents had taken place since January 1939, fifty-seven in London, seventy in the provinces. One person had been killed and fifty-five injured. Altogether sixty-six people had been convicted of related offences and a mass of bomb-making paraphernalia had been confiscated. The haul included fifty-five sticks of dynamite and gelignite, over a thousand detonators, two tons of potassium chlorate and iron oxide and seven gallons of sulphuric acid.

In Scotland the situation was a little better. The Glasgow City Police led by Chief Constable Percy Sillitoe, had raided an assembly hall used by the IRA on 14 May and made several arrests. Over six hundred sticks of dynamite and five hundred detonators were recovered.

In spite of the new legislation the attacks continued and became more bloody than ever. The left luggage offices at Victoria station and King's Cross were blown up on 26 July. One man had both his legs torn off and later died. Seven other bystanders were injured. The week was one long series of outrages. Three banks in Piccadilly Circus were bombed and Madame Tussaud's Waxworks was hit by a balloon bomb. The central Post Office in Liverpool was wrecked on 27 July while three other explosions in the city caused chaos. The House of Lords passed the Prevention of Violence Bill two days later.

The new Act had the immediate effect of increasing the traffic of passengers bound for Eire. As the police continued their searches in the Irish communities many of the IRA sympathizers decided to flee the country before they were served with deportation orders. Within a matter of days of its becoming law the police had deported more than fifty suspects under its provisions. In Ireland Éamonn de Valera issued two proclamations invoking the Offences Against the State Act which gave the Garda more powers of arrest and detention, which were designed to prevent the English Campaign from spreading across the Irish Sea. These measures seemed to have little effect. The attention of the public was temporarily diverted to Hitler in Europe but the IRA offensive was closer to home. On 25 August a bomb in a bicycle carrier-basket exploded in the early afternoon in Coventry's busy Broadgate shopping area. Five people were killed instantly and a further sixty injured by the blast and broken glass.

This terrible act of terrorism had been a mistake. The IRA member entrusted with delivering the bomb to its final target had panicked as he cycled across an unfamiliar city. He abandoned his bicycle in the busy thoroughfare and fled to Ireland the same day.[43] The newspapers demanded prompt action and the police made a search of every Irish house in Coventry. IRA prisoners were attacked in Dartmoor Prison and the police were inundated with tips. Within a fortnight most of the Coventry 'Active Service Unit' had been rounded up and charged with the murder of just one of the Broadgate victims, Elsie Ansell.

A twenty-nine-year-old labourer, Joseph Hewitt, was sent for trial in Birmingham, along with his wife and widowed mother-in-law. Also accused were James McCormack (using the name Richards), who was also twenty-nine years old and a labourer, and Peter Barnes, a thirty-two-year-old clerk. The trial lasted three days, at the end of which Barnes and 'Richards' were found guilty and sentenced to death. As soon as the sentence was announced in the press a whole spate of new attacks were sparked off. Pillar boxes burst into flames, post offices were bombed and a mail train attacked, but the executions took place anyway the following year on 7 February, 1940.

The case stirred up a great controversy because both men had only participated in the plot at an early stage and both thought the target was to be one of those indicated in the S-Plan, namely, a power station. This distinction was too fine for the Birmingham Assizes and the men were hanged at Winson Green Gaol. The IRA responded by raiding a British military depot at Ballykinkar in County Down and successfully escaped with two hundred rifles and a good stock of ammunition.

Throughout the English Campaign Cecil Liddell had liaised with Special Branch and tried to fathom the strength of the IRA in Britain. He was assisted by Joyce Huggins, his devoted secretary, and John Stephenson, later Lord Justice Stephenson, a barrister recruited for wartime service by Guy Liddell. All parties were agreed that the Irish connection was a potential Achilles heel for the United Kingdom and that it was unlikely that the Abwehr had overlooked the possibility of exploiting the situation.

'B' Division had already established that the Abwehr had been crippled by the September 1939 internments and were anxious to make contact with extremist groups opposed to the government. The senior German agent in Britain, SNOW, was allegedly motivated by his strong sympathies for the Welsh Nationalist cause and his saboteur-in-chief, Gwilym Williams, GW, had also been recruited from the same organization. Cecil Liddell reasoned that if the Abwehr were prepared to go to so much trouble for an untried group that had yet to prove their effectiveness, an alliance between the IRA and the Abwehr was a real possibility, which could prove a grave threat. Unlike the Welsh Nationalists the IRA had demonstrated their ability on many occasions to mount and execute clandestine attacks in the heart of enemy territory.

The Abwehr had indeed been watching the progress of the English Campaign with interest. After the discovery of the S-Plan the German Nazi party newspaper *Voelkischer Beobachier* commented:

> 'This action programme makes a fantastic impression. The bomb attacks carried out to date and the terrorist activities announced in the S-Plan show that the Irish Republicans are in earnest, for all their fantasy.'

In fact, the Abwehr had already established links with the IRA leadership in Dublin and were preparing to develop them further. The Hamburg Abstelle had sent Oskar Pfaus, a German-American who had lived for some years in the United States, to Dublin in February 1939. It was as a result of this first mission to Ireland that Jim O'Donovan was invited to visit the Reich and cement Abwehr/IRA relations.

On the outbreak of war in September 1939 Ireland had declared her intention of remaining neutral. This placed the Republic in a curious position. It was a member of the British Commonwealth and in spite of its stand on 'non-belligerency' Irish subjects were quite free to join British regiments, an opportunity that thousands of Irish citizens took up. The neutral status of the Republic also offered the Germans some advantages. The German Embassy at 58 Northumberland Road, Dublin, was a useful base of operations though the Ambassador, Dr Eduard Hempel, was reluctant to compromise his diplomatic mission by tolerating overt espionage. His staff consisted of the Counsellor, SS Major Henning Thomson, Herr Bruchhans, Herr Mueller and two female secretaries. A late addition to the diplomats was Dr Carlheinz

Petersen, the German News Agency representative in Dublin, who was appointed Press Attaché. The embassy communicated with Berlin on a teleprinter landline that happened to be routed through London, something MI5 did not fail to notice and take advantage of. There was also a powerful short-wave transmitter which became a source of constant aggravation to the Allies, who pressed the Irish authorities to confiscate it.

Cecil Liddell understandably assumed that the German Embassy was packed with intelligence officers in diplomatic cover but there was actually little evidence to show that any of the Germans were engaged in illegal activities. In fact, Dr Hempel made sure that they all studiously avoided being tricked into a compromising situation by the British who, of course, were anxious to bring Ireland into their sphere of influence. Each opponent overestimated the strength of the other.

The Germans suspected everyone in Dublin of being in the pay of the British Secret Service while MI5 simply feared the worst. For their part the Irish kept the diplomatic missions of both under permanent surveillance. The Garda Special Branch were responsible for most of these duties though the Irish Secret Service, G2, had been mobilized in a counterespionage role to protect the Republic's neutrality. This department operated under the umbrella of the Department of Defence and consisted of around forty officers seconded from other duties. They were housed in the main Department of Defence building in Dublin's Park Gate and were led by Colonel Liam Archer, an uncompromising Irishman who reported to de Valera and the Interior Minister, Joseph Walshe. G2 combined the roles of MI5 and MI6 and relied on the Garda Special Branch to carry out fieldwork and enquiries beyond the range of the few G2 branch offices.

The first lesson that Liddell and Stephenson learnt in their relationship with G2 was that they could rely on virtually no exchange of opinions or information. The second lesson was that Whitehall had no good contacts in the Irish capital. Before Partition the business of intelligence had been largely left to the military authorities, who had failed to make any impression on the scene. SIS had kept clear of Ireland since November 1919 and the Bloody Sunday murders. Liddell was expected to step into this void and develop a good relationship with G2. Colonel Archer made it clear that the kind of links that MI5 had in mind were out of the question. Guy Liddell relayed the message that the Irish Ministry of the Interior would consider any foreign intelligence presence on their soil as a serious breach of their neutral status and would take appropriate action. Meanwhile Liddell's Irish section grew, taking in Waldemar Caroe, a 'B' Division officer of

Norwegian extraction, and two secretaries, Vera Sutherland and Monica Mooney.

It was not long after the start of the war that MI5 understood just how deeply the Irish government felt about the issue. They refused to return RAF aircrews forced to land in the Republic and explained that these badly-needed men would be interned for the duration. Nothing the Liddells said made any impression. G2 would not tolerate any interference, an attitude shared by the Dublin Cabinet. If the Secret Intelligence Service and the Security Service were reluctant to venture over the Irish Sea, the NID had no such qualms and filled a part of the gap. The DNI responded to the challenge, and the rumours of U-boats sheltering in Ireland's West Coast, by sending a Naval Attaché to join the British diplomatic staff in Dublin. Captain Grieg, the DNI's nominee, set about the development of a coast-watching force and in this endeavour received a degree of co-operation (in the sense that he was not arrested immediately) from the Irish government. It was not part of his brief to enter the realms of counter-espionage but nevertheless he established fairly friendly relations with G2.

The coast-watchers produced irregular reports of enemy activity which were circulated under the appropriate code name POTATOES in Whitehall but it took an SIS aerial survey, conducted by Sidney Cotton, to confirm that at least for the time being there was no immediate danger of Nazi raiders taking advantage of the long and isolated Irish coastline.

In April 1940 the very thing that Cecil Liddell feared most took place: a German agent was arrested in Ireland, charged with the relatively trivial offence of illegal entry, and then released after payment of a £3 fine.

The first MI5 knew of the event was via the British diplomatic representative in Dublin, Sir John Maffey, who reported to Whitehall that the *Irish Times* of 15 April had published an interesting story under the headline 'German's Strange Journey to Ireland'. A sixty-one-year-old Austrian had appeared in a Dublin District Court the previous day and had admitted landing on the Waterford coast from a small boat on 9 February, 1940. He claimed his name was Ernst Weber-Drohl but his passport and marriage certificate had been lost when his small boat had been capsized by a wave. He denied being a member of the Nazi Party and spun an elaborate story about his plans to find his children, who he believed were somewhere in Ireland. The prosecution commented that the accused's story 'was difficult to check and even more difficult to believe'. Nevertheless, the District Judge was persuaded that Weber-Drohl was harmless and he was freed by the court.

For their part the Irish Special Branch shared MI5's concern about Weber-Drohl. His claim that he had joined a tramp steamer in Antwerp bound for Ireland was unlikely. A Dublin physiotherapist confirmed that Weber-Drohl was a member of the European Union of Chiropractors and that he had been in correspondence with the 'Doctor' trying to help the Austrian trace his two children and their mother, whom he had known during a brief residence in Ireland in 1907. The police had traced his movements from the Westland Row hotel in which he had been arrested after a tip-off back to Kilkenny between Waterford and Dublin. There was little evidence about Weber-Drohl's activities between his arrival on 9 February and his arrest but again there was little to prove that he had acted against the State. In his summing-up the District Judge noted that 'the Irish government had no expenses in the matter'.

Apparently, Weber-Drohl had been a well-known athlete and had made his first visit to Ireland during the International Exhibition in 1907 and had then gone to the United States. He explained the large amount of dollars on his person by saying that his wife, who had relations in Switzerland, had lent him her life savings for his search.

If the District Judge believed his story, G2 did not, and arranged for the elderly Austrian to be arrested and interned just three days after the Court Hearing.

It was later established that Weber-Drohl had been recruited by the Nuremburg Abstelle because he had once been billed as a wrestler in Ireland as 'Atlas the Strong'. In spite of many unforeseen incidents, such as the loss of his transmitter overboard, Weber-Drohl had found Jim O'Donovan, the IRA representative who had contacted Hamburg the previous year, and had delivered a quantity of dollars and a set of detailed instructions about how to enlarge on the S-Plan. His role had been limited to that of a courier and he did at least succeed in following his orders. Shortly after he had been interned the German Ambassador began pressing for his release and after a while the Irish government relented and allowed 'Atlas the Strong' a period of freedom to demonstrate his phenomenal strength to the public.

The Internment Order on Weber-Drohl came as a great relief to MI5 but they were refused access to him and denied a sight of the G2 interrogation reports. Eventually in May 1945 Weber-Drohl was flown from Baldonnel airfield by the USAF to Frankfurt where he was received by CSDIC staff from Bad Nenndorf.

Three weeks later a second German agent was arrested. He was Willy Preetz, using the genuine Irish passport of 'Paddy Mitchell'. He too was arrested after a tip-off, just three weeks after he had arrived by U-boat in Dingle Bay. In the meantime, he had taken lodgings in the harbour area and then rented a shop in Westland Row. Above it he had a transmitter but his downfall was the purchase of a car. Local gossip about the car led the police to call on 'Mr Mitchell' who was taken straight to Mountjoy Prison.

It turned out that Preetz had been visiting his parents-in-law when war had been declared in September 1939. He had made his way back to Germany via a Belgian cement freighter with the assistance of a passport in the name of 'Paddy Mitchell' which had been obtained for him by a Sligo policeman. The neutral Belgians had briefly interned Preetz and then deported him back to Germany where he had been recruited by the Abwehr. Before the war he had been a steward on the Nord-Deutsche Lloyd Line based in Hamburg and had married Sarah Reynolds, a young Irish girl from Tuam in Galway. His background made him ideal material for the Abwehr and the Hamburg Abstelle had not lost the opportunity to train him in wireless procedure and send him off to Ireland. Again, Cecil Liddell was prevented from visiting the detainee.

The following month the Irish police arrested three Abwehr agents. Two of them, Herbert Tributh and Dieter Gaertner, were South African students who had been caught by the war in Germany. They were both anti-British and detained with an Indian named Henry Obed in a remote country lane by the local Garda. All three were sentenced to seven years' imprisonment and sent to Mountjoy.

These three were of particular interest to Liddell and Stephenson because the two South Africans, who were found with their original, valid passports, were due to continue their journey to the United Kingdom and they were thought to be in a position to offer valuable intelligence about future Abwehr intentions. Again, all requests for access to the spies were turned down.

By the end of 1940 no less than six Abwehr agents were under arrest. The last to join his comrades at Mountjoy was Walter Simon, a fifty-eight-year-old intelligence veteran who was already well known to MI5 because of a conviction in February 1939 at Tonbridge. He had received two consecutive sentences of three months for breaching the Aliens Registration Act and had been interrogated by Colonel Hinchley-Cooke. Walter Simon had been landed by U-boat in Dingle Bay in County Kerry on 13 June, three weeks before the Tributh, Gaertner and Obed trio landed in Baltimore Bay from a sailing boat.[44] He was carrying the papers of Karl Anderson, a naturalized British subject who had been born in Sweden. He claimed that he was a seaman who had persuaded a ship sailing from Rotterdam to take him to Ireland and that he was

266

therefore a refugee. He explained the large amount of money he was carrying, £215 15s 10d and $1,910, by saying that he had withdrawn all his savings from a Rotterdam bank before escaping to Ireland. The Special Criminal Court at Collins' Barracks did not believe him, especially after Commander Butler of the Irish Special Branch produced a photograph of Walter Simon taken in Wandsworth Prison sixteen months earlier. When 'Anderson' was asked to comment he merely said, 'Yes – that's a very nice picture!'

Simon was convicted of illegal entry into Ireland and interned at Mountjoy Prison. His mission had been completely wasted. His wireless set had been found by the police hidden on the beach soon after his arrest and he had given MI5 the satisfaction of proving that Hermann Christian Simon was the same person as 'Karl Anderson', the hapless 'refugee' who had managed to escape Nazi tyranny on a fishing boat.

Colonel Archer was delighted by the progress G2 had made in 1940 but there was one nagging worry. They had evidence that at least one German agent had come to the Republic and had evaded capture. The probability was that he had returned to Germany or gone on to Britain but there was no certainty of this.

The evidence of Lieutenant Krause's existence had been seized during a raid on a house in Templeogue Road in Dublin on 22 May, 1940. The house, named 'Konstanz', was owned by Stephen Held, a forty-three-year-old businessman with strong IRA connections. A parachute, a wireless transmitter and various German Great War medals had been found in a locked room. Nearly $20,000 had been recovered from a locked safe. The London *Times* reported the raid on 25 May but Krause was to remain at liberty in Ireland for another seventeen months. His continued presence was yet another wedge between MI5 and G2. The elusive German had succeeded where the earlier agents had failed. He had made definite contact with the IRA and the capture of his code book suggested that he was also keeping a regular radio schedule with Hamburg.

The first arrest of 1941 came when two policemen in County Waterford challenged a young stranger outside the small village of New Ross on 12 March. They opened his suitcase and found several bundles of banknotes and an Afu transmitter. By that evening 'Hans Marschner' was under arrest at the Bridewell Interrogation Centre being questioned by Commander Butler, a former aide to the President and wartime recruit into G2, and 'Captain Grey'.

'Captain Grey' was in fact Dr Richard Hayes, who had been brought into the Irish Secret Service by Colonel Archer, who suspected that the

Abwehr might be planning to use Eire as a base for operations against Britain. 'Doc' Hayes was Director of the National Museum and a brilliant linguist. During his service with G2 he developed a talent for cryptology which was later to pay unexpected dividends. He and his children spent hours examining the Abwehr code books recovered from Held's house and eventually succeeded in recreating authentic German cyphers.

The interrogation of 'Hans Marschner' revealed him to be Sergeant Gunther Schütz, a twenty-nine-year-old German from Schweidnitz. He began by claiming that he was a South African student and gave a home address in Webster Gardens in west London, a point that Cecil Liddell pursued with special interest.

The Webster Gardens address was a lodging-house used as a refuge by the Abwehr and had also been the subject of B1(a)'s attention since January 1940 when RAINBOW came under control. Schütz and RAINBOW had met at the lodgings in 1938 and had become friends (see Chapter VII). The two Liddells discussed the situation at length and decided to make no comment to G2 about the conclusions of their enquiries at 41 Webster Gardens. They were now more anxious than ever to gain access to the internees sitting out the war in Mountjoy Prison. Schütz could give valuable information on how RAINBOW's reports were being received in Hamburg and the case had close links with other B1(a) cases. It was crucial to the whole double cross system that the Webster Gardens safe house stay high in the opinion of the Abwehr. To date all the indications were that there were no suspicions about it. When TATE landed in September 1940 the address had been given to him as a lifeline.

The G2 enquiry was answered by Liddell with the comment that Schütz was indeed known there. He had spent a year at the house while he was attending the German Commercial School at Eaton Rise in Ealing before the war. The name Hans Marschner was completely unknown. Schütz was indeed a valuable arrest. He had been recruited by the Hamburg Abstelle on his return from London and had then been posted to Spain to operate an Abwehr post-box. At the end of 1940 he had been recalled to Hamburg and assigned a mission in Northern Ireland.

It was later established that Schütz had instructions to make daily weather reports and observe coastal convoy movements. The first attempt to drop him into County Waterford had occurred in January 1941 and had been abandoned because of bad weather. His plane had returned to its base in Holland. As well as his wireless and aerial Schütz carried £1,000, some of it in forged £5 notes, and $3,000 in currency. He had also been given a spade, a small compass and a microscope.

The microscope was a giveaway. G2 had no difficulty in concluding that the agent had been equipped with it to read microdots, which had just come into vogue with the Germans. Sure enough, several of the punctuation marks on a newspaper cutting from an English botany article were revealed as instructions to penetrate the Belfast shipbuilding yards.

'Doc' Hayes was also interested in Schütz's choice of reading material. He had a small English pocket edition of *Just a Girl* which was the basis of his cyphers. The method of coding a message was elaborate. If a transmission had to be made on the fourteenth day of the third month (the day after his arrest), he would select page 143. He would then turn back an agreed number of pages and prepare his message from a particular line.

Schütz had also been issued with the address of the German Embassy in Northumberland Road, Dublin, and another emergency safe house – 46 Merrion Square. This was an address already under G2 observation. The owner was a German businessman, Werner Unland, who had fled to Dublin from England just before the outbreak of the war. His mail had been intercepted since that date but little evidence had been accumulated against him. The most suspicious part of his mail had been the amount of payments he received from such diverse countries as Hungary, Spain and Belgium. Werner Unland was arrested in May 1941 and sentenced to five years for espionage. The evidence against him had been not only his mail but also the fact that his address had been found on Schütz.

Schütz's arrest was considered something of a *coup* for both MI5 and G2 because it had led to proof against Unland but apparently did not jeopardize Webster Gardens. RAINBOW continued to communicate with his cover address without interruption until June 1943. He also contributed to the picture that G2 were building up about the Abwehr's methods. During his interrogations at the Arbour Hill Military Prison Schütz had been searched and it had been discovered that the lining of his jacket was rather discoloured. The shoulder pads were sent for chemical analysis and found to contain an ingredient for secret writing. A solution was made up by soaking part of the impregnated cloth with water and then using the result as ink.

Schütz was eventually sent to Sligo Prison in the northwest of Ireland and was then transferred to join the other interned agents at 'Internment Camp No 3', the hospital wing of Mountjoy Prison.

After the arrest of Werner Unland, G2 underwent a change of command. Colonel Archer was promoted to the post of Assistant Chief-of-Staff of the swelling Irish defence forces and Dan Bryan was appointed the new G2 Chief. Bryan continued to maintain 'frostiness' between G2 and MI5 but a certain thaw was detectable. Many of the earlier 'misunderstandings' had now been sorted out and Liddell was resigned to getting minimum co-operation. Nevertheless G2's performance to date had been impressive. As yet there was little to show that Eire had become a major base for the Abwehr and relations between Hamburg and the IRA seemed precarious. The worst had not happened.

In July 1941 'B' Division were able to improve their picture of the Irish scene with a new recruit to the double cross system. He was an Irishman, Joseph Lenihan, who had landed by parachute near Dublin and had made his way up to Ulster with his two wireless transmitters, a large quantity of secret ink and £400. Once in British territory he contacted the police, who passed him on to the RSLO Belfast. Lenihan was dubbed BASKET and put to sending letters to his Abwehr cover address. Unfortunately, his case was not entirely successful because B1(a) had to scrap the idea of using his radios. BASKET's instructions had been to set up a weather station in Sligo but this was quite impossible as it would have meant bringing G2 into the scheme. In any event such an operation would have been in complete contradiction to the standing orders of Exterior Minister Joseph Walshe who was always anxious to protect Eire's neutrality.

In spite of the lack of total success with BASKET Cecil Liddell had now gained more confidence. Domestic double agents were achieving impressive results in Britain and the Twenty Committee were satisfied that MI5 had taken control of the Hamburg Abstelle's operations directed against the United Kingdom.

G2 had also made some sensational *coups*. In June 1941 a leading member of the IRA had been kidnapped by his own organization. His name was Stephen Hayes and he was suspected, wrongly, of having given information to the Irish Special Branch. Hayes was tortured and questioned by the IRA Adjutant-General, Sean McCaughey, for two months and then forced to sign a 'confession'. On 8 September, 1941 Hayes escaped his captors and surrendered himself to the astonished police. With the IRA Chief-of-Staff in custody the Irish Special Branch under Superintendent Gantley set about dismembering the illegal organization. Hayes poured out detail after detail about the IRA's activities and told G2 the full story about the elusive 'Lieutenant Krause' who had been sought since Held's arrest the previous year. Hayes was sentenced to five years' imprisonment in June 1942 for 'the maintenance of an illegal force'. He appeared as a prosecution witness against

McCaughey who later died during a hunger strike in Maryborough Prison after the war.

'Krause' was an alias used by Dr Hermann Goertz, a figure well known to MI5 and G2. Hayes explained that Goertz had parachuted into County Meath in May 1940 and had announced himself to the IRA as their liaison with the Abwehr, a sort of espionage ambassador. He had been forced to go into hiding after Held's arrest but the Garda had never managed to trap him. A raid was mounted on a house in Blackheath Park, a district in Dublin's suburb of Clontarf, and seventeen months of freedom for Goertz were abruptly ended.

The arrest of Goertz tied up one remaining loose end of German espionage activity in Ireland and paved the way for better relations between MI5 and G2. Goertz was a seasoned Abwehr operator (see Chapter III) but found that trying to deal with the IRA was an impossible mission. He had intended to use the IRA as an invading force against the British in Ulster but no operation ever got beyond the planning stage. He remained convinced that in spite of all the betrayals and conspiracies the Republicans could contribute a great deal to the war. His wireless had been lost on arrival so he had to rely on very uncertain methods of communication with Germany, which inevitably meant long delays in exchanging messages. He wrote reports to several neutral letter-boxes and had also made contact with Dr Hempel in Dublin, though the Ambassador had discouraged regular links for fear of British entrapment. There was good reason for his suspicions. A Dutch deserter had visited the Embassy in September 1941 and had offered his services to the Germans. He said his name was Jan van Loon and that he had used his leave in Belfast to travel down to Dublin. He was interviewed by Herr Mueller who declined his offer. As soon as he left the Embassy he was arrested and interned with the other G2 prisoners.

Goertz underwent a long interrogation at the hands of 'Doc' Hayes, Major Joseph Guilfoyle and Lieutenant Ben Byrne and was then sent to a special internment camp near Athlone which had once been a British Army barracks. It was here that Hayes devised and executed an extraordinary counter-intelligence operation.

The statements made to G2 inquisitors were far from complete and Schütz's daring escape from Mountjoy Prison dressed as a woman on 28 February, 1942 proved that the detainees still had good contacts on the outside. Schütz remained free until 30 April when he was arrested in the home of Mrs Caitlin Brugha, an IRA activist and widow of a former Defence Minister. Hayes decided to pump Goertz for information and allowed him to think that he had corrupted a quartermaster at the

Athlone camp, Sergeant Power. Goertz bribed him to deliver messages in code to the Dublin Legation but in fact the letters were taken straight to the G2 office in the Defence Department building in Dublin's Park Gate.

Hayes and his five children spent hours deciphering the messages and gradually discovered the key. He then started a regular correspondence with Goertz but the hapless German always believed he was in touch with Hamburg! The operation was so successful that Hayes was confident enough to award the elderly Abwehr agent the Iron Cross and promote him to the rank of Major. At one point Jan van Loon received confirmation via this channel that he had been enrolled in the Waffen SS.

The deception worked well and Goertz was prevented from making several escape attempts from his internment. One unexpected result of this was a growing suspicion of a traitor amongst the prisoners. The unfortunate Henry Obed was accused by his comrades of informing on them and he was ostracized in spite of his denials.

Even after the war Goertz believed that he had genuinely been communicating with Hamburg and had directed the activities of a network in Northern Ireland code-named ULRIKE which was broadcasting German propaganda on an illegal transmitter.

Goertz stayed in prison until September 1946, when he was released on parole. He went to live in Dublin and became Secretary of the Save the German Children Fund but in May 1947 he was refused asylum in Ireland. He was told that he would be flown back to Germany where he would have to face interrogation from the Allies. On 23 May, 1947 he took poison in the Aliens Registration Office at Dublin Castle and later died at the Mercer's Hospital.

While Hayes spent much of 1943 building up the Goertz deception the rest of G2 concentrated on their counter-espionage activities and managed to plant a reliable agent in the American Embassy, an act that virtually completed Irish surveillance on all the foreign missions.

The British representative alone escaped this attention because his office was too small and was known not to contain any MI5 or MI6 officers. The full British diplomatic staff consisted of Sir John Maffey, two Secretaries and a Registrar. Relations between the two countries had improved since the days when the Dublin government refused to return downed British aircrew and even arrested a coast-watcher from NID. Nevertheless, G2 attached telephone taps to all the landlines and followed all diplomatic staff.

Towards the end of 1943 the Irish government came under increasing pressure to expel Dr Hempel and his staff but every Allied intervention was rebuffed. As a compromise the Germans were cut off from access to the overseas telephone exchange and a vital part of their short-wave radio confiscated. Thus, when Churchill and the American Ambassador, David Gray, a relation through marriage to Roosevelt, charged that Eire had become a hotbed of Fifth Columnists and Nazi parachutists the charges could all be refuted.

Two further parachutists did land in December 1943 but neither got very far. The first was John O'Reilly, a twenty-eight-year-old Irishman who had been interned in the Channel Islands by the Germans. He had volunteered his services, just as Eddie Chapman had (see Chapter VIII), and had gone to Berlin. Instead of being enrolled as an agent O'Reilly joined the Rundfunk's English language service and became a well-known broadcaster under the alias 'Pat O'Brien'. The Bremen Abstelle eventually recruited him as a wireless operator and he was dropped near Moveen in County Clare early in the morning of 16 December, 1943. He was arrested the same day. O'Reilly escaped from Arbour Hill Prison in July 1944, having told a warder that he had buried a vast sum of Abwehr money before his capture. Three days after his break-out he was denounced by his father, a retired policeman who had arrested Sir Roger Casement on Good Friday 1916. O'Reilly was released after the war and opened the Parachute Bar.

The second agent was thirty-five-year-old John Kenny who landed near Kilfeanagh, three miles from Kilkee, but he was badly injured during the drop. His parachute dragged him across rough ground for some distance and he was forced to give himself up.

By the end of 1943 G2 had put twelve Abwehr agents behind bars and the atmosphere between the Allies and Dublin had begun to thaw a little more although de Valera rejected Ambassador Gray's formal request from the United States government for the expulsion of the German diplomats. At the same time, though, he offered a compromise suggestion which was just what the Allies had been hoping for. De Valera authorized Colonel Bryan to invite a representative of the OSS to come to Dublin and liaise with G2 so that everyone could be satisfied by the local security measures.

Earlier in the war General William Donovan, the Chief of OSS, had paid a courtesy visit to Dublin, and had laid the groundwork for a further visit by David Bruce in 1942. As the Chief of OSS operations in Europe, Bruce (later US Ambassador to London 1961-1969) called on Joseph Walshe at the Department of External Affairs and arranged for a Vice-Consul at the American Embassy to be kept in touch with security matters.

The choice for this post fell on 'Spike' Marlan, a former student at Trinity College, Dublin. He was a Jew, which was to cause some comment among the strictly Catholic intelligence community in G2, and had no experience whatever of counter-espionage work. He quickly made an enemy of Ambassador Gray, who was wildly indiscreet and openly critical of de Valera. Marlan did his best to instil a sense of security into the Embassy staff but he failed to stop Gray airing his suspicions and opinions about various Irish government personalities on an open radio-telephone link to London.

In February 1944 the British government announced new restrictions on diplomatic communications overseas in an attempt to reduce the chance of a leak about OVERLORD. The United Kingdom was effectively cut off from the rest of the world, with the exception of the thousands of Irishmen who crossed over to England each week. The risk of the Germans discovering some of the Allies' invasion secrets appeared considerable, but they ignored the opportunity.

In an effort to reassure themselves the Americans sent a delegation to Dublin consisting of Hubert Will (Chief of the X2 Counter-Intelligence Branch of OSS in Europe) and Lieutenant Edward Lawler. They flew to Belfast and then caught a train south to Dublin. They were met at the station by Colonel Bryan and entertained at the Royal Hibernian Hotel. The Americans suspected that Dr Hempel's Legation was a centre of Abwehr operations and were particularly anxious to discover if G2 were monitoring German wireless transmissions or tapping the telephones there.

Bryan evaded all their questions, merely pointing out that the Germans no longer had the use of their diplomatic pouch, and their short-wave radio had been rendered unserviceable. Whenever Bryan was pressed on a point, such as the placing of a G2 informant inside the Legation or the interception of the cable traffic, the G2 Chief replied that such action would be a violation of German sovereignty. The OSS men noted however that Bryan did not actually deny that his organization had taken these precautions.

The following day Colonel Bryan and Dr Hayes conferred with the Irish Prime Minister who gave his approval to a secret agreement drawn up between OSS and G2. The treaty would allow Ed Lawler to remain in Dublin and enable him to study the security arrangements made by G2. For their part the Americans agreed to respect the confidence and keep what they learnt a secret, even from SHAEF.

Lawler proved to be an excellent liaison officer and established a close relationship with Colonel Bryan. He soon discovered that G2 had already taken almost every possible precaution. The telephones at the German Legation were tapped and every letter intercepted. The only improvement he could suggest was the inspection in secret of the Germans' waste paper. By April 1944 Lawler was satisfied that he could find no flaw in G2's arrangements and was sure that the D-Day preparations would not be leaked via Dublin.

Postscript

This book has looked at the Security Service from its beginnings in 1909 until the end of the Second World War. For most of this time it was under the aegis of one man, Vernon Kell, who created it and shaped and fashioned it into the delicate instrument which it became.

Great Britain had had several intelligence organizations since the nineteenth century; MO5 was created to fill a gap. Its initial brief was to assess the United Kingdom's vulnerability to foreign espionage, to watch for sabotage and for those anxious to undermine the established system of government. Its powers were therefore principally investigative: its weapon was the card-index. It was responsible for looking, listening and learning, rather than for action. It could watch, notice, remember, collate and cross-reference, but powers of cross-examination, arrest and prosecution lay with the police. It had also to be careful not to tread on the toes of its other partners – SIS, DNI and Special Branch.

Under Kell the Security Service grew from one man and a clerk in 1909 to a complex organization with many Divisions, sections and ramifications. During that time the world of espionage also changed and so did the values and ideals of many in society. But the greatest change came after Kell had left.

Kell was a cautious, circumspect individual who had relied on a few well-trained colleagues, whom he had personally hand-picked, to do most of the work: Guy Liddell, Tar Robertson, Max Knight, Dick White and Jasper Harker were among his stalwarts. With these few trusted lieutenants he managed many magnificent *coups,* and his handling of aliens at the beginning of both world wars was masterly.

With old age, however, came increasing caution and a marked disinclination for any reduction in standards. Although he knew war was inevitable by the end of the Thirties, he was starved by the Treasury of the funds which might have enabled him to create a system which could expand organically. When the politicians deemed it necessary to overhaul MI5, the decision came too late and the changes that were made were too extreme and too sudden not to endanger the integrity of an intelligence service in a country already at war. Kell was summarily dismissed, and the rigid criteria on which he had always insisted disappeared with him. For example, Kell would never employ a Catholic or someone without an entirely stable home life. He justified his discrimination by saying that the Roman Church had the best intelligence service in the world, and he had no intention of letting it penetrate the Security Service. The importance he placed on a staff member's family, he felt, was simply common sense: if an officer could not run his own life, how could he be entrusted with the security of the nation? By contrast, Sir David Petrie, the D-G appointed to replace Kell in November 1940, chose a practising Catholic solicitor, Richard Butler, as his Personal Assistant. Among the flood of recruits of mid-1940 were journalists, intellectuals, playboys and even known homosexuals – men whom Kell would never have considered.

With hindsight one can see that MI5 underestimated the appeal of Communism in those circles from which men and women were mobilized and drafted into the British intelligence and security community during the war. This was a little surprising in view of the considerable attention the organization had rightly paid to the rise of Communism both nationally and internationally, from 1917 onwards. MI5's success with the Arcos operation had indeed dealt a crippling blow to the Comintern and their ambitions around the world. The fact, incidentally, that the raid was partly organized by Guy Liddell underlines the absurdity of the allegations that have been made against him.

The Security Service took great pains to infiltrate King Street and follow the machinations of the CPGB, but they remained unaware of the number of underground CPGB members and NKVD recruits. There were three important cases of secrets being leaked to the Soviets during and just before the war, and one CPGB member was executed for Treachery. MI5 was penetrated by two Soviet agents (an art historian and a lawyer). An even better placed agent in MI6 (a former journalist) achieved excellent results, and several agents were run in SOE. Soviet interest in British intelligence services was hardly surprising, but wartime screening was naturally aimed at excluding Fascist rather than leftist sympathizers.

The most obvious example of this is Anthony Blunt, who volunteered his services to the War Office in 1938. In reply he received, by the same post, but in two separate envelopes, an official refusal of his offer and an acceptance. Ignoring the refusal, Blunt took a posting in 1939 to Minley Manor and began a Staff Officer's intelligence course. He lasted less than a week before being summoned to London to attend an interview with the DDMI. The DDMI explained that MI5 had discovered two potentially damaging facts about Blunt. One was a LIU copy of a postcard to Blunt from a leftist magazine declining an article he had written. The other was a report on his 1935 holiday in Russia. Blunt was able to persuade the DDMI that MI5's fears were groundless, and received a second posting to Minley Manor to complete his course. At the end of the course Blunt reported for duty to Mytchett Place, the headquarters of the Field Security Police, and from there was sent to Boulogne with the ill-fated British Expeditionary Force. Six months later he was evacuated and, following a recommendation from an MI5 officer, was recruited into MI5's 'D' Division.

At this stage Blunt was constantly in contact with his Soviet case officer, whom he only knew by his code name GEORGE, and his replacement, HENRY. Twenty-three years later Blunt was able to identify HENRY from MI5's copy of his passport photograph as Anatoli Gorski, an NKVD officer under diplomatic cover at the Russian Embassy. Both HENRY and Guy Burgess urged Blunt to move from his somewhat dull desk job with Brigadier Harry Allen to 'B' Division, the real centre of MI5's activities. After some two months with 'D', Blunt was appointed Personal Assistant to Guy Liddell, then Director of 'B' Division. He lasted little longer there, following hostility from Miss Huggins, Liddell's long-serving secretary.

Liddell moved Blunt from his private office into B1(b) and set him to work rifling the diplomatic pouches of neutral countries. He remained in this sensitive post until 1944 when he was transferred to SHEAF Ops 'B' at Norfolk House, the headquarters of the D-Day deception planners.

Later, during Blunt's debriefing by MI5, he stated that he was unaware of any other Soviet source inside the Security Service. His chief collaborator had been Guy Burgess whom he had occasionally employed as a link with a Swiss diplomatic source, code-named ORANGE. ORANGE was a senior Swiss envoy who passed on items of political gossip to Burgess in the belief that the information was going to the Foreign Office. In fact, it was going to Moscow, via B1(b).

Although Blunt was holding frequent meetings in various inconvenient locations around London in the evenings with HENRY (and later PETER), it was Guy Burgess who remained the key organizer of the Cambridge-orientated ring. The fear that there was at least one

Soviet agent inside MI5 at this time had originally been voiced in 1941 by Max Knight. A routine B5(b) report on the CPGB had been spotted by Blunt who reported the contents to his Russian case officer. One of the agents referred to in the report was 'M8', a cryptonym identifying the agent as being one from Max Knight's stable. The secret report mentioned a book written by M8, and Blunt immediately realized that M8 was none other than Tom Driberg, then a *Daily Express* journalist and a CPGB member. Driberg was promptly summoned to King Street and told by Harry Pollitt, the CPGB General Secretary, that his Party membership had been withdrawn. When Driberg demanded to know why, Pollitt accused him of being M8. Driberg naturally denied the charge, never before having heard his own code name. But when the incident was reported to Knight the MI5 officer realized there could only be one explanation – a hostile agent inside the Security Service. Knight was appalled and launched an investigation to track down the source, but he never succeeded. Blunt was furious at the way in which his information had been handled and complained that the network had been unnecessarily put at risk.

In fact, the ring survived until the culmination of the HOMER investigation which, in 1951, led to the defection of Maclean and the unplanned escape of Burgess. While Blunt had talent-spotted a number of potential recruits at Cambridge, it had been Burgess's responsibility to put them in contact with the Soviet case officers and maintain the occasional contact. Burgess had been living under increasing strain towards the end, and when he had finally left he had done so without removing all the incriminating papers that he had allowed to accumulate in his flat.

Following the departures of Burgess and Maclean, MI5 urgently wanted to search Burgess's flat, and to save the time of asking Special Branch to apply for a warrant, arranged for Blunt to meet them on the premises. Blunt collected a key from Burgess's flat-mate, Jack Hewit, and let two MI5 representatives into the flat. To speed up the search Blunt was asked to help, and was left alone to go through the sitting-room while the other two men ransacked the bedroom. To his horror Blunt found two particularly compromising letters, which he quickly pocketed. One was from himself, addressed to Burgess. The other was an indiscreet plea from Philby. If either had been found by MI5 it would have provided damning evidence.

Blunt's removal of these letters from under the noses of MI5 enabled him to avoid immediate exposure, but the haul from Burgess's bedroom was to prove a treasure trove for the investigators. A mass of secret papers were recovered from some suitcases and there could be no mistaking their sources. Disappointingly for MI5 two of the sources were beyond reach; Maclean was thought to be in Moscow, and John Cairncross initially denied having given Burgess classified material. Cairncross was a Cambridge modern languages graduate who had joined the Treasury, and had been transferred to GC & CS at Bletchley for wartime service dealing with German Air Force intercepts. Cairncross underwent a further interview in the United States, where he was lecturing, and made a full statement on his role as a Soviet agent. Although he was able to fill in a number of gaps about Burgess, he was unaware of Blunt's talent-spotting and thus failed to name Blunt as a suspect. Cairncross wisely decided not to return to England and went to live in Rome when the American Department of Immigration declined to renew his visa.

The two principal MI5 investigators, Arthur Martin and Jim Skardon, continued their interviews and settled on three further suspects: Anthony Blunt, one of Blunt's university friends who had worked in the Admiralty during the war and another former MI5 officer who had worked in 'A' Division's legal section. Blunt repeatedly denied any knowledge of Burgess's illicit activities and the other former MI5 officer, a barrister, died of a brain tumour before further action could be taken.

In 1963 the tip Arthur Martin needed so badly did fortuitously appear. Michael Straight, a wealthy American and another of Blunt's recruits, had been offered a prestigious White House-sponsored job in the Arts. Straight had left the United States government in 1941, and had broken with Blunt and Burgess in 1948. When Straight learned that his name had been put forward by the Kennedys he volunteered a statement to the FBI. He explained that prior to 1948 he had passed to his Soviet contact non-classified economic reports from the American banking community, of which he was a member. He also stated that his first introduction to intelligence work had been at the hands of Anthony Blunt. He named two other possible Soviet agents. The first, Blunt's university friend mentioned above, had already come under MI5 suspicion, but had denied passing the Russians wartime Admiralty secrets. The second, Leo Long, another Cambridge CPGB member who had 'gone underground', admitted having once been a Soviet agent but assured MI5 that he had long since abandoned Marxism. He had held a sensitive post in Military Intelligence during the war but had long since ceased to have access to secrets.

Although quite unequivocal, Straight's evidence was clearly not enough to obtain a criminal conviction against Blunt, so the Director-General, Sir Roger Hollis, negotiated a formal immunity from prosecution from the Attorney-General, Sir John Hobson. Hollis consulted his two senior advisors, Anthony Simkins and Martin Furnival Jones, and then authorized Arthur Martin to confront Blunt with the information from Straight. As expected Blunt flatly denied the charge, but when Martin made the verbal offer of immunity he agreed to co-operate. Blunt was then handed over for intensive debriefing to MI5's Soviet affairs expert.

Some months later the MI5 debriefer told Blunt that Straight was coming to London and had asked for a private meeting with the art historian. Intrigued and a little embarrassed, Blunt agreed to receive Straight, but to his amazement Straight avoided the subject of his FBI statement and proceeded to discuss a seventeenth-century painting he had recently acquired. The two men never met again.

Over a whole series of exhausting interviews Blunt described his talent-spotting at Cambridge and gave the names of all the Soviet agents he had been aware of. To the undoubted disappointment of MI5, all had previously been identified. Blunt was questioned about dozens of potential suspects and confirmed the involvement of one of the two Cambridge CPGB members named by Straight. A confrontation arranged between Blunt, his debriefer and the other suspect took place in Brown's Hotel. The interview lasted five hours, by the end of which the suspect had admitted little but had convinced Blunt and MI5 that he had been a Soviet agent. Blunt also confirmed an MI5 suspicion that Burgess had been blackmailing a wartime War Office Duty Clerk, Tom Wylie, who had died of alcoholism after the war.

Inevitably Blunt was drawn into MI5's efforts to determine whether there was still a long-term Soviet source within the Security Service, which seemed all the more likely in view of his assurance that neither Burgess nor PETER had urged him to stay on in MI5 after the war. The presence of such an agent, some officers thought, was in any case the only rational explanation for a series of events which had benefited the Russians. The officers conducting that particular enquiry arranged to have Blunt closely questioned, but their efforts positively to identify a suspect failed.

Certainly, the problem facing them was daunting. Blunt's belated confession had shown the extent of the Soviet network headed by Burgess, and it had also provided circumstantial evidence of a remaining 'mole'. But who was he? To date no less than five former British wartime intelligence officers had been confirmed as Soviet agents: Philby, Burgess, Blunt, Cairncross and Long. It was quite obvious to the two principal MI5 'mole-hunters', Ian Carrel and John Day, that the Security Service remained an important KGB target. Leo Long's personal file revealed that after the war, when he was serving as Deputy Director of Military Intelligence in Germany, he had applied for a transfer to MI5. He was given an interview, but his application failed. Although he had subsequently gone into civilian life, had others succeeded?

The further the mole-hunters delved, the more complicated the picture became. The NKVD had recruited a number of ideologically motivated sympathizers during the Twenties and Thirties, and a number of them had succeeded, like Philby and Long, insinuating themselves into sensitive posts where they might be of special advantage to Moscow. The roll-call of people who admitted they may have been approached on behalf of the Russians, or even unconsciously used by them, was impressive: Alistair Watson, the Admiralty scientist who, as we have seen, was interviewed at Brown's Hotel; Bernard Floud MP, who subsequently committed suicide; Jenifer Hart, the wife of Herbert Hart; Sir Dennis Proctor, a former Permanent Under-Secretary at the Ministry of Power.

The fact that each had been active in left-wing politics during a period of Soviet recruitment at English universities may have accounted for their names being passed by 'talent spotters' to the NKVD. Prior to the new enquiries initiated in the early Sixties the Security Service had only the vaguest idea of the extent of the pre-war Soviet networks. When interviewed on the subject most denied ever having passed classified information although a few conceded that they might, inadvertently, have been indiscreet while discussing sensitive issues with such acquaintances as Guy Burgess.

Several of those interviewed were in posts which gave regular access to secret documents, and two such individuals in the Foreign Office resigned quietly.

In 1969 a third member of the Diplomatic Corps, Edward Scott, was interviewed. Scott had resigned prematurely in March 1961 after he had been involved with a Czech housemaid whilst serving as the Chargé d'Affaires at the British Embassy in Prague. Eight years later, when Josef Frolik defected, MI5 officers learned that Scott had been conducting covert meetings with Czech intelligence officers in London. Once again, the espionage suspect denied having passed secrets and he was released without charge.

MI5's chief concern during this enquiry was to establish the extent of the damage, as opposed to putting traitors in the dock, and for this reason the names of Blunt and Long were not made public for more than sixteen years. However, their damage-control exercise did not achieve any tangible results in respect of Soviet penetration of the Security Service.

Drastic loyalty checks were made to ensure there were no 'loose ends'. An atmosphere of distrust and suspicion enveloped the organization at this time and some, finding it intolerable, resigned as soon as they had been cleared, including Graham Mitchell, a completely loyal MI5 officer who had first joined 'F' Division's anti-Fascist section in 1939. Sir Roger Hollis had decreed that no one, however senior, would be exempt from the investigation, himself included. The fact that the Director-General had submitted to intensive questioning was later to be widely misunderstood and misrepresented. When Hollis reached retirement age in 1966, after nine years in the post, he stepped down and was succeeded by his Deputy D-G, Martin Furnival Jones.

In spite of the very far-reaching internal investigations and the creation of a joint MI5/SIS committee to review security, some MI5 officers retained doubts over the affair and took unusual steps to keep the matter open. The absolute credibility of MI5, enabling the Prime Minister of the day to accept the D-G's advice and act on it, is a national asset of incalculable importance, and this credibility was now seen to be at stake. It was therefore decided in 1974 to pass all the relevant files to a respected senior personage who was plainly outside the control of the Security Service. The chosen adjudicator was Lord Trend, the recently retired Secretary of the Cabinet. The Trend Report analysed all the evidence and concluded that the original MI5 enquiry had been sufficiently comprehensive.

Chapman Pincher's main contention in his book *Their Trade is Treachery*, which caused such a furore early in 1981, was that Sir Roger Hollis had been suspected of being a Soviet 'mole' at the time when he was Director-General of the Security Service. It was a sensational allegation. Pincher was of course correct in stating that Hollis had been the subject of an investigation by his old department, though the fact was not sinister, as he made it seem; but wrong when he said Lord Trend had been called in to investigate Hollis further. He was also wrong when he claimed the Trend Report had concluded that Sir Roger 'was the likeliest suspect' for a Soviet agent inside MI5. Interestingly enough, Pincher's allegations were all concerned with people who were recruited before or during the war.

In a sense the war was a watershed for British counter-intelligence. The 'regulars' who ran MI5 before the war were, with few exceptions, amateurs by the standards of today. Their great assets were robust common sense and uncomplicated patriotism – admirable qualities in the world as it was then. They would have been out of their element in the increasingly technological and multinational intelligence world of today.

Indeed, most of the leading wartime MI5 personalities were demobilized when the war ended. The rewards were limited, and only a few stayed on. Guy Liddell died of a heart attack in 1958 having retired from the Security Service and been appointed Chief Security Officer at Harwell. Tar Robertson left in 1949 for a similar job at the Foreign Office's Government Communications Headquarters in Cheltenham. Both were pre-war 'regulars'. On the other hand, the three men who were to climb right to the top, largely because of their wartime experience, had entered the organization almost by chance: Dick White, Roger Hollis and Martin Furnival Jones. White owed his recruitment to Malcolm Cumming whom he met while travelling to Australia, Hollis joined Colonel Alexander having spent some years in the Far East with British American Tobacco, and Martin Furnival Jones might easily have remained a solicitor with Slaughter & May if he had not been rescued by friends from a staff post in wartime Ulster.

Did the influx of new talent in the early part of the war reduce MI5's capacity to protect the Realm? Certainly not at the time. The Security Service not only overcame the difficulties created by this flood of new personnel; it coped successfully with eighteen months of constant reorganization and relocation, survived with inadequate funds, and went on to score many notable successes, as we have seen. When the time finally came, in 1945, to re-create a peacetime Security Service, however, few wished to remain in the organization.

Notes

1   Hodder & Stoughton, London 1940.
2   L. Chester, S. Fay and H. Young. *The Zinoviev Letter* (Heinemann, London 1967).
3   This was by no means the last MI5 heard of Wilfred Macartney. On his release from prison he published *Walls have Mouths* (Gollancz 1936) and *Zigzag* (Gollancz 1937). He was one of the first volunteers to join the International Brigade in the Spanish Civil War and eventually became the first Commander of the British Battalion. He was accidently wounded in the elbow in January 1937 just before the Battalion's first action. He then returned to London.
    After the war Macartney was again prosecuted under the Official Secrets Act, this time with Eddie Chapman as co-defendant. Chapman had sold the story of his wartime exploits as ZIGZAG to a French newspaper. The article was withdrawn and both men were given nominal fines (see Chapter VII).
4   Denis Pritt was Labour MP for North Hammersmith (1935-1950) as well as a Soviet sympathizer. He fronted several pro-Russian groups such as the Reichstag Fire Enquiry Commission and the Society for Cultural Relations with the USSR. He was expelled from the Labour Party in 1940 after persistently supporting the USSR during the war in Finland.
5   In 1939 Miss Sissmore made an 'office marriage' to Group Captain Archer, the RAF liaison officer in 'D' Division.
6   MacGibbon & Kee, London 1968.
7   Bernard Harrison, London.
8   The reference to 'Marie Louise' was to cause considerable embarrassment for this name was shared by Captain von Rintelen's daughter. Von Rintelen had spied for Germany during the Great War and had been imprisoned for espionage in America. He became a close friend of his old adversary, 'Blinker' Hall, and wrote *The Dark Invader* and *The Return of the Dark Invader*. Rumours forced him to issue a public denial of any connection during the subsequent well-publicized proceedings.
9   This was by no means the last of Baillie-Stewart. The US Army reported in May 1945 that he had been arrested near Berchtesgaden. He was wanted for assisting 'Lord Haw-Haw' and was duly interviewed in Brussels by Captain Spooner of the Intelligence Corps (better known as Reg Spooner of MI5, later Deputy Commander of Special Branch). He subsequently pleaded Guilty in January 1946 to a charge of aiding the enemy under the 1939 Defence Regulations and was

sentenced to five years by Mr Justice Oliver. In May 1949 he was released from Parkhurst and went to live in Ireland as 'James Scott' and later as 'Patrick Stewart'. He died in Dublin in June 1966.

[10] A list of prominent Anglo-German Fellowship members is shown on p.95 at the end of Chapter V. By the end of 1936 the Fellowship boasted a membership of over a thousand. By September 1939 there were practically none.

[11] See p.95 for a list of members of the Link.

[12] Part of the sentence was served at Maidstone Prison where Goertz came into contact with Baillie-Stewart. When Baillie-Stewart was released in March 1937 he travelled to Berlin via Vienna and Czechoslovakia.

[13] This address was already known to the Security Service and the LIU as a post-box for the Abwehr Abstelle in Hamburg.

[14] The State Department Security Division and the NYPD Alien Squad, eventually handed Rumrich over to the FBI where he was received by FBI Special Agent Leon G. Turrou. In 1938 Turrou published a highly inaccurate account of the affair entitled *Nazi Spies in America*. Hoover sacked him.

[15] Lonkowski was caught with classified aircraft blueprints by US Customs at the *Europa's* dock in New York. In an incredible blunder the German agent was released and asked to return the following day for questioning. He disappeared back to Germany via Canada.

[16] Walter Schellenberg claimed during his post-war interrogations to have been the editor of *Informationsheft Grossbritannien* but no confirmation was obtained. Also suspected as the Nazi expert on British Intelligence was Walter zu Christian, another SS officer in the RSHA's Amt VI.

[17] Best and Stevens were not the only SIS officers to fall into enemy hands. Apart from Captain Kendrick (the Head of Station in Vienna in 1938), the SIS Far East expert, Mr H. Steptoe, was actually interned by the Japanese if 1941 but exchanged the following year without incident.

[18] One such Dutch intelligence officer was Colonel Oreste Pinto, who quite unjustifiably dubbed himself 'Spycatcher' after the war.

[19] See David Lampe, *The Last Ditch* (Cassell, London 1968).

[20] *Invasion 1940* (Hart-Davis, London 1957); *Operation Sealion* (OUP, Oxford 1958)

[21] Lady Pearson's home, Brickendonbury, near Hertford, became one of SOE's first Special Training Schools (see Chapter VII).

[22] The designation 'Top Secret' was introduced as a replacement for the traditional 'Most Secret' for the benefit of the Americans.

[23] Son of Sir Arthur Comyns Carr KC, Liberal MP for Islington, and a financial journalist.

[24] This 'Herr Müller' was later identified as Captain Hans Dierks, Head of the Naval Intelligence section of the Hamburg Abstelle. He was killed in a road accident in Stavanger in 1940 while taking Robert Petter, Karl Drücke and Vera Erikson to their plane. (See Chapter IX.)

[25] 'Dr Rantzau' was identified as Major Nikolaus Ritter, Great War officer who went to America in 1927, returning in 1937 to join the Abwehr.

[26] Kühlenthal remained ignorant of the deception and died in 1975.

[27] Name altered by request.

[28] Zilliacus became Labour MP for Gateshead in 1945. The Labour Party expelled him for his pro-Soviet views in May 1949.

[29] Later Lord Rea and Deputy Speaker in the House of Lords.

[30] TREASURE was not assigned a regular male B1(a) case officer for fear of rape allegations.

[31] Douglas Hyde, *I Believed* (Heinemann, London 1950).

[32] Pierrepoint describes the incident in *Executioner Pierrepoint* (Harrap, London 1968), but changes Richter's name to 'Otto Schmidt'.

[33] The following month the *Ulea* was torpedoed en route for Oban carrying a cargo of copper-pyrites from Huelva.

[34] Sir Wintringham Stable MC KC was MI5's neighbour although he never knew it. He too had a flat in Rugby Mansions, W14. (See the cases of TREASURE and BRUTUS.)

[35] Among the Clipper passengers on their way to New York was Somerset Maugham, who had been forced to flee his villa on Cap Ferrat. During the Great War he had been an SIS recruit and so was able to deliver an impressive account of conditions under the Vichy regime.

[36] A former Consul in Palma, Hillgarth co-ordinated SIS, NID and SOE in Spain until 1943 when he was appointed Chief of Naval Intelligence, Eastern Theatre.

[37] The events of MINCEMEAT are well documented by Duff Cooper, *Operation Heartbreak* (Hart-Davis. London 1951), Ewen Montagu, *The Man Who Never Was* (Evans, London 1953), and Ian Colvin, *The Unknown Courier* (Kimber, London 1953).

[38] A feature film with the same title was released in 1958, and accounts of the exercise also appeared in the *RAPC Journal*, Volume V, 1946, and in *Moonlight on a Lake in Bond Street* by Stephen Watts (Bodley Head, London 1961).

[39] See *Ambassador On Special Mission* by Lord Templewood (Collins, London 1946) and *Wartime Mission in Spain* by Carlton Hayes (Macmillan, London 1945).

[40] Admiral Darlan, the Commander-in-Chief ot the French Fleet, was shot by a twenty-year-old Frenchman named Fernand Bonnier on Christmas Eve 1942. The assassin was captured seconds after the shooting, smoking gun in hand. He never denied his guilt but the remarkable speed of his court martial and execution – he was shot by firing squad fifty-three hours after the assassination – helped to create many rumours of a massive plot to murder the politically enigmatic Admiral.

[41] A sixteen-year-old youth from Dublin named Brendan Behan was convicted for this incident. His subsequent experiences led him to write *Borstal Boy*.

[42] Ironically the S-Plan was not the product of the German General Staff. It had been written by Jim O'Donovan, an IRA activist based in Dublin, and close friend of Sean Russell, the IRA Chief-of-Staff. He did make two trips to Hamburg during 1939 to contact the Abwehr but neither visit resulted in the S-Plan, which he wrote alone.

[43] The anonymous Irishman escaped and was never caught. He was interviewed by a *Sunday Times* reporter in 1969 and the resulting article was published on 6 July, 1969.

[44] All three had been landed from the yacht *Soizic* which had been requisitioned by the Abwehr from a French owner in Brest. The yacht successfully evaded British Naval inspections and for this reason was well thought of as a method of 'agent insertion' for a short time. See the case of Karel Richter. Chapter IX.

Index